C# 2008 and 2005 Threaded Programming
Beginner's Guide

Exploit the power of multiple processors for faster, more responsive software.

Gastón C. Hillar

BIRMINGHAM - MUMBAI

C# 2008 and 2005 Threaded Programming
Beginner's Guide

First published: January 2009

Production Reference: 1200109

Published by Packt Publishing Ltd.
32 Lincoln Road
Olton
Birmingham, B27 6PA, UK.

ISBN 978-1-847197-10-8

www.packtpub.com

Cover Image by Vinayak Chittar (vinayak.chittar@gmail.com)

Credits

Author

Gastón C. Hillar

Reviewers

Bogdan Brinzarea-Iamandi

Jerry L. Spohn

Ron Steckly

Senior Acquisition Editor

David Barnes

Development Editor

Shilpa Dube

Technical Editor

Rakesh Shejwal

Editorial Team Leader

Akshara Aware

Copy Editor

Sumathi Sridhar

Project Team Leader

Lata Basantani

Project Coordinator

Rajashree Hamine

Project Editorial Manager

Abhijeet Deobhakta

Indexer

Monica Ajmera

Proofreaders

Chris Smith

Ron Steckly

Production Coordinator

Rajni R. Thorat

Cover Work

Rajni R. Thorat

About the Author

Gastón C. Hillar has been working with computers since he was eight. He began programming with the legendary Texas TI-99/4A and Commodore 64 home computers in the early 80s.

He has a Bachelor degree in Computer Science, graduated with honors, and an MBA (Master in Business Administration), graduated with an outstanding thesis.

He has worked as developer, architect, and project manager for many companies in Buenos Aires, Argentina. He was project manager in one of the most important mortgage loan banks in Latin America for several years. Now, he is an independent IT consultant working for several Spanish, German, and Latin American companies, and a freelance author. He is always looking for new adventures around the world.

He also works with electronics (he is an electronics technician). He is always researching about new technologies and writing about them. He owns an IT and electronics laboratory with many servers, monitors, and measuring instruments.

He is the author of more than 40 books in Spanish about computer science, modern hardware, programming, systems development, software architecture, business applications, balanced scorecard applications, IT project management, Internet, and electronics, published by Editorial HASA and Grupo Noriega Editores.

He usually writes articles for leading Spanish magazines "Mundo Linux", "Solo Programadores", and "Resistor".

He lives with his wife, Vanesa, and his son, Kevin. When not tinkering with computers, he enjoys developing and playing with wireless virtual reality devices and electronics toys with his father, his son, and his nephew Nico.

You can reach him at gastonhillar@hotmail.com

Acknowledgement

When writing this book, I was fortunate to work with an excellent team at Packt Publishing Ltd, whose contributions vastly improved the presentation of this book. David Barnes helped me to transform the idea into the final book and to give my first steps working with the Beginner's Guide. Rajashree Hamine made everything easier with her incredible time management. Shilpa Dube helped me realize my vision for this book and provided many sensible suggestions regarding the text, the format, and the flow. The reader will notice her excellent work. Rakesh Shejwal made the sentences, the paragraphs, and the code easier to read and to understand. He has added great value to the final drafts.

I would like to thank my technical reviewers Bogdan Brinzarea-Iamandi, Jerry L. Spohn, and Ron Steckly and proofreaders Chris Smith and Ron Steckly, for their thorough reviews and insightful comments. I was able to incorporate some of the knowledge and wisdom they have gained in their many years in the software development industry. The examples and the code include the great feedback provided by Bogdan Brinzarea. Bogdan helped me a lot to include better and shorter code to simplify the learning process.

I wish to acknowledge Hector A. Algarra, who always helped me to improve my writing.

Special thanks go to my wife, Vanesa S. Olsen, my son Kevin, my nephew, Nicolas, my father, Jose Carlos, who acted as a great sounding board and participated in many hours of technical discussions, my sister, Silvina, who helped me when my grammar was confusing, and my mother Susana. They always supported me during the production of this book.

About the Reviewers

Bogdan Brinzarea-Iamandi has a strong background in Computer Science holding a Master and Bachelor Degree from the Automatic Control and Computers Faculty of the Politehnica University of Bucharest, Romania, and also an Auditor diploma from the Computer Science department at Ecole Polytechnique, Paris, France. His main interests cover a wide area from embedded programming, distributed and mobile computing, and new web technologies.

Currently, he is employed as Supervisor within the team of the Alternative Channels Sector of the IT Division in Banca Romaneasca, a Member of the National Bank of Greece. He is Project Manager for Internet Banking and he coordinates other projects related to new technologies and applications to be implemented in the banking area.

Bogdan is also the author of two AJAX books, the popular *AJAX and PHP: Building Responsive Web Applications* and *Microsoft AJAX Library Essentials*, also published by Packt.

Jerry Spohn is a Manager of Development for a medium-sized software development firm in Exton, Pennsylvania. His responsibilities include managing a team of developers and assisting in architecting a large multi-lingual, multi-currency loan account system, written in COBOL and JAVA. He is also responsible for maintaining and tracking a system-wide program and database documentation web site, in which he uses DotNetNuke as the portal for this information.

Jerry is also the owner of Spohn Software LLC., a small consulting firm that helps small businesses in the area with all aspects of maintaining and improving their business processes. This includes helping with the creation and maintenance of web sites, general office productivity issues, and computer purchasing and networking. Spohn Software, as a firm, prefers to teach its clients how to solve their problems internally, rather than acquire a long-term contract, thereby making the business more productive and profitable in the future.

Jerry currently works and resides in Pennsylvania, with his wife, Jacqueline, and his two sons, Nicholas and Nolan.

Ron Steckly has been developing various platforms for the past several years, recently adopting .NET as his platform of choice. He graduated from U.C. Berkeley with highest distinction in 2004. He recently moved back to sunny Northern California after living for several years in Manhattan. He is currently working as a Web Application Engineer at Empirical Education in Palo Alto, CA and authoring a book on using MySQL with .NET for Packt Publishing. In his spare time, he enjoys studying mathematics (particularly combinatorics), statistics, economics, and new programming languages.

I would like to thank my good friends Johannes Castner, Josh Brandt-Young, and David Aaron Engle for all their kindness and patience over the years.

To my son, Kevin

Table of Contents

Preface   **1**

Chapter 1: Taking Advantage of Multiprocessing and Multiple Cores   **7**

Mono-processor systems: The old gladiators   **8**

Single core: Only one warrior to fight against everybody   8

Doing a tiny bit of each task   9

The performance waterfall   **11**

Multi-processor systems: Many warriors to win a battle   **13**

Estimating performance improvements   16

Avoiding bottlenecks   21

Taking advantage of multiple execution cores   23

Scalability   27

Load balancing: Keeping everybody happy   29

Operating systems and virtual machines   31

Parallelism is here to stay   31

Summary   **33**

Chapter 2: Processes and Threads   **35**

Processes—any running program   **35**

Time for action – Coding a simple CPU-intensive loop   37

Time for action – Changing the cores available for a process   39

Relating processes to cores   41

Time for action – Changing a process priority   42

Linear code problems in multiprocessing systems   44

Time for action – Running many processes in parallel   44

Time for action – Testing parallelism capabilities with processes   48

Time for action – Using the Process Explorer   51

Threads—Independent parts of a process   **53**

Time for action – Listing threads with Process Explorer   55

Time for action – Analyzing context switches with Process Explorer   57

Multiple threads in servers	59
Multiple threads in clients	59
Summary	**63**
Chapter 3: BackgroundWorker—Putting Threads to Work	**65**
RTC: Rapid thread creation	**65**
Time for action – Breaking a code in a single thread	67
Time for action – Defining the work to be done in a new thread	73
Asynchronous execution	**75**
Time for action - Understanding asynchronous execution step-by-step	76
Synchronous execution	**78**
Showing the progress	**78**
Time for action – Using a BackgroundWorker to report progress in the UI	79
Cancelling the job	**84**
Time for action – Using a BackgroundWorker to cancel the job	85
Time for action – Using a BackgroundWorker to detect a job completed	87
Time for action – Working with parameters and results	89
Working with multiple BackgroundWorker components	**94**
Time for action – Using many BackgroundWorker components to break	94
the code faster	94
BackgroundWorker and Timer	**104**
BackgroundWorker creation on the fly	**105**
Time for action – Creating BackgroundWorker components in run-time	105
Summary	**110**
Chapter 4: Thread Class—Practical Multithreading in Applications	**113**
Creating threads with the Thread class	**113**
Time for action – Defining methods for encryption and decryption	114
Time for action – Running the encryption in a new thread using the	119
Thread class	119
Decoupling the UI	122
Creating a new thread	124
Retrieving data from threads	125
Sharing data between threads	**125**
Time for action – Updating the UI while running threads	126
Sharing some specific data between threads	130
A BackgroundWorker helping a Thread class	132
Time for action – Executing the thread synchronously	133
Main and secondary threads	135
Passing parameters to threads	**136**
Time for action – Using lists for thread creation on the fly I	136
Time for action – Using lists for thread creation on the fly II	138
Creating as many threads as the number of cores	141
Receiving parameters in the thread method	142
Summary	**146**

Chapter 5: Simple Debugging Techniques with Multithreading | 147

Watching multiple threads | 147

Time for action – Understanding the difficulty in debugging | 148

concurrent threads | 148

Debugging concurrent threads | 150

Time for action – Finding the threads | 151

Understanding the information shown in the Threads window | 153

Time for action – Assigning names to threads | 154

Identifying the current thread at runtime | 157

Debugging multithreaded applications as single-threaded applications | 159

Time for action – Leaving a thread running alone | 159

Freezing and thawing threads | 161

Viewing the call stack for each running thread | 162

Showing partial results in multithreaded code | 164

Time for action – Explaining the encryption procedure | 164

Showing thread-safe output | 167

Time for action – Isolating results | 167

Understanding thread information in tracepoints | 169

Summary | 172

Chapter 6: Understanding Thread Control with Patterns | 173

Starting, joining, pausing, and restarting threads | 173

Time for action – Defining methods for counting old stars | 174

Avoiding conflicts | 178

Splitting image processing | 179

Understanding the pixels' color compositions | 180

Time for action – Running the stars counter in many concurrent threads | 181

Creating independent blocks of concurrent code | 186

Using flags to enhance control over concurrent threads | 189

Rebuilding results to show in the UI | 190

Testing results with Performance Monitor and Process Explorer | 192

Time for action –Waiting for the threads' signals | 195

Using the AutoResetEvent class to handle signals between threads | 197

Using the WaitHandle class to check for signals | 198

Summary | 201

Chapter 7: Dynamically Splitting Jobs into Pieces—Avoiding Problems | 203

Running split jobs many times | 203

Time for action – Defining new methods for running many times | 204

Time for action – Running a multithreaded algorithm many times | 205

Using classes, methods, procedures, and functions with

multithreading capabilities | 207

Time for action – Analyzing the memory usage | 207

Understanding the garbage collector with multithreading | 209

Time for action – Collecting the garbage at the right time | 210

Controlling the system garbage collector with the GC class | 212
Avoiding garbage collection problems | 213
Avoiding inefficient processing usage problems | 214
Retrieving the total memory thought to be allocated | 217
Generalizing the algorithms for segmentation with classes | **218**
Time for action – Creating a parallel algorithm piece class | 218
Time for action – Using a generic method in order to create pieces | 221
Creating the pieces | 222
Time for action – Creating a parallel algorithm coordination class | 223
Starting the threads associated to the pieces | 225
Accessing instances and variables from threads' methods | 225
Time for action – Adding useful classic coordination methods | 226
Summary | **230**

Chapter 8: Simplifying Parallelism Complexity | **231**
Specializing the algorithms for segmentation with classes | **231**
Time for action – Preparing the parallel algorithm classes for the | 232
factory method | 232
Defining the class to instantiate | 234
Preparing the classes for inheritance | 236
Time for action – Creating a specialized parallel algorithm piece subclass | 237
Creating a complete piece of work | 240
Writing the code for a thread in an instance method | 240
Time for action – Creating a specialized parallel algorithm | 241
coordination subclass | 241
Creating simple constructors | 244
Time for action—Overriding methods in the coordination subclass | 245
Programming the piece creation method | 247
Programming the results collection method | 247
Time for action – Defining a new method to create an algorithm instance | 248
Forgetting about threads | 249
Time for action – Running the Sunspot Analyzer in many concurrent | 249
independent pieces | 249
Optimizing and encapsulating parallel algorithms | 252
Achieving thread affinity | 252
Avoiding locks and many synchronization nightmares | **253**
Summary | **256**

Chapter 9: Working with Parallelized Input/Output and Data Access | **257**
Queuing threads with I/O operations | **257**
Time for action – Creating a class to run an algorithm in an | 258
independent thread | 258
Time for action – Putting the logic into methods to simplify multithreading | 260
Avoiding Input/Output bottlenecks | 262
Using concurrent streams | 263

Controlling exceptions in threads 264
Time for action – Creating the methods for queuing requests 265
Using a pool of threads with the ThreadPool class 266
Managing the thread queue in the pool 268
Time for action – Running concurrent encryptions on demand using a 270
pool of threads 270
Converting single-threaded tasks to a multithreaded pool 272
Encapsulating scalability 273
Thread affinity in a pool of threads 274
Parallelizing database access **276**
Summary **278**

Chapter 10: Parallelizing and Concurrently Updating the User Interface **279**
Updating the UI from independent threads **279**
Time for action – Creating a safe method to update the user interface 280
Creating delegates to make cross-thread calls 281
Figuring out the right thread to make the call to the UI 282
Avoiding UI update problems with a delegate 283
Retrieving results from a synchronous delegate invoke 284
Time for action – Invoking a user interface update from a thread 285
Providing feedback when the work is finished 287
Time for action – Identifying threads and giving them names 288
Time for action – Understanding how to invoke delegates step-by-step 289
Decoding the delegates and concurrency puzzle 293
Time for action – Creating safe counters using delegates and avoiding 294
concurrency problems 294
Taking advantage of the single-threaded UI to create safe counters 296
Reporting progress to the UI from independent threads **298**
Time for action – Creating the classes to show a progress bar column in a 299
DataGridView 299
Time for action – Creating a class to hold the information to show in the 302
DataGridView 302
Time for action – Invoking multiple asynchronous user interface updates 304
from many threads 304
Creating a delegate without parameters 306
Invoking a delegate asynchronously to avoid performance degradation 307
Time for action – Updating progress percentages from worker threads 309
Providing feedback while the work is being done 311
Summary **314**

Chapter 11: Coding with .NET Parallel Extensions **315**
Parallelizing loops using .NET extensions **315**
Time for action – Downloading and installing the .NET Parallel Extensions 316
No silver bullet 319
Time for action – Downloading and installing the imaging library 319

Time for action – Creating an independent class to run in parallel without 321
side effects 321
Counting and showing blobs while avoiding side effects 325
Time for action – Running concurrent nebula finders using a 327
parallelized loop 327
Using a parallelized ForEach loop 330
Coding with delegates in parallelized loops 331
Working with a concurrent queue 332
Controlling exceptions in parallelized loops 333
Time for action – Showing the results in the UI 334
Combining delegates with a BackgroundWorker 337
Retrieving elements from a concurrent queue in a producer-consumer scheme 337
Time for action – Providing feedback to the UI using a producer-consumer 339
scheme 339
Creating an asynchronous task combined with a synchronous parallel loop 340
Time for action – Invoking a UI update from a task 342
Providing feedback when each job is finished 344
Using lambda expressions to simplify the code 344
Parallelizing loops with ranges 345
Parallelizing queries   346
Time for action – Parallelized counter 346
Parallelizing LINQ queries with PLINQ 348
Specifying the degree of parallelism for PLINQ 349
Parallelizing statistics and multiple queries 349
Summary 352
Chapter 12: Developing a Completely Parallelized Application 353
Joining many different parallelized pieces into a complete application 353
Time for action – Creating an opacity effect in an independent thread 354
Running code out of the UI thread 356
Time for action – Creating a safe method to change the opacity 357
Blocking the UI—Forbidden with multithreading code 359
Time for action – Creating a class to run a task in an independent thread 360
Time for action – Putting the logic into methods to simplify running tasks 361
in a pool of threads 361
Time for action – Queuing requests, running threads, and updating the UI 364
Combining threads with a pool of threads and the UI thread 369
Time for action – Creating a specialized parallel algorithm piece subclass 370
to run concurrently with the pool of threads 370
Time for action – Creating a specialized parallel algorithm coordination 373
subclass to run concurrently with the pool of threads 373
Time for action – Overriding methods in the brightness adjustment 375
coordination subclass 375
Time for action – Starting new threads in a new window 377
Creating threads inside other threads 380

Time for action – Showing new windows without blocking the user
interface   381
                                                                             381
Multiple windows and one UI thread for all of them   383
Rationalizing multithreaded code   **384**
Summary   **388**
Index   **389**

Preface

Most machines today have multiple core processors; to make full use of these, applications need to support multithreading. This book will take your C# development skills to the next level. It includes best practices alongside theory and will help you learn the various aspects of parallel programming, thereby helping you to build your career. The book covers various aspects of parallel programming—right from planning, designing, preparing algorithms and analytical models up to specific parallel programming systems. It will help you learn C# threaded programming, with numerous examples and clear explanations packed with screenshots to aid your understanding of every process. After all of the code is written, it is bundled in .zip files for easy availability and use.

What this book covers

Chapter 1 acknowledges the advantages of parallel programming with C# for the coming years. It also elaborates on the challenges associated with parallel processing and programming.

Chapter 2 focuses on the fundamentals of the operating system scheduler and how a single application can be divided into multiple threads or different processes. It also explains the different ways of using threads to work in clients and servers.

Chapter 3 shows how to develop applications that are able to create background threads, start and cancel threads, and launching multiple threads using the BackgroundWorker components. It also discusses the differences between multiple threads using BackgroundWorker and Timers.

Chapter 4 introduces the powerful Thread class, using which one can create independent and very flexible threads. It also discusses the differences between multiple threads, using BackgroundWorker and employing the Thread class, and ways to create high performance applications.

Chapter 5 focuses on debugging applications with many concurrent threads and coordinating the entire debugging process. It also explains the differences between single-threaded debugging and multithreading debugging for threads created using BackgroundWorker and employing the Thread class and many tricks that help simplifying the debugging process.

Chapter 6 takes a closer look at working with independent blocks of code when concurrency is not allowed, managing and coordinating those using new techniques different from the ones offered by the Thread class. It also explains how to apply parallel algorithms to image processing, and the solutions to the most common problems when working with components not enabled for multithreading.

Chapter 7 shows how to improve the memory usage in heavy multithreading applications, managing and coordinating the garbage collection service, and using an object-oriented approach for splitting jobs into well-managed pieces, easily and dynamically. It also covers developing highly optimized multithreaded algorithms.

Chapter 8 elaborates on using object-oriented capabilities offered by the C# programming language, using design patterns for simplifying the parallelism complexity, and avoiding synchronization pains. It also covers the principles of thread affinity, and how to avoid the undesirable side effects related to concurrent programming.

Chapter 9 takes a closer look at using object-oriented capabilities offered by the C# programming language for achieving great scalability in converting single-threaded algorithms to multithreaded scalable jobs, while avoiding the pains of multithreading. It emphasizes the use of pools and parallelized input/output operations in many ways.

Chapter 10 focuses on providing a more responsive user interface, using synchronous and asynchronous delegates. It explains how to combine parallelized operations with a precise user interface feedback while avoiding some multithreading pains. It also shows how to combine a pool of threads with a responsive user interface.

Chapter 11 walks through parallelizing the execution of code, taking advantage of the .NET Parallel Extensions. It explains how to combine different execution techniques with automatically parallelized structures that will be available in Visual Studio 2010. The chapter also shows how to transform a single-threaded imaging library into a parallelized algorithm, and how to combine the .NET Parallel Extensions with a responsive user interface.

Chapter 12 helps you in creating a whole application from scratch with completely multithreaded code offering a responsive user interface for every event. It demonstrates on how to join all the pieces in a complete application, parallelize the execution as much as possible to offer great scalability, an impressive performance, and an incredibly responsive user interface. It shows how to combine different parallelized tasks with multiple-window UIs, always offering the best possible performance, and the most responsive UI.

What you need for this book

You need prior knowledge of C# programming language and .NET Framework, as this book helps developers to find out how to improve their applications' performance and responsiveness. However, you do not need to be a C# guru to understand the book. In order to execute the code included in most chapters you need Visual C# 2005, 2008 or 2010 (CTP). Nevertheless, in order to run the examples in the last two chapters, you need Visual C# 2008 or 2010 (CTP), as you will be using many features available in these new releases.

You can use Visual C# Express Editions for most of the exercises. However, the Threads Window and many multithreading debugging features are not available in these editions. Thus, you will not be able to run some debugging exercises included in the book. Therefore, you are encouraged to use at least a Trial or Standard Edition, instead of working with the Express Editions.

You need a computer with at least two cores (dual-core) or two microprocessors installed in order to achieve significant results for most experiences, as we will be focusing on multi-core development. You can run the exercises in single-core microprocessors, but you will not be able to understand the improvements you are achieving.

Who is this book for

Whether you are a beginner to working with threads or an old hand who is looking for a reference, this book should be on your desk.

This book is for people who are interested in working with C#. This book will help you to build scalable, high performance software using parallel programming techniques.

The book will prove beneficial to C++ programmers who are interested in moving to C#, and to beginner programmers that are interested in learning C#. Students learning introductory threaded programming in C# will also gain benefits from this book.

Conventions

In this book, you will find a number of styles of text that distinguish between different kinds of information. Here are some examples of these styles, and an explanation of their meaning.

Code words in text are shown as follows: "Therefore, the main thread continues with its next statements as if the method `RunWorkerAsync()` is completed successfully."

A block of code will be set as follows:

```
if (bakCodebreaker.CancellationPending)
{
    // The user requested to cancel the process
    e.Cancel = true;
    return;
}
```

New terms and **important words** are introduced in a bold-type font. Words that you see on the screen, in menus or dialog boxes for example, appear in our text like this: "the code now disables the **Start** button and enables the **Stop** button ".

 Warnings or important notes appear in a box like this.

 Tips and tricks appear like this.

Practical, hands-on actions and instructions are introduced with a Time For Action heading, and use numbered steps to make it easier to read:

Time for action – Uploading a document

1. Action 1
2. Action 2
3. Action 3

When instructions need some extra explanation so that they make sense, they are followed with...

What just happened?

... which explains how the task or instructions you just completed work, so that you learn how Moodle works as you complete useful activities.

You will also find some other learning aids in the book, including:

Pop quiz

These are short questions intended to help you test your own understanding.

Have a go hero

These set practical challenges and give you ideas for experimenting with what you have learned.

Reader feedback

Feedback from our readers is always welcome. Let us know what you think about this book, what you liked or may have disliked. Reader feedback is important for us to develop titles that you really get the most out of.

To send us general feedback, simply drop an email to feedback@packtpub.com, making sure to mention the book title in the subject of your message.

If there is a book that you need and would like to see us publish, please send us a note in the **SUGGEST A TITLE** form on www.packtpub.com or email suggest@packtpub.com.

If there is a topic that you have expertise in and you are interested in either writing or contributing to a book, see our author guide on www.packtpub.com/authors.

Customer support

Now that you are the proud owner of a Packt book, we have a number of things to help you to get the most from your purchase.

Downloading the example code for the book

Visit http://www.packtpub.com/files/code/7108_Code.zip to directly download the example code.

The downloadable files contain instructions on how to use them.

Errata

Although we have taken every care to ensure the accuracy of our contents, mistakes do happen. If you find a mistake in one of our books—maybe a mistake in text or code—we would be grateful if you would report this to us. By doing this you can save other readers from frustration, and help to improve subsequent versions of this book. If you find any errata, report them by visiting http://www.packtpub.com/support, selecting your book, clicking on the **let us know** link, and entering the details of your errata. Once your errata are verified, your submission will be accepted and the errata added to the list of existing errata. The existing errata can be viewed by selecting your title from http://www.packtpub.com/support.

Piracy

Piracy of copyright material on the Internet is an ongoing problem across all media. At Packt, we take the protection of our copyright and licenses very seriously. If you come across any illegal copies of our works in any form on the Internet, please provide the location address or web site name immediately so we can pursue a remedy.

Please contact us at copyright@packtpub.com with a link to the suspected pirated material.

We appreciate your help in protecting our authors, and our ability to bring you valuable content.

Questions

You can contact us at questions@packtpub.com if you are having a problem with some aspect of the book, and we will do our best to address it.

1
Taking Advantage of Multiprocessing and Multiple Cores

We already know how to develop applications using the C# programming language. However, modern computers are prepared for running many operations in parallel, concurrently. C# is an advanced programming language. Thus, users and our bosses expect a C# application to offer great performance and a responsive user interface.

So, let's take our C# development skills to the next level. We want to take full advantage of modern hardware. For that reason, the first thing we have to do is try and understand how modern computers differ from older computers. Let's understand the parallelization revolution. The only requirement to be able to develop parallelized C# applications is to understand the basics of the C# programming language and the Visual Studio IDE. We will cover the rest of the requirements in our journey through the parallel programming world!

We must understand some fundamentals related to the multiprocessing capabilities offered by modern computers. We will have to consider them in order to develop applications that take full advantage of parallel processing features. In this chapter, we will cover many topics to help us understand the new challenges involved in parallel programming with modern hardware. Upon reading it and following the exercises we shall:

- Begin a paradigm shift in software design
- Understand the techniques for developing a new generation of applications
- Have an idea of the performance increases we can achieve using parallel programming with C#
- Perform accurate response time estimation for critical processes

Mono-processor systems: The old gladiators

The **mono-processor** systems use an old-fashioned, classic computer architecture. The microprocessor receives an input stream, executes the necessary processes and sends the results in an output stream that is distributed to the indicated destinations. The following diagram represents a mono-processor system (one processor with just one **core**) with one user, and one task running:

This working scheme is known as **IPO (Input; Processing; Output)** or **SISD (Single Instruction, Single Data)**. This basic design represents the von Neumann machines, developed by this outstanding mathematician in 1952.

Single core: Only one warrior to fight against everybody

These days, systems with a single processing core, with just one logical processor, are known as **single core**.

When there is only one user running an application in a mono-processor machine and the processor is fast enough to deliver an adequate response time in **critical** operations, the model will work without any major problems.

For example, consider a robotic servant in the kitchen having just two hands to work with. If you ask him to do one task that requires both his hands, such as washing up, he will be efficient. He has a single processing core.

However, suppose that you ask him to do various tasks—wash up, clean the oven, make your lunch, mop the floor, cook dinner for your friends, and so on. You give him the list of tasks, and he works down the tasks. But since there is so much washing up, its 2 pm before he even starts making your lunch—by which time you get very hungry and make it yourself. You need more robots when you have multiple tasks. You need multiple execution cores, many logical processors.

Each task performed by the robot is a critical operation, because you and your friends are very hungry!

Let's consider another case. We have a mono-processor computer and it has many users connected, requesting services which the computer must process. In this case, we have many input streams and many output streams, one for each connected user. As there is just one microprocessor, there is only one input channel and only one output channel. Therefore the input streams are en-queued (**multiplexing**) for their processing, and then the same happens with the output streams but is inverted, as shown in the following diagram:

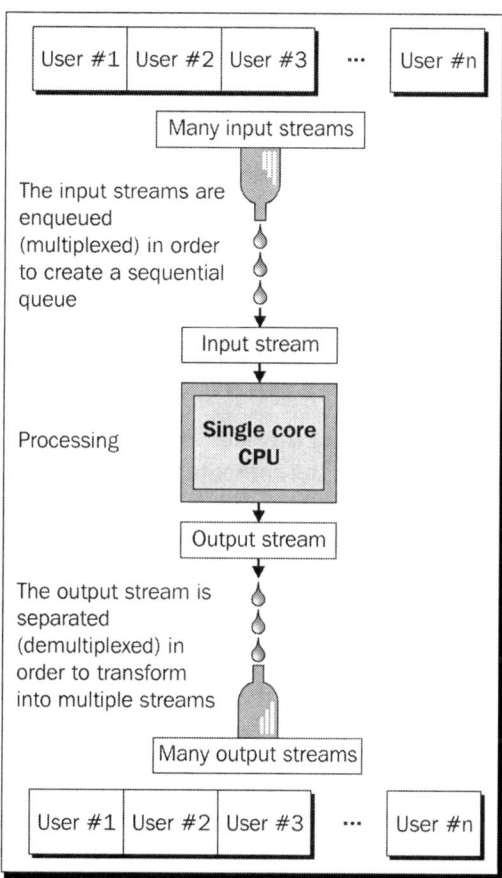

Doing a tiny bit of each task

Why does the robot take so long to cook dinner for you and your friends? The robot does a tiny bit of each task, and then goes back to the list to see what else he should be doing. He has to keep moving to the list, read it, and then start a new task. The time it takes to complete the list is much longer because he is not fast enough to finish so many tasks in the required time. That's **multiplexing**, and the delay is called **von Neumann's bottleneck**. Multiplexing takes additional time because you have just one robot to do everything you need in the kitchen.

The systems with concurrent access by multiple users are known as **multi-user** systems.

If the processor is not fast enough to deliver an adequate response time in every critical operation requested by each connected user, a bottleneck will be generated in the processor's input queue. This is well known in computer architecture as von Neumann's bottleneck.

There are three possible solutions to this problem, each consisting of upgrading or increasing one of the following:

- The processor's speed, by using a faster robot. He will need less time to finish each task.
- The processor's capacity to process instructions concurrently (in parallel), that is, adding more hands to the robot and the capability to use his hands to do different jobs.
- The number of installed processors or the number of processing cores, that is, adding more robots. They can all focus on one task, but everything gets done in parallel. All tasks are completed faster and you get your lunch on time. That is multitasking.

No matter which option we pick, we must consider other factors that depend particularly on the kind of operations performed by the computer and which could generate additional bottlenecks. In some cases, the main memory speed access could be too slow (the robot takes too much time to read each task). In some other cases, the disks subsystem could have bad response times (the robot takes too much time to memorize the tasks to be done), and so on. It is important to make a detailed analysis on these topics before taking a decision to troubleshoot bottlenecks.

Moreover, sometimes the amount of data that needs to be processed is too large and the problem is the transfer time between the memory and the processor. The robot is too slow to move each hand. Poor robot! Why don't you buy a new model?

In the last few years, every new micro-architecture developed by microprocessor manufacturers has focused on improving the processors' capacity to run instructions in parallel (a robot with more hands). Some examples of these are the continuous duplication of processing structures like the **ALU (Arithmetic and Logic Unit)** and the **FPU (Floating Point Unit)**, and the growing number of processing cores that are included in one single physical processor. Hence, you can build a super robot with many independent robots and many hands. Each sub-robot can be made to specialize in a specific task, thus parallelizing the work.

Computers used as servers, with many connected users and running applications, take greater advantage of modern processors' capacity to run instructions in parallel as compared to those computers used by only one user. We will learn how to take full advantage of those features in the applications developed using the C# programming language. You want the robot to get your lunch on time!

The performance waterfall

Considering all the analysis we have done so far to develop new algorithms for the applications of critical processes, we can conceive the performance waterfall shown in the following image:

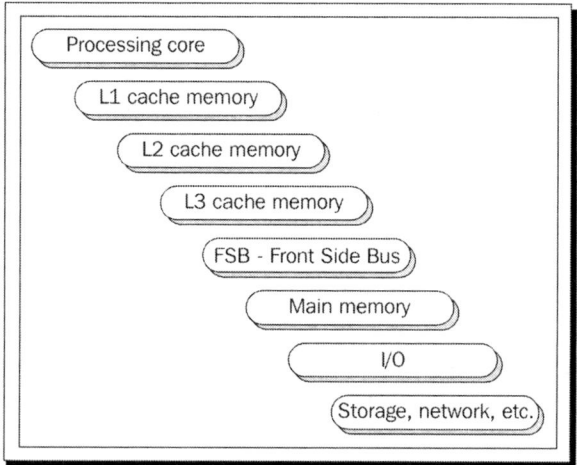

FSB (Front Side Bus)

The FSB is a bus that transports the data between the CPU and the outside world. When the CPU needs data from memory or from the I/O subsystem, the FSB is the highway used for that information interchange.

This performance waterfall will help us understand how we can take full advantage of modern multiprocessing. The topmost part of the waterfall represents the best performance. Hence, we lose speed as we go down each step. It is not a linear relationship, and the hardware infrastructure in which the application runs will determine the exact performance loss with each step represented in the above figure. However, the cascade is the same for every case, neither dependent on the kind of application being developed nor the hardware being used.

We must design the algorithms bearing in mind to keep the steps, down to the bottom of the performance waterfall, minimal. We should go downstairs as an exception and not as a rule. For example, a good decision consists of recovering all the necessary information from the disk subsystem or the network in one pass. Then, we can take everything to memory and begin processing without having to search for the data in every iteration.

A small performance problem in a mono-processing application multiplies its defects in its translation to a concurrent model. Therefore, we must consider these details.

As a rule or as a design pattern, the best approach when optimizing a critical process consists of running its tasks in the higher steps of the performance waterfall most of the time. It should visit the main memory in some iteration, but as little as possible. Each step down from the top means losing a small portion of the performance.

Let's draw an example of this. We have a state-of-the-art laser printer capable of printing 32 pages per minute. It is in an office on the sixth floor, but the paper ream stays on the first one. When the printer finishes with a page, a person must step down the six floors to take another sheet of paper and put it in the printer's paper feed tray. It takes about five to ten minutes for this person to bring each sheet of paper to the printer, as he goes downstairs, then he goes upstairs, on the way, he spends some time talking to a neighbor, and then he arrives back to the office with the sheet of paper. In addition, he could feel thirsty and go for a drink. As we can see, he wasted the state-of-the-art printer's performance (the execution core) because the paper tray was not fed quickly enough. The problem is that he brings a small quantity each time he arrives at the office (the hard disk and the I/O subsystem).

The printer's work would be more efficient if the person could feed it with a paper ream containing 500 sheets. The person could bring another paper ream with 500 sheets from the first floor when the printer's paper feed tray has only 50 sheets left (bringing it to the cache memories L1, L2, or L3).

What happens if we have eight printers working in parallel instead of only one? In order to take full advantage of their performance and their efficient printing process, all of them must have a good number of sheets in their respective paper feed trays. This is the goal we must accomplish when we plan an algorithm for parallelism.

 In the rest of the book, we will consider the performance waterfall for many examples and will try to achieve optimal results. We will not leave behind the necessary pragmatism in order to improve performance within a reasonable developing time.

Have a go hero – Researching micro-architectures and applications

A group of researchers need some consulting services of an IT professional specialized in parallel computing. They are not very clear in explaining the kind of research they are doing. However, you decide to help them.

They want to find the best computer micro-architecture needed to parallelize an application.

Research the new micro-architectures that are being prepared by leading PC microprocessor manufacturers, and the schedules for their release, particularly on these topics:

- Are they increasing the processors' speed?

- Do they mention upgrades about the processor's capacity to process instructions concurrently (in parallel)?
- Are they talking about increasing the number of processing cores?

Multi-processor systems: Many warriors to win a battle

On one hand, systems with multiple processors are a solution to von Neumann's bottleneck; on the other hand, it is necessary to know their detailed features in order to break some myths about them. They do not offer an immediate performance improvement for all applications! The dilemma is that systems with multiple processors are not always the most appropriate solution to a performance problem.

There are two basic procedures for distributing tasks in systems with multiple processors:

- ◆ **Symmetrical multiprocessing**. This is also known as **SMP**. Any available processor or core can execute tasks. The most used and efficient one is the 'n' way symmetrical multiprocessing, where 'n' is replaced by the number of installed processors. With this procedure, each processor can execute a task isolated from the rest, and also when particular software is not optimized for multiprocessing systems. In the following image we can see how this scheme of assigning a task to a processor works. You have eight robots in the kitchen. When a robot is free, he goes back to the list to see what else he should be doing and starts working on the new task ('8' way symmetrical multiprocessing):

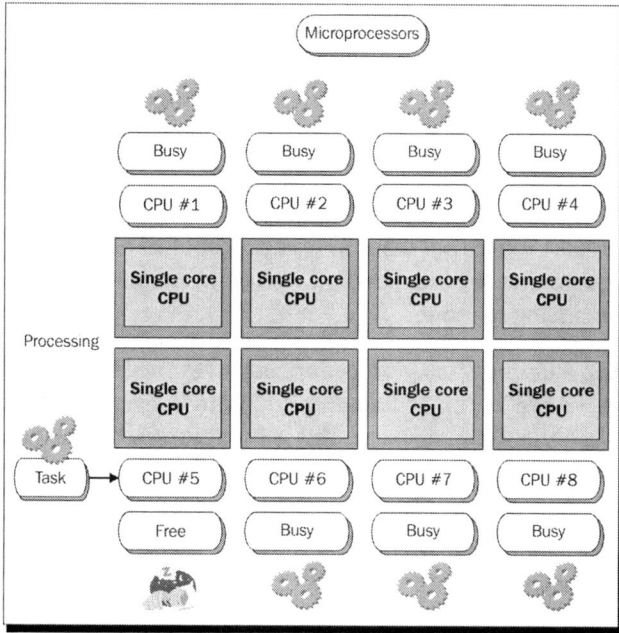

♦ **Asymmetrical multiprocessing**. This is also known as **AMP** or **ASMP**. Usually, one processor acts as the main processor. It works as a manager and is in charge of distributing the tasks to the other available processors, using different kinds of algorithms for this purpose. In the following image, we can see how this scheme assigns a task to a processor. You have nine robots in the kitchen. One of them is in charge of tasks' distribution (the manager robot). He is always reading the list and watching the other robots' work (the worker robots, processors dedicated to run tasks). When a robot is free, the manager robot tells him what to do next:

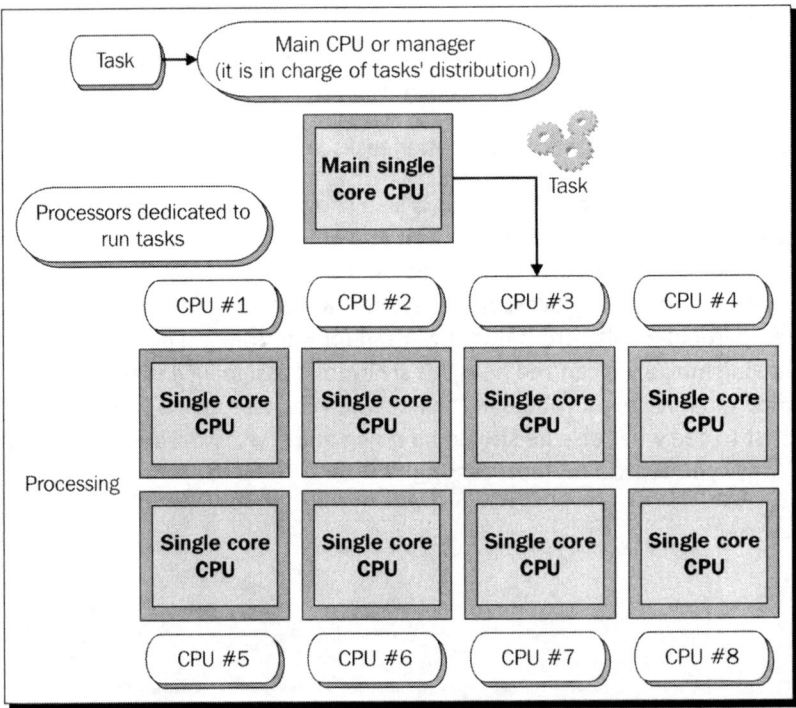

The robots are expensive! You do not want to waste a robot to distribute the tasks. You would rather have robots that are independent. You want robots arranged similar to a symmetrical multiprocessing scheme.

The 'n' way symmetric multiprocessing procedure achieves the best performance and the best resources usage, where 'n' can be two or more. With it, every available processor can execute tasks in an absolutely dynamic way. This is the reason why most multiprocessing systems use this approach.

 We will learn programming techniques that combine the advantages of the SMP and AMP approaches.

A symmetric multiprocessing system with many users connected or numerous tasks running provides a good solution to von Neumann's bottleneck. The multiple input streams are distributed to the different available processors for their execution, and they generate multiple concurrent output streams, as shown in the following image:

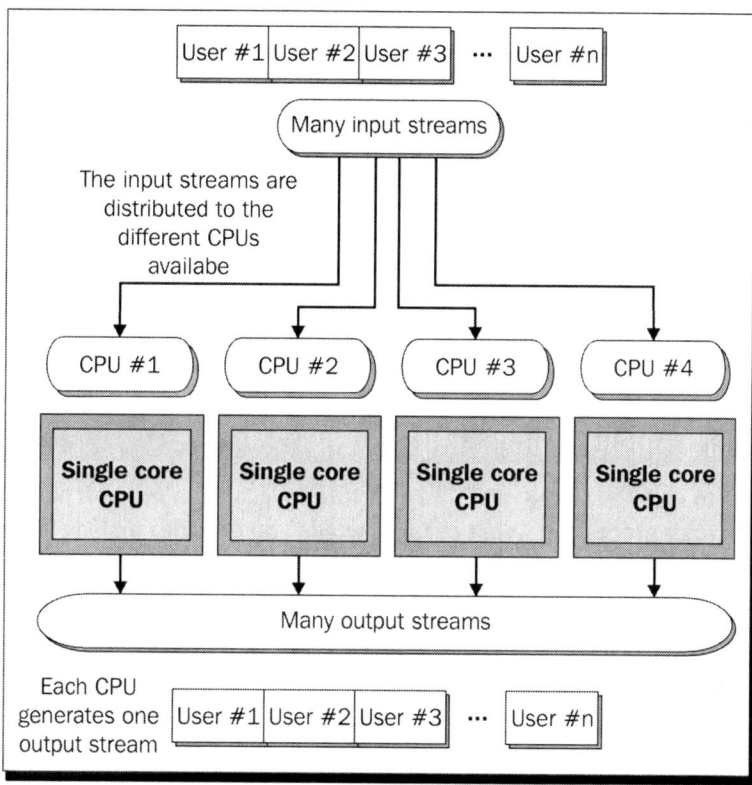

But what if there is so much washing up that it takes a single robot several days to complete? A bottleneck will be generated again. Are his hands as fast as necessary? Are his legs too slow? Is he a lazy robot?

We have to take into account that if the response time of a processor to a user's request is not quick enough, a bottleneck will be generated again. However, it can also be generated by other problems along the performance waterfall. We must delve deeper into the process in order to understand these potential performance issues.

Therefore, while the number of users or the number of tasks being executed in a multiprocessing system increases, it is more likely to run out of processing capacity, among other things. If this happens, each user's tasks being executed will take longer to run, and for that reason, the response time will worsen.

Under these circumstances, there are two possible approaches to keep the response time untouched:

- Replacing the existing processors with new ones (buying super-robots): In order to apply this solution, there should be processors with better performance ratios than the ones that are currently used, or with more execution cores (to achieve more parallelism). Besides, they have to be compatible with the motherboard and with the sockets used by them. The great disadvantage of this approach is that the old processors are thrown out of the way. Besides, it is also expensive.
- Adding new processors to work with the existing ones (buying new robots to help the existing ones): In order to apply this solution, there should be free sockets in the motherboard.

[These solutions apply only when the information systems are optimized to take full advantage of a dynamically growing parallelism capability.]

Have a go hero – Multi-processing systems

It is a good idea to look inside the micro-architectures available in modern personal computers with multiprocessing. What changes would you consider making in the applications in order to take full advantage of them?

Estimating performance improvements

One of the most common mistakes in designing or upgrading systems with multiple processors is making linear projections in their processing speed. It is very common to consider that each additional processor in the system will increase the performance in a way that is directly proportional to its processing capacity.

For instance, when we have a system with just one processor, and if we add three more, we will not have four times the performance. This is because each time we add a processor, the time they dedicate to coordinate their work and the task assignment process increases. Therefore, because of the increased processing power spent on managing tasks, their performance will not increase linearly.

The additional robots added to the kitchen must talk among themselves to coordinate their work.

The coordination costs and the performance increment depend upon a number of factors, including:

- The operating system and its management procedures for coordinating and distributing processes and threads among multiple processors: It is the robots' accuracy to assign the appropriate task to the most capable robot model for a particular task.

- The level of optimization for running multiple processors offered by applications: This is one of the most relevant points, even when we are using an 'n' way symmetric multiprocessing scheme. In this book, we will learn to reach high levels of optimizations for concurrency in our software. This can be correlated to the robots' abilities to work with other robots in the same tasks.

- The microprocessors' micro-architecture: This corresponds to the robots' speed to move hands and legs, and so on.

- The speed of the memory subsystem shared by the microprocessors: It is the robots' communications interface.

- The speed of the I/O buses shared by the microprocessors: It is the robots' efficiency and precision to manage their hands and legs to do each task (moping the floor and cooking, among others).

All these items represent a problem when we design or upgrade a machine, because we need answers to these questions:

- How many microprocessors do we need when the number of users increased? How many robots do you need according to the number of friends/tasks?

- How many microprocessors do we need to increase an application's performance? How many robots do you need to accelerate the wash up time?

- How many microprocessors do we need to run a critical process within a specific time period? How many robots do you need to clean the oven in five minutes?

We need a reference, similar to the one offered in the following table in which we can see the coordination cost and the relative performance for an increasing number of processors:

Number of processors	Coordination cost		Relative performance	
	In relative processors	In percentage	In relative processors	In percentage
1	0.00	0%	1.00	100%
2	0.09	5%	1.91	95%
3	0.29	10%	2.71	90%
4	0.54	14%	3.46	86%
5	0.84	17%	4.16	83%

Number of processors	Coordination cost		Relative performance	
	In relative processors	In percentage	In relative processors	In percentage
6	1.17	19%	4.83	81%
7	1.52	22%	5.48	78%
8	1.90	24%	6.10	76%
9	2.29	25%	6.71	75%
10	2.70	27%	7.30	73%
11	3.12	28%	7.88	72%
12	3.56	30%	8.44	70%
13	4.01	31%	8.99	69%
14	4.47	32%	9.53	68%
15	4.94	33%	10.06	67%
16	5.42	34%	10.58	66%
17	5.91	35%	11.09	65%
18	6.40	36%	11.60	64%
19	6.91	36%	12.09	64%
20	7.42	37%	12.58	63%
21	7.93	38%	13.07	62%
22	8.46	38%	13.54	62%
23	8.99	39%	14.01	61%
24	9.52	40%	14.48	60%
25	10.07	40%	14.93	60%
26	10.61	41%	15.39	59%
27	11.16	41%	15.84	59%
28	11.72	42%	16.28	58%
29	12.28	42%	16.72	58%
30	12.85	43%	17.15	57%
31	13.42	43%	17.58	57%
32	14.00	44%	18.00	56%

This table was prepared taking into account an overall average performance test with many typical applications well optimized for multiprocessing, and the most modern processors with multiple execution cores used in workstations and servers. These processors were all compatible with AMD64 or EMT64 instruction sets, also known as x86-64. We can take these values as a reference in order to have an idea of the performance improvement that we will see in optimized applications.

As we can see in the following image, the coordination cost grows exponentially as the number of processors or cores increases:

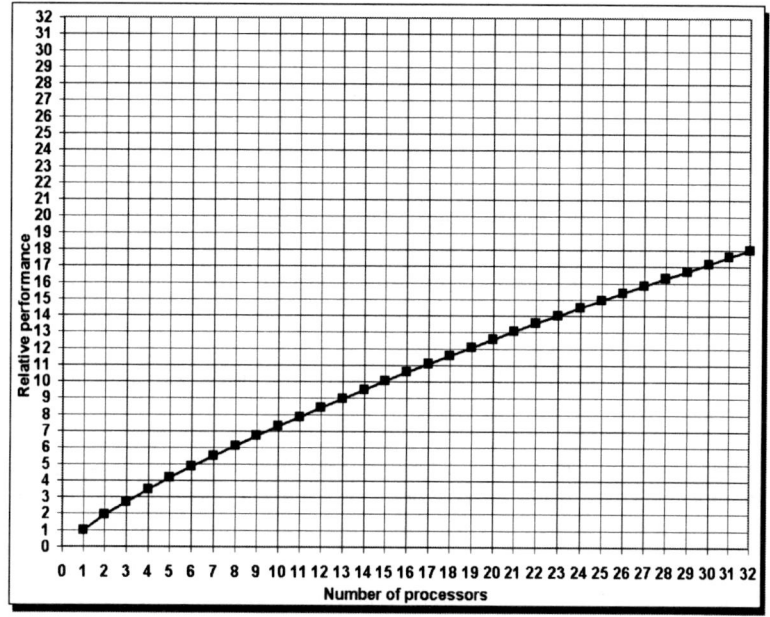

As we can see in the following image, the relative performance grows logarithmically as the number of processors or cores increase:

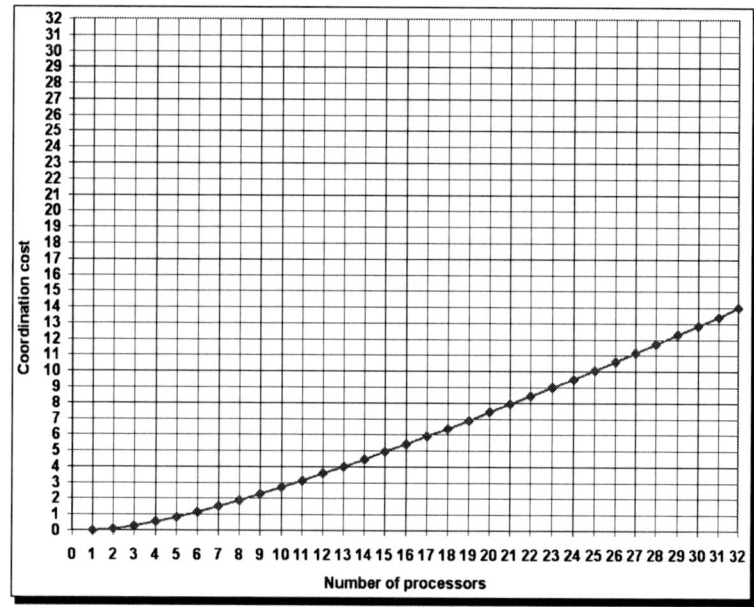

The formulas used to calculate the values presented in the table and the graphs:

Coordination cost = 0.3 x logarithm (number of processors) x (number of processors - 1)

Relative performance = number of processors – coordination cost

The percentages are the result of the division between the coordination cost or the relative performance and the total number of microprocessors installed.

Nowadays the problem is that, without many concurrent users, multiple processor systems have not proved to be as useful as expected. The use of machines equipped with more than one processor, in workstations used by just one user, is meaningful when the applications executed are designed to work with multiple processors.

Most applications designed for a single user are not optimized to take full advantage of multiple processors. Therefore, if the code is not prepared to use these additional processors, their performance will not improve, as was explained earlier.

But, why does this happen? The answer is simple. The process for developing applications that take full advantage of multiple processors is much more complex than traditional software development (this book will show how to make this task much easier). With the exception of specialized applications requiring a lot of processing capacity and those dedicated to resolving complex calculations, most applications have been developed using a traditional, linear programming scheme.

Nevertheless, the release of physical microprocessors with multiple logical execution cores leads to the widespread availability of multiprocessing systems and an urgent need to take full advantage of these micro-architectures.

A system with multiple processors can be analyzed and measured by the following items:

- Total number of processors and their features—the total number of robots and their features

- Processing capacity (discounting the coordination overload)—the robots' speed to work on each task (without communicating)

- Micro-architecture and architecture (the number of execution cores in each physical microprocessor and the number of physical microprocessors with each micro-architecture)—the sub-robots in each robot, the number of hands, legs, and their speed

- Shared memory's bus bandwidth–the maximum number of concurrent communications that the robots can establish

- I/O bus bandwidth—the robots' efficiency, precision, and speed to manage their hands and legs concurrently to do each task

 **Bandwidth between processors**

This bus allows the processors to establish a fluid communication between them. It is also known as the inter-processor bus. In some micro-architectures, this bus is the same as the FSB. It competes with the outputs to the microprocessor's outside world and therefore steals available bandwidth. The great diversity in micro-architectures makes it difficult to foretell the performance of the applications optimized for multiprocessing in every running context that is possible in modern computing world.

We are considering neither the storage space nor the amount of memory. We are focused on the parameters that define the operation and the performance of multiple processors.

Have a go hero – Calculating an estimated performance improvement

The group of researchers will ask you many questions regarding the performance improvements that you can achieve in your new applications. You must be prepared to answer those questions.

Take some applications developed in any programming language and measure their performance. Using the procedure and the formulas explained, calculate an estimated performance improvement that can be achieved by optimizing them.

The numbers are a temptation to begin recoding old-fashioned linear programming applications, aren't they? Let's go on to study the technical concepts we will use in the rest of the book. We need them in order to begin coding lots of practical samples.

Avoiding bottlenecks

Many bottlenecks can arise in systems with multiple processors, besides the von Neumann's one (that is reduced, but still alive). The problems appear when the system runs out of processing capacity.

The following list enumerates the components in which the bottlenecks may appear with some possible solutions:

- Shared memory's bus

    Some possible solutions for a bottleneck here can be:

    - Increase each processor's cache memory
    - Increase each processor's cache memory levels (levels 1, 2, 3, and 4 in some cases)

- ❑ Replace the processors with others having more cache memory and/or more levels

- ❑ Replace the processors with others having a memory controller integrated in the physical microprocessor

- ❑ Use a motherboard providing dedicated buses to shared memory

◆ Inter-processor bus

To avoid a bottleneck in the inter-processor bus, we can replace the motherboard and the processors with another set offering a bus with a wider bandwidth between them. It is expensive to troubleshoot this because you are replacing two of the most expensive components of the system.

◆ I/O shared bus (that is, hard disks)

Some possible solutions for a bottleneck here can be:

- ❑ Increase the amount of the system's physical memory dedicated to work as a cache memory for the I/O subsystem, for example, the disks' cache

- ❑ Use a faster I/O bus; it could involve changing cards or adding new ones for the chosen bus; in some cases, the only way is to replace the motherboard

- ❑ Use a motherboard providing dedicated buses to shared I/O

◆ Network (wireless or cabled)

Some possible solutions for a bottleneck here can be:

- ❑ Increase the buffers dedicated to the network or enhance the amount of physical system's memory committed to work as a cache memory for the network subsystem

- ❑ Reduce network accesses

- ❑ Increase the number of network cards

- ❑ Increase the network speed

◆ Storage subsystem performance

Some possible solutions to improve the performance here can be:

- ❑ Increase the amount of the system's physical memory dedicated to work as a cache memory for the storage subsystem

- ❑ Use a faster I/O bus; it could implicate changing cards or adding new ones for the chosen bus; in some cases, the only way is to replace the motherboard

- ❑ Improve the storage configurations (for example, using disk arrays)

It is very important to take all these bottlenecks into account in order to develop applications that take full advantage of the available parallelism in modern computers. We will design the applications' architecture using algorithms that avoid these bottlenecks.

Have a go hero – Detecting bottlenecks

It is a good idea to detect bottlenecks in many applications using the tools provided by the operating system to monitor different subsystems. What changes would you consider making in your system to avoid them? Do you think you have enough memory to avoid continuous slow accesses to the hard disks?

There is a lot of software in the market that does not use the power offered by the available computers. We can improve the performance of this software.

Taking advantage of multiple execution cores

One of the techniques for improving the processing capacity consists of increasing the microprocessors' working frequency (**over-clocking**), which raises the number of instructions capable of processing in the same period. This technique has been used for many years and evolved from the legendary 8086/8088 with its poor 4.77 MHz (Megahertz) to the many GHz (Gigahertz) of modern microprocessors.

Nevertheless, microprocessor manufacturers are increasingly facing difficulties in raising the frequencies because the manufacturing process becomes more complex and the generated heat is difficult to dissipate in an efficient and inexpensive way.

Consider our robot instance again. You want to buy a single robot, but want him to clean the oven in 5 seconds. That is possible, but he needs plutonium as an energy source because he must move his arms and legs at a very high speed. Besides, he needs an ambient temperature of 5°F (5 degrees Fahrenheit) or -15°C (-15 degrees Celsius). Why? Because metals moving at very high speeds generate heat. You do not want a burnt robot. Moreover, plutonium is very expensive. Something similar happens with modern microprocessors.

Therefore, the other alternative is to develop new micro-architectures; incorporating first duplicated, and then quadruplicated processing structures, and so on. In this way, there are many sub-processors in one single microprocessor's package. These sub-processors are known as execution cores or processing cores.

Microprocessors with multiple execution cores, also known as multi-core, offer many complete execution cores that are interconnected in a single package. Their physical look is very similar to a conventional single core microprocessor. Nevertheless, they are equivalent to something like two or more microprocessors inside a single piece of silicon, as well as many pieces of silicon interconnected between themselves under the same physical package. Of course, we are avoiding deep technical issues.

 At present, most available modern computers have at least microprocessors with two execution cores (dual core). Therefore, they are computers with multiprocessing capabilities.

Ever since the rise of multiple execution cores, the possibilities of combining the communication architectures, the different cores owned, and shared resources have been multiplying. As with everything in life, in each possibility, there is a trade-off between manufacturing costs and performance. For this reason, a new land appeared in the microprocessors' world.

In some cases, each execution core includes L1 and L2 cache memories, as shown in the following image:

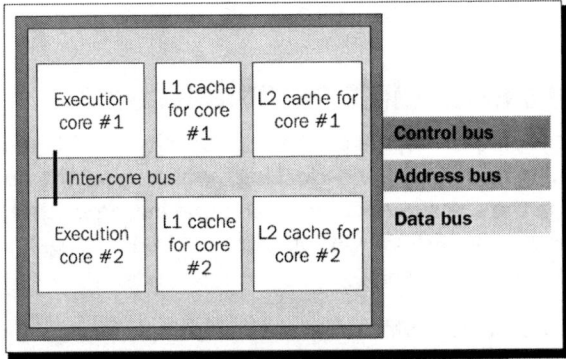

In other cases, L2 cache memories are shared between two or more cores. Therefore, each core will have access to the whole L2 cache, as shown in this image:

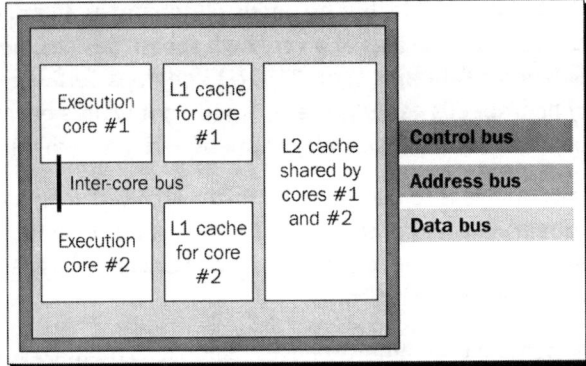

The greater the number of resources included in each core and the fewer the resources shared with the others, the greater the processing speed achieved by each core. On the other hand, sharing resources between cores benefits applications not optimized for multiprocessing because they use a single execution core.

The robots' communications interface must be as efficient as possible, since you want the robots to do many different tasks.

Achieving efficient external memory accesses is one of the most important matters with these micro-architectures. The communication with external memory has a great overhead with respect to time, as compared to the internal cores' speed. When we design the most critical algorithms for our applications, we must minimize the external memory accessed in order to achieve the best performance. It is one of the main subjects to consider in designing applications that will be developed with parallelism in mind.

There are two options available to speed up the tasks done by the robots, taking into account the washing up example:

- Divide the washing up into as many parts as the number of robots available and have the robots do their own portion of the global task
- Have a big pile of washing up, and have each robot pick items up from that pile when they have room in their sinks to do that washing up

The internal bus is very important, because it transports data between the different execution cores. Many microprocessors use one or more dedicated buses for that task with very high working speeds, while others establish those communications through the FSB (a less efficient way). When the microprocessor has more than two cores, the architecture could be any possible merger between the known architectures for single and dual core microprocessors. There are some microprocessors built by two pair of cores, each one using a dedicated bus for the data interchange between both the cores, but with both pairs talking through the FSB. The following diagram illustrates this micro-architecture:

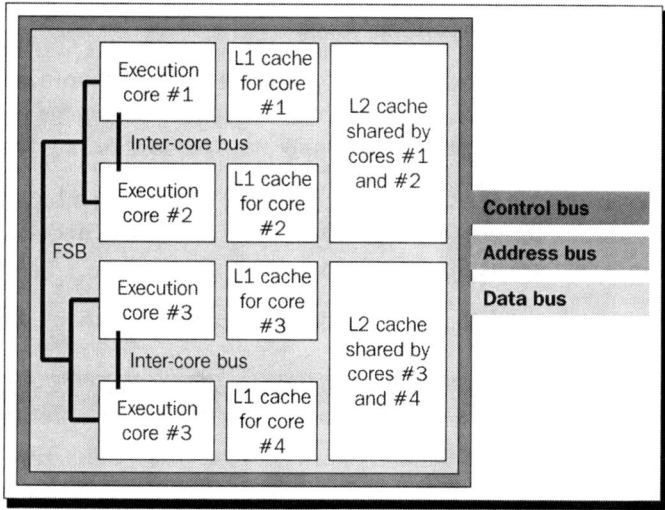

When we are optimizing applications to take full advantage of these micro-architectures, one of the things that we should minimize is the information going through the FSB. Besides, we must consider this in evaluating the optimized applications efficiency. If we don't, we will probably draft wrong conclusions about them and we will try to optimize already maximized performances (according to the underlying hardware architecture).

A system with asymmetric multiprocessing based in many independent physical processors has many FSBs to access external memory, one for each physical processor. However, a system with a microprocessor having multiple cores has to share the FSB which acts as a great single door to the outside world and to the external memory. Therefore, the tasks for coordinating the activities in the execution cores require additional time to avoid conflicts in the shared FSB. This is an important difference between multiprocessing using independent physical microprocessors and multiple cores in one physical microprocessor.

The probability that a FSB will become a bottleneck is very high when applications are not optimized to take full advantage of cache memories included in each core. Therefore, when the software is running over these micro-architectures, it should avoid frequent accesses to the main memory.

Besides, many asymmetric multiprocessing systems use duplicated communication channels with the main memory. This feature is not available in many multi-core microprocessors. It makes it nearly impossible to predict the performance of applications in completely different systems architectures. However, designing them with parallelism in mind will take full advantage of any feature present in the system.

Nowadays, microprocessors with multiple execution cores are widespread. However, we can find many of them arranged in an 'n' way asymmetric multiprocessing system such as an eight-core system with two physical quad-core microprocessors. It is something very attractive in high range workstations and servers.

In the coming years, microprocessors are going to include more and more processing cores. Modern operating systems are already optimized to take advantage of their parallel processing capabilities. We must optimize our applications to take full advantage of them.

Analyzing the micro-architectures used in modern microprocessors is a topic for an entire book. However, we needed some knowledge about them in order to understand the parallel processing capabilities that are useful for our goals.

Do not expect plutonium robots! They will still be very expensive to maintain.

Have a go hero – Counting cores

Look at the computers that you will be able to use with the researchers. How many microprocessors do they have? How many cores does each microprocessor have? You can use CPU-Z in order to find this information. You can download this free software from http://www.cpuid.com/.

In the following image, you can see the information provided by CPU-Z for a computer with a microprocessor providing four cores:

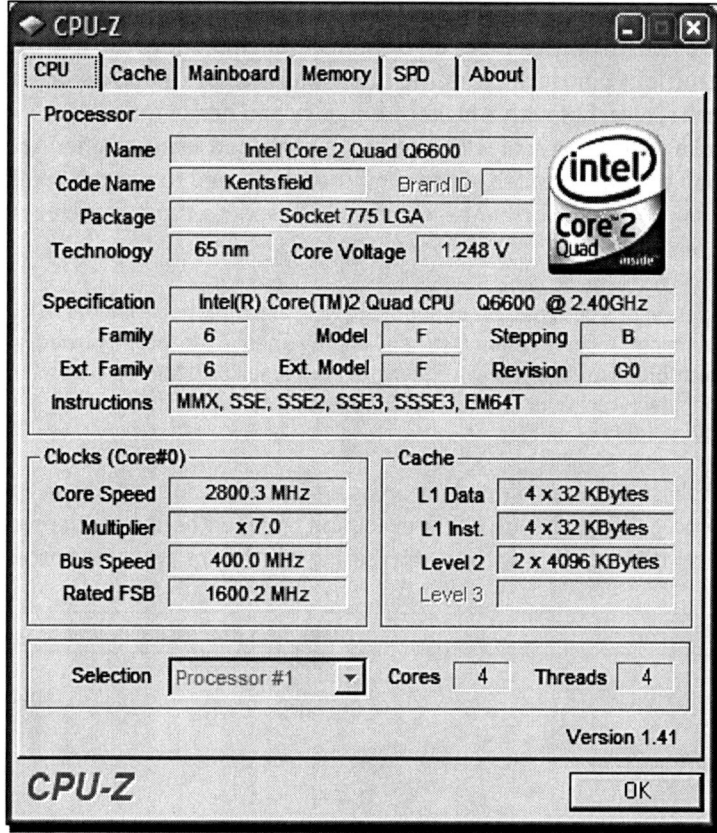

At the bottom of the window, the **Cores** item displays number **4**.

Scalability

Talking about information systems, scalability is an application's ability to upgrade its performance, its response time, or the number of users to which it can provide services. We can measure scalability from many points of views:

- Processing capacity—the robots can do the tasks in lesser time
- Features and services (new functions, new cards, and new hardware)—the robots can do new tasks (prepare squeezed orange juice)
- Storage capacity—the robots can save tasks for each day of the month
- Memory—the robots remember more tasks without having to go back to the list every minute

We will analyze scalability taking into account the processing capacity, leaving behind other hardware resources, which could break down scalability, as the ones mentioned earlier.

We have two possible ways to scale applications designed for mono-processing. One way is to use a microprocessor with a more efficient micro-architecture, capable of executing many more instructions per clock cycle. The other way is to use a microprocessor with the same micro-architecture, but with a higher frequency and hence more clock cycles. So, if we cannot find a microprocessor with one of the explained features offering a better performance than the one installed in the computer dedicated to run the application, we will not be able to improve its performance, enhance its response time, or increase the number of concurrent users.

 Applications designed for mono-processing are completely limited to the microprocessor manufacturers' improvements. Moreover, nowadays, microprocessors' working frequencies have stabilized. Microprocessors manufacturers tend to offer more processing cores, hence more parallelism capabilities.

The following table shows the complete processing power exploitation of an application designed for mono-processing with linear execution code, without considering parallelism. The table presents this situation with the increasing number of available processing cores:

Number of cores	Maximum processing power usage
1	100.00%
2	50.00%
3	33.33%
4	25.00%
6	16.33%
8	12.50%
12	8.33%
16	6.25%
24	4.16%
32	3.13%
48	2.08%
64	1.56%

The numbers are scary and demonstrate the need to tame multiprocessing quickly.

On the other hand, with applications designed to take full advantage of parallelism, multiprocessing, and multiple execution cores, scalability depends on the total number of processors or cores we can incorporate. Because applications are optimized for parallelism, each added processor will offer an immediate enhancement in performance despite the added management costs explained earlier. Hence, we will be able to achieve better performance using applications optimized for parallelism.

 If an application optimized for parallelism requires more processing capacity than the one offered by the most powerful microprocessor available in the market, and it would be scalable, then we can add other microprocessors or cores. We can also achieve more scalability distributing work to many computers. Our focus in this book will be on the first case.

Mounting a computer with eight processing cores (two microprocessors with four cores in each) is more likely than asking a microprocessor manufacturer to develop an exclusive processor working at 20 GHz.

We will be able to generate applications with a dynamic scalability concept, according to the number of available or configured working processing cores.

Have a go hero – Detecting scalability problems

If you have a computer with a multi-core microprocessor, you will be able to get some hands-on experience on the problems related to scalability. It is a good idea to monitor many applications you usually run and check each execution core load using Windows Task Manager. Are the applications taking full advantage of the processing power installed in your computing system? Are all the tasks using the full processing power?

Load balancing: Keeping everybody happy

The mechanism used for distributing the workload between many processors or cores that are part of a multiprocessing system is known as **load balancing**. Its main goal is to achieve the best possible performance by maintaining an equal workload between all the available processors or cores. It is also responsible for detecting with high accuracy the need to scale up (to increase the number of processors or cores).

If an inefficient workload distribution was applied, one of the cores would be overloaded with requests while the others would remain underutilized. For that reason, the load balancing algorithm has a critical role in the response time offered by the running application.

You do not want a robot to rebel! You want them to be happy! Therefore, you apply a carefully chosen load balancing procedure to distribute the tasks to the robots.

There are four traditional procedures for load balancing:

◆ **Random selection**: Each request is assigned to a core randomly. One robot may kill you.

◆ **Task distribution**: The tasks are distributed into each available core keeping a balance. This mechanism is known as **PLB (Processing Load Balancing)**. The robot that mops the floor will kill you.

◆ **Round robin**: Each request is assigned once to each core in the order of arrival, irrespective of the time it takes to accomplish the task. The round begins when a request arrives and is assigned to the first core, the next to the second, the following one to the third, and so on. When there are no more cores available, and a new request arrives, it is assigned to the first core and the round begins again. For example, if we apply this algorithm with a dual core CPU, request #1 goes to core #1, request #2 goes to core #2, request #3 goes to core #1, request #4 goes to core #2, and so on. One day, robot "A" will kill you. The other day, robot "B" will kill you. But, perhaps, some day, all of them will be happy. And, some other day, they will all be queued to kill you.

◆ **User defined (programmed by the user)**: Using any of the three algorithms mentioned above, the system tends to a uniform workload only if the distributed tasks consume the same processing power and take the same time for completion. Therefore, they can lack the necessary balance. So, another option is to introduce user-defined algorithms. We can develop small components or applications in order to measure each core workload and assign tasks considering the results. Although this algorithm could bring the best response time in some applications, it transforms an 'n' way symmetrical multiprocessing system in an asymmetric multiprocessing one, using one core to manage the task distribution process instead of leaving it to the algorithms applied by the operating system. You will be there an entire day watching the robots. In a week's time, there will be no more robots in your kitchen!

 Every algorithm has its advantages and trade-offs.

Have a go hero – Thinking about load balancing

Take some processes and routines with poor performance results and redesign them to achieve better results with 2, 4, 8, and 16 execution cores. Which load balancing algorithm do you consider the best option for each application?

Operating systems and virtual machines

Why do we need to consider so many aspects related to hardware architecture in order to develop applications that take full advantage of parallelism? The answer is simple! Which is the most efficient way to reach Rome from our position? We need a map showing all the different possible ways to develop an accurate answer. The same happens when developing applications for multiprocessing. We need to know certain details about the way multiprocessing works in order to develop efficient methods to take full advantage of it. If we do not do this, any efforts made to take advantage of parallelism will not increase the application's performance.

There are great differences between parallelism and linear mono-processing programming. Hence, before starting with the necessary paradigm shift necessary for achieving the best results, it is very important to understand the underlying hardware architectures in which our optimized applications will be running.

We are talking about hardware, which is supposed to be a responsibility of modern operating systems. In some cases, as with the Java programming language, it is the responsibility of a virtual machine, which provides an even more isolated environment.

C# is a high-level, object-oriented language that provides a very good level of isolation from hardware. Nevertheless, when we are optimizing the applications for parallelism, we must obtain certain information about the hardware in order to adapt some aspects of the application to take full advantage of available resources.

This is the point where the first complications appear. The operating system isolates the applications from the underlying hardware, generating an intermediate manager. Its kernel is the lowest level layer above the hardware and manages memory, processors, and many other hardware, in a low-level way. Therefore, it is in charge of administering the different available processors or cores and distributing the workload in the most efficient way. It reduces our possibility to control certain variables and make them dependent on the operating system with which we are working.

The results achieved by the same applications in different Windows versions such as Vista, 2008, 2003, and XP can be quite different. It happens because each new release tends to be more optimized for the most recent hardware and hence for providing more efficient multiprocessing with multi-core microprocessors. For this reason, the operating system is also responsible for the performance results.

Parallelism is here to stay

Multiprocessing is not new. It has been available for many years, although always limited to powerful servers and sophisticated specific workstations because of its expensive and difficult-to-find components.

Nowadays, microprocessor manufacturers tend to add more execution cores to every new microprocessor instead of increasing their working frequency. They also improve the instructions per clock cycle ratio. But the focus is on the parallelism capabilities. They are continuously improving the execution of instructions in parallel. Therefore, the multi-core revolution is here and hence, we will see more and more cores in one physical microprocessor. For this reason, the time has arrived to take full advantage of parallel architectures available in modern computers. Linear code has reached its end.

We will go through lots of samples covering the most useful situations in which we will need to take full advantage of the available processing cores with C# 2.0 and 3.0.

 We are at an inflection point wherein, as developers, we must use the parallel processing power available in current and future computers. We must not lose the opportunity to take full advantage of parallelism.

Have a go hero – Preparing minds for parallelism

Exercise your mind to prepare for parallelism. This group of researchers seems to have many complex algorithms in mind:

- Take some applications you have developed using C# and check which processes should be recoded in order to improve these applications' performance. Think and write using some kind of pseudo-code, with part of those processes executed in parallel. Moreover, redesign the applied algorithms in order to reduce the results dependencies between instructions.

- Think about new solutions in which you believe it is convenient to use parallelism to improve performance. Divide the processes into many independent ones from a conceptual point of view, without focusing on design and technical details.

- Take some processes and routines with poor performance results and redesign them thinking of some way to achieve better results with 2, 4, 8, and 16 execution cores. Write them using some kind of pseudo-code.

- Take some actions you do during the day and try to describe the parallel tasks you execute under certain circumstances. Doing it will help you understand how human beings apply parallelism every second. Then you will be able to transfer this thinking model to help you achieve better results in designing applications using this new paradigm.

Summary

We learned a lot in this chapter about multiprocessing and multiple cores. Specifically, we understood the performance waterfall in a computing system. We acknowledged the advantages of parallel programming with C# for the coming years. We learned the challenges associated with parallel processing and programming. Now, we are able to detect bottlenecks and prepare for scalability and efficient load balancing.

Now that we've learned about the principles of multiprocessing and multiple cores, we're ready to learn the main components of a parallel program, the processes and the threads, which is the topic of the next chapter.

2

Processes and Threads

In order to be able to develop applications using parallel programming in C#, we must understand their main low-level components, the processes, and the threads. We must also study how they work and interact. In this chapter, we will walk through them and follow the exercises given:

- Learning the parallel programming fundamentals
- Understanding the different ways in which we can divide applications into smaller pieces to improve parallel processing
- Learning how the operating system works and interacts with those pieces
- Understanding the problems related to old-fashioned linear algorithms
- Optimizing the software architecture according to the kind of computer in which it is prepared to run servers, high-load workstations, or clients
- Continuing to generate a paradigm shift in our software design process

Processes—any running program

A **process** is a running program. When we run an executable program (`.exe` extension) in any Windows version, a new process is generated in memory. The list of processes available can be seen by displaying the **Windows Task Manager** and selecting the **Processes** tab, as shown in the following image:

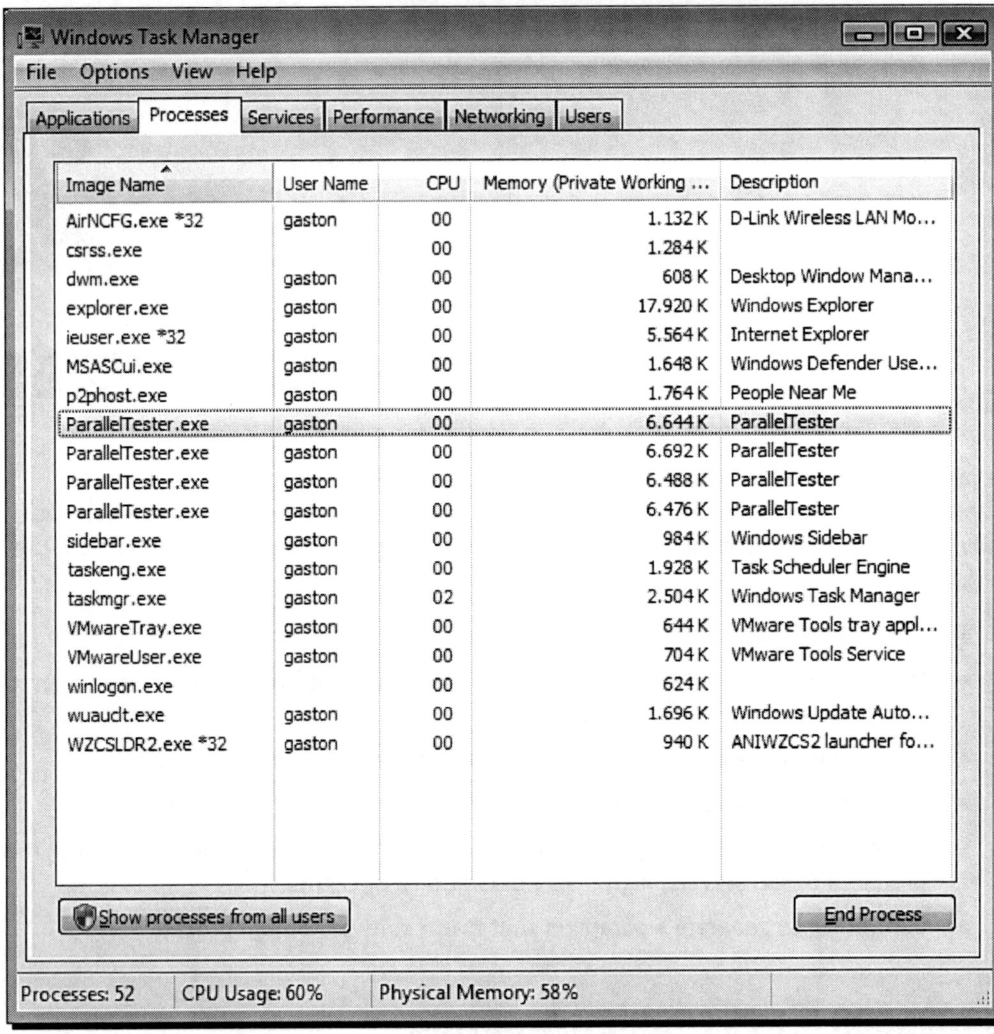
Windows Task Manager
File Options View Help
Applications Processes Services Performance Networking Users
Image Name | User Name | CPU | Memory (Private Working ... | Description
AirNCFG.exe *32 | gaston | 00 | 1.132 K | D-Link Wireless LAN Mo...
csrss.exe | | 00 | 1.284 K |
dwm.exe | gaston | 00 | 608 K | Desktop Window Mana...
explorer.exe | gaston | 00 | 17.920 K | Windows Explorer
ieuser.exe *32 | gaston | 00 | 5.564 K | Internet Explorer
MSASCui.exe | gaston | 00 | 1.648 K | Windows Defender Use...
p2phost.exe | gaston | 00 | 1.764 K | People Near Me
ParallelTester.exe | gaston | 00 | 6.644 K | ParallelTester
ParallelTester.exe | gaston | 00 | 6.692 K | ParallelTester
ParallelTester.exe | gaston | 00 | 6.488 K | ParallelTester
ParallelTester.exe | gaston | 00 | 6.476 K | ParallelTester
sidebar.exe | gaston | 00 | 984 K | Windows Sidebar
taskeng.exe | gaston | 00 | 1.928 K | Task Scheduler Engine
taskmgr.exe | gaston | 02 | 2.504 K | Windows Task Manager
VMwareTray.exe | gaston | 00 | 644 K | VMware Tools tray appl...
VMwareUser.exe | gaston | 00 | 704 K | VMware Tools Service
winlogon.exe | | 00 | 624 K |
wuauclt.exe | gaston | 00 | 1.696 K | Windows Update Auto...
WZCSLDR2.exe *32 | gaston | 00 | 940 K | ANIWZCS2 launcher fo...
Show processes from all users
End Process
Processes: 52
CPU Usage: 60%
Physical Memory: 58%

Each process has its own independent memory space. Therefore, if there is any problem inside it, it will not affect the rest of the running processes—when the operating system does not have bugs. Besides, each process has its own address space, and that is the reason why it cannot access the memory of other running processes. Older Windows versions did not work that way, but that is history; we are talking about current Windows versions, such as Vista, XP, 2003, and 2008, in both 32 and 64 bit releases.

> The running processes require processing resources, also known as CPU time.

In modern operating systems prepared for multiprocessing, as in modern Windows versions, when we have more than one core or processor installed in the computer, we can tell the operating system which ones should be available to be used for a process. This operation is known as **affinity**.

Time for action – Coding a simple CPU-intensive loop

You are a very good C# developer. However, you will have to work with computers using multi-core processors. You must understand how processes work. You do not understand why the researchers need huge processing power.

We are going to build a new C# application that executes a CPU-intensive loop and then run it without the **IDE (Integrated Development Environment)** in the background.

 We need a computer with at least two cores or two microprocessors installed in order to achieve significant results for this experiment.

1. Create a new C# Project using the Windows Forms Application template in Visual Studio or Visual C# Express. The IDE is going to create a very simple one with a main Windows form as a **UI (User Interface)**. Use `ParallelTester` as the project's name.

2. Change the form's name to `frmParallelPerformance`.

3. Open Windows Form `Form1` (`frmParallelPerformance`) in the form designer, add the following controls, and align them as shown in the image:

- One button (**butStart**)
- One Progress Bar (**pgbLoopProgress**)
- One Label (**lblSeconds**)

4. Add the following private variables:

```
// The number at which the iteration begins
private long priBegin;
// The number at which the iteration ends
private long priEnd;
// The total number of times the code in the loop will run
private long priTotalIterations;
```

5. Create the following constructor with two parameters:

```
public frmParallelPerformance(long pariBegin, long pariEnd)
{
    InitializeComponent();
    priBegin = pariBegin;
    priEnd = pariEnd;
    priTotalIterations = pariEnd - pariBegin + 1;
}
```

6. Open the `Click` event in the **butStart** button and enter the following code:

```
// Save the start time
DateTime loStartTime = DateTime.Now;
/* This code will not generate a result.
 * Its main purpose is to consume processing power and also to
   update the progress bar */

// This variable will hold a number to iterate from 1 to
   36,000,000
long liNumber;
// This variable will hold a char generated from the number in
   liNumber
ichar lcChar;
// This variable will hold the conversion from the char type to
   string
String lsConverted;
// This loop will run priTotalIteration times
for (liNumber = priBegin; liNumber <= priEnd; liNumber++)
{
    // lcChar holds a char as a result of modulus applied to
       liNumber
    lcChar = (char)(liNumber % 255);
    // The char is converted to a string and stored in lsConverted
    lsConverted = lcChar.ToString();
    // The progress is communicated to the progressbar
    pgbLoopProgress.Value = (int)((liNumber - priBegin) * 100 /
    priTotalIterations);
    // Allow Windows process events and display the advances in
       the progressbar
```

```
        Application.DoEvents();
    }

    // Save the ending time
    DateTime loEndTime = DateTime.Now;
    TimeSpan loDifference = (loEndTime - loStartTime);
    // Show the time to complete the loop in seconds
    lblSeconds.Text = string.Format("{0} seconds to complete",
                     loDifference.Seconds);
```

7. Double-click on **Program.cs** in the **Solution Explorer**. The IDE will open the
   main entry point for the application. Replace the main procedure with the
   following function:

```
static int Main(string[] args)
{
    Application.EnableVisualStyles();
    Application.SetCompatibleTextRenderingDefault(false);
    if (args.Length < 2)
    {
      // The application needs two arguments. Use the default
          values.
        Application.Run(new frmParallelPerformance(1, 36000000));
    }
    else
    {
      // Run the main form with the two parameters that set the
          iteration bounds (begin and end)
        Application.Run(new frmParallelPerformance(
        long.Parse(args[0]), long.Parse(args[1])));
    }
    return 0;
}
```

What just happened?

The code required to run a CPU-intensive loop to test the behavior of one or more processes
with one or more cores is now held in the main form. Now, we can start this application with
the default parameters or by using specific beginning and ending values.

Time for action – Changing the cores available for a process

Now, we will change the processor affinity while our application is running. This way, we are
going to understand the way Windows works with multiprocessing:

1. Build and run the application. A window will appear with a button and a progress bar.

2. Click on the button. You will see the progress bar filling up, as shown in the following image:

3. Once finished, you will see the label showing the seconds it took to complete the loop. Close the window and return to the IDE.

4. Close Visual Studio or Visual C# and run the generated executable (`ParallelTester.exe`). A window will appear again, with a button and a progress bar.

5. Close any other applications that could distort the performance-measuring results.

6. Launch the **Windows Task Manager**.

> To start Windows Task Manager, you can take any of the following actions:
>
> Press *Ctrl + Alt + Delete*, and then click Task Manager.
>
> Press *Ctrl + Shift + Esc*.
>
> Right-click on an empty area of the taskbar, and then click **Task Manager**.

7. Select the **Processes** tab and order the processes by name. Go to the process named `ParallelTester.exe`.

8. Right-click on this process. A context menu will appear.

9. Click on **Set Affinity....** A dialog box will appear showing a checkbox for each core or processor available, beginning with number 0, as shown in the following image for a computer with 2 cores, using a dual-core microprocessor:

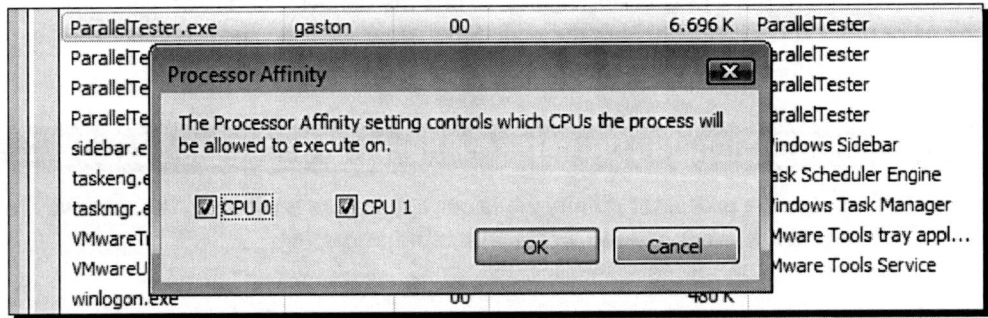

10. Check the CPUs that you want the process to run on and click **OK**.

11. Depending on the number of cores or processors available in your computer, run the application many times, setting its affinity from 1 to n, where n is the number of CPUs appearing in the dialog box shown before. For example, if your computer has four cores, you will run the application four times, measuring the time it takes to complete the process, with the following affinities set:

- CPU 0 only
- CPU 1 and CPU 2
- CPU 1, CPU 2, and CPU 3
- CPU 1, CPU 2, CPU 3, and CPU 4

12. Run two instances of the application, first of all with 1 on one core and 1 on another, then with both on the same core (CPU 0). They will take nearly twice the time for completion.

What just happened?

This way, we could check how an application behaves with different numbers of available cores. By default, Windows assigns every available core to the application. Besides our goals with this example, the above-mentioned action can be done to test the approximate response of an optimized application with fewer cores than the ones available in our computer. If we were using a quad-core microprocessor, we could have an idea of its response time with a dual-core microprocessor setting its affinity to CPU 1 and CPU 2, instead of the default.

Relating processes to cores

The application took nearly the same time to process the 36,000,000 iterations, regardless of the affinity settings. Hence, although the number of cores available was increased, the performance did not increase. Why did that happen? It's very simple. The algorithm was not optimized for taking advantage of multiple cores and hence did not consider the available parallel processing capabilities.

The `for` loop used in the code presented above is a classic linear programming structure, but does not succeed in scaling performance with computers capable of parallel processing. No matter how many cores we give to the process, it takes the same time to complete the loop from 1 to 36,000,000. These are the default values when no parameters are specified.

The code is a good example of an algorithm in which we must execute processes on many elements, and it shows how inefficient code may be in a multiprocessing environment, when it is not optimized for such an environment. The code used in the example is the most common way to execute a process on many elements without parallelism.

The code contained in the `for` loop is executed 36 million times, generating a Unicode character between 0 and 255 in the variable `lsConverted` of `String` type. When these kinds of loops are executed in a computer with only one processing core (mono-processing), the operating system CPU performance analysis tool shows a nearly uninterrupted 100% CPU usage until the loop ends. The iteration processes are the ones that usually make the user wait because there are many tasks to be done before the user retrieves application control.

When running two instances on a single core, even though it appears that both instances run simultaneously, they are actually multiplexing. The CPU does a bit of one process, then a bit of another, and then back again.

Let's recollect the robots in the kitchen. The same happens when you ask a single robot with just two arms to do two tasks, wash up and make your lunch at the same time. The robot does a tiny bit of each task. Therefore, it takes twice the time to finish both the tasks.

Time for action – Changing a process priority

Each process has a priority assigned in order to be taken into account when competing for processing resources (CPU time). The operating system scheduler has the responsibility to manage the tasks queue for each available processor or core. The priority assigned to a process determines a better or worse probability to take the first turn for accessing a processor or the core processing time. The possible priority values for the processes in any modern Windows version are the following (with their corresponding numerical values):

- Realtime. Numerical value 24. You want the robot to finish preparing the dinner as soon as possible. Do not do anything else until you finish preparing my dinner!

- High. Numerical value 13. You want the robot to finish the dinner, but you also want it to wash up every five minutes.

- Above Normal. Numerical value 10. You are very hungry. The robot must pay special attention to your dinner.

- Normal. Numerical value 8. You are hungry, but you can wait for the dinner's normal time.

- Below Normal. Numerical value 6. You can wait a few hours for the dinner to be ready.

- Low. Numerical value 4. You let the robot finish the dinner when it wants to.

We are going to change a process priority while it is running using the Task Manager:

1. Close Visual Studio or Visual C# and run the generated executable (`ParallelTester.exe`).

2. Close any other applications that could distort the performance-measuring results.

3. Launch the Windows Task Manager.

4. Select the **Processes** tab and order the processes by their names. Go to the process named **ParallelTester.exe**.

5. Right-click on this process. A context menu will appear.

6. Click on **Set Priority**. Another menu will appear showing the aforementioned items, beginning with **Realtime** and with **Normal** as the default selection, as shown in the following image:

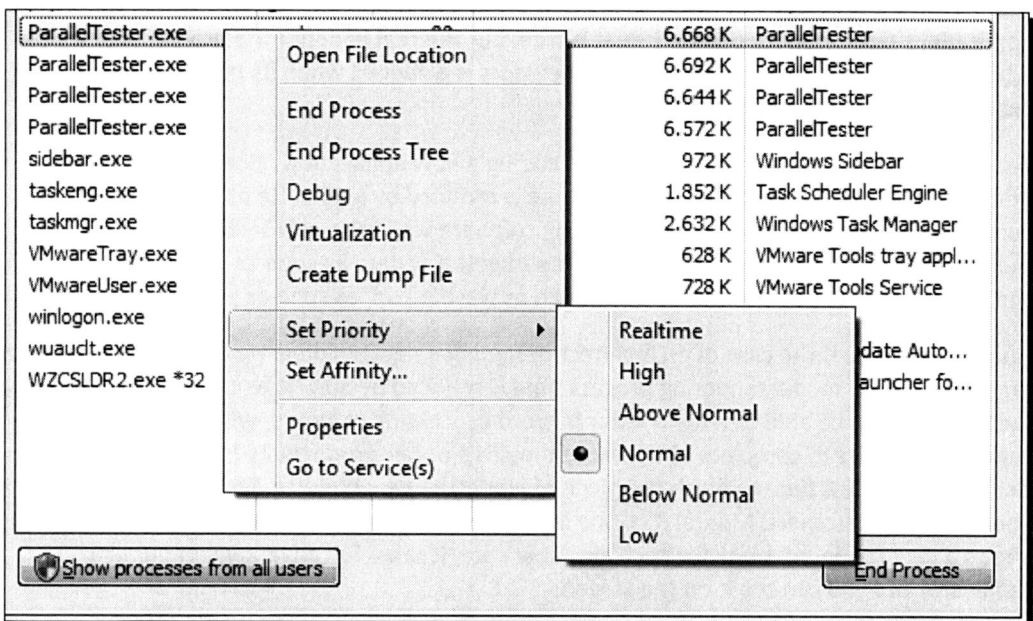

7. Run the application many times (clicking on the button to execute the iteration), setting its process priority to each available option. You will run the application six times, measuring the time it takes to complete the process.

What just happened?

This way, we could check how an application behaves with different priorities assigned to its process. By default, Windows will assign the normal priority to the application's process.

The scheduler does not change its behavior much with different priorities. We must not forget that we still have the same algorithm that is not optimized for taking advantage of multiple cores. There is no silver bullet!

[Changing the process priority did not automatically optimize it for multiprocessing.]

Run many instances of the application concurrently and change their respective priorities. The application with the highest priority will take less time to run as compared to the others.

Linear code problems in multiprocessing systems

When the new microprocessors including multiple execution cores in one physical package arrived, the main marketing focus given by the microprocessor manufacturers was to let the users run many concurrent tasks, without the need to wait for new releases of the applications optimized for parallelism. It is true, but the real benefit for a professional user who has invested in multiple core microprocessors is achieved when its main tasks are executed in the least possible time.

For example, a developer who has finished coding a new application release would be grateful when the compiling and building time is reduced by a 40%. He or she would not consider it important to use word processing software while the new release is compiled and built, because his or her desire is to finish realizing the system as soon as possible. You want the robots to finish just one of the tasks, such as washing up, as soon as possible!

Another example is the case of an architect designing a new building. He or she would be grateful if the 3D model rendering process time is reduced by 30%. It would not be so useful for him or her to be able to write a letter in word processing software, while waiting for the rendering process to complete at the same time. His or her productivity increases when he or she requires less time to finish the piece of work (the new building design) so that he can show it to his customers. Mental Ray, one of the best-known renderers in 3D applications shows a new rendering block for each available core. It takes full advantage of parallel hardware, and you can see it on the screen.

Hence, the most important topic is optimizing the applications destined to run on client PCs and workstations with access to multiprocessing.

Time for action – Running many processes in parallel

We are not yet able to take full advantage of multiprocessing, but we know how to set a process affinity. This way, we should be able to take full advantage of every available core.

We are going to do that and monitor the CPU usage when running many instances of our simple application in a multiprocessing computer using the Task Manager:

1. Close Visual Studio or Visual C# and run as many instances of the generated executable (`ParallelTester.exe`) as there are available cores or processors are in the system. For example, if you have a dual core microprocessor, you will run it twice, and if you have a quad core microprocessor, you will run it four times. Do not click the buttons yet.

2. Close any other applications that could distort the performance-measuring results.

3. Launch the Windows Task Manager.

4. Select the **Performance** tab, and in the main menu select **View | CPU History | One Graph All CPUs**. This way, it will show one graph with the sum of the multiple CPU usage.

5. Resize and move the windows in order to make all of them visible at the same time (including the Task Manager's window). You must be able to watch the multiple progress bars advancing.

6. Click on the application's buttons one after the other, as fast as possible, to execute the iterations concurrently and watch the CPU usage graph in the Task Manager, as shown in the following image when run in a quad-core microprocessor (with four applications, and hence four processes, running concurrently):

7. Repeat the experiment running the applications many times (clicking on the buttons to execute the iteration concurrently).

8. Now, go to the Task Manager, select the **Performance** tab, and in the main menu select **View | CPU History | One Graph per CPU**. This way, it will show one graph for each core or processor available and the sum of the multiple CPU usage on the left.

9. Click on the application's buttons one after the other, as fast as possible, to execute the iterations concurrently and watch the CPU usage graphs for each core in the Task Manager, as shown in the following image when run in a quad-core microprocessor (with four applications, and hence four processes, running concurrently):

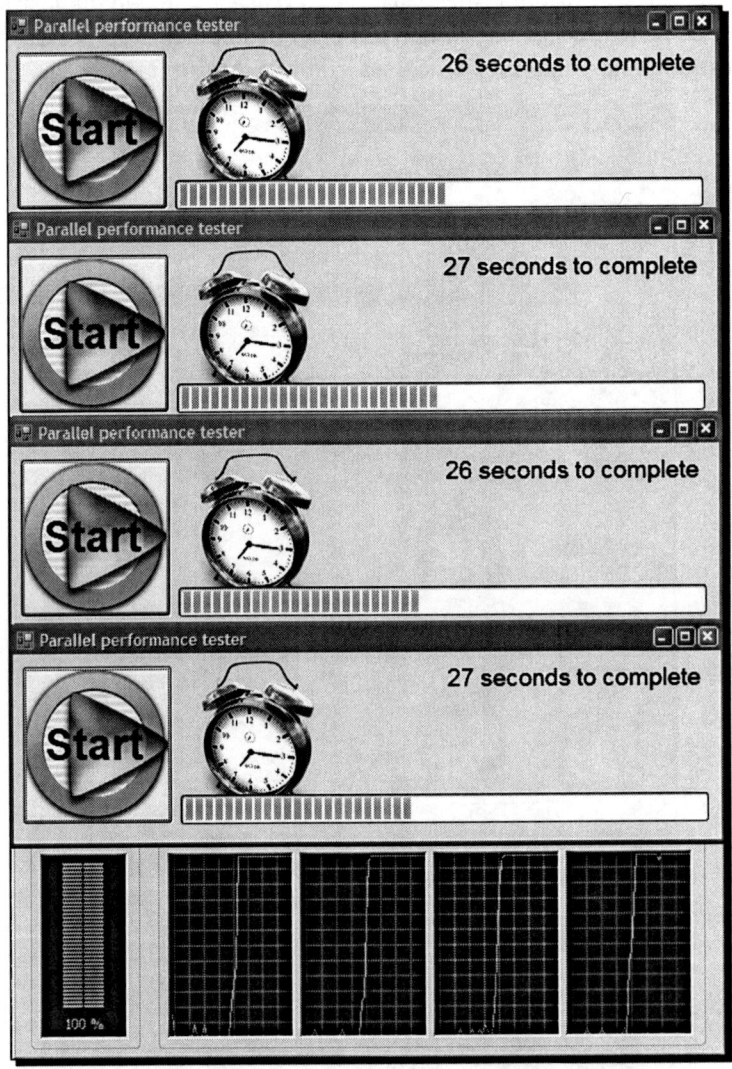

10. Repeat the experiment running the applications many times (clicking on the buttons to execute the iteration concurrently).

11. Repeat the experiment assigning each process an affinity setting so that one core is assigned to each different process. Do not forget to pay attention to the times displayed.

12. Now, click on the button on one application. Look at the time it takes to complete the iteration.

13. Repeat the experiment running all the applications. Look at the time it takes to complete all the iterations running concurrently.

What just happened?

The results of this experiment will be slightly different depending on the micro-architecture of the CPUs installed in the system.

The application took nearly the same time to process the 36,000,000 iterations running individually as running many times concurrently. For example, if we used a quad core system, we would be able to run four instances of the application, each one processing 36,000,000 iterations, which means, 36,000,000 x 4 = 144,000,000 iterations in nearly the same time it took to process 36,000,000.

Why did that happen? It's very simple if we continue considering a quad core system. As the algorithm was not optimized for taking advantage of multiple cores to consider the available parallel processing capabilities, we used four independent processes, four instances of the same application running in parallel. Each one was assigned to one core and took full advantage of the concurrent processing power.

Therefore, we could divide applications into multiple independent processes to take full advantage of the available parallel processing capabilities. In some cases, this is the best alternative, in others we must use multiple threads.

As we can see in this simple example, we can take full advantage of the parallel processing power. It is possible to reduce the time needed for a process to complete. Moreover, we will go ahead with it, no matter the number of cores.

Time for action – Testing parallelism capabilities with processes

Now, we are going to use our C# application with command-line arguments that will tell it the iteration bounds (where to begin and where to end). This way, we will be able to know whether it is possible or not to achieve a better performance for our simple application dividing its task into as many processes as available cores.

1. Depending on the number of cores or processors available in the system, calculate the beginning and end of the iterations for each application's instance. Remember that the application must process 36,000,000 iterations. The following table shows an example for a quad core system in which each instance will process 9,000,000 iterations (9,000,000 x 4 = 36,000,000):

Instance number	Beginning	End
1	1	9,000,000
2	9,000,001	18,000,000
3	18,000,001	27,000,000
4	27,000,001	36,000,000

2. Close any other applications that could distort performance-measuring results.

3. Repeat the following steps (4 to 5) as many times as the available cores or processors in the system. You can also create a batch file to run the application with the desired parameters.

4. Start a Windows command line, and go to the executable's folder.

5. Run the application with the beginning and end as two command-line parameters. Do not click on the button yet. For example, in a quad core system, you will launch four instances with the following commands:

```
ParallelTester 1 9000000
ParallelTester 9000001 18000000
ParallelTester 18000001 27000000
ParallelTester 27000001 36000000
```

6. If everything is done the right way, Windows desktop will show as many windows as the cores that are available in the system. Launch the Windows Task Manager and select the **Performance** tab, and in the main menu select **View | CPU History | One Graph All CPUs**. This way, it will show one graph with the sum of the multiple CPUs' usage.

7. Resize and move the windows in order to make all of them visible at the same time (including the Task Manager's window). You must be able to watch the multiple progress bars advancing.

8. Click on the applications' buttons one after the other, as fast as possible, to execute the iterations concurrently and watch the CPU usage graph in the Task Manager, as shown in the following image when run in a quad-core microprocessor (with four applications, and hence four processes, running concurrently):

9. Repeat the experiment, running the applications many times (clicking on the buttons to execute the iteration concurrently).

10. Now, go to the Task Manager, select the **Performance** tab, and in the main menu select **View | CPU History | One Graph per CPU**. This way, it will show one graph for each core or processor available and the sum of multiple CPU usages on the left.

11. Click on the applications' buttons one after the other, as fast as possible, to execute the iterations concurrently and watch the CPU usage graphs for each core in the Task Manager, as shown in the following image when run in a quad-core microprocessor (with four applications, and hence four processes, running concurrently):

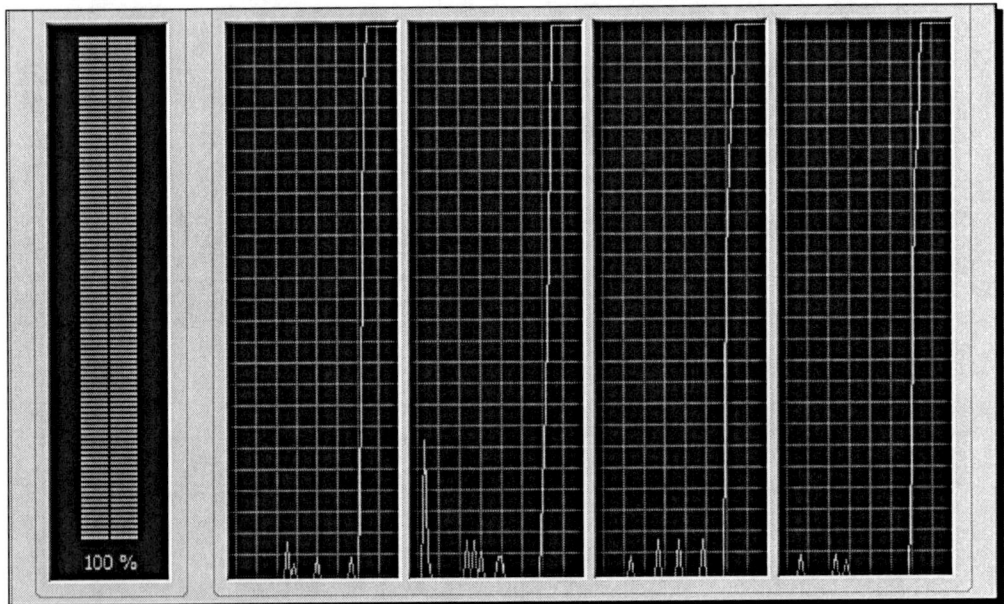

12. Repeat the experiment, running the applications many times (clicking on the buttons to execute the iteration concurrently).

13. Repeat the experiment assigning each process an affinity setting so that one core is assigned to each different process. Do not forget to look at the times measured by the application.

What just happened?

Again, the results of this experiment will be slightly different depending on the micro-architecture of the CPUs installed in the system.

We could take advantage of multiple cores using many concurrent processes and dividing the work assigned to each. However, it seems something difficult to use in real life applications. It appears to be more useful in batch processing routines.

Time is valuable, therefore we must continue in our parallel programming adventure. There are some important concepts to learn about processes and threads.

Nowadays, applications designed for execution in client PCs, with a linear execution programming technique will not reap great benefits when they find themselves with multiple execution cores. Most of them will waste many installed hardware resources and much processing power. On the other side, this sounds logical, because the additional design and programming costs required for preparing an application for multiprocessing were not profitable until recently. The massive use of multiple core microprocessors changes the rules, and now it makes sense to improve applications running on the client side.

 It is very important to prepare applications to take full advantage of this new generation of microprocessors and computers. Most PCs are now prepared for parallelism.

Time for action – Using the Process Explorer

Each process can have many child processes (sub-processes). This situation happens when one process launches another and defines itself as the parent. If the parent process ends, the entire process tree will end (every child process with the main process).

There are many other topics related to processes, but they have more to do with the operating system structure and are beyond our interests, because they are strictly related to the specific ways in which the different Windows versions work.

Processes can establish communications between them. They have the possibility to exchange information, known as **IPC (Inter-Process Communication)** and to call procedures from one process to another one. Nevertheless, use of IPC consumes more processing time as compared to the same communication done inside the same process space. Therefore, while it has some advantages and reasons for its existence, we should avoid using it when we are lagging behind in achieving the best performance.

Often, the information provided by Windows Task Manager is not enough to see and understand the processes status. Among other issues that we will analyze later, it allows us neither to see the complete processes tree nor detailed information about the processes contained by a parent process.

Process Explorer is an excellent utility that will help us a lot in offering valuable information to understand and to analyze performance issues. It was developed by Mark Russinovich, of Sysinternals (www.sysinternals.com).

You can download Process Explorer free of cost by visiting the following URL: `http://technet.microsoft.com/en-us/sysinternals/bb896653.aspx`.

We are going to use Process Explorer to obtain information about the running processes instead of the Windows Task Manager:

1. Run the `procexp.exe` file (included in `ProcessExplorer.zip`). A window with a complete running processes tree list and its icons will appear, similar to the one shown in the following image:

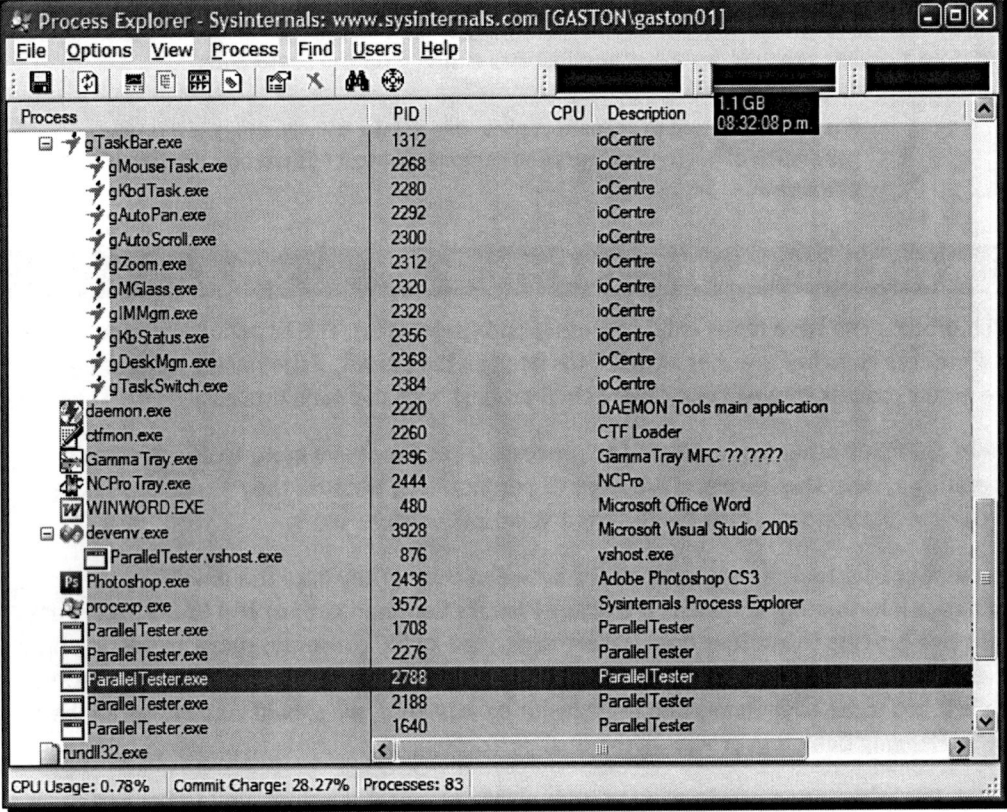

2. Navigate to your computer processes tree.

3. Run one of the sample applications used before and right-click on the process name to see the options available in the context menu. It has options similar to the ones found in the Windows Task Manager plus many others.

4. Right-click to select **Properties**. A dialog box will appear showing a lot of information about the running process and its resources. Look through the many tabs offered by this dialog box.

Process Explorer will help us get detailed information about the running processes and their resources. We need more sophisticated tools than Windows Task Manager in order to optimize applications for parallelism. Process Explorer will tell us everything we need to know about each process.

Threads—Independent parts of a process

A process contains one or more threads. The creation of a process implies the generation of a main thread, but more threads can be created according to the needs. Each thread represents the basic unit to which the operating system assigns the processor's time. Each thread belongs to a process, and hence shares its context and is also able to access the memory space of the entire private process.

Each thread generated by a process can execute any part of its code, including parts being executed by other threads.

Each thread can be assigned to a different core or processor, always limited to the ones available for the owner process through its affinity settings.

Hence, if there are available resources for that, the threads will be able to run concurrently taking full advantage of the parallelism offered by multiprocessing.

Threads are like processes, except that they can access all the variables of the process. Thus, they can communicate inside the same private unique process space. For example, they can access the main thread variables and communicate with them on a cost lower than that incurred by many processes to exchange information. Therefore, they simplify the execution of code in parallel, while decoupling different tasks in order to bring the user a much more natural experience and a better response time.

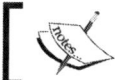 Working with multiple threads in the same process is known as **multithreading**.

Threads have their own stack, a copy of the registers, including the legendary program counter, and a local private storage space.

Let's correlate this with our robot example again. You have a huge amount of washing up to do, and you need it done as quickly as possible. One way is to just get a faster robot (a single-core CPU). But you have four robots. You can get the job done faster by giving each robot a kitchen sink to work at (memory space) and a quarter of the dishes (data to work on). This is similar to having multiple processes.

Another option would be to get a really big sink, and have all the four robots stand around it, and have each one do a bit of washing up. You could even have each of them do a slightly different task (one puts it in the water, one brushes it, and another takes it out of the water). This is known as multithreading—a single process with one memory store and one lot of data, but several threads of action operating on it at once.

We can see a representation of the relation between processes and threads in the following image:

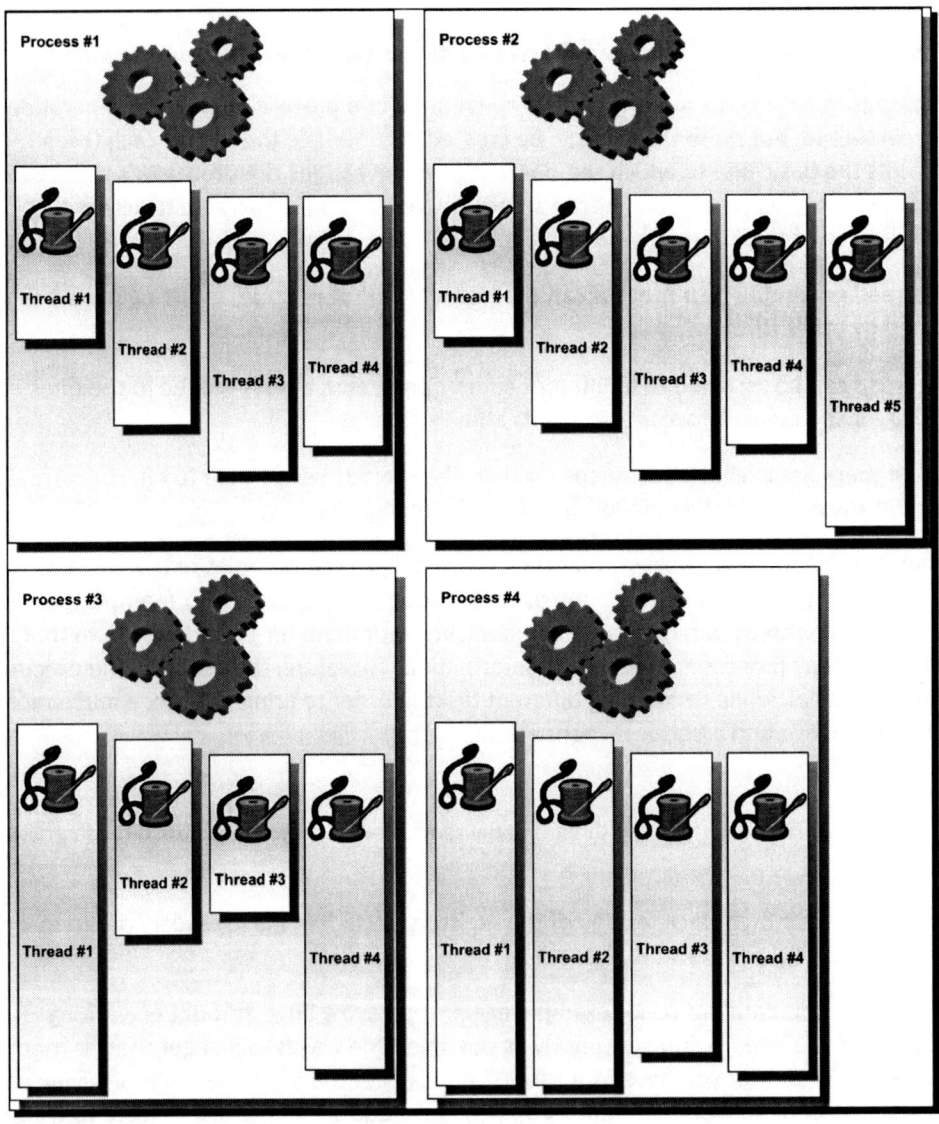

Time for action – Listing threads with Process Explorer

Each process can have many threads. The Windows Task Manager does not show a list of threads owned by each process. For that reason, it is not useful to understand the threads' status.

Instead of the incomplete Windows Task Manager, we are going to use the Process Explorer, a utility we installed in our last example, to obtain information about the running threads:

1. Run the Process Explorer.
2. Navigate into your computer processes tree.
3. Repeat the following steps (4 to 6) with many different processes from the list.
4. Right-click and select **Properties**. A dialog box will appear showing a lot of information about the running process and its resources.
5. Select the **Threads** tab. Process Explorer will show a list with the threads created by the process, like the one in the following image:

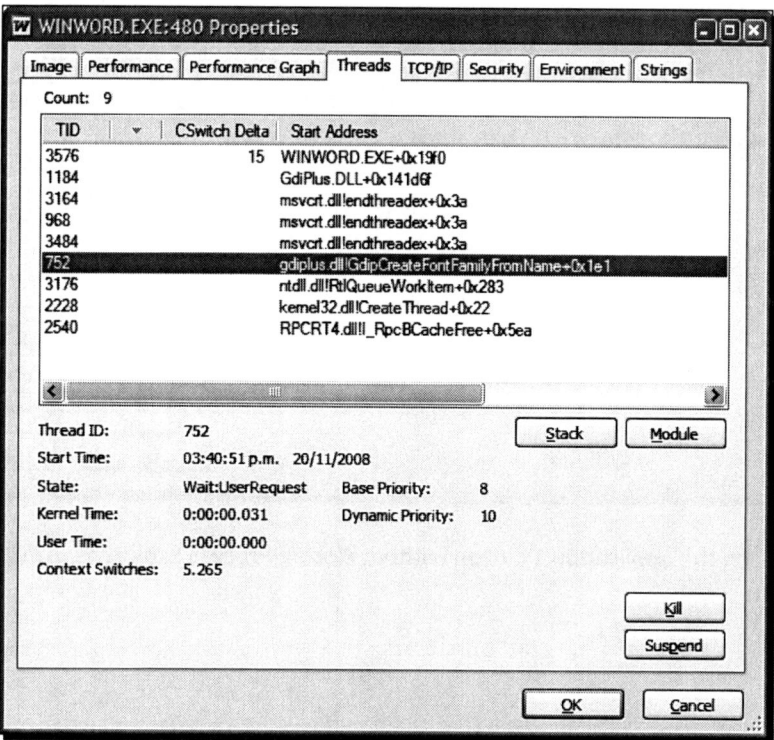

6. Navigate through the different threads and watch their properties shown by the Process Explorer. Then, close the dialog box.

7. Run the `ParallelTester.exe` application used earlier.

8. Move to its process name, right-click on it and select **Properties**. Select the **Threads** tab. As shown in the following image, you will see a list with four threads:

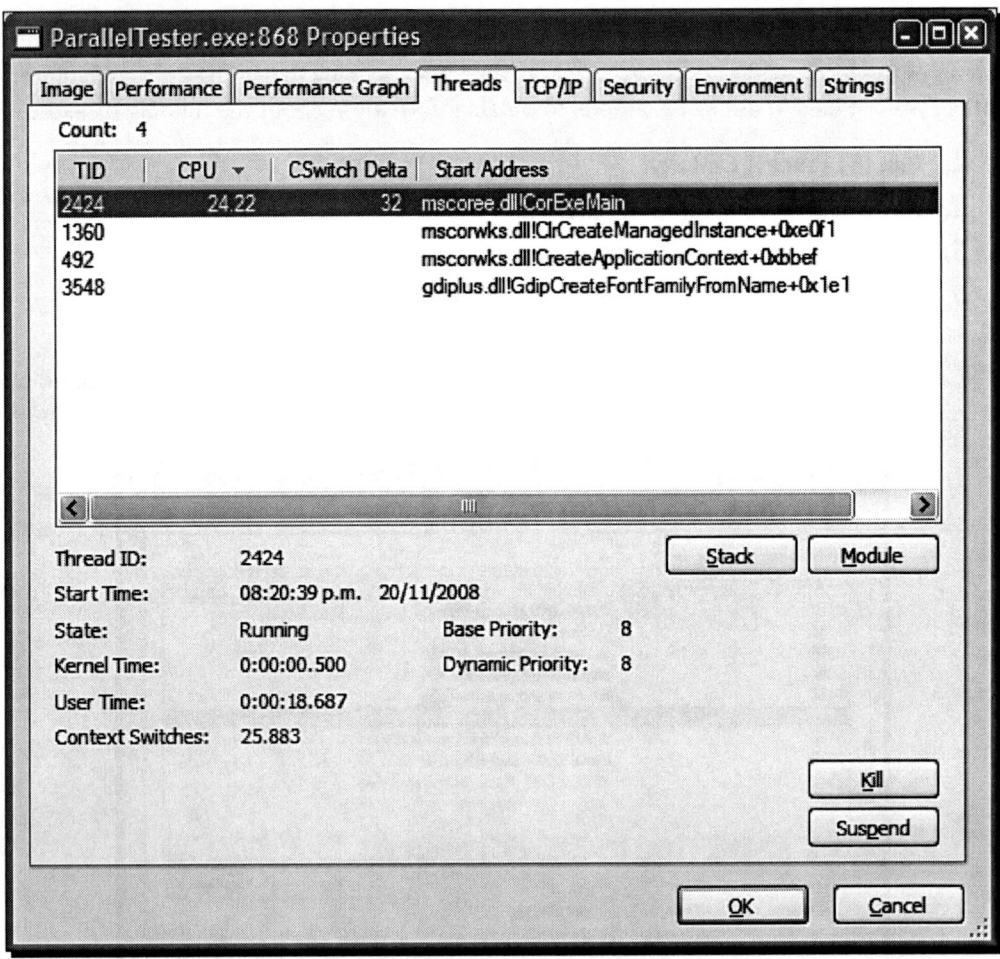

9. Click on the application's button without closing Process Explorer's dialog box.

10. You will find that the thread with a great deal of activity is **mscoree.dll!CorExeMain**, the application's main thread. The other threads are created automatically by the C# IDE when we generate a new Windows application based on a Windows Form.

Have a go hero – Searching multithreaded applications

Repeat the exercise with the processes for other applications in order to find out whether they use multiple threads to take advantage of parallelism or not, always using the Process Explorer. You will see a lot of interesting information about the processes and the threads that is not shown by the Task Manager. Moreover, you will be surprised with the results.

Once you are finished with the aforementioned exercise, use Windows Task Manager to monitor the CPU usage of available cores or processors in many applications that take some time to achieve different tasks. Try to guess which applications are taking full advantage of multiple cores and which are not, using just Windows Task Manager. Then, check the validity of your predictions using Process Explorer to see the number of threads and their activity. You will again be surprised with the results. There are many applications that you will expect to be prepared for multiprocessing, but which you will find are not.

Time for action – Analyzing context switches with Process Explorer

When a single robot does a tiny bit of each task, it is multiplexing. This is known as a **context switch**. They take time, because the robot must switch from one task to another and return to the point where it had left the task. The same happens with the cores and the threads.

Now, we are going to use Process Explorer to analyze context switches in a core:

1. Run the `procexp.exe` file. A window with a complete running processes tree list with its icons will appear.

2. Select **View | System Information** in the main menu. A window with information similar to the one offered by Windows Task Manager will be shown, but will have complete information.

3. Check **Show one graph per CPU**.

4. Position the mouse pointer over one of the graphics under the title **CPU Usage History** and leave it still for a few seconds.

5. The name of the processes that are being executed by the core will appear, as seen in the following image:

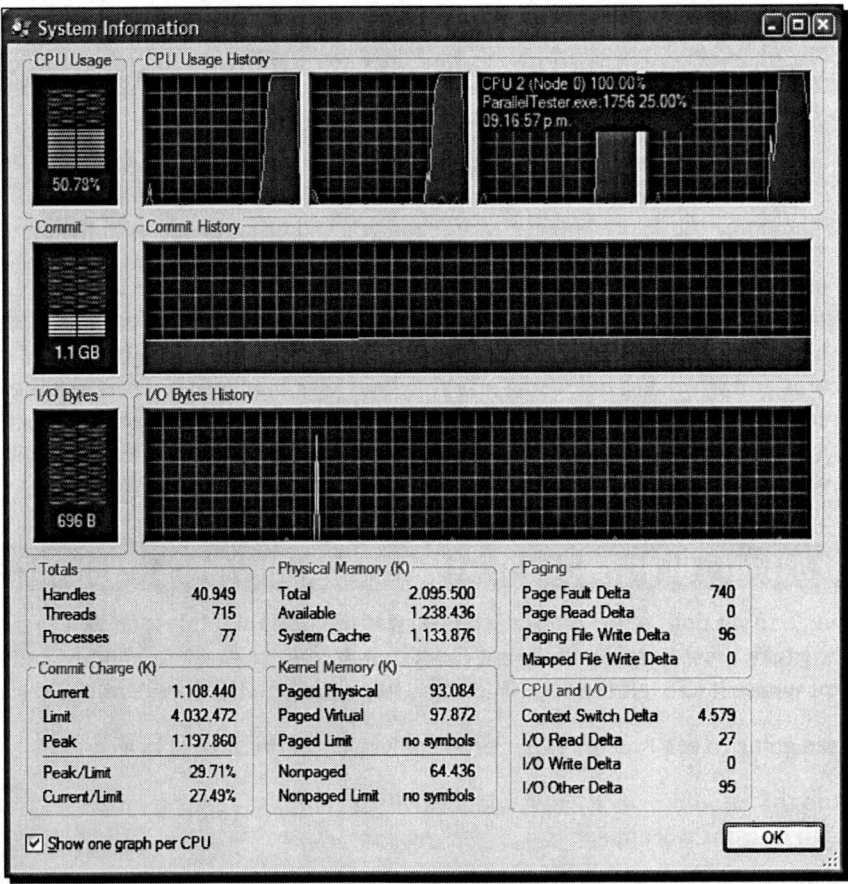

What just happened?

Process Explorer shows a lot of useful information, a very important item being the context switch delta. It reports the number of context switches that have occurred in each process in between the refresh interval configured for Process Explorer. By default, that is 1 second.

The lower this number is, the more efficient the use of the available cores by the application. Using more threads than available cores will inevitably generate an important context switch delta.

 When a thread is scheduled (selected to run), its context switch count is incremented.

Multiple threads in servers

If we have an application destined to offer a service that accomplishes a complex calculation for many client computers, we will create a new thread to process the calculation for each client requesting it. As we are expecting an important client concurrency this simple way, with minimal changes and no algorithm redesign at all, we can take full advantage of parallelism. This is so because it is parallelism based on simultaneous requests that each launch a new thread.

As servers are destined to attend to multiple simultaneous requests, we can easily adjust this kind of application to parallelism, without the need to redesign every algorithm. Database engines, among others, are not limited to the described optimization. If one user runs a query that can be parallelized to accelerate the results, it will be split into as many threads as the available cores that exist in order to achieve the best performance. However, not all the applications destined for servers are optimized with this fine-tuning.

Applications designed using old standards such as COM, Microsoft Transaction Server, and COM+ for creating remote objects generated many threads in servers. This way, inclusive of old programming languages without multithreading capabilities, we could achieve some kind of parallelism in the server from a main application. This was an old-fashioned manner to take advantage of server parallelism.

The ideal optimization of an application destined to be executed in a server is to split its algorithms into as many threads as the available cores to respond to each request, but in a dynamic way, thereby helping the scheduler.

If all the available cores are busy, it will not be worth splitting the algorithm, as there will be many context switches.

Multiple threads in clients

The first thing we must consider is an asymmetric situation. On one side we have a software application and on the other many available execution cores.

We can achieve excellent results with simple changes in applications, applying the design patterns that we will learn in the following chapters.

We will take as an example an application that carries out a transformation to a bitmap image or a vector graph. Using the classic procedure, a linear process would start from the beginning and continue to the end of the transformation procedure.

Instead, we can change the application's design to begin splitting this transformation into two very independent blocks, each covering one half of the process. Then, it will launch two threads to cover both the halves. This way, each execution core will take one thread, and it will be possible to take advantage of the installed hardware in a much more efficient manner and with minimal coordination costs between the two cores.

A very important issue to consider is that each thread should work with a memory segment that is as independent as possible from the one used by the other core. It implies a new way of thinking about the critical process development strategies. However, the benefits are surprising, as we experienced with the examples shown in this chapter.

Another classic example is that of an application that executes a batch process with data retrieved from a database. Using the classic procedure, a linear process would start retrieving from the beginning to and continue the end of the records retrieved.

Instead, we can change the application's design to begin splitting this original records list into many independent arrays, each covering one fractional part of the process. Then, it will launch many threads to cover the different parts. Just as happened in the previous case, each execution core will take one thread, and it will be possible to take advantage of the installed hardware in a much more efficient manner, with minimal coordination costs between the different cores.

The following diagram represents a process block composed of sequential and linear code, which is transformed into multiple threads with a coordinator:

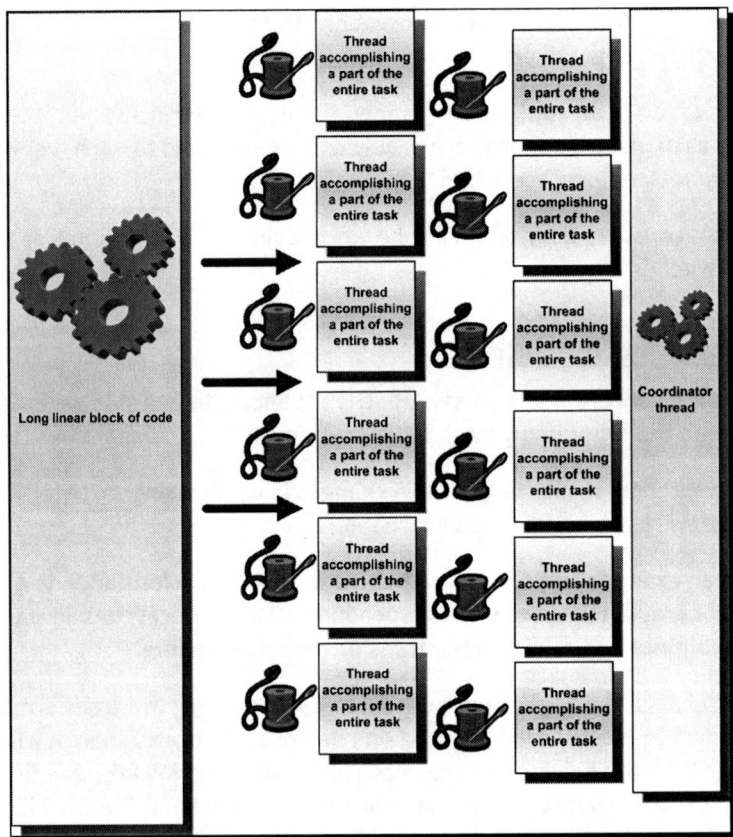

Each slower robot does a bit of the washing up instead of having a single faster robot.

This scheme is much more suitable for microprocessors with multiple execution cores and allows a more efficient use of the available hardware resources. Besides, it offers an unlimited scalability.

Nevertheless, we should consider those changes that bring new obstacles for achieving the maximum efficiency. The famous bottlenecks enter at this stage without any invitation. Therefore, we should avoid them systematically.

We will use another example. We have to process a list in which we need to sum up a total. We will use pseudo-code to show how it would be coded using a classic linear approach. We are not going to do it using C# 2.0 or 3.0 yet. Remember, our focus is on the paradigm shift.

```
Function CalculateSum(Items: List)
Returns Result: Double
{
Item: ItemClass;
Sum: Double = 0;

    For Each Item in Items
    {
      Sum += Item.Sum;
    }
    Result = Sum;
}
```

The `CalculateSum()` function will iterate through each one of the different items on the list it receives as a parameter, and it will generate a result. If the list has 10,000 (ten thousand) items, we will have to wait for the application to finish its iteration in order to obtain the result. It will only take advantage of one execution core.

If we have a microprocessor with four execution cores, the approach should be splitting this function into four parts, in addition to one dedicated to coordinating the beginning and the end result. This is shown in the following pseudo-code:

```
Function CalculateSum(Items: List)
Returns Result: Double
{
    Item: ItemClass;
    Sum: Double = 0;
    Sum1: Double;
    Sum2: Double;
    Sum3: Double;
    Sum4: Double;
```

```
        ThreadId1: ThreadId;
        ThreadId2: ThreadId;
        ThreadId3: ThreadId;
        ThreadId4: ThreadId;

        RunInNewThread(ThreadId1, CalculatePartialSum(Items, 1, 4, Sum1);
        RunInNewThread(ThreadId2, CalculatePartialSum(Items, 2, 4, Sum2);
        RunInNewThread(ThreadId3, CalculatePartialSum(Items, 3, 4, Sum3);
        RunInNewThread(ThreadId4, CalculatePartialSum(Items, 4, 4, Sum4);

        While Not (ExecutionFinishedInThread(ThreadId1) AND
         ExecutionFinishedInThread(ThreadId2) AND
         ExecutionFinishedInThread(ThreadId3) AND
         ExecutionFinishedInThread(ThreadId4) )
         {
             Nothing
         }

        Result = Sum1 + Sum2 + Sum3 + Sum4;
     }
Function CalculatePartialSum(Items: List, PartToProcess: Integer,
        SumParts: Integer, SumVariable: Double)
        Returns Nothing
     {
       Item: ItemClass;
       SumVariable = 0;

       For each Item in Items CorrespondingTo PartToProcess of
        SumParts
       {
          SumVariable += Item.Sum;
       }
     }
```

As we can see, here, programming is a bit more complicated than in the classic linear way. However, once we are used to the parallel programming design patterns, things will be easier and the benefits will make it worthwhile. The CalculateSum() function now creates four independent threads. Each thread will iterate through one part of the total list and will calculate a partial sum, a subtotal.

The main thread is going to monitor the completion of the four threads and, when they finish calculating the partial sums, it will calculate the total sum of the four partial sums. This pseudo-code algorithm will take full advantage of the four processing cores, and will reduce the time needed to carry out the sum to approximately 25% of the time that the first presented pseudo-code would require.

It would not take exactly 25% of the time required by the first algorithm, because as we explained earlier, there is a coordination cost, and there is no other option than to execute it in one thread. There are very few processes capable of taking full advantage (100%) of parallel architectures, because there is always some task needed to initialize, distribute tasks, coordinate the execution, and compose the result from the different parts.

Of course, the pseudo-code shown in the previous list is a simple example. We could improve it by defining the number of parts in which the process should be split to dynamically create the threads. In the example, we split the code into four threads in a static way. This is not the best approach, because we would not take full advantage of a computer with eight cores (two quad core processors) this way. We must have scalability in mind.

Have a go hero – Redesigning algorithms using pseudo-code

Write the algorithms you redesigned in the previous chapter using a pseudo-code similar to the one used in this chapter.

You must prepare for creating high-performance parallelized algorithms. The researchers are hackers!

Summary

We learned a lot in this chapter about processes and threads. Specifically, we covered:

- ◆ Understanding the differences between processes and threads
- ◆ Learning the need to use multiple threads in a single application in order to take full advantage of parallel processing capabilities in modern computers
- ◆ Acknowledging the need to leave behind linear programming techniques
- ◆ Learning the different ways threads use to work in clients and servers

We also discussed different ways to achieve a paradigm shift to develop an efficient concurrent programming technique.

Now that we've learned about the way a single application can be divided into multiple threads or different processes, and the fundamentals of the operating system scheduler, we're ready to program code to be executed in the background, in different threads—which is the topic of the next chapter.

3

BackgroundWorker—Putting Threads to Work

In order to be able to create and control threads in our applications, C# offers a very interesting component, the **BackgroundWorker**. In this chapter, we will study this component in detail, and we will begin developing multithreaded applications that take full advantage of multiprocessing. Reading this and following the exercises we shall:

- ◆ Develop applications that are able to execute tasks in the background while keeping alive the graphical user interface, offering the user a more real-life experience
- ◆ Learn to create independent threads using a simple component
- ◆ Understand the differences between synchronous and asynchronous execution
- ◆ Develop applications that are able to show the progress of their many concurrent running tasks in the graphical user interface
- ◆ Learn to start and cancel background tasks
- ◆ Develop applications capable of launching multiple background tasks when necessary

RTC: Rapid thread creation

Since the introduction of .NET 2.0 (C# 2005), a new component has become a part of Visual C# that simplifies the execution of tasks in independent threads, separated from the main thread. It is the BackgroundWorker (`System.ComponentModel.BackgroundWorker`), and it allows us to begin working with many threads and taking advantage of parallelism with very little effort. So, let us go on with its detailed analysis.

One of the main advantages of components in C# and the .NET working environment is the possibility to define their properties, values, and events in design time without the need to write lots of code.

Historically, multithreaded programming terrified developers because of the extreme complexity of the code needed to initialize, coordinate, stop, and free those threads.

The easiest way to begin experimenting with multithreading in .NET and learn the basic principles is using the BackgroundWorker component. It allows us to define certain properties in design time and introduce the code for the `DoWork` event handler. It represents an easy and rapid way to generate a new thread, independent of the main thread (the one that runs the main application's flow), without having to use more flexible or more complicated methods. Therefore, it is worth meeting this very interesting component.

Remember that components are not like controls. We can see and work with components in design time, but they are not going to be visible at runtime. Therefore, we will not see a graphical representation of the BackgroundWorker in the application's Windows form. We will see it as an icon in design time to simplify tasks related to it such as defining its properties' values and accessing its events, as shown in the following image:

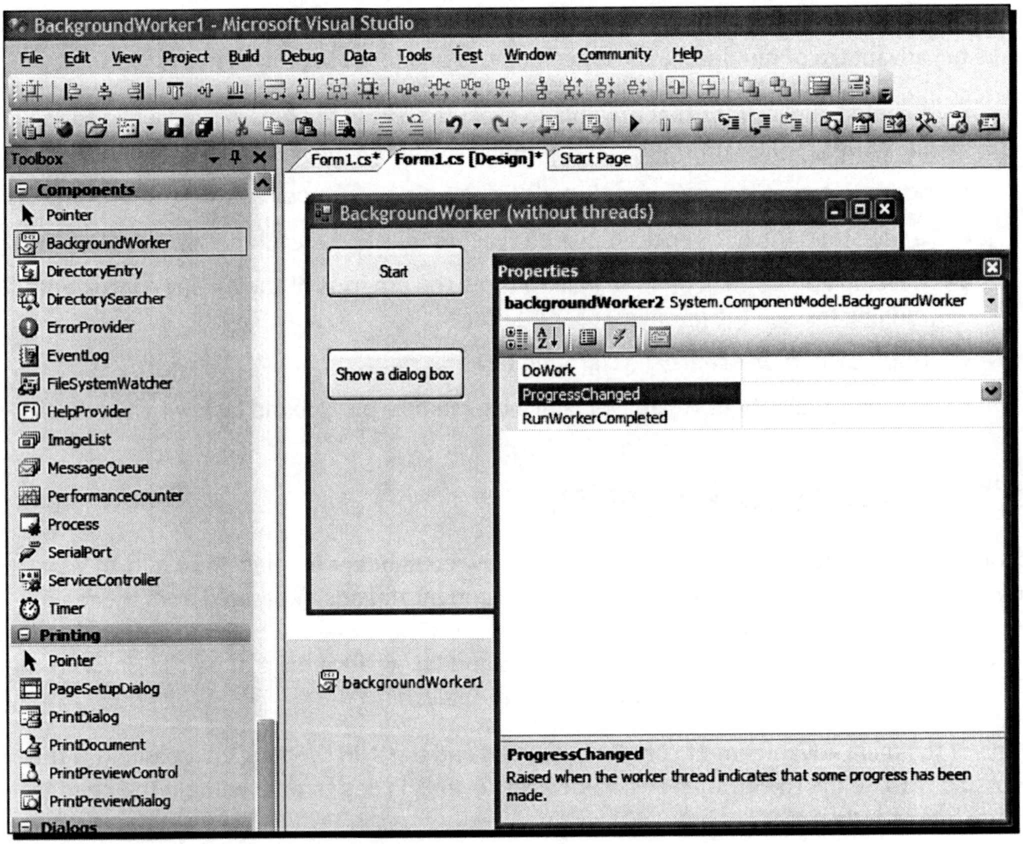

We will find the BackgroundWorker component in the IDE Toolbox. It has been available since .NET 2.0 (Visual C# 2005 and 2008). The component is designed for running operations that take some time to give a response to the user in the UI and offers the possibility of cancelling the job. In order to accomplish these goals, it runs in a new independent thread. It is therefore a very good option for generating many threads without the need to understand additional issues requiring much more code that can frighten developers used to linear code algorithms.

Time for action – Breaking a code in a single thread

The work to be done and run in a new thread is programmed in the `DoWork` event handler. To understand how it works, the best we can do is to see it in action and experience the difference between the code running in the same thread (the application's main thread) and in another thread.

Imagine that we must create a **Codebreaker Application**. There is a code of four Unicode characters, and we want to break it by a brute force attack. Therefore, we must loop through each Unicode character until we have a match, then move on to the next character and so on.

However, as the application will take some time to break the code, we do not want to get caught by a guard during the hacking process. Therefore, we will add some pictures that will simulate a fishes game. We must be able to hide our hacking application and show the fishes game by clicking on a button.

First, we are going to build a new C# application, and we will program a classic linear programming loop with some processing in order to run the code in the same thread (the application's main thread):

 We need a computer with at least two cores or two microprocessors installed in order to achieve significant results for the forthcoming experiments and for the examples in the rest of this book.

1. Create a new C# Project using the Windows Forms Application template in Visual Studio or Visual C# Express. The IDE is going to create a very simple one with a main windows form as a UI. Use `CodeBreakerApplication` as the project's name.

2. Open Windows Form `Form1` in the form designer, add the following controls and align them as shown in the image:

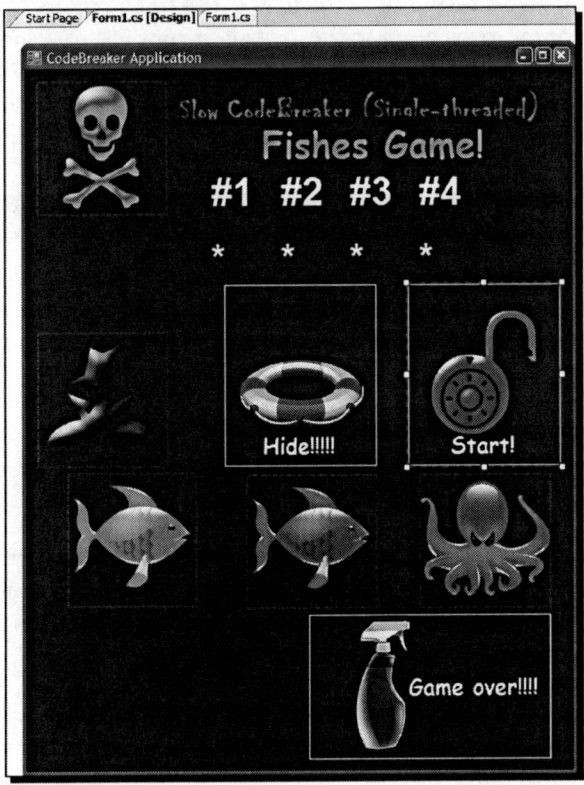

- ◆ Two picture boxes showing a skull and an agent (`picSkull` and `picAgent`).
- ◆ Three picture boxes showing fishes and an octopus (`picFish1`, `picFish2`, and `picFish3`).
- ◆ Four labels with their `Text` property set to "**#1**"; "**#2**"; "**#3**", and "**#4**" (**lblLabelChar1**, **lblLabelChar2**, **lblLabelChar3**, and **lblLabelChar4**).
- ◆ Four labels with their `Text` property set to "*****" (**lblOutputChar1**, **lblOutputChar2**, **lblOutputChar3**, and **lblOutputChar4**).
- ◆ One Label with its `Text` property set to "**Slow CodeBreaker (Single-threaded)**" and a scary font (**lblCodeBreaker**).
- ◆ One Label with its `Text` property set to "**Fishes Game!**" and a funny font (**lblFishesGame**).
- ◆ One button showing an open lock and its `Text` property set to "**Start!**" (**butStart**). This is the button that will run the main loop, which will find the code.

- ◆ One button showing a help or S.O.S. icon and its `Text` property set to **"Hide!!!!!"** (**butStart**). This button must hide all the controls related to the Codebreaker and show the fishes game. You will click this button when the guard is coming!

- ◆ One button showing a funny icon and its `Text` property set to **"Game over!!!!"** (**butGameOver**). This button must hide all the controls related to the fishes game and show the Codebreaker again. You will click this button when the guard has gone and you will feel safe to go on breaking the code!

3. Add the following line in the `public partial class frmMain : Form` definition to declare two private variables:

```
// The simulated code to be broken
private string prsCode;
// The list of Label controls that show the characters of the
 code being broken
private List<Label> prloOutputCharLabels;
```

4. Add the following procedure, `SimulateCodeGeneration`. It will simulate the code that must be broken:

```
private void SimulateCodeGeneration()
{
    // A Random number generator
    Random loRandom = new Random();
    // The char position being generated
    int i;

    prsCode = "";
    for (i = 0; i <= 4; i++)
    {
        // Generate a Random Unicode char for each of the 4
            positions
        prsCode += (char)(loRandom.Next(65535));
    }
}
```

5. Add the following procedure, `setFishesVisibility`. It will change the visibility of the controls related to the fishes game:

```
private void setFishesVisibility(bool pbValue)
{
    // Change the visibility of the controls related to the
        fishes game
    picFish1.Visible = pbValue;
    picFish2.Visible = pbValue;
    picFish3.Visible = pbValue;
    lblFishesGame.Visible = pbValue;
    butGameOver.Visible = pbValue;
}
```

6. Add the following procedure, `setCodeBreakerVisibility`. It will change the visibility of the controls related to the code breaking procedure:

```
private void setCodeBreakerVisibility(bool pbValue)
{
    // Change the visibility of the controls related to the
        code breaking procedure
    picSkull.Visible = pbValue;
    picAgent.Visible = pbValue;
    lblCodeBreaker.Visible = pbValue;
    lblLabelChar1.Visible = pbValue;
    lblLabelChar2.Visible = pbValue;
    lblLabelChar3.Visible = pbValue;
    lblLabelChar4.Visible = pbValue;
    lblOutputChar1.Visible = pbValue;
    lblOutputChar2.Visible = pbValue;
    lblOutputChar3.Visible = pbValue;
    lblOutputChar4.Visible = pbValue;
    butStart.Visible = pbValue;
    butHide.Visible = pbValue;
}
```

7. Add the following procedure, `showFishes`. It will show the fishes game, and will hide everything related to the code breaking procedure. You need that in order to avoid many years in jail:

```
private void showFishes()
{
    // Hide all the controls related to the code breaking
        procedure
    setCodeBreakerVisibility(false);
    // Change the window title
    this.Text = "Fishing game for Windows 1.0";
    // Make the fishes visible
    setFishesVisibility(true);
    // Change the window height
    this.Height = 700;
}
```

8. Add the following procedure, `showCodeBreaker`. It will hide the fishes game (you do not want to play), and will show everything related to the code breaking procedure. You need that in order to break the code:

```
private void showCodeBreaker()
{
    // Hide all the controls related to the fishes game
    setFishesVisibility(false);
    // Change the window title
    this.Text = "CodeBreaker Application";
    // Make the code breaker controls visible
    setCodeBreakerVisibility(true);
```

```
    // Change the window height
    this.Height = 415;
}
```

9. Add the following function, checkCodeChar. It will return true if the received character and position matches the one in the code. It will help us in our simulation, and we can then replace it with a real decoder. But we do not want to be in jail for many years, so let's just simulate:

```
private bool checkCodeChar(char pcChar, int piCharNumber)
{
    // Returns a bool value indicating whether the piCharNumber
       position of the code is the pcChar received
    return (prsCode[piCharNumber] == pcChar);
}
```

10. Add the following code in the form constructor (after InitializeComponent()):

```
// Generate a random code to be broken
   simulateCodeGeneration();
// Create a new list of Label controls that show the characters
   of the code being broken
prloOutputCharLabels = new List<Label>(4);
// Add the Label controls to the List
prloOutputCharLabels.Add(lblOutputChar1);
prloOutputCharLabels.Add(lblOutputChar2);
prloOutputCharLabels.Add(lblOutputChar3);
prloOutputCharLabels.Add(lblOutputChar4);
```

11. Open the Load event in the form and enter the following code:

```
// Hide the fishes game and show the Codebreaker
showCodeBreaker();
```

12. Open the Click event in the button **butGameOver**, and enter the following code:

```
// Hide the fishes game and show the Codebreaker
showCodeBreaker();
```

13. Open the Click event in the button **butHide**, and enter the following code:

```
// Hide the Codebreaker and show the fishes game
showFishes();
```

14. Open the Click event in the button **butStart**, and enter the following code:

```
// This code will break the simulated code
// This variable will hold a number to iterate from 1 to
   65,535 - Unicode character set
int i;
// This variable will hold a number to iterate from 0 to 3 (the
   characters positions in the code to be broken)
int liCharNumber;
```

```
// This variable will hold a char generated from the number in i
char lcChar;
// This variable will hold the current Label control that shows
   the char position being decoded
Label loOutputCharCurrentLabel;

for (liCharNumber = 0; liCharNumber < 4; liCharNumber++)
{
    loOutputCharCurrentLabel =
     prloOutputCharLabels[liCharNumber];
    // This loop will run 65,536 times
    for (i = 0; i <= 65535; i++)
    {
        // myChar holds a Unicode char
        lcChar = (char)(i);
        loOutputCharCurrentLabel.Text = lcChar.ToString();
        //Application.DoEvents();
        if (checkCodeChar(lcChar, liCharNumber))
        {
            // The code position was found
            break;
        }
    }
}
MessageBox.Show("The code has been decoded successfully.",
                this.Text);
```

15. Build and run the application. A window will be shown with the scary Codebreaker
    controls, as shown in the following image:

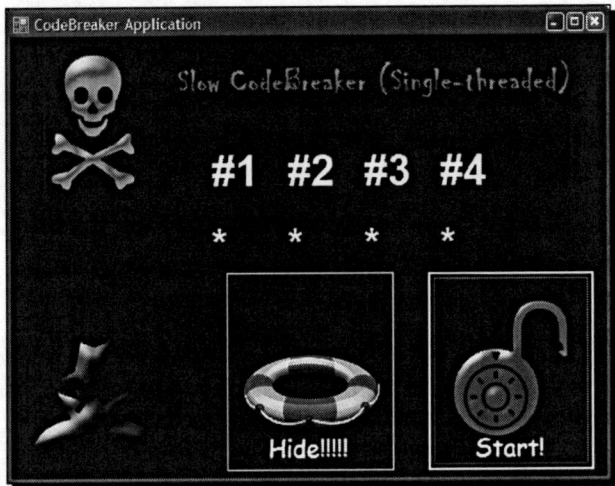

16. Click on the **Start** button. While the loop is running and the code is being broken by
    brute force, try clicking on the **Hide!!!!!** button. It will not be possible.

What just happened?

If a guard comes past when you are trying to break the code, you will be caught and shot (perhaps dead or in jail).

Why? Because we do not have a multithreaded application, we lose control over the graphical user interface.

The code programmed in the **butStart** click event handler runs in the main thread. Therefore, when the user clicks on this button, he or she loses control over the UI and cannot click on the other button to hide the Codebreaker-related controls.

The code is quite simple. It generates the 65,536 Unicode characters four times, and calls the checkCodeChar function in order to determine whether it is part of the code or not. It tries to display the progress showing each tested character in the window, but as it is a single threaded application, it fails in this objective. Again, as the loop is run in the main thread of the process created when the application is executed, we lose control over the UI. We cannot move the window, change its size, or push a button. The main thread is processing the intensive loop and consuming all the processing time of a single core. Hence, it cannot show information in the main window.

For this reason, when the guard comes, you are dead. Hence, let's make a multithreaded application and save human lives!

Time for action – Defining the work to be done in a new thread

A loop like the one used in the aforementioned example is an ideal task to run in an independent thread. That way, we could keep control over the UI and have the possibility of cancelling the job, displaying its progress, hiding the Codebreaker controls, and displaying our fishes game. Hence, we can avoid being shot by the guard (death or jail).

Now, we are going to make some changes to the application, and we will process that loop using a BackgroundWorker in order to run the code in an independent thread:

1. Open the project, CodeBreakerApplication.
2. Add a BackgroundWorker component to **frmMain (bakCodebreaker)**.
3. Open the DoWork event in the BackgroundWorker **bakCodeBreaker**, and paste the same code entered previously in the Click event in the button, **butStart**. (This is the code that is going to be run when the BackgroundWorker is started.) Then, comment out the following lines of code:

```
// loOutputCharCurrentLabel.Text = lcChar.ToString();
// MessageBox.Show("The code has been decoded successfully.",
    this.Text);
```

You must comment out these lines of code because, as the BackgroundWorker creates a new thread in which the loop is going to run, it cannot make changes to the user interface. There are mechanisms for doing that, and we will learn them later.

4. Open the `Click` event in the button **butStart**, and enter the following code:

```
// Start running the code programmed in BackgroundWorker DoWork
   event handler
// in a new independent thread and return control to the
   application's main thread
bakCodebreaker.RunWorkerAsync();
```

5. Build and run the application.

6. Click on the **Start** button. While the loop is running, and the code is being broken by brute force in a new thread created by the BackgroundWorker component, try to click on the **Hide!!!!!** button. It worked, and while the Codebreaker code is still working in the background, you will see the **Fishes Game!** being displayed in the Window, as shown in the following image:

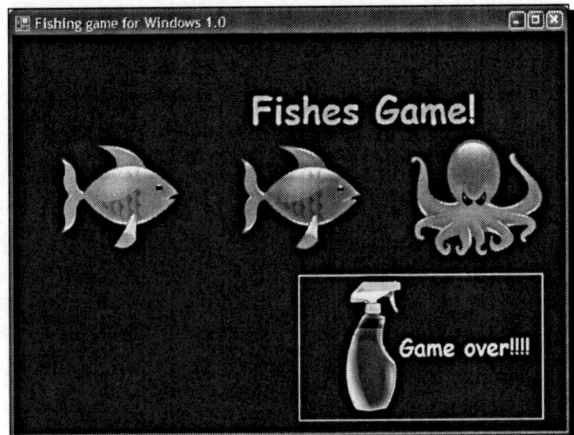

7. Move the window, change its size, maximize it, and do anything else you want to. While you do these operations, the code programmed in the `DoWork` event will keep on executing in another thread.

What just happened?

Now, we are safe from the guards! We can click on the **Hide** button, and the window shows the two fishes and the octopus with the **Game over!!!!** button, but continues processing the Codebreaker in the other thread.

The code programmed in the `DoWork` event handler runs in an independent thread. Therefore, when the user clicks on the **Start** button, a new thread is created, and he or she does not lose control over the UI. While the Codebreaker is running, the user can move the mouse cursor over other buttons, change the window size, and use other user interface components similar to the buttons.

 Using the BackgroundWorker component, executing code in another thread becomes very simple, and the application is more responsive.

However, we cannot see the progress of the code being broken. We will have a remedy for that later.

Have a go hero – Adding UI elements and monitoring the application

Create a new version of the application, but using four BackgroundWorker components instead of using only one. Each BackgroundWorker must find the match for one position of the four characters code. This way, they will run simultaneously.

Use the Process Explorer to view the running threads for the example, and monitor its activities. Apply all the things we have learned in the previous chapter. Also, use the Windows Task Manager.

Make the decoding process for each character more intensive in order to represent a real brute force attack, and not just a character matching. Doing this, you will learn a lot about the advantages of threading, and you will advance a few steps towards parallel programming. However, do not use this knowledge to hack any site or code on the Internet, because guards are everywhere, and you could get caught no matter how many threads your application uses!

Asynchronous execution

Calling the BackgroundWorker `RunWorkerAsync()` method, the advantages of threading begins running the code programmed in the `DoWork` event handler in a new independent thread. This mechanism is known as **asynchronous execution**.

When an asynchronous method is called, it runs in an independent way, and the program flow goes on with the instruction after to the method call even though its code has not finished its execution. The code in the asynchronous method runs concurrently with the main program flow.

Time for action - Understanding asynchronous execution step-by-step

We are going to run our last example step-by-step in order to understand the asynchronous execution, and how the main thread's code goes on running:

1. Open the project, `CodeBreakerApplication`.

2. Define a breakpoint in the line `bakCodebreaker.RunWorkerAsync();` in **butStart** `Click` event code.

3. Define a breakpoint in the line `showFishes();` in the **butHide** `Click` event code.

4. Press *F5* or select **Debug | Start Debugging** in the main menu.

5. Click on the **Start** button. The line with the breakpoint defined is shown highlighted as the next statement that will be executed.

6. Press *F10* or select **Debug | Step Over** in the main menu a few times. As you can see, the next statement that will be executed in the main thread is not in the BackgroundWorker `DoWork` event handler. It remains in the **butStart** `Click` event code.

7. Now, click on the **Hide** button.

8. Press *F10* or select **Debug | Step Over** in the main menu many times. As you can see, the thread created by the BackgroundWorker keeps running while the next statement that will be executed in the main thread is not in the BackgroundWorker `DoWork` event handler. It remains in the **butHide** `Click` event code, as shown in the following image:

```
Object Browser  Form1.cs [Design]  Form1.cs

CodeBreakerApplication.frmMain

        // Change the window height
        this.Height = 415;
    }

    private bool checkCodeChar(char pcChar, int piCharNumber)
    {
        // Returns a bool value indicating whether the piCharNumber position of the code is the pcChar received
        return (prsCode[piCharNumber] == pcChar);
    }

    private void butStart_Click(object sender, EventArgs e)
    {
        // Start running the code programmed in BackgroundWorker DoWork event handler
        // in a new independent thread and return control to the application's main thread
        bakCodebreaker.RunWorkerAsync();
    }

    private void butHide_Click(object sender, EventArgs e)
    {
        // Hide the Codebreaker and show the fishes game
        showFishes();
    }
```

What just happened?

Running the application step-by-step, we could not enter the code in the BackgroundWorker `DoWork` event handler. However, the code was running because the Codebreaker thread did its job. It happened because the BackgroundWorker starts an asynchronous execution of the code in another thread. Therefore, the main thread continues with its next statements as if the method `RunWorkerAsync()` had completed successfully. Hence, that method does not execute code in a linear, synchronous way.

 As we learned in the previous chapter, threads have their own program counter. The main thread has its program counter, and runs independent of the program counter of the new thread created during the asynchronous execution of the code contained in the `DoWork` event handler.

The execution flow in the main thread is synchronous. The main thread and the one created by BackgroundWorker run concurrently.

Nevertheless, not everything that shines is gold. Asynchronous code execution brings many new headaches to programmers because it ends with many implicit warranties related to synchronous and linear code execution. We will be talking about them, and will provide simple solutions for the most common problems.

When we worked with a single thread, we used to be the only owners of all the available elements in the programming context, the instances, the variables, the collections, the arrays, the controls that compose the graphical user interface, and the components, among many others. However, when we work with multiple threads and asynchronous execution, we are sharing this world, in many ways, with strangers. Hence, there may be some code that runs concurrently, affecting the values for some variables, or accomplishing changes in the objects' instances that we were going to work on.

For this reason, a paradigm shift is very important indeed. We must stop thinking we are alone with our code. The same happened when home computers were not connected to a network, some decades ago. They did not use a hard drive, and the user was a complete and unique owner of everything that was executed. Things like memory swapping did not take place then. On the other side, nowadays, it would be difficult to find a modern computer without some kind of Internet connection. The antivirus, antispyware, anti-malware, and many other anti-threats that could interrupt the digital ecosystem harmony appeared. Therefore, every action is accompanied by those anti whatever threat.

The same happens with multithreading and asynchronous execution. New threats appear and they can make the most perfectly designed code for a single thread produce completely unexpected and incomprehensible results when executed in a multithreading environment.

When we program with multithreading, we are not alone, and we must be very careful with the things we change henceforth in the thread's context in which we are coding the behavior.

Many techniques must be applied in order to avoid the different problems related to concurrent programming. We are going to analyze them with concrete examples through this book, case by case.

Synchronous execution

On the other hand, we are used to **synchronous execution** when we work with a single thread. This mechanism executes the next instruction once the current instruction processing is completed.

When a synchronous method is called, it runs in the same thread, and the program flow goes into the method's code. Once it returns from the method with or without a result, it goes on with the instruction next to the method call. There is no code in the method left for later execution, because it had finished when it returned the control to the caller. The main program has to wait for the method to complete its execution in order to go on with the next set of instructions.

This is what happens when you debug a single-threaded application, step-by-step.

In a single-threaded application, the synchronous execution takes place as we observed in classic linear programming. When a line of code executes, nothing else runs.

However, in a multithreaded application, like the ones using one or more BackgroundWorker components, asynchronous execution comes into picture.

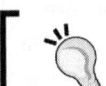

We must master this important change in the way methods are called and new independent threads are created on the fly, in order to get used to parallel and concurrent programming in C#.

Showing the progress

Users may get impatient when processes are delayed for more than a few seconds. In such cases, they need to know how long it will take them to finish. A good evidence of that is the replacement of messages like "Hold on..." by animated dialog boxes with progress bars, entertaining the users while they wait for the process, and showing them some kind of approximation of the time required to finish it.

Reporting the progress is one of the main problems when we work with only one thread, and make intensive use of the processing power. If you are still alive, and the guard did not catch you when using the single-threaded Codebreaker application, you will be able to make changes to the application to show the code as it is being decoded, and report the decoding progress for each character. This way, you will be able to decide whether to hide the Codebreaker when the guard is coming or wait for the process to finish; the application will give you the necessary feedback. Your life depends on good feedback from the application; therefore the changes are very important indeed.

As we work in the same thread that updates the user interface, if we send orders to make changes in a control to show any kind of progress, it will probably show the update whenever the main thread retrieves control (usually, when the process has already finished). Hence, as it is not useful to watch when the process has finished, it is necessary to update the progress report regularly.

> As a rule, we cannot make calls to a control since the thread used is different from the one that created it. If that happened, an **InvalidOperationException** would be raised. In order to make these calls safely, we must use **delegates** and asynchronous calls, known as **callbacks**. Both of them require certain knowledge that we will acquire in the forthcoming chapters.

As we learned in the beginning of this chapter, the BackgroundWorker is a component that tries to simplify the task of generating code for execution in a new thread. Therefore, it offers us a straightforward way to report progress and simplifies updating any control in the user interface that shows this progress, without any need to use delegates or asynchronous calls (callbacks). The last two are indeed much more complex ways to achieve the same results.

In order to show the progress of an operation using the BackgroundWorker component, we must assign the `true` value to its property `WorkerReportsProgress`. Its type is `bool`, and it tells whether the code executed in the new thread will report some kind of progress or not. If the value is `true`, the BackgroundWorker will trigger the `ProgressChanged` event handler.

This event facilitates updating the user interface. Therefore, it allows changes to control values, without having to consider the problems generated when we want to do it from a thread different from the one that created the control (the application's main thread).

Time for action – Using a BackgroundWorker to report progress in the UI

We are going to make some changes to our second example to take advantage of the features offered by the BackgroundWorker component to report progress in the user interface without delegates or callbacks. This way, we will be safe from the guards:

1. Open the project, `CodeBreakerApplication`.

2. Add four ProgressBar controls to **frmMain** (**pgbProgressChar1**, **pgbProgressChar2**, **pgbProgressChar3**, and **pgbProgressChar4**).

3. Set the BackgroundWorker `bakCodebreaker WorkerReportsProgress` property to `true`.

4. Add the following lines of code to the procedure `setCodeBreakerVisibility`. It will change the visibility of the new controls related to the progress of the code breaking procedure:

```
// Change the visibility of the controls related to the progress
    of the code breaking procedure
pgbProgressChar1.Visible = pbValue;
pgbProgressChar2.Visible = pbValue;
pgbProgressChar3.Visible = pbValue;
pgbProgressChar4.Visible = pbValue;
```

5. Add the following lines of code in the form class declaration to declare a new private variable:

```
// The list of ProgressBar controls that show the progress of
    the character being decoded
private List<ProgressBar> prloProgressChar;
```

6. Add the following code in the form constructor (after `InitializeComponent()`):

```
// Create a new list of ProgressBar controls that show the
    progress of each character of the code being broken
prloProgressChar = new List<ProgressBar>(4);
// Add the ProgressBar controls to the list
prloProgressChar.Add(pgbProgressChar1);
prloProgressChar.Add(pgbProgressChar2);
prloProgressChar.Add(pgbProgressChar3);
prloProgressChar.Add(pgbProgressChar4);
```

7. Add the following code after the end of the form class definition. The new `CodeBreakerProgress` class will have properties that will help provide many values related to the progress for updating the user interface:

```
public class CodeBreakerProgress
{
    // The char position in the 4 chars code
    private int priCharNumber;
    // The Unicode char code
    private int priCharCode;
    // The decoding process percentage completed
    private int priPercentageCompleted;

    public int CharNumber
```

```
    {
        get
        {
            return priCharNumber;
        }
        set
        {
            priCharNumber = value;
        }
    }

    public int CharCode
    {
        get
        {
            return priCharCode;
        }
        set
        {
            priCharCode = value;
        }
    }

    public int PercentageCompleted
    {
        get
        {
            return priPercentageCompleted;
        }
        set
        {
            priPercentageCompleted = value;
        }
    }
}
```

8. Open the `DoWork` event in the BackgroundWorker **bakCodebreaker**, and enter the following code at the beginning, before the `for` loop:

```
// This variable will hold a CodeBreakerProgress instance
CodeBreakerProgress loCodeBreakerProgress =
    new CodeBreakerProgress();
// This variable will hold the last percentage of the
    iteration completed
int liOldPercentageCompleted;

liOldPercentageCompleted = 0;
```

9. Now, in the same aforementioned event, add the following code before the `if (checkCodeChar(lcChar, liCharNumber))` line:

```
// The percentage completed is calculated and stored in
   the PercentageCompleted property
loCodeBreakerProgress.PercentageCompleted =
 (int)((i * 100) / 65535);
loCodeBreakerProgress.CharNumber = liCharNumber;
loCodeBreakerProgress.CharCode = i;

if (loCodeBreakerProgress.PercentageCompleted >
    liOldPercentageCompleted)
{
    // The progress is reported only when it changes with regard
       to the last one (liOldPercentageCompleted)
    bakCodebreaker.ReportProgress(loCodeBreakerProgress
     .PercentageCompleted, loCodeBreakerProgress);
    // The old percentage completed is now the percentage
       reported
    liOldPercentageCompleted = loCodeBreakerProgress.
     PercentageCompleted;
}
```

10. Now, in the same event, add the following code before the `break;` line:

```
// The code position was found
loCodeBreakerProgress.PercentageCompleted = 100;
bakCodebreaker.ReportProgress(loCodeBreakerProgress.
    PercentageCompleted, loCodeBreakerProgress);
```

11. Open the `ProgressChanged` event in the BackgroundWorker **bakCodebreaker**, and enter the following code (this is the code that is going to be run when the method `ReportProgress` is called during the loop):

```
// This variable will hold a CodeBreakerProgress instance
CodeBreakerProgress loCodeBreakerProgress =
 (CodeBreakerProgress)e.UserState;

// Update the corresponding ProgressBar with the percentage
   received in the as a parameter
prloProgressChar[loCodeBreakerProgress.CharNumber].Value =
 loCodeBreakerProgress.PercentageCompleted;
// Update the corresponding Label with the character being
   processed
prloOutputCharLabels[loCodeBreakerProgress.CharNumber].Text =
 ((char)loCodeBreakerProgress.CharCode).ToString();
```

12. Do not forget to remove the breakpoints.

13. Build and run the application.

14. Click on the **Start** button. You will see the progress bars filling up, showing how the process advances from 0 to 65,535 Unicode characters and the characters being tested. Now you have more information to decide whether to hide the application or not, according to the approximate distance from the guards, as shown in the following image:

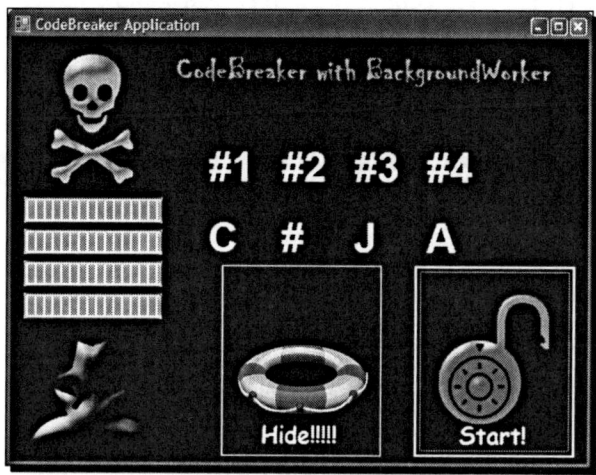

15. While the code is being broken, you can move the window, change its size, maximize it, or perform any such action. Show the dialog box, move it, and close it. While you do these operations, the progress bar goes on filling up.

What just happened?

The code programmed in the loop reports the progress only if the percentage completed increased by a unit or more. Otherwise, we would be triggering 65536 events in order to report only 100 different percentages and we could cause a stack overflow. That would be very inefficient and would make the loop take longer to complete its execution. Hence, with the conditional progress report, the event will be triggered only 100 times, running the code programmed in the BackgroundWorker **bakCodebreaker_ProgressChanged** event handler.

Now, you have more information to be safe from the guards and to complete your work. However, we still have some problems. For example, the application does not show the final code when it ends, and sometimes the progress bars will not show that it has completed 100 percent. We must be sure to have the right results, because we will be in great trouble if the code is not the expected one.

It is very easy to report the progress of a time-consuming process running in another thread using the BackgroundWorker component features. Nevertheless, we must pay attention to the number of times we trigger the ProgressChanged event. Reporting the progress must not generate exaggerated additional processing time in order to improve the efficiency.

In this example, we call the BackgroundWorker component `ReportProgress` method with two parameters, as in the following line of code:

```
bakCodebreaker.ReportProgress(loCodeBreakerProgress.
    PercentageCompleted, loCodeBreakerProgress);
```

The first parameter is an `int`, and defines the percentage completed. The second can be any object. Therefore, we send an instance of the `CodeBreakerProgress` class, with the values assigned to its many properties. This way, we can send more information than just a simple percentage and display the code being broken.

Have a go hero – Reporting progress in many ways

Create a new application that needs to run a time-consuming process. Use one or many BackgroundWorker components in order to run it in independent threads and report the progress as we have done in this chapter.

Add some controls that show the progress reported in different ways. For example, you can show the percentage completed as a number in a label or a text box.

Also, add some controls, such as a checkbox and a textbox, to this example. Then, run it in order to test the possibility of adding text while the BackgroundWorker is running and reporting the progress. Also, try to check and uncheck the checkbox while the progress bar and the other controls, showing the percentage completed, are updated. You will be able to see how the user experience changes when using multithreaded applications.

Add new buttons that show new Windows forms with many controls and use them while running the loop. As you can see, there are no interferences between the user interface update and the progress report, because we use the features provided by the BackgroundWorker component to simplify this process.

Cancelling the job

Executing a time-consuming process in an independent thread allows us to work in concurrent tasks and show the progress easily. Besides, one of the great advantages of doing this is the possibility to allow the user to go on using the controls in the graphical user interface without the usual aforementioned restrictions of single-threaded applications. For example, perhaps he or she wishes to cancel the process if it takes more time than expected.

The BackgroundWorker component simplifies the task of cancelling the execution of the code running in the thread it creates without having to make a big programming effort. In order to ease the cancellation of the execution of the code programmed in the BackgroundWorker DoWork event handler, we must assign the true value to its property WorkerSupportsCancellation. Its type is bool and it tells whether the code executed in the new thread will support cancellation through a call to the BackgroundWorker method CancelAsync(). This method simply assigns the true value to the BackgroundWorker property CancellationPending. Hence, the code being executed in the DoWork event handler must regularly check this property's value to determine whether it has to go on working or not.

Again, we can do it without the need to use either delegates or asynchronous calls (callbacks).

Time for action – Using a BackgroundWorker to cancel the job

You are using a wireless connection to detect intruders in your hacking network while breaking the code. If an intrusion is detected spying your network, you must abort the code breaking process, and you will avoid the detection of your location by the spies. Hiding the controls does not stop the code breaking process. Therefore, it is very important to provide the application with a fast cancellation procedure. Hurry up, the FBI is on your tail!

We are going to make some changes to our example to allow the user to cancel the loop at any time without delegates or callbacks, using the features provided by the BackgroundWorker component:

1. Open the project, CodeBreakerApplication.

2. Set the BackgroundWorker **bakCodebreaker** WorkerSupportsCancellation property to true.

3. Add a button control **butStop**. Set its Text property to "**Stop**".

4. Add the following line of code to the procedure setCodeBreakerVisibility. It will change the visibility of the new button:

   ```
   // Change the visibility of the new stop button
      butStop.Visible = pbValue;
   ```

5. Open the DoWork event in the BackgroundWorker bakCodebreaker, and enter the following code before the line lcChar = (char)(i); and in the beginning of the for loop (the code now adds support for a premature cancellation):

   ```
   if (bakCodebreaker.CancellationPending)
   {
       // The user requested to cancel the process
       e.Cancel = true;
       return;
   }
   ```

6. Open the `Click` event in the button **butStart**, and add the following lines of code at the beginning (the code now disables the **Start** button and enables the **Stop** button):

```
// Disable the Start button
butStart.Enabled = false;
// Enable the Stop button
butStop.Enabled = true;
```

7. Set the button **butStop Enabled** property to `false`. Hence, the button will be disabled when the Windows form is shown for the first time.

8. Open the `Click` event in the button **butStop**, and enter the following code:

```
// Disable the Stop button
butStop.Enabled = false;
// Enable the Start button
butStart.Enabled = true;
// Call the asynchronous cancellation (it will assign the true
    value to the BackgroundWorker bakCodebreaker
    CancellationPending property
bakCodebreaker.CancelAsync();
```

9. Build and run the application.

10. Click on the **Start** button. But wait! The wireless network analyzer tells you they are detecting your hacking activity. Click the **Stop** button now! The Codebreaker will cancel its execution, and you will be safe. The thread created by the BackgroundWorker will stop running. The result is shown in the following image:

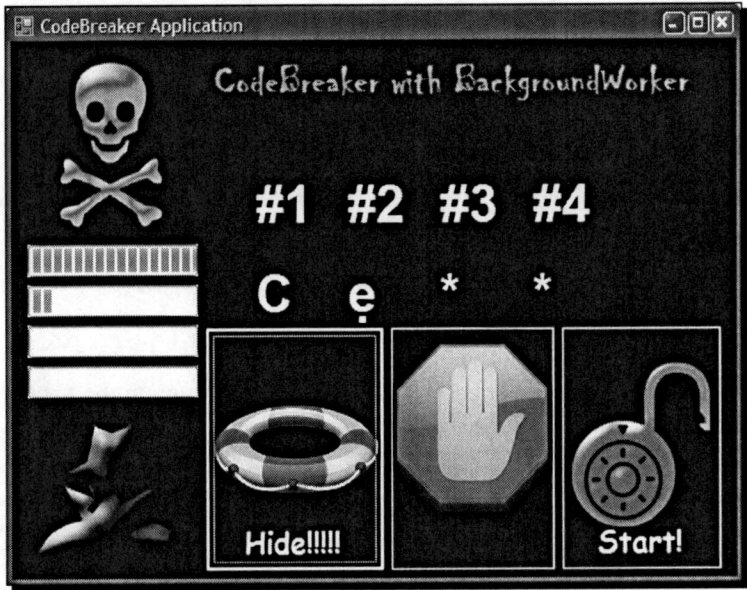

11. Now, click on the **Start** button and let the process finish.

What just happened?

Earlier, you could avoid the guards, and now you are able to escape from the wireless spies!

We could develop an application able to execute a time-consuming task in the background, while keeping the graphical user interface alive, offering the user a more real-life experience. Besides, we could offer the user the possibility to start and to stop the process whenever he wanted to. We did everything using the BackgroundWorker component features.

However, the application has a defect. When we click on the **Start** button and let the process finish, the **Stop** button will not be shown disabled. Besides, we cannot see the final code on the screen. We must create a remedy for this.

Time for action – Using a BackgroundWorker to detect a job completed

You must know the exact code because if you fail just one login process, you will be jailed for the rest of your life. But you want to go on learning parallel programming, therefore, let's enhance our application.

We are going to make some changes to our example to detect when the job running in the independent thread was completed without cancellation, using the features provided by the BackgroundWorker component:

1. Open the project `CodeBreakerApplication`.

2. Open the `RunWorkerCompleted` event in the BackgroundWorker **bakCodebreaker**, and enter the following code:

```
if (!e.Cancelled)
{
    // Only when the thread was not cancelled
    // Only when the thread completed its loop
    // Show a message box announcing the job completion
    MessageBox.Show("The code has been decoded successfully.",
                    this.Text);
    // Disable the Stop button
    butStop.Enabled = false;
    // Enable the Start button
    butStart.Enabled = true;
}
```

3. Build and run the application.

4. Click on the **Start** button and let the process finish. Now you will know when the code was decoded. A message box will appear, as shown in the following image:

5. Now, click on the **Start** button. After a few seconds, click on the **Stop** button (the wireless network alarm sounds). The thread created by the BackgroundWorker will stop running, but the message box will not appear because you stopped the thread.

What just happened?

You know when the code breaking process has finished successfully. But you still can't see the actual code in the window. And you need this immediately in order to logon to the system.

Now, the application can alert the user when the background task finishes and make the necessary changes in the user interface controls such as disabling the **Stop** button and enabling the **Start** button. We did not include this code in the end of the `for` loop in the `DoWork` event handler because we would have been changing a control related to the user interface.

 Remember that we cannot make changes to the user interface from a thread different from the main thread.

For this reason, we used the event that the BackgroundWorker triggers when it finishes running the code in its own thread, `RunWorkerCompleted`.

We checked the `bool` value of `e.Cancelled` to determine whether the thread was cancelled by the user or not. If the thread was cancelled by the user, the application would not display a message box that would state that the thread had successfully finished its execution.

We achieved our goal with the use of neither delegates nor callbacks, because the BackgroundWorker component offers interesting features to simplify the most common multithreading patterns.

Time for action – Working with parameters and results

Suppose that you have to define the number of Unicode characters that the code breaking process must use in the decoding process. A spy told you that using Unicode characters greater than 32,000 was not allowed. The process can run faster, and you can avoid the guards and the wireless spies.

We want to define the number of Unicode characters that the application must use in the decoding loop programmed for the BackgroundWorker component. We cannot use a traditional mechanism for passing parameters because the execution starts asynchronously, and in an independent thread.

In order to accomplish this, we can use another way to call the `RunWorkerAsync` method by passing an `Object` type parameter. Therefore, the parameter can be of any type, and we will have it available in the code programmed in the `DoWork` event handler by accessing the `Argument` property of the parameter `e` (`e.Argument`, type: `Object`).

 We must use the typecasting (type conversion) options in order to take full advantage of the `e.Argument` property and the `RunWorkerAsync` method call with a parameter.

On the other hand, we must obtain a result from the code executed in the independent thread (the code). In order to accomplish this, we can use the `Result` property of the parameter `e` (`e.Result`, type: `Object`). It is available in the code programmed both in the `DoWork` and in the `RunWorkerCompleted` event handlers.

Again, we must use the typecasting (type conversion) options in order to take full advantage of the `e.Result` property.

We are going to make some changes to our example to define the number of Unicode characters that the application must try (compare) in the codebreaking loop and show the broken code as a result, using the features provided by the BackgroundWorker component:

1. Open the project `CodeBreakerApplication`.

2. Replace the 65,535 value in the `SimulateCodeGeneration` procedure by 32,000; the line `prsCode += (char)(loRandom.Next(65535));` should become:

   ```
   prsCode += (char)(loRandom.Next(32000));
   ```

3. Open the `Click` event in the button **butStart**, and enter the following lines of code replacing the line `bakCodebreaker.RunWorkerAsync();` (the code now passes a parameter to the `RunWorkerAsync` method):

   ```
   // Only use the first 32,000 Unicode characters for the decoding
       process
   backgroundWorker1.RunWorkerAsync(32000);
   ```

4. Open the `DoWork` event in the BackgroundWorker **bakCodebreaker**, and enter the following code at the beginning, before the `for` loop:

   ```
   // This variable holds the last Unicode character to be processed
   int liTotal = (int)e.Argument;
   // This variable will hold the broken code
   string lsBrokenCode = "";
   ```

5. In the same event, change the second `for` with the following lines:

   ```
   // This loop will run (liTotal + 1) times
   for (i = 0; i <= liTotal; i++)
   ```

6. Then, change the line of code `loCodeBreakerProgress.PercentageCompleted = (int)((i * 100) / 65535);` with this one:

   ```
   loCodeBreakerProgress.PercentageCompleted =
     (int)((i * 100) / liTotal);
   ```

7. Add the following line of code in the `if (checkCodeChar(lcChar, liCharNumber))` block, but before the `break;`:

   ```
   // The broken code is concatenated in lsBrokenCode
   lsBrokenCode += lcChar.ToString();
   ```

8. Add the following line of code at the end of the `DoWork` event:

   ```
   e.Result = lsBrokenCode;
   ```

9. Open the `RunWorkerCompleted` event in the BackgroundWorker
`bakCodebreaker,` and add the following lines of code in the
`if (!e.Cancelled)` statement:

```
// The process has finished, therefore the 4 ProgressBar controls
   must show 100%
pgbProgressChar1.Value = 100;
pgbProgressChar2.Value = 100;
pgbProgressChar3.Value = 100;
pgbProgressChar4.Value = 100;
// Show the broken code in the labels
lblOutputChar1.Text = ((String)e.Result)[0].ToString();
lblOutputChar2.Text = ((String)e.Result)[1].ToString();
lblOutputChar3.Text = ((String)e.Result)[2].ToString();
lblOutputChar4.Text = ((String)e.Result)[3].ToString();
```

10. Build and run the application.

11. Click on the **Start** button and let the process finish. Now, you will have the code
shown in the window. Be careful, the guard is coming! Close the dialog box, click
on the **Hide!!!!!** button, and show the fishes! The results should be as shown in the
following image:

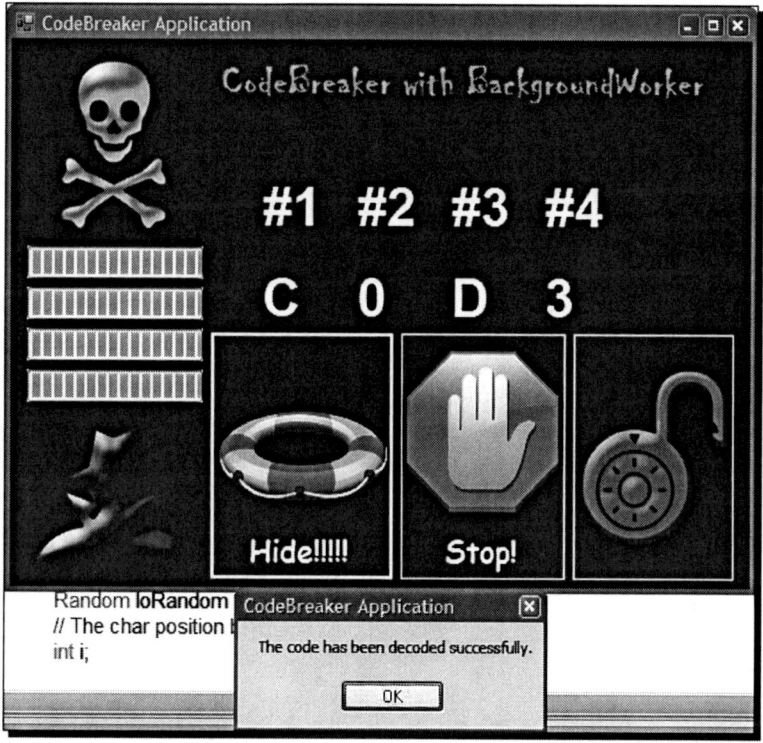

What just happened?

You have the code, and you are sure it is the final code because you know the process has finished successfully! However, using the decoding process necessary to obtain each character of the code, it will take a long time to process, and you will be unsafe from the guards. We have to think of a solution for this.

Now, the application passes parameters and results between different threads. As we can see, it is not a direct technique, but an indirect one. However, it is quite simple because we use the features incorporated in the BackgroundWorker component.

Nevertheless, we must be extremely careful with the typecasting used with the `Object` type. A wrong usage of typecasting will generate exceptions during the execution.

In the following line of code, in the BackgroundWorker `DoWork` event, we define the number of Unicode characters the loop must create in order to check in each code character position:

```
int liTotal = (int)e.Argument;
```

The typecasting to an `int` is necessary because `e.Argument` is an object, and we used it to pass an `int` parameter in this line of code:

```
bakCodebreaker.RunWorkerAsync(32000);
```

We changed the `for` loop bounds, and we concatenated each found character in the new string variable `lsBrokenCode` with this line of code:

```
lsBrokenCode += lcChar.ToString();
```

Once the loops are finished and the code is broken, it is assigned to `e.Result` (types: `DoWorkEventArgs` for `e` and `Object` for `Result`):

```
e.Result = lsBrokenCode;
```

When the BackgroundWorker finishes its job without cancellation, we show the broken code in the `RunWorkerCompleted` event, in the labels typecasting the `e.Result` property that we receive in the parameter `e` (type: `RunWorkerCompletedEventArgs`).

Have a go hero – Enhancing the application

A multimillionaire hacker watches your notebook, and realizes you are working with a multithreading application. He wants to contract you to make a new version in which you must limit the Unicode characters because he wants to break different codes with diverse constraints.

Add a control like a text box with a spinner to tell the thread the number of Unicode characters to be shown in the immediate window. Make the necessary changes to the code to take into account the value entered in the control for the loop, as we have already learned to do using the features provided by the BackgroundWorker component.

Then, use the `e.Result` property to return the following results:

♦ The number of Unicode characters the application needs to check in order to break the code

♦ The number of seconds the loop took to finish

♦ The number of seconds the loop took to break each character

 You can use an instance of a new Class with these properties in order to pass many values in the `e.Result` property using the proper typecasting. We made something like that in one of the previous examples.

Later, pass a parameter to the `RunWorkerAsync` method, and then use the `e.Argument` property to send the task the following values:

♦ The first number of Unicode character to be used in the decoding process, for each character position.

♦ The last number of Unicode character to be used in the decoding process, for each character position.

♦ The maximum number of seconds that the loop must be running. If the loop takes more than that the maximum number, it must automatically stop its execution, returning the aforementioned results. You have taken the time the guard takes to come. Therefore, you want to have the entire control over the application.

 You can use an instance of a new Class with these properties in order to pass many values in the `RunWorkerAsync` parameter using the proper typecasting with the `e.Argument` property.

Make the changes to the user interface, adding controls to set the aforementioned parameters.

Then, add a new BackgroundWorker to the application and program its code to query the value of the property `IsBusy` of the BackgroundWorker **bakCodebreaker**. Use the technique explained for reporting progress in order to change the Windows form background color, when the BackgroundWorker `backgroundWorker1` is working (`IsBusy == true`).

Change the code in the **Start** and the **Stop** buttons, and check the value of the `IsBusy` property before starting or cancelling the work.

Use the Process Explorer to view the running threads for the example and monitor its activities. Apply all the things we have learned in the previous chapter. Also, use the Windows Task Manager.

Working with multiple BackgroundWorker components

We can work with many BackgroundWorker components in order to run many concurrent threads. As we learned in the previous chapters, the performance results will depend upon the number of cores or processors available in the computer in which we run the application and many other factors we will study in the forthcoming chapters.

[Remember that each BackgroundWorker will create its own new independent thread.]

Time for action – Using many BackgroundWorker components to break the code faster

Using the real algorithms, the process for breaking the four Unicode characters code is very intensive, and requires more time than expected. You have many threats, the guards, the wireless network spies, and many others you do not know. Breaking the code must take minimum time possible. So far, we have been using multithreading to have a more responsive application, but now, we must make execution faster.

We are going to take the code presented in our previous examples and divide it into four BackgroundWorker components. With this example, we will learn how multiple BackgroundWorker components co-exist and create new independent threads, and hence achieve an incredible performance enhancement:

1. Open the project, `CodeBreakerApplication`.

2. Add three new BackgroundWorker components (**bakCodeBreaker2**, **bakCodeBreaker3**, and **bakCodeBreaker4**), to create four independent threads. Set the **True** value for their properties **WorkerReportsProgress** and **WorkerSupportsCancellation**, in design time, as shown in the following image:

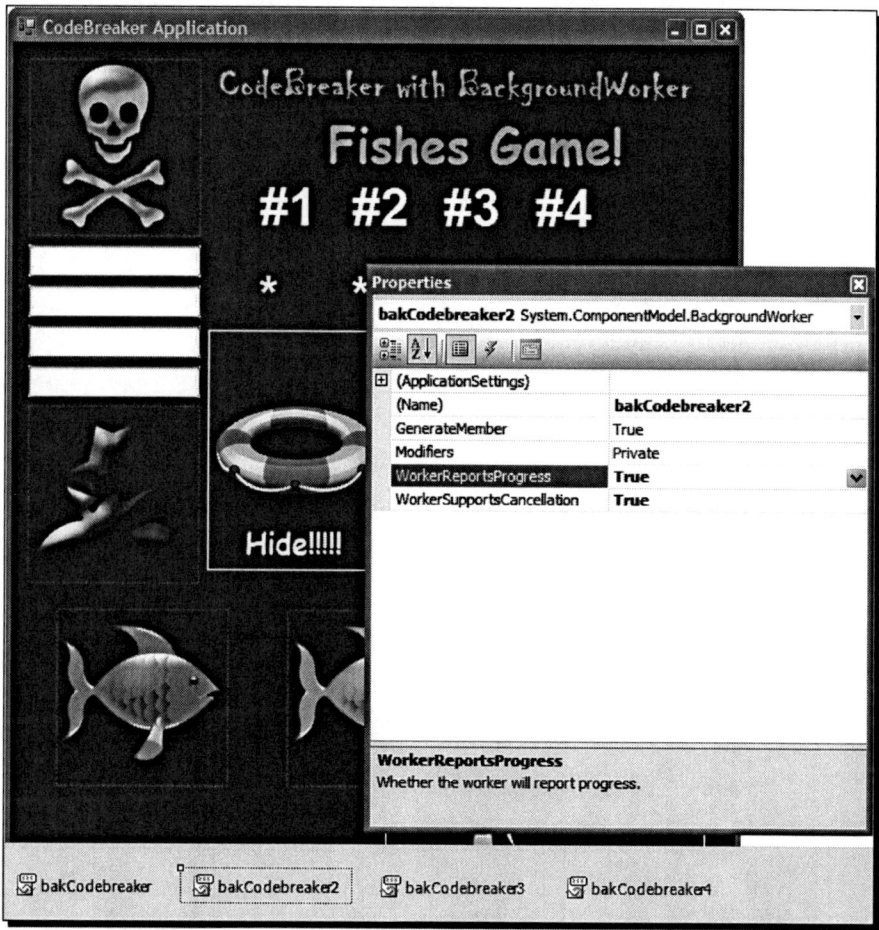

3. Add the following code after the end of the form class definition. The new `CodeBreakerParameters` class will have properties that will help provide many values that will be available as parameters for the four BackgroundWorker components:

```
public class CodeBreakerParameters
{
    // The first char position in the 4 chars code to process
    private int priFirstCharNumber;
```

```
        // The last char position in the 4 chars code to process
            private int priLastCharNumber;
        // The maximum number of the Unicode character
        private int priMaxUnicodeCharCode;
        public int FirstCharNumber
        {
            get
            {
                return priFirstCharNumber;
            }
            set
            {
                priFirstCharNumber = value;
            }
        }

        public int LastCharNumber
        {
            get
            {
                return priLastCharNumber;
            }
            set
            {
                priLastCharNumber = value;
            }
        }
        public int MaxUnicodeCharCode
        {
            get
            {
                return priMaxUnicodeCharCode;
            }
            set
            {
                priMaxUnicodeCharCode = value;
            }
        }
    }
```

4. Again, add the following code at the end of the form class definition. The new `CodeBreakerResult` class will have properties that help in providing many values available as parameters for the four BackgroundWorker components' `RunWorkerCompleted` events:

```
public class CodeBreakerResult
{
    // The first char position in the 4 chars code to process
    private int priFirstCharNumber;
```

```csharp
        // The last char position in the 4 chars code to process
        private int priLastCharNumber;
        // The part of the broken code
        private string prsBrokenCode;

        public int FirstCharNumber
        {
            get
            {
                return priFirstCharNumber;
            }
            set
            {
                priFirstCharNumber = value;
            }
        }

        public int LastCharNumber
        {
            get
            {
                return priLastCharNumber;
            }
            set
            {
                priLastCharNumber = value;
            }
        }

        public string BrokenCode
        {
            get
            {
                return prsBrokenCode;
            }
            set
            {
                prsBrokenCode = value;
            }
        }
    }
}
```

5. Open the `Click` event in the button **butStart**, and add the following lines of code before the line `bakCodebreaker.RunWorkerAsync();` (now the code will set the parameters for the four BackgroundWorker components, and will run them asynchronously):

```csharp
    // Start running the code programmed in each BackgroundWorker
    DoWork event handler in a new independent thread and return
    control to the application's main thread
    // First, create the CodeBreakerParameters for each
```

```
          BackgroundWorker and set its parameters
CodeBreakerParameters loParameters1 =
   new CodeBreakerParameters();
CodeBreakerParameters loParameters2 =
   new CodeBreakerParameters();
CodeBreakerParameters loParameters3 =
   new CodeBreakerParameters();
CodeBreakerParameters loParameters4 =
   new CodeBreakerParameters();
loParameters1.MaxUnicodeCharCode = 32000;
loParameters1.FirstCharNumber = 0;
loParameters1.LastCharNumber = 0;
loParameters2.MaxUnicodeCharCode = 32000;
loParameters2.FirstCharNumber = 1;
loParameters2.LastCharNumber = 1;
loParameters3.MaxUnicodeCharCode = 32000;
loParameters3.FirstCharNumber = 2;
loParameters3.LastCharNumber = 2;
loParameters4.MaxUnicodeCharCode = 32000;
loParameters4.FirstCharNumber = 3;
loParameters4.LastCharNumber = 3;
bakCodebreaker.RunWorkerAsync(loParameters1);
bakCodebreaker2.RunWorkerAsync(loParameters2);
bakCodebreaker3.RunWorkerAsync(loParameters3);
bakCodebreaker4.RunWorkerAsync(loParameters4);
```

6. Now, in the same aforementioned event, remove the line `bakCodebreaker.RunWorkerAsync();`.

7. Open the `Click` event in the button **butStop**, and add the following lines of code (now the code will cancel the four BackgroundWorker components, `bakCodebreaker` and the three Backgroundworker components added in these lines):

```
bakCodebreaker2.CancelAsync();
bakCodebreaker3.CancelAsync();
bakCodebreaker4.CancelAsync();
```

8. Now, we will create generic procedures for handling these three BackgroundWorker components programmed events, receiving the same parameters as the corresponding event handler:

   - `DoWorkProcedure` for `DoWork` event
   - `RunWorkerCompletedProcedure` for `RunWorkerCompleted` event
   - `ProgressChangedProcedure` for `ProgressChanged` event

9. Paste the BackgroundWorker **bakCodebreaker** DoWork event handler code in a new private procedure, and then make the following changes as explained:

```
private void DoWorkProcedure(object sender, DoWorkEventArgs e)
```

10. Add the following variable definitions in the beginning:

```
// This variable will hold the broken code
string lsBrokenCode = "";
CodeBreakerParameters loCodeBreakerParameters =
    (CodeBreakerParameters)e.Argument;
```

11. Replace the line int liTotal = (int)e.Argument; with this (now the event handler procedure needs more parameters, and we created a class to manage them):

```
int liTotal = loCodeBreakerParameters.MaxUnicodeCharCode;
```

12. Replace the line that defines the first loop with this one (now the loop takes into account the parameters received through a CodeBreakerParameters instance):

```
for (liCharNumber = loCodeBreakerParameters.FirstCharNumber;
     liCharNumber <= loCodeBreakerParameters.LastCharNumber;
     liCharNumber++)
```

13. Replace the pending cancellation check with this line (we use the sender parameter typecast because the same procedure is employed by the four BackgroundWorker components:

```
if (((BackgroundWorker)sender).CancellationPending)
```

14. Replace the call to the ReportProgress method by the following line (again, we use the sender parameter typecasted for generalization):

```
((BackgroundWorker)sender).ReportProgress(loCodeBreakerProgress.
  PercentageCompleted, loCodeBreakerProgress);
```

15. Replace the call to the ReportProgress method when the checkCodeChar function returns true with this line:

```
((BackgroundWorker)sender).ReportProgress(loCodeBreakerProgress.
  PercentageCompleted, loCodeBreakerProgress);
```

16. Replace the line e.Result = lsBrokenCode; with the following lines (now we must return more than one result, therefore we use an instance of the CodeBreakerResult class created earlier):

```
// Create a new instance of the CodeBreakerResult class and set
   its properties' values
CodeBreakerResult loResult = new CodeBreakerResult();
loResult.FirstCharNumber = loCodeBreakerParameters.
                           FirstCharNumber;
```

```
loResult.LastCharNumber = loCodeBreakerParameters.LastCharNumber;
loResult.BrokenCode = lsBrokenCode;
// Return a CodeBreakerResult instance in the Result property
e.Result = loResult;
```

17. Enter the following code to create the new `RunWorkerCompleted` procedure:

```
private void RunWorkerCompletedProcedure(object sender,
    RunWorkerCompletedEventArgs e)
{
    if (!e.Cancelled)
    {
        // Obtain the CodeBreakerResult instance contained in the
            Result property of e parameter
        CodeBreakerResult loResult = (CodeBreakerResult)
                                        e.Result;

        int i;

        // Iterate through the parts of the result resolved by
            this BackgroundWorker
        for (i = loResult.FirstCharNumber; i <=
            loResult.LastCharNumber; i++)
        {
            // The process has finishes, therefore the
                ProgressBar control must show a 100%
            prloProgressChar[i].Value = 100;
            // Show the part of the broken code in the label
            prloOutputCharLabels[i].Text = loResult.
            BrokenCode[i - loResult.FirstCharNumber].ToString();
        }
    }
}
```

18. Enter the following code to create the new `ProgressChangedProcedure` procedure:

```
private void ProgressChangedProcedure(object sender,
    ProgressChangedEventArgs e)
{
    // This variable will hold a CodeBreakerProgress instance
    CodeBreakerProgress loCodeBreakerProgress =
        (CodeBreakerProgress)e.UserState;
    // Update the corresponding ProgressBar with the percentage
        received as a parameter
    prloProgressChar[loCodeBreakerProgress.CharNumber].Value =
        loCodeBreakerProgress.PercentageCompleted;
    // Update the corresponding Label with the character being
        processed
```

```
prloOutputCharLabels[loCodeBreakerProgress.CharNumber].Text =
    ((char)loCodeBreakerProgress.CharCode).ToString();
}
```

19. Now, you have to program the code for the three event handlers of the four BackgroundWorker components. As we have used procedures, we will use the same code for the four BackgroundWorker components.

20. Add the following code in the four BackgroundWorker components' `DoWork` event handlers:

```
DoWorkProcedure(sender, e);
```

21. Add the following code in the four BackgroundWorker components' `ProgressChanged` event handlers:

```
ProgressChangedProcedure(sender, e);
```

22. Add the following code in the four BackgroundWorker components' `RunWorkerCompleted` event handlers:

```
RunWorkerCompletedProcedure(sender, e);
```

23. Build and run the application.

24. Click on the **Start** button and let the process finish. Now, you will have the code shown in the window using four independent threads, one for each part of the code, and with generic procedures that do not repeat the code in the event handlers. By making some changes to the algorithms used to check each character and using performance measures, you will find this new version faster than ever. Wow, you have 10 mails requiring the use of your new abilities. Be careful; they can be jealous hackers! Remember that you can still switch to the fishes when the guard is coming. The results are as shown in the following image:

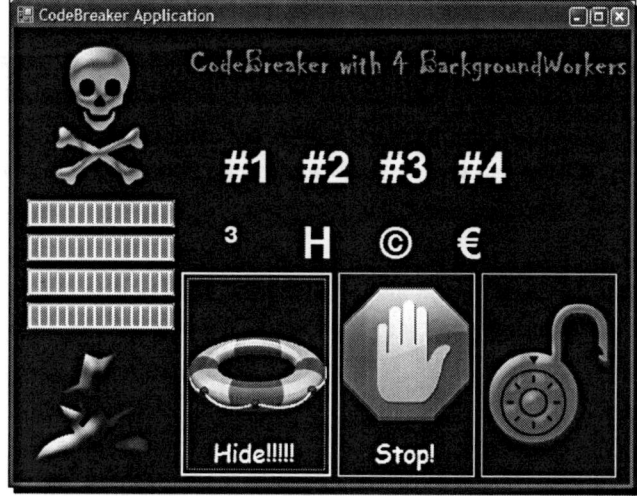

What just happened?

Now, there are four multimillionaire hackers looking for you! Your code breaking procedure is very fast, and they want you working for them thanks to multithreading.

As we have seen, it is easy to split a process into many threads using the features provided by the BackgroundWorker component. The results of the execution of the previous example will depend on the number of cores or processors available in the computer. The ideal situation is to start as many BackgroundWorker components as the number of cores available. This way, we can achieve the best performance for each thread and take the CPU usage to a value around 95%.

Now, we do not need to run many instances of an application to take advantage of parallel processing capabilities. Using the BackgroundWorker and everything we have learned so far, we can quite easily split a process into many threads.

However, we had to make some important changes to the code because we needed to generalize the behavior of four BackgroundWorker components without writing the same piece of code four times.

We created new classes for passing parameters and obtaining results because we needed many parameters and many results. As you can see, with typecasting, C# offers us excellent alternatives to generalize the code.

The key was the sender parameter. Remember that this parameter available in the event handlers offers a reference to the component (the BackgroundWorker) that triggers the event. Typecasting the sender parameter to a BackgroundWorker, we could generalize the code in the different event handlers and create procedures for each one.

There were many changes. But once the code patterns are practiced and learned, it will be easier to work with concurrent programming structures.

Have a go hero – Monitoring and enhancing the application

As of now, the application uses four BackgroundWorker components, and hence four independent threads. It does not give the user a message about the end of the codebreaking global process.

Add another BackgroundWorker to show a message box telling the user the process has finished, disabling the **Stop** button and enabling the **Start** button, when the four BackgroundWorker components complete their work. You can use the IsBusy() function.

Use the Process Explorer to view the running threads for the example and monitor its activities. Apply all the things we have learned in the previous chapter. Also, use the Windows Task Manager. You will have a better understanding of the differences between multiple processes and multithreaded applications, when monitoring the application running concurrently with the four BackgroundWorker threads, in a computer with a quad-core microprocessor and using the Process Explorer. This is shown in the following image:

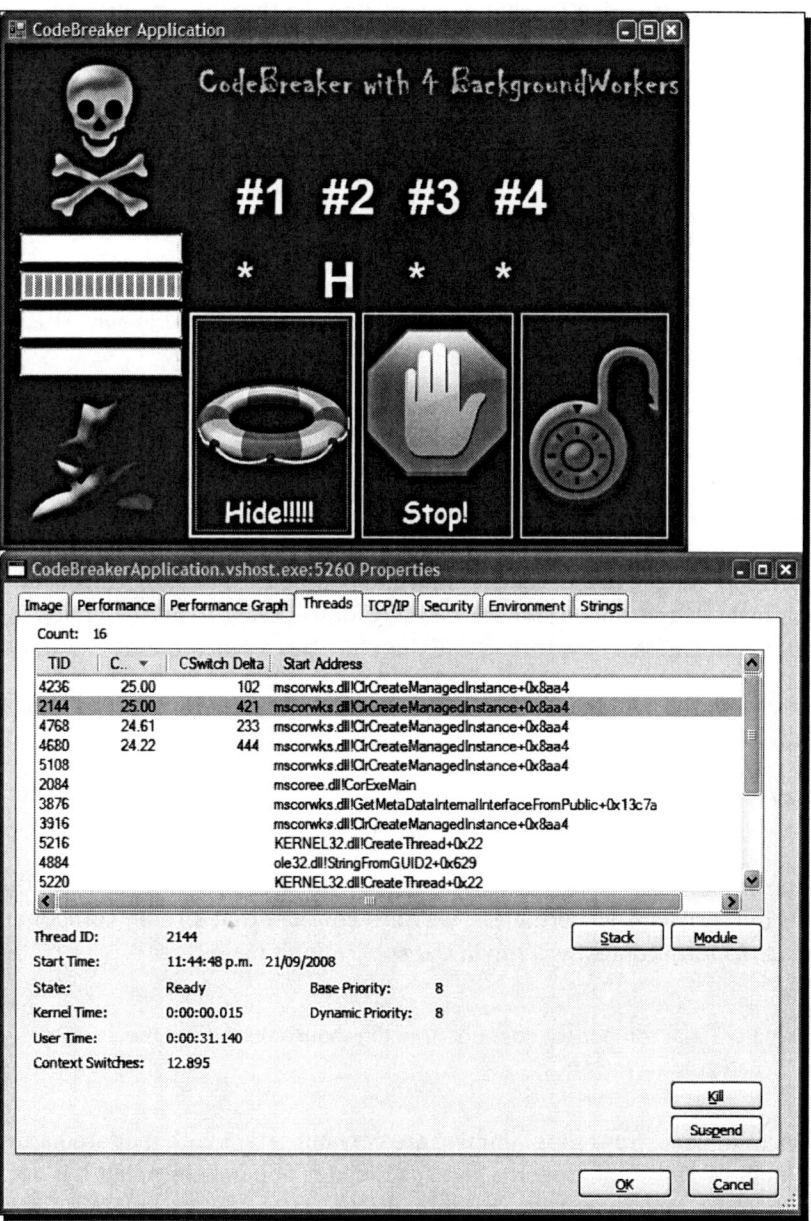

Monitor the application using one, two, three, and four threads running concurrently.

Enhance the application using the patterns we have learned in the previous example using only one BackgroundWorker component. Change the code to add the possibility to start and stop the threads running in each BackgroundWorker.

Monitor the application starting and stopping one, two, three, and four threads running concurrently, and pay attention to what happens with the threads' activities and CPU usage in the Process Explorer.

Run the application in different computers with different microprocessors and use the Process Explorer to monitor their behavior and measure their performance.

BackgroundWorker and Timer

At first sight, developers who have already worked with the Timer component can find certain similarities between the Timer and the BackgroundWorker. However, they are completely different, and they have different purposes.

The Timer is a component prepared for triggering an event at specified intervals. When the event is triggered, the code written in its handler is executed. We can specify the interval for triggering the event, and also, as with any other event, we can program the code in its handler. It is very useful for executing a block of code at specified intervals. However, this is done in the application's main thread, and hence, during all the time that the code corresponding to the Timer event is running, the execution of instructions in the application's main thread will be stopped, waiting for the event to finish. It happens because the Timer does not create a new thread and therefore has a synchronous execution.

On the other hand, the BackgroundWorker component has an asynchronous execution, as we have experienced in the examples.

The best way to compare the way they work is using them and checking the execution sequence, and debugging the applications statement by statement.

However, sometimes, the use of many BackgroundWorker components combined with Timer components can be useful. Nevertheless, we must consider that a Timer component created under a Windows form context will run in the application's main thread.

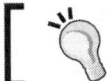 The Timer component does not have the same objectives as the BackgroundWorker.

The advantages of concurrent programming are very important with modern hardware. The use of multiple Timer components gives us the idea of parallelism, but it is not true parallelism, because they share the main thread.

BackgroundWorker creation on the fly

In the previous chapters, we were talking about the ideal situation, consisting of the alignment between the number of cores or processors available and the number of threads into which a process is divided, in order to achieve the best possible performance, according to hardware resources. As we can see, the BackgroundWorker is a very noble component, and helps us a lot when we need a simple way to create new threads and control certain aspects of their behavior, as well as provide feedback about the component's progress to the user interface. However, as we have developed the examples inserting the BackgroundWorker components in design time, we should find a way to create many of them dynamically in runtime.

Time for action – Creating BackgroundWorker components in run-time

The hackers who contracted you have many notebooks with processors having different numbers of execution cores. It is said that one of them has a 128 core computer (that can hack everything you can imagine). The hacker has been looking for a multithreading expert to take full advantage of the powerful computer, but did not find anyone. The hacker wants to break a 128 Unicode characters code using 128 threads. Come on, let's help the hacker!

We are going to create a new version of our Codebreaker application creating the BackgroundWorker components in runtime, without any design-time prerequisites, and assign the event handlers with the relevant code:

1. Open the project, `CodeBreakerApplication`.

2. Remove the existing four BackgroundWorker components; we will create them at runtime.

3. Remove the event handlers' code for the four BackgroundWorker components (now removed).

4. Add the following lines of code in the form class declaration to declare four new private variables:

```
// 4 BackgroundWorker components
private BackgroundWorker bakCodebreaker;
private BackgroundWorker bakCodebreaker2;
private BackgroundWorker bakCodebreaker3;
private BackgroundWorker bakCodebreaker4;
```

5. Add the following lines of code in the form constructor (now we are creating the four BackgroundWorker components in runtime, and we will assign them the events programmed in the previously created procedures):

```
// Create 4 new BackgroundWorker component
bakCodebreaker = new System.ComponentModel.BackgroundWorker();
// Attach an event handler making reference to the procedure that
    contains the code that will be triggered by the DoWork event
bakCodebreaker.DoWork += new DoWorkEventHandler(DoWorkProcedure);
// Attach an event handler making reference to the procedure that
    contains the code that will be triggered by the
    ProgressChanged event
bakCodebreaker.ProgressChanged +=
 new ProgressChangedEventHandler(ProgressChangedProcedure);
// Attach an event handler making reference to the procedure that
    contains the code that will be triggered by the
    RunWorkerCompleted event
bakCodebreaker.RunWorkerCompleted +=
 new RunWorkerCompletedEventHandler(RunWorkerCompletedProcedure);

// Set up its properties
bakCodebreaker.WorkerReportsProgress = true;
bakCodebreaker.WorkerSupportsCancellation = true;

bakCodebreaker2= new System.ComponentModel.BackgroundWorker();
// Attach an event handler making reference to the procedure that
    contains the code that will be triggered by the DoWork event
bakCodebreaker2.DoWork +=
 new DoWorkEventHandler(DoWorkProcedure);
// Attach an event handler making reference to the procedure that
    contains the code that will be triggered by the
    ProgressChanged event
bakCodebreaker2.ProgressChanged +=
 new ProgressChangedEventHandler(ProgressChangedProcedure);
// Attach an event handler making reference to the procedure that
    contains the code that will be triggered by the
    RunWorkerCompleted event
bakCodebreaker2.RunWorkerCompleted +=
 new RunWorkerCompletedEventHandler(RunWorkerCompletedProcedure);

// Set up its properties
bakCodebreaker2.WorkerReportsProgress = true;
bakCodebreaker2.WorkerSupportsCancellation = true;
```

```
bakCodebreaker3 = new System.ComponentModel.BackgroundWorker();
// Attach an event handler making reference to the procedure that
    contains the code that will be triggered by the DoWork event
bakCodebreaker3.DoWork += new
 DoWorkEventHandler(DoWorkProcedure);
// Attach an event handler making reference to the procedure that
    contains the code that will be triggered by the
    ProgressChanged event
bakCodebreaker3.ProgressChanged +=
 new ProgressChangedEventHandler(ProgressChangedProcedure);
// Attach an event handler making reference to the procedure that
    contains the code that will be triggered by the
    RunWorkerCompleted event
bakCodebreaker3.RunWorkerCompleted +=
 new RunWorkerCompletedEventHandler(RunWorkerCompletedProcedure);


// Set up its properties
bakCodebreaker3.WorkerReportsProgress = true;
bakCodebreaker3.WorkerSupportsCancellation = true;


bakCodebreaker4 = new System.ComponentModel.BackgroundWorker();
// Attach an event handler making reference to the procedure that
    contains the code that will be triggered by the DoWork event
bakCodebreaker4.DoWork +=
 new DoWorkEventHandler(DoWorkProcedure);
// Attach an event handler making reference to the procedure that
    contains the code that will be triggered by the
    ProgressChanged event
bakCodebreaker4.ProgressChanged +=
 new ProgressChangedEventHandler(ProgressChangedProcedure);
// Attach an event handler making reference to the procedure that
    contains the code that will be triggered by the
    RunWorkerCompleted event
bakCodebreaker4.RunWorkerCompleted +=
 new RunWorkerCompletedEventHandler(RunWorkerCompletedProcedure);


// Set up its properties
bakCodebreaker4.WorkerReportsProgress = true;
bakCodebreaker4.WorkerSupportsCancellation = true;
```

6. We do not need to enter new code to define the contents of the event handlers because we are using the procedures we wrote in the previous example (generalization benefits).

7. Build and run the application. You will see no differences with the BackgroundWorker components created at design time. Now, you can control the BackgroundWorker creation whenever you want!

What just happened?

Now, they want you to show them how to create the BackgroundWorker components dynamically according to the number of available processors or cores.

In this case, we created the BackgroundWorker component completely with code. We set up its properties and attached its event handlers at runtime. Hence, there are no limitations for working with many threads depending on the underlying hardware configuration. This technique allows us to make decisions at runtime. In some cases, two BackgroundWorker components will be enough, but in others, perhaps the application may find it convenient to create 32 BackgroundWorker components.

We must pay attention to the first lines of code in the form class constructor. We attached event handlers making reference to the procedure that contains the event code. For example, in this line:

```
bakCodebreaker.DoWork += new DoWorkEventHandler(DoWorkProcedure);
```

Using the += operator applied to DoWork and passing the procedure name as a parameter of DoWorkEventHandler, we attached the DoWork event handler.

The great advantage of doing it this way is the flexibility at runtime. If we fix the number of BackgroundWorker components at design time, we will have some difficulties in achieving scalability for our application.

But, you want to figure out how many cores the processor has at runtime in order to create the best number of BackgroundWorker components, and hence threads. It is very easy to do that in C#, with the following property:

```
Environment.ProcessorCount
```

Using it, you can determine the best number of concurrent threads. And they will love you!

Have a go hero – Enhancing the code

Of course, the code shown in the previous examples can be enhanced. We used the `sender` parameter to know dynamically in which BackgroundWorker we are positioned. This way, it was possible to use the same procedure for many BackgroundWorker components, which could be generated dynamically and could also be attached to the event handlers.

Develop a new version of this application example. But, instead of using many BackgroundWorker components already defined in design time, create them according to the number of available processors using code in runtime. Also, make the necessary changes for each event procedure to process a different part with a beginning and an ending character.

Make some changes to this new application, and let the user specify the total number of characters the Unicode code to be broken has. The application must divide that total number by the number of BackgroundWorker components and show the results in dynamically created label controls.

Add the possibility of independently starting and stopping the BackgroundWorker threads. We learned how to do that.

Using your C# programming language skills and everything learned in this chapter add the possibility of resuming the BackgroundWorker threads that were stopped (not to start all over again, but to resume).

Again, use the Process Explorer to view the running threads for all the examples and monitor their activities. Apply all the things we have learned in the previous chapter. Also, use the Windows Task Manager. You will be able to have a better understanding of the differences between multiple processes and multithreaded applications.

Pop quiz

1. The BackgroundWorker's `DoWork` event handler runs:

    a. In the application's main thread

    b. In a new independent thread

    c. In a new process

2. The Timer component:
   a. Is the same as the BackgroundWorker component
   b. Runs in the main application's thread
   c. Creates a new independent thread

3. The BackgroundWorker component `RunWorkerAsync`:
   a. Starts a new thread with asynchronous execution
   b. Starts a new thread with synchronous execution
   c. Runs the code in the `DoWork` event handler synchronously

4. Using the BackgroundWorker component:
   a. You can change the user interface controls properties freely
   b. You cannot make any changes to the user interface controls because you need delegates
   c. You can change the user interface controls using the `ProgressChanged` event handler

5. Which of the following lines of code passes parameters to a BackgroundWorker?
   a. `backgroundWorker1.RunWorkerAsync(90000000);`
   b. `backgroundWorker1.ReportProgress(90000000);`
   c. `backgroundWorker1.DoWork +=`
      `new DoWorkEventHandler(backgroundWorker1, 90000000);`

Right answers:

1. a.
2. b.
3. a.
4. c.
5. a.

Summary

We learned a lot in this chapter about working with threads using the BackgroundWorker component. Specifically, we covered:

- Developing applications that are able to create background threads using the BackgroundWorker component, and showing the progress taking advantage of the methods provided by this component for that action

- ◆ Programming the threads' code to be executed by the BackgroundWorker
- ◆ Understanding the differences between synchronous and asynchronous execution and how they are related to threads
- ◆ Reporting the progress of multiple threads in the user interface
- ◆ Starting and cancelling threads created using BackgroundWorker instances
- ◆ Launching multiple threads using many BackgroundWorker components and certain code patterns

We also discussed the differences between multiple threads using BackgroundWorker and Timers, and the way to create a responsive UI.

Now that we've learned about a simple way to create many threads in a C# application using the BackgroundWorker component, we're ready to do these things using a much more flexible but more complex technique, the Thread Class—which is the topic of the next chapter.

4

Thread Class—Practical Multithreading in Applications

In order to have very precise control over the concurrently running threads in our applications, we do not need to work with Windows **API (Application Programming Interface)**; instead we can use the **Thread class**. In this chapter, we will study this class in detail and we will develop more complex multithreaded applications that take full advantage of multiprocessing. Reading it and following the exercises, we shall be:

- ◆ Developing applications with great control over the multiple running threads, offering an exciting performance enhancement
- ◆ Learning to create independent and very flexible threads using a very powerful class
- ◆ Finding out how to start, control, and coordinate multiple threads
- ◆ Discovering how to send parameters to and retrieve data from threads
- ◆ Learning to share data between many threads
- ◆ Finding out how to combine asynchronous and synchronous execution in order to have an exhaustive control over the running threads and their tasks
- ◆ Developing applications capable of launching multiple threads when necessary

Creating threads with the Thread class

So far, we have used the BackgroundWorker component to create new threads independent of the main application thread. The applications can respond to UI events while processing continues and take full advantage of multiple cores, thus running faster. But there are some restrictions when we must control and coordinate the execution of many threads that are not intended to just run in the background. How can we use threading and the `Thread` class to make an application capable of taking full control of the synchronous and asynchronous execution of concurrent threads?

We can work with many instances of the `Thread` class (`System.Threading.Thread`) in order to run many concurrent threads with more control capabilities than the ones created using the BackgroundWorker component. As we learned in the previous chapters, the performance results will depend upon the number of cores or processors available in the computer in which we run the application, and many other factors, which we will study in the following chapters. However, the `Thread` class offers many fine-tuning capabilities, when we cannot achieve the desired performance using multithreading.

As with the BackgroundWorker component, each `Thread` class will create its own new independent thread. However, as it is a class and not a component, everything requires writing code, and there is no design-time component.

The `Thread` class does a great job of offering great flexibility while offering a simple way to initialize, coordinate, run, stop, and free multiple threads.

Time for action – Defining methods for encryption and decryption

Unfortunately, the FBI finally discovered your brute force attack. The problem was that the first version took too much time to break the code because it was single-threaded. Now, the FBI wants you to cooperate with them in an encryption project using your multithreading knowledge and as a reward, they will acquit you of all your charges.

They are working with a new cellular phone capable of sending SMS (text messages) with access to the complete Unicode character set. The cellular phone is a single core device. You have to work in a very fast and efficient encryption engine capable of encrypting the incoming text messages and leaving them in an output queue. This engine is going to run in a huge server with many multi-core processors. They want you to use a very fine-tuned multithreading application, capable of working with as many threads as the cores available in the computer in which the engine is being executed.

First, we are going to build a new C# application, and we will define and test the methods for encrypting and decrypting a string:

1. Create a new C# Project using the Windows Forms Application template in Visual Studio or Visual C# Express. Use `SMSEncryption` as the project's name.

2. Open Windows Form `Form1` in the form designer, add the following controls, and align them as shown in the following image:

- One picture box showing a cell phone.

- One picture box showing the world connected.

- One picture box showing a recorder.

- Three labels with their `Text` property set to **SMS Encryption Engine**, **Original SMS Messages**, and **Encrypted SMS Messages**.

- Two textboxes with their **Multiline** property set to **True** and their **MaxLength** property set to **0** (**txtOriginalSMS** and **txtEncryptedSMS**). Use an elegant font.

- One button showing some messages or a conversation; its `Text` property set to **Test** (**butTest**). This is the button that will test the encryption and decryption methods.

3. Add the following function—Encrypt. It will encrypt the string received as a parameter and return a string with the resulting encoded message with unrecognizable characters:

```
public string Encrypt(string psText)
{
    string lsEncryptedText;
    string lsEncryptedTextWithFinalXOR;
    // A Random number generator
    Random loRandom = new Random();
    // The char position being encrypted
    int i;
    char loRandomChar;

    lsEncryptedText = "";
    for (i = 0; i <= (psText.Length - 1); i++)
    {
        loRandomChar = (char)(loRandom.Next(65535));
        // Current char XOR random generated char
        lsEncryptedText += ((char)(psText[i] ^ loRandomChar)).
         ToString();
        // Random generated char XOR 65535 - i
        // It is saved because we need it later for the
           decryption process
        lsEncryptedText += ((char)(loRandomChar ^ (65535 -
         i))).ToString();
        // Another random generated char but just to add garbage
           to confuss the hackers
        loRandomChar = (char)(loRandom.Next(65535));
        lsEncryptedText += loRandomChar.ToString();
    }

    lsEncryptedTextWithFinalXOR = "";
    // Now, every character XOR 125
    for (i = 0; i <= (lsEncryptedText.Length - 1); i++)
    {
        lsEncryptedTextWithFinalXOR += ((char)(lsEncryptedText[i]
         ^ 125)).ToString();
    }

    return lsEncryptedTextWithFinalXOR;
}
```

4. Add the following function—Decrypt. It will decrypt the encrypted string received as a parameter and return a string with the resulting decoded message:

```
public string Decrypt(string psText)
{
    // The decrypted text to return
    string lsDecryptedText;

    // The char position being decrypted
    int i;
    // The random char
    char loRandomChar;

    lsDecryptedText = "";
    for (i = 0; i <= (psText.Length - 1); i+=3)
    {
        // Retrieve the previously random generated char
        //    XOR 125 XOR 65535 - i (but previous i)
        loRandomChar = (char)(psText[i +1] ^ 125 ^ (65535 -
        (i / 3)));
        // Char XOR random generated char
        lsDecryptedText += ((char)(psText[i] ^ 125 ^
        loRandomChar)).ToString();
    }

    return lsDecryptedText;
}
```

5. Open the Click event in the button butTest and enter the following code:

```
// The encrypted text
string lsEncryptedText;

// For each line in txtOriginalSMS TextBox
foreach (string lsText in txtOriginalSMS.Lines)
{
    lsEncryptedText = Encrypt(lsText);
    // Append a line with the Encrypted text
    txtEncryptedSMS.AppendText(lsEncryptedText +
    Environment.NewLine);
    // Append a line with the Encrypted text decrypted to test
    //    everything is as expected
    txtEncryptedSMS.AppendText(Decrypt(lsEncryptedText) +
    Environment.NewLine);
}
```

6. Build and run the application.

7. Enter a short text in the Textbox labeled **Original SMS Messages**, and click on the **Test** button. The encrypted message will appear in the Textbox labeled **Encrypted SMS Messages**. The decrypted message too will become visible in the bottom Textbox, but will be the result of decrypting the encrypted message to test the algorithm. The results will look similar to the following image:

What just happened?

The FBI agents liked the encryption algorithm. However, they think it will be too slow if you run it using just one thread, as there will be more than 1,000,000 messages per second to be encrypted using this algorithm. Nevertheless, they offer you a computer with 16 quad-core microprocessors (64 cores).

The code required to encrypt and decrypt a message is now held in the functions named Encrypt and Decrypt.

The encryption algorithm uses a random number generator and many **XOR (Exclusive OR)** operations. It also adds garbage in the text in order to confuse potential hackers.

 Remember that in C#, the XOR operation is specified by the ^ operator and can be applied to numbers. Thus, we needed many typecastings to char type and then we called the ToString() method.

One of the most exciting properties of the XOR operation is the possibility to return to the original value when it is applied twice. For example, in the following lines of code:

```
int liOriginalValue = 120;
int liFirstXOR = liOriginalValue ^ 250;
int liSecondXOR = liFirstXOR ^ 250;
```

The value assigned to `liSecondXOR` will be the same that is in `liOriginalValue`, that is, 120.

As the encryption algorithms uses the complete Unicode character set, with 65,536 possible characters. The resulting text is unreadable and very confusing, as it is not limited to the classic 256 characters code.

As we have tested the decryption of the previously encrypted message, we are sure it is working fine. We are now going to run the encryption algorithm in a new thread created using the `Thread` class.

Time for action – Running the encryption in a new thread using the Thread class

As your freedom is dependent on this application, you want to minimize the risks! Therefore, you want to use the `Thread` class to have a very exhaustive control over the execution of the different threads. But, first, you want to make the encryption function run in just one thread. Later, you will align the threads with the number of cores.

Now, we are going to make some changes to the application, and we will encrypt the messages in a new independent thread created and configured using the `Thread` class:

1. Open the project, `SMSEncryption`.

2. Add a button control (**butRunInThread**). Set its `Text` property to **Run in a thread**.

3. Add the following line of code at the beginning (as we are going to use the `System.Threading.Thread` class):

```
using System.Threading;
```

4. Add the following line in the form class definition to declare three new private variables:

```
// The thread
private Thread proThreadEncryption;
// The string list with SMS messages to encrypt (input)
private List<string> prlsSMSToEncrypt;
// The string list with SMS messages encrypted (output)
private List<string> prlsEncryptedSMS;
```

5. Open the `Click` event in **butRunInThread** and enter the following code to run the encryption process in a new thread created using the `Thread` class:

```
// Prepare everything the thread needs from the UI
// For each line in txtOriginalSMS TextBox
prlsSMSToEncrypt = new List<string>(txtOriginalSMS.
 Lines.GetLength(0));
// Add the lines in txtOriginalSMS TextBox
prlsSMSToEncrypt.AddRange(txtOriginalSMS.Lines);

// Create the new Thread and use the ThreadEncryptProcedure
    method
proThreadEncryption = new Thread(new
 ThreadStart(ThreadEncryptProcedure));

// Start running the thread
proThreadEncryption.Start();
// Join the independent thread to this thread to wait until
    ThreadProc ends
proThreadEncryption.Join();
// When the thread finishes running this is the next line that is
    going to be executed
// Copy the string List generated by the thread
foreach (string lsEncryptedText in prlsEncryptedSMS)
{
    // Append a line with the Encrypted text
    txtEncryptedSMS.AppendText(lsEncryptedText +
     Environment.NewLine);
}
```

6. Build and run the application.

7. Enter or copy and paste a long text in the `Textbox` labeled **Original SMS Messages** and click on the **Run in a thread** button. The encrypted message will appear in the `Textbox` labeled **Encrypted SMS Messages**. However, the code runs in a different thread. The results will be similar to what is shown in the following image:

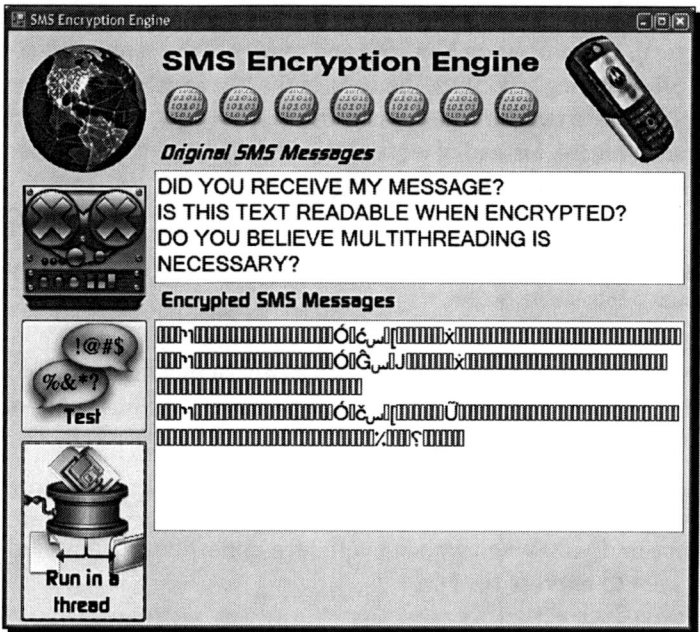

What just happened?

The FBI agents are getting impatient! You explain that you were working on separating the encryption execution into many threads to take full advantage of parallel processing capabilities. However, they do not see any changes or improvements in the new version. So, hurry up and learn about the Thread class to show them a performance improvement that amazes them.

Now, when the user clicks the **Run in a thread** button, the encryption runs in a new thread, but with synchronous execution, because we do not want to run a background thread, but we want to create as many numbers of threads as the number of available cores. We are looking for a performance enhancement as we are developing an encryption engine.

As we are not using a BackgroundWorker component, which simplified the UI decoupling, we must do that work in code.

The following lines declare the two private string lists that will work as an input (prlsSMSToEncrypt) and as an output (prlsEncryptedSMS) for the new independent thread:

```
private List<string> prlsSMSToEncrypt;
private List<string> prlsEncryptedSMS;
```

When started, the thread will execute the code in the `ThreadEncryptProcedure` procedure (without parameters). This procedure is private and resides in the same class as the two aforementioned private string lists. Thus, the code in the `ThreadEncryptProcedure` procedure can access these two variables to take the input strings, encrypt them, and add them to the output string list. Instead of working against the UI controls, we decouple the UI and avoid the problems related to multithreading with the UI.

It is quite simple. We prepare the input data for the thread, and the thread leaves a collectable output.

The `ThreadEncryptProcedure` procedure does a very simple task without touching the UI controls. When it creates a new `List<string>`, it passes the number of items (capacity) as a parameter in order to optimize the execution:

```
prlsEncryptedSMS = new List<string>(prlsSMSToEncrypt.Count);
```

It is a good practice to do this when working with lists, collections, or any kind of arrays. Remember, you want to impress the FBI!

Then, for each string in the input string list (`prlsSMSToEncrypt`), it encrypts the string and adds it to the output string list, (`prlsEncryptedSMS`).

Besides decoupling the UI, we have not made great changes to the loop in order to run it in a new independent thread.

Decoupling the UI

When the user clicks the **Run in a thread** button, the following lines prepare everything the thread needs from the UI:

```
prlsSMSToEncrypt = new List<string>(txtOriginalSMS.
  Lines.GetLength(0));
prlsSMSToEncrypt.AddRange(txtOriginalSMS.Lines);
```

First, we create a new `List<string>`. As mentioned earlier, we pass the number of items (capacity) as a parameter in order to optimize the execution, calling the `GetLength` method for the lines in the `txtOriginalSMS` `TextBox`.

Then, we employ the very useful `AddRange` method to add all the strings in the string array, `txtOriginalSMS.Lines`, to our new `List<string>`. Now we have everything the thread needs as an input in a private `List<string>`, which it can access without problems.

Mastering the use of lists, arrays, and collections is a must when working with multithreading.

This is a very simple way to share data with a new independent thread without complications. However, we must be very careful, as we must learn more things in order to change data in the same variables accessed from many threads.

When we access variables from multiple threads, they must be of **thread safety** types. Thread safety types are the ones that are safe for multithreaded operations. If you have any doubt about a type, you can check whether it is of a thread safety type or not in the C# documentation. It offers a section describing the thread safety, as shown in the following image for the Int32 type:

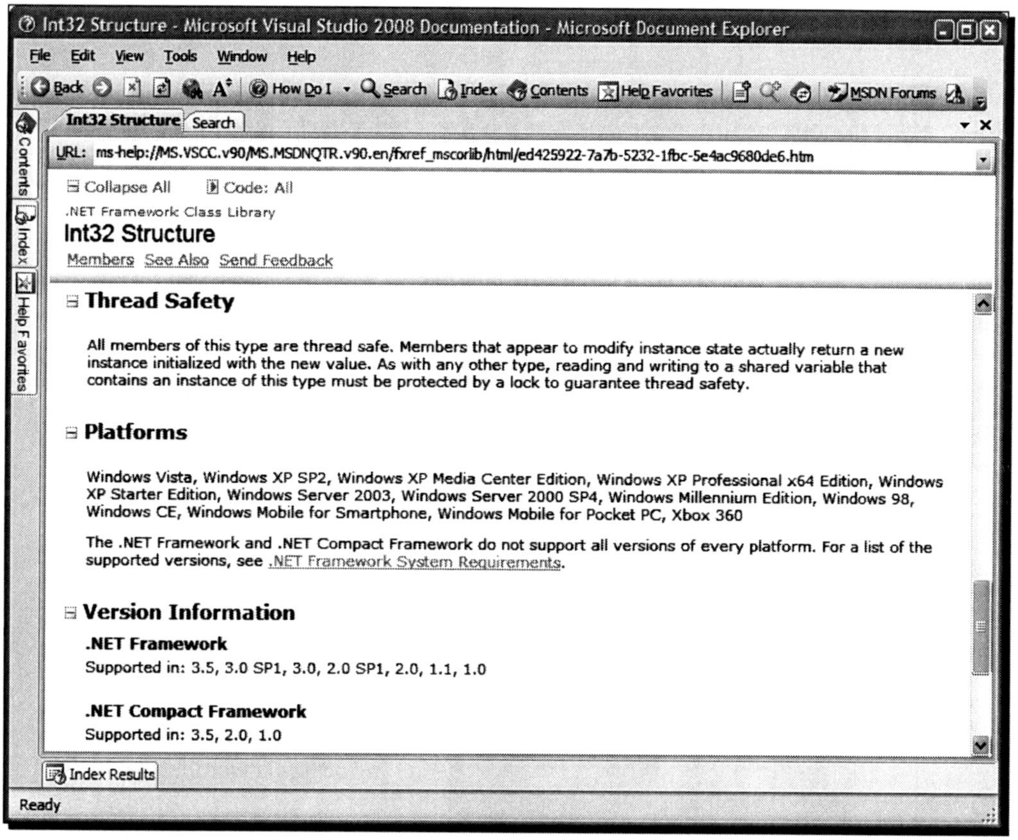

Int32 Structure - Microsoft Visual Studio 2008 Documentation - Microsoft Document Explorer

File   Edit   View   Tools   Window   Help

Back | How Do I ▾ | Search | Index | Contents | Help Favorites | MSDN Forums

Int32 Structure / Search

URL: ms-help://MS.VSCC.v90/MS.MSDNQTR.v90.en/fxref_mscorlib/html/ed425922-7a7b-5232-1fbc-5e4ac9680de6.htm

Collapse All   Code: All

.NET Framework Class Library

Int32 Structure

Members   See Also   Send Feedback

Thread Safety

All members of this type are thread safe. Members that appear to modify instance state actually return a new instance initialized with the new value. As with any other type, reading and writing to a shared variable that contains an instance of this type must be protected by a lock to guarantee thread safety.

Platforms

Windows Vista, Windows XP SP2, Windows XP Media Center Edition, Windows XP Professional x64 Edition, Windows XP Starter Edition, Windows Server 2003, Windows Server 2000 SP4, Windows Millennium Edition, Windows 98, Windows CE, Windows Mobile for Smartphone, Windows Mobile for Pocket PC, Xbox 360

The .NET Framework and .NET Compact Framework do not support all versions of every platform. For a list of the supported versions, see .NET Framework System Requirements.

Version Information

.NET Framework
Supported in: 3.5, 3.0 SP1, 3.0, 2.0 SP1, 2.0, 1.1, 1.0

.NET Compact Framework
Supported in: 3.5, 2.0, 1.0

Index Results

Ready

Creating a new thread

This line declared the `proThreadEncryption` variable with the `Thread` type:

```
private Thread proThreadEncryption;
```

When the user clicks the **Run in a thread** button, the following lines create an instance of the `Thread` class specifying the method it must execute in the new thread when it is started. In order to accomplish this, we use the `ThreadStart` **delegate** because we do not need to send parameters or other data to the thread for initialization purposes:

```
proThreadEncryption = new Thread(new
  ThreadStart(ThreadEncryptProcedure));
```

Once the thread is created, it does not start running the code in the specified `ThreadEncryptProcedure` procedure until we call the `Start` method. We do not want to send parameters to the procedure. Therefore we use `Start()` method:

```
proThreadEncryption.Start();
```

This method tells the scheduler to start running the code in the new independent thread with an asynchronous execution. However, as it is executed asynchronously, we lose control over the time when the code in the thread begins running. It can be 100 milliseconds, 200 milliseconds, or 2 seconds.

In this case, we do not want to start an independent thread and lose control over its execution time, but we want to start it with a synchronous execution and wait till it finishes in the main thread. In order to do so, we call the `Join` method in the next line:

```
proThreadEncryption.Join();
```

It makes the new thread run the `ThreadEncryptProcedure` procedure code. Once it finishes its execution, it returns the control to the main thread and goes on with the next statement, as shown in the following image:

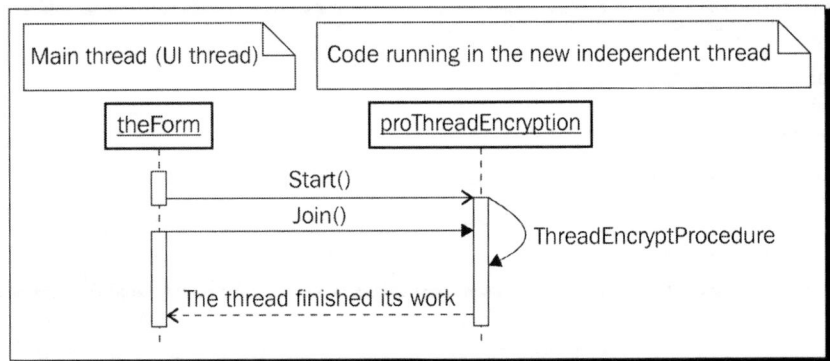

It works as if we were calling a classic method, but in another thread.

Separating the code in a new thread using the `Thread` class is easy if we follow this simple code pattern.

Retrieving data from threads

Since it was joined with the main thread, the statements after the call to the `Join` method are executed as soon as the thread finishes its execution. These lines collect the encrypted strings generated in the `prlsEncryptedSMS` string list and append them, one per line in the `txtEncryptedSMS` TextBox:

```
foreach (string lsEncryptedText in prlsEncryptedSMS)
{
    txtEncryptedSMS.AppendText(lsEncryptedText +
    Environment.NewLine);
}
```

As the thread left the results of its processing in a private variable, also accessible from the main thread, we can use it to show the results in the UI controls.

This is a very simple way to retrieve data from threads, leaving the results in a variable, accessible from both the main and the secondary threads.

 Nevertheless, remember that we cannot change a variable from concurrent threads without taking into account the other threads that can read or write its value concurrently. Therefore, the aforementioned solution can only be applied when we need independent results from many concurrent threads.

This is one of the main advantages of threads over processes. It is very easy to share data between threads without much effort. However, it has some trade-offs; it requires more memory than the same algorithm run in a single thread without the need to decouple the UI.

Sharing data between threads

So far, we have used the BackgroundWorker component and the `Thread` class to execute code in independent threads. The `Thread` class allows us to have great control over the thread while the BackgroundWorker component offers a very simple way to update the UI without using complicated delegates or call-backs. How can we combine this component and this class in an application to make it faster to complete while being responsive?

If we want to work with a BackgroundWorker component to show some feedback or progress to the UI controls, while one or more thread created using the `Thread` class is running, we must find a way to share data between threads.

We made something like that in our last example. But we must use some techniques in order to avoid confusion between the different ways in which this useful component, the BackgroundWorker, and this flexible and powerful class, the `Thread` class work.

 We can do it using the `Thread` class, but there is a BackgroundWorker component ready to help us. Thus, let's be pragmatic and use the best of both the worlds.

Time for action – Updating the UI while running threads

You need more time to finish the final release for your extremely efficient encryption engine. You therefore decide to distract the FBI agents by showing some small improvements in the application. You want to display some feedback in the UI while the thread is encrypting. But, you do not want to lose too much performance in that because they are expecting an impressive encryption speed. However, you do not know how to do it using threads, and you do not want to lose time. Hence, the BackgroundWorker is here to help you!

Now, we are going to make some changes to the application, adding a BackgroundWorker to display progress. In order to accomplish that, we must share data between two threads:

1. Open the project, `SMSEncryption`.

2. Add a label control (**lblNumberOfSMSEncrypted**). Set its `Text` property to **0**, and set its `TextAlign` property to **TopRight**. Add another label control, and set its `Text` property to **Number of SMS Messages encrypted**.

3. Add a BackgroundWorker component (**bakShowEncryptedStrings**) to create a new independent thread capable of talking to the UI, as we learned in the previous chapter. Set the `WorkerReportsProgress` property in design-time to **True**.

4. Add the following lines in the form class definition to declare three new private variables:

```
// The number of the last encrypted string
private int priLastEncryptedString;
// The number of the last encrypted string shown in the UI
private int priLastEncryptedStringShown;
// The number of the previous last encrypted string shown in the
    UI
private int priOldLastEncryptedStringShown;
```

5. Add the following line of code at the beginning of the `ThreadEncryptProcedure` procedure:

```
priLastEncryptedString = 0;
```

6. Add the following line of code after the line `prlsEncryptedSMS.` `Add(lsEncryptedText);` in the `ThreadEncryptProcedure` procedure:

```
priLastEncryptedString++;
```

7. Open the `DoWork` event in the BackgroundWorker **bakShowEncryptedStrings** and enter the following code:

```
// Initialize the last encrypted string shown
priLastEncryptedStringShown = 0;
// Initialize the last encrypted string shown before
priOldLastEncryptedStringShown = 0;
// The iteration
int i;
// The last encrypted string (saved locally to avoid changes in
   the middle of the iteration)
int liLast;

// Wait until proThreadEncryption begins
while ((priLastEncryptedString < 1))
{
    // Sleep the thread for 10 milliseconds)
    Thread.Sleep(10);
}

while (proThreadEncryption.IsAlive || (priLastEncryptedString
      > priLastEncryptedStringShown))
{
    liLast = priLastEncryptedString;
    if (liLast != priLastEncryptedStringShown)
    {
        ((BackgroundWorker)sender).ReportProgress(liLast);
        priLastEncryptedStringShown = liLast;
    }

    // Sleep the thread for 2 seconds (2000 milliseconds)
    Thread.Sleep(2000);
}
```

8. Open the `ProgressChanged` event in the BackgroundWorker **bakShowEncryptedStrings**, and enter the following code:

```
// The iteration
int i;
// Show the number of SMS messages encrypted by the concurrent
    proThreadEncryption thread
lblNumberOfSMSEncrypted.Text = priLastEncryptedString.ToString();
// Append each new string, from priOldLastEncryptedStringShown to
    the received parameter in e.ProgressPercentage - 1
for (i = priOldLastEncryptedStringShown;
     i < (int)e.ProgressPercentage; i++)
{
    // Append the string to the txtEncryptedSMS TextBox
    txtEncryptedSMS.AppendText(prlsEncryptedSMS[i]
     + Environment.NewLine);
    // Let the UI update
    Application.DoEvents();
}
// Update the old last encrypted string shown
priOldLastEncryptedStringShown = priLastEncryptedStringShown;
```

9. Open the `Click` event in the button **butRunInThread**, and enter the following code before the line `proThreadEncryption.Start();` (we must start the BackgroundWorker before starting the encryption thread):

```
// Start the BackgroundWorker with an asynchronous execution
bakShowEncryptedStrings.RunWorkerAsync();
```

10. In the same aforementioned event, comment the line `proThreadEncryption.Join();` (now we do not want the thread to join the main thread).

11. Build and run the application.

12. Enter or copy and paste a very long text (with more than 5,000 lines) in the `Textbox` labeled **Original SMS Messages**, and click on the **Run in a thread** button. You will see the strings representing the messages encrypted appearing in the `Textbox` labeled **Encrypted SMS Messages** as the number of messages encrypted increases. The results will look similar to what is shown in the following image:

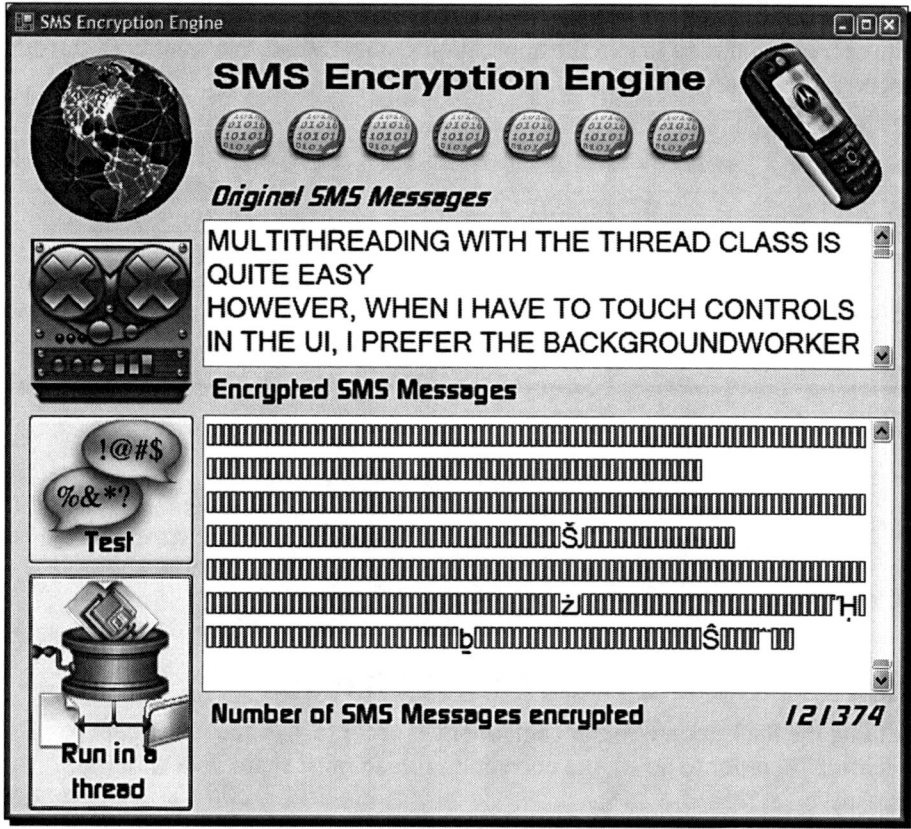

What just happened?

Wow, the FBI agents are amazed with the counter and the encrypted messages appearing at high speed. They realize you are working with concurrent threads, and they accept your request for more time in order to complete the final release of the encryption engine.

Now, when the user clicks the **Run in a thread** button, the encryption runs in a new thread, but with an asynchronous execution. At the same time, the BackgroundWorker component creates a new thread to give some feedback to the UI and also runs asynchronously. Thus, we have two concurrent threads with an asynchronous execution, doing completely different tasks in parallel.

For this reason, we added the following lines:

```
bakShowEncryptedStrings.RunWorkerAsync();
proThreadEncryption.Start();
```

First, we start the BackgroundWorker component thread, and then we start the encryption thread, created with the `Thread` class.

Therefore, we commented the line `proThreadEncryption.Join();` because we do not want the encryption thread to join the application's main thread. We want both threads to run concurrently and asynchronously, as shown in the following image:

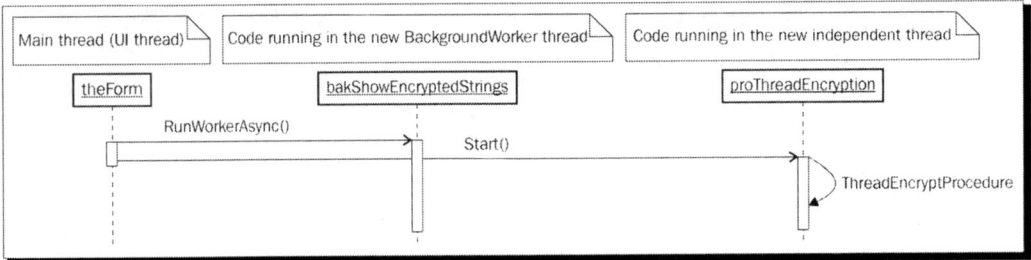

 With these examples, we have learned and seen the differences between executing a thread in a synchronous and an asynchronous way. We must master this in order to have complete control over many concurrent threads.

Sharing some specific data between threads

We are using the BackgroundWorker component in order to give some feedback to the UI controls. In order to do so, the encryption thread must share data with the BackgroundWorker thread.

We use the same technique that we used in the previous example. However, this time, we have concurrency. While the encryption thread is adding encrypted strings to the `prlsEncryptedSMS` string list, the BackgroundWorker thread looks at the number of the last encrypted string and calls the `ReportProgress` method, sending it as a parameter.

 Remember that too many calls to the `ReportProgress` method can generate a stack overflow exception. Because this method runs code that upgrades the `TextBox` adding lines, it takes a lot more time than encrypting. If we have 100,000 messages to encrypt, and we make 100,000 calls to the `ReportProgress` method, it is highly probable that a stack overflow will be generated. The code in this method runs in the main thread, and for this reason, we must sacrifice some UI feedback to achieve a better overall performance and avoid exceptions.

Thus, the code in the `DoWork` and the `ReportProgress` event handlers is quite complex.

We define three new private variables:

```
private int priLastEncryptedString;
private int priLastEncryptedStringShown;
private int priOldLastEncryptedStringShown;
```

The encryption thread initializes `priLastEncryptedString` and then increments its value each time it adds an encrypted string to the `prlsEncryptedSMS` string list. This value is useful for the BackgroundWorker thread.

The code executed by the BackgroundWorker thread concurrently with the encryption thread, defined in its `DoWork` event handler, initializes `priLastEncryptedStringShown` and `priOldLastEncryptedStringShown`.

Then, it waits until the encryption thread has some results. This is necessary because both threads are launched asynchronously, at nearly the same time. It is a `while` loop, but with a call to the `Thread.Sleep` method, with 10 milliseconds of inactivity for the thread:

```
while ((priLastEncryptedString < 1))
{
    Thread.Sleep(10);
}
```

Since the variable `priLastEncryptedString` has a value lower than 1, the encryption thread has not added any value yet.

The `Thread.Sleep` method suspends the current thread (the thread in the actual context) for a specified time in milliseconds (0.001 seconds). As it suspends the thread execution, it does not consume CPU cycles. Hence, it does not waste processing power.

 Never use loops without instructions to wait for some time in a thread, because you will be wasting processing power. Instead, use the `Thread.Sleep` method when you have to pause a thread.

When the encryption thread finishes encrypting the first string, adds it to the corresponding string list, and increments the value of `priLastEncryptedString`, the BackgroundWorker thread will move on to the next statements of the code in the `DoWork` event handler. Hence, it will enter in this other loop:

```
while (proThreadEncryption.IsAlive || (priLastEncryptedString
        > priLastEncryptedStringShown))
{
    liLast = priLastEncryptedString;
    if (liLast != priLastEncryptedStringShown)
    {
```

```
        ((BackgroundWorker)sender).ReportProgress(liLast);
        priLastEncryptedStringShown = liLast;
    }
    Thread.Sleep(2000);
}
```

The loop (and the thread) will go on running while the encryption thread is running, or while there are encrypted strings to be shown. We know when the `proThreadEncryption` thread is not running, or not calling its `IsAlive` method. It returns a `bool` value.

The first line in the loop saves the value of `priLastEncryptedString` in `liLast`. Why? Is that necessary? It is necessary because the value is changing concurrently on another thread (the encryption thread)—we are not alone. We must save the value to work with the captured value in the rest of the comparisons and assignments.

If the last encrypted string is not the last string shown, we use the well known `sender` parameter typecast to a BackgroundWorker to call the `ReportProgress` method with the last string shown as a parameter.

Once the `ReportProgress` method returns, with an asynchronous event triggered to update the UI, we save the last string shown and make the thread suspend its execution for 2 seconds (2,000 milliseconds). This is necessary in order to avoid a probable stack overflow. Because the execution of the aforementioned code is faster than the code programmed in the `ProgressChanged` event handler, we must give some time to the UI controls to get updated.

 When we call the `Thread.Sleep` method, the current thread suspends its execution for a specified time, though the other threads keep running. That is the reason why the counter shows big steps when we run the application with several text lines. The encryption thread works without suspensions.

A BackgroundWorker helping a Thread class

Thus, the BackgroundWorker component helps the `Thread` class to update the UI controls. The BackgroundWorker `ProgressChanged` event handler does the rest of the job.

First, it updates the number of SMS messages encrypted with this line:

```
lblNumberOfSMSEncrypted.Text = priLastEncryptedString.ToString();
```

And then it casts the `e.ProgressPercentage` property received as a parameter to an `int` in order to obtain the last encrypted string, instead of a progress percentage.

Then, it appends each new string with a loop from `priOldLastEncryptedStringShown` (the previous last encrypted string shown) to the received last encrypted string (in `e.ProgressPercentage` property). We access the `prlsEncryptedSMS` string list in an element number that the encryption thread is not modifying (because it is already encrypted). Therefore, we can append the string to the `TextBox` without problems, and then we call the `Application.DoEvents` method to let the controls be updated and show the progress:

```
for (i = priOldLastEncryptedStringShown; i < (int)
    e.ProgressPercentage; i++)
{
    txtEncryptedSMS.AppendText(prlsEncryptedSMS[i]
    + Environment.NewLine);
    Application.DoEvents();
}
```

Finally, the string previous to the last encrypted string is now the last encrypted string shown.

```
priOldLastEncryptedStringShown = priLastEncryptedStringShown;
```

 We cannot do that when the value is being modified concurrently by another thread. There are methods and techniques for such a situation. We will learn these later.

Combining a BackgroundWorker with some threads created with the `Thread` class, we can easily give feedback to the UI and achieve a great performance with a responsive application.

Time for action – Executing the thread synchronously

You have some doubts about the `Join` method and how it works with the `Thread` class. As the FBI agents offered you a cappuccino, you believe that there is some time for experiments, before achieving the best performance.

Now, we are going to make a small change to the application to call the `Join` method again and make a synchronous execution of the encryption thread:

1. Open the project, `SMSEncryption`.
2. Open the `Click` event in the button **butRunInThread** and uncomment the line `proThreadEncryption.Join();` (now the thread joins the main thread).
3. Build and run the application.

4. Enter or copy and paste a very long text (with more than 5,000 lines) in the Textbox labeled **Original SMS Messages** and click on the **Run in a thread** button. You will see the strings representing the messages encrypted in the Textbox once the encryption process finishes after some processing time, without any feedback. The results will be as shown in the following image:

What just happened?

The FBI agents bring you the cappuccino. You have some time to relax. Thanks to multithreading!

Now, when the user clicks the **Run in a thread** button, the encryption runs in a new thread, but again with a synchronous execution. Doesn't the BackgroundWorker component run concurrently? Yes, but the main thread is waiting for the encryption thread to finish. Then, it will take control again over the execution of the rest of the statements. And, the code programmed in the BackgroundWorker ProgressChanged event handler runs in the main thread. Therefore, the execution is blocked until the encryption thread completes its execution. All this can be explained with the help of the following diagram:

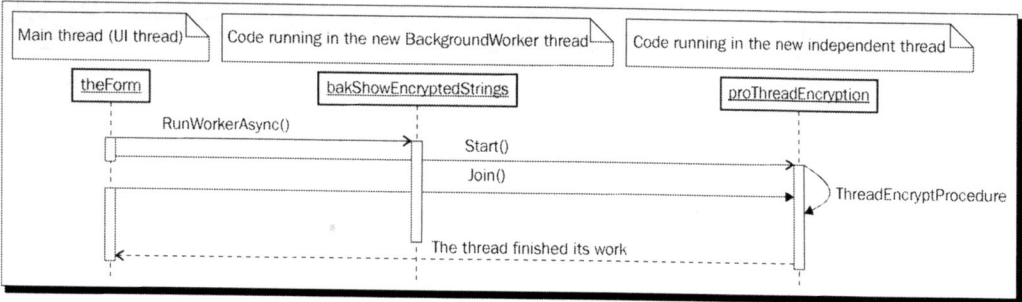

 It is very important to understand the differences between synchronous and asynchronous execution of threads to keep control of the concurrency.

Main and secondary threads

As we can see, there is a great difference between calling the `Start` method and the `Join` method for a `Thread` class instance.

When we call the `Start` method, the thread is sent to the scheduler for its execution. As mentioned earlier, it does not mean an immediate execution.

 When we call the `Start` method for many threads, one after the other, or when combined with a BackgroundWorker thread as in our example, we are not sure which one is going to run faster. We cannot assume one of them will reach some statement first, because the execution speed will depend upon the processor or the core, it is assigned to and its capabilities. If it needs more context switches than the other thread, it will take longer to reach the same statement.

This is one of the most important issues with concurrency. It all depends on something that we do not know how to predict sometimes. Therefore, we must consider every possible situation according to the code that will be executed concurrently.

When we call the `Join` method, the thread is attached to the other thread, and it will not execute anything else until the thread method finishes its execution.

Using them with their variations, we can take complete control of a multithreading application. That is one of the most difficult things to achieve for traditional and classic linear code programmers.

Have a go hero – Concurrent encryption algorithms

Of course, the code shown in the previous examples can be enhanced, and you can delight the FBI agents with some additional work. Perhaps, they could contract you!

Develop a new version of this application example. Let the user specify different encryption algorithms, for example, using a combo box. The encrypting thread must change its behavior according to the user selection. Take into account everything we have learned about sharing data between threads.

Enhance this new application, running two or three different encryption algorithms concurrently (in two or three independent threads), showing the results in the UI at the same time, using two or three BackgroundWorker components as we learned.

Again, use the Process Explorer to view the running threads for all the examples and monitor their activities. Apply all the things we have learned in the previous chapter. Also, use the Windows Task Manager.

Passing parameters to threads

So far, we have used the BackgroundWorker component combined with the `Thread` class to provide a fast execution and UI feedback. How can we combine multiple `Thread` class instances with many BackgroundWorker components to create an application that runs as fast as possible in modern computer architectures?

We can work with dynamic lists and the `Environment.ProcessorCount` property to create threads on the fly according to the available cores or processors. However, we need some technique to distribute the SMS messages that must be encrypted to the many encrypting threads. At the same time, we must provide feedback through many BackgroundWorker components. It sounds complex and it is complex.

To achieve this goal, we must pass specific parameters to the common procedure that the many threads will run. We want to re-use the procedure because we want it to be dynamically organized according to the number of available cores at runtime.

Time for action – Using lists for thread creation on the fly I

It is time! You must finish the application. One FBI agent tells you he had a quad-core notebook, and he wanted to test the application on the notebook before running it on the server. You cannot hardcode the threads and you need to do it completely dynamically. The lists are the best solution for this problem and your key to freedom! Let's use them. It is not difficult.

Now, we are going to make some big changes to the application, modifying variables to be lists, or lists of lists, so they can be accessed by multiple threads created dynamically. In order to accomplish that, we must share data between the many threads:

1. Open the project, SMSEncryption.

2. Add the following line in the form class definition to declare a new private variable (we need to know the number of processors or cores):

```
// The number of processors or cores available in the computer
   for this application
private int priProcessorC0.ount = Environment.ProcessorCount;
```

3. Change the definition for the following private variables in the form class definition to make them lists:

```
// The string list with SMS messages encrypted (output)
private List<List<string>> prlsEncryptedSMS;
// The number of the last encrypted string
private List<int> priLastEncryptedString;
```

4. Add the following line in the form class definition to declare a new private variable that will hold the list of the Thread class instances:

```
// The threads list
private List<Thread> prloThreadList;
```

What just happened?

The variables required to grow dynamically, according to the number of cores found in the computer, have been added to the application.

The priProcessorCount variable is the most important, because it holds the number of available cores. If we manually change the number in this variable, the application is going to create that number of threads and split the encryption accordingly. The idea is to parallelize as much as possible.

 One potential problem of manually assigning a value greater than the number of available cores to the priProcessorCount variable is that the increasing context switches needed by the operating system scheduler will degrade performance. Therefore, you must be wary of wrong fine-tuning.

We are now going to change the code in the different procedures and events to allow the multiple threads to encrypt the strings as fast as possible.

Time for action – Using lists for thread creation on the fly II

Wow, another cappuccino! Gracefulness or impatience? Never mind. Let's finish the application, and they will be very happy with you.

Now, we must rewrite some procedures and events. It is going to be easier rewriting these than making the changes, as we are replacing single variables by lists. In order to accomplish this, we must create a thread with a parameter indicating its number:

1. Open the project, SMSEncryption.

2. Replace the definition for ThreadEncryptProcedure with the following (now it receives a parameter):

```
private void ThreadEncryptProcedure(object poThreadParameter)
```

3. Replace the code in the ThreadEncryptProcedure procedure with the following:

```
string lsEncryptedText;
// Retrieve the thread number received in object
   poThreadParameter
int liThreadNumber = (int) poThreadParameter;
// ThreadNumber + 1
int liStringNumber;

// Create a new string list for the prlsSMSToEncrypt
   corresponding to the thread
prlsEncryptedSMS[liThreadNumber] = new List<string>
 ((prlsSMSToEncrypt.Count / priProcessorCount));
priLastEncryptedString[liThreadNumber] = 0;

liStringNumber = 0;
int i;
// steps the thread number
string lsText;
// Iterate through each string in the prlsSMSToEncrypt string
   list stepping by priProcessorCount
// To distribute the work among each concurrent thread
for (i = liThreadNumber; i < prlsSMSToEncrypt.Count; i +=
     priProcessorCount)
{
    lsText = prlsSMSToEncrypt[i];
    lsEncryptedText = Encrypt(lsText);
    // Append a string with the Encrypted text
    prlsEncryptedSMS[liThreadNumber].Add(lsEncryptedText);

    priLastEncryptedString[liThreadNumber]++;
    liStringNumber++;
}
```

4. Replace the code where the threads were initialized and started in the `Click` event handler in the button **butRunInThread**, after the line `prlsSMSToEncrypt.AddRange(txtOriginalSMS.Lines);`, with the following:

```
// Thread number
int liThreadNumber;
// Create the thread list and string lists
prloThreadList = new List<Thread>(priProcessorCount);
prlsEncryptedSMS = new List<List<string>>(priProcessorCount);
priLastEncryptedString = new List<int>(priProcessorCount);

// Initialize the threads
for (liThreadNumber = 0; liThreadNumber < priProcessorCount;
     liThreadNumber++)
{
    // Just to occupy the number
    prlsEncryptedSMS.Add(new List<string>());
    // Just to occupy the number
    priLastEncryptedString.Add(0);
    // Add the new thread, with a parameterized start (to allow
        parameters)
    prloThreadList.Add(new Thread(new ParameterizedThreadStart
                    (ThreadEncryptProcedure)));
}

// Now, start the threads
for (liThreadNumber = 0; liThreadNumber < priProcessorCount;
     liThreadNumber++)
{
    prloThreadList[liThreadNumber].Start(liThreadNumber);
}

// Start the BackgroundWorker with an asynchronous execution
bakShowEncryptedStrings.RunWorkerAsync();
```

5. Open the `DoWork` event in the BackgroundWorker **bakShowEncryptedStrings**, and make the following code replacements to the existing code:

- Replace `priLastEncryptedString` with `priLastEncryptedString[0]`
- Replace `proThreadEncryption` with `prloThreadList[0]`

6. Open the `ProgressChanged` event in the BackgroundWorker **bakShowEncryptedStrings** and make the following code replacements to the existing code:

- Replace `priLastEncryptedString` with `priLastEncryptedString[0]`
- Replace `prlsEncryptedSMS[i]` with `prlsEncryptedSMS[0][i]`

7. Build and run the application.

8. Enter or copy and paste a very long text (with more than 20,000 lines) in the `Textbox` labeled **Original SMS Messages** and click on the **Run in a thread** button. You will see the strings representing the messages encrypted by **thread 1** appearing in the `Textbox` labeled **Encrypted SMS Messages**, while the number of messages encrypted by **thread 1** increase. The results will be similar to what is shown in the following image:

What just happened?

The FBI agents are amazed with the encrypting speed you've achieved! They ask you for some changes in the UI, and you will be free. However, they like your multithreading knowledge, and they have a huge parallel processing capacity installed. They can call you again at any time. See you later, some time soon!

It is true that the code has become more complex. But, running this application in a quad-core computer improves the performance incredibly.

 In order to achieve the best performance results, if you are using Windows XP or Windows Server 2003, you will have to check for an installed patch. There is a known bug in these Windows versions with multiple core microprocessors that can dramatically reduce the performance in multithreaded applications. The patch can be downloaded from `http://support.microsoft.com/kb/896256`. It is not necessary for Windows Vista or Windows Server 2008. You must remember that this patch was not included in Windows XP SP2.

Now, when the user clicks the **Run in a thread** button, the encryption runs in as many threads as the available cores in the computer with an asynchronous execution. At the same time, the BackgroundWorker component starts running concurrently displaying the results just for the first thread.

The private string list that works as an input for the many threads is the same as in the previous examples (`prlsSMSToEncrypt`), but is accessed in a different way by each thread.

The private string list that work as an output (`prlsEncryptedSMS`) is now a list of string lists. Thus, each thread can work in its own output:

```
private List<List<string>> prlsEncryptedSMS;
```

Creating as many threads as the number of cores

Of course, there is a new thread list that will be aligned with the value in the `priProcessorCount` variable:

```
private List<Thread> prloThreadList;
```

It replaces the line that declared the `proThreadEncryption` variable with the `Thread` type.

When the user clicks the **Run in a thread** button, the following lines create an instance of the `Thread` class specifying the method it must execute in the new thread when started. In order to accomplish this, we use the `ParameterizedThreadStart` **delegate** because we need to send a parameter with the number of the thread to identify each thread in the method it runs:

```
for (liThreadNumber = 0; liThreadNumber < priProcessorCount;
    liThreadNumber++)
{
    prlsEncryptedSMS.Add(new List<string>());
    priLastEncryptedString.Add(0);
    prloThreadList.Add(new Thread(new ParameterizedThreadStart
                    (ThreadEncryptProcedure)));
}
```

Once each thread is created, it does not start running the code in the specified `ThreadEncryptProcedure` procedure until we call the `Start` method. But, first we initialize the threads, and then we call the `Start` procedure for each one. We want to send parameters to the procedure, the thread number. Therefore we use `Start` with one parameter:

```
for (liThreadNumber = 0; liThreadNumber < priProcessorCount;
liThreadNumber++)
{
    prloThreadList[liThreadNumber].Start(liThreadNumber);
}
```

This method tells the scheduler to start running the code in the new threads (one per available core). Then, we want to run the BackgroundWorker thread concurrently to report the UI with feedback from the first created thread (thread number 0):

```
bakShowEncryptedStrings.RunWorkerAsync();
```

In a dual-core or dual processor computer, we will have two encrypting threads and one BackgroundWorker thread.

In a quad-core or quad processor computer, we will have four encrypting threads and one BackgroundWorker thread.

It makes the new threads run the `ThreadEncryptProcedure` procedure code (with the thread number as a parameter), and when they finish its execution, it returns the control to the main thread and goes on with the next statement.

Separating the code into many concurrent threads using the `Thread` class and sending parameters to them is easy if we follow this simple code pattern and we have good knowledge of working with lists or dynamic arrays.

Receiving parameters in the thread method

We did not want to use many methods, one for each new thread. We wanted to share the same method and differentiate among the threads using a parameter with a number that identifies each.

There are many ways to distribute the work in many concurrent threads working on the same algorithm, taking the same input and producing almost the same output. We used one of them, and we will learn many more in the following chapters.

The parameter that is sent when calling the `Start` method for the thread instance is received in the `object poThreadParameter` parameter, as shown in the following declaration:

```
private void ThreadEncryptProcedure(object poThreadParameter)
```

Therefore, we must use typecasting to convert it to an `int`:

```
int liThreadNumber = (int) poThreadParameter;
```

With the thread number and the total number of threads (the value in the `priProcessorCount` variable) that will be sharing the work to be done, we can easily distribute the work of a list to be processed (encrypted). A simple way to do it is to make each thread take the input it must process and leave the rest untouched.

This is done in the iteration, which goes through the string list from the thread number (hence, each thread will begin in a different number) to the total number of strings to encrypt, stepping up the value in the `priProcessorCount` variable (the total number of threads):

```
for (i = liThreadNumber; i < prlsSMSToEncrypt.Count;
     i += priProcessorCount)
```

For example, let's suppose that there are four threads. They will work on these strings from the list:

- Thread #1: 0; 4; 8; 12; 16; 20; ...
- Thread #2: 1; 5; 9; 13; 17; 21; ...
- Thread #3: 2; 6; 10; 14; 18; 22; ...
- Thread #4: 3; 7; 11; 15; 19; 23; ...

Here, we always consider that they will run concurrently.

The string list capacity for `prlsEncryptedSMS [liThreadNumber]` is determined by the total number of strings to be encrypted divided by the total number of threads (the value in the `priProcessorCount` variable):

```
prlsEncryptedSMS[liThreadNumber] = new List<string>((
    prlsSMSToEncrypt.Count / priProcessorCount));
```

It can be wrong by 1, but it does not matter in this case (reserving capacity is better), because the thread increments a variable with the number of processed strings:

```
priLastEncryptedString[liThreadNumber]++;
```

The code in the BackgroundWorker was modified to show only the progress of the first thread.

Have a go hero – Concurrent UI feedback

As mentioned earlier, there is still some work to be done. The FBI wants to see all the code being encrypted and not just the work done by the first thread. Remember, they have a computer with 16 quad-core microprocessors (64 cores).

Using everything we have learned, develop a new version of this application that shows the progress for each dynamically created thread. Show the progress in numbers, in a progress bar, and in text boxes (adding the encrypted SMS messages). For all these controls, as many concurrent threads as the number of available cores are running in the application.

Then, use the Thread class instances control procedures we learned in order to create a final collection procedure that takes the results of all the running threads and shows the complete list of encrypted messages.

Enhance the application changing the string lists with instances of a new class, with the following information:

◆ Caller ID
◆ Destination number
◆ SMS message

Encrypt all the fields and compute the total number of characters sent.

Show the incoming and outgoing SMS messages with their information in a grid with many columns, instead of using text boxes.

Switch off the web cam. The FBI is looking for you for a new mission!

Pop quiz

1. A Thread class instance Start method:
   a. Starts a new thread with synchronous execution
   b. Begins running the code in the thread method
   c. Starts a new thread with asynchronous execution

2. The BackgroundWorker component combined with the `Thread` class:

   a. Are incompatible

   b. Are useful to work with many threads, while easily updating the UI

   c. Cannot update the UI without callbacks

3. A `Thread` class instance:

   a. Can send parameters to the method it runs in a new thread

   b. Cannot send parameters to the method it runs in a new thread

   c. Can only send integer parameters to the method it runs in a new thread

4. `List<>` variables:

   a. Are forbidden with concurrent threads

   b. Are very useful with concurrent threads

   c. Are not thread safe

5. `List<List<string>>` is:

   a. A list of string lists

   b. An invalid type

   c. A list of string

Right answers:

1. c.

2. b.

3. a.

4. b.

5. a.

Summary

We learned a lot in this chapter about working with threads, managing and coordinating them using the features offered by the `Thread` class. Specifically, we covered:

- Developing applications that are able to provide a great control over the multiple running threads, created using the `Thread` class, offering an exciting performance enhancement

- Programming the threads' code to be executed by the `Thread` class instance when started

- Creating independent and very flexible threads using the very powerful `Thread` class

- Starting, controlling, and coordinating multiple threads with great flexibility

- Sending parameters and retrieving data of any types from threads

- Sharing data between many threads

- Combining asynchronous and synchronous execution

- Matching the number of available cores with the number of concurrent threads to take full advantage of parallel processing capabilities in modern computers

We also discussed the differences between multiple threads, using BackgroundWorker and employing the `Thread` class, and ways to create high performance applications.

Now that we've learned about a more advanced way to control concurrent threads in a C# application using the `Thread` class, we're ready to study some specific debugging techniques related to multithreading and parallel programming—which is the topic of the next chapter.

5
Simple Debugging Techniques with Multithreading

In order to solve problems that arise in concurrently running threads in our applications, we need new debugging techniques suitable for the new parallelism environments that occur in Visual C#. In this chapter, we will learn many tricks and debugging procedures that will help us find solutions to multithreaded application problems and have a better understanding of the execution of parallel threads. Reading the chapter and following the exercises we shall:

- ◆ Learn some tricks to prepare multithreaded code to simplify the debugging and troubleshooting processes
- ◆ Become skilled at watching and understanding the execution of multiple concurrent threads
- ◆ Find out how to freeze some threads to stop concurrency and simplify the process for debugging one thread at a time
- ◆ Learn to set and control breakpoints with multithreaded applications
- ◆ Discover how to inspect values when multiple threads are accessing the variables that hold them
- ◆ Develop multithreaded applications that show partial results to help us in the debugging process

Watching multiple threads

So far, we have used the BackgroundWorker component and then the `Thread` class to create new threads independent of the main application thread. The applications can respond to UI events, while the processing continues, and take full advantage of multiple cores, and can thus run faster. However, we are used to debugging applications that run in just one thread (the main thread), and there are many changes in the debugging process that generate great confusion when following the classic procedures running many concurrent threads. How can we successfully debug applications that are running many concurrent threads?

We can use some techniques when we have to control and coordinate the debugging process of many concurrent threads. As we have learned from the previous chapters, when an application is multithreaded, we are not alone. There is code running everywhere at any given time in the same application process context. Therefore, when we are debugging an application step-by-step, in each step, the other concurrent threads can make several changes to many things we are inspecting or debugging. It sounds very confusing (and indeed, it is). Fortunately, the IDE offers us many tools that can help us a lot in the debugging process of a multithreaded application and can save us a lot of time and headaches.

Time for action – Understanding the difficulty in debugging concurrent threads

Your cellular phone rings! The FBI agents have detected a problem with the encryption engine. When the application receives the same messages many times during a certain period, the encryption process generates exactly the same results, as shown in the following image:

Thus, hackers could easily break the code once they discover this important bug. They ask for your help again, but this time, very gently. Of course, you want to cooperate because you do not want the FBI agents to get angry with you again. However, you need to debug the multithreaded encryption engine, and you have never done that! Let's create a solution for this problem!

First, we are going to try to debug the multithreaded application the same way we do with a single-threaded application to understand the new problems we might face:

    1. Open the project, SMSEncryption.

2. Define a breakpoint in the line `int liThreadNumber = (int) poThreadParameter;` in the `ThreadEncryptProcedure` procedure code.

3. Press *F5* or select **Debug | Start Debugging** in the main menu.

4. Enter or copy and paste a long text (with more than 5,000 lines) in the `Textbox` labeled **Original SMS Messages** and click on the **Run in a thread** button. The line with the breakpoint defined is shown highlighted as the next statement that will be executed.

5. Press *F10* or select, **Debug | Step Over** in the main menu two or three times (depending on the number of cores you have in the computer). As you can see, the next statement that gets executed is the same even when you try to go on with the next one. It seems that the statement is not being executed. However, inspecting the value of `poThreadParameter` (the parameter passed to the `ThreadEncryptProcedure` procedure) shows that it changes each time you step over the statement, as shown in the following image:

```
Object Browser  Form1.cs  Form1.cs [Design]
SMSEncryption. frmSMSEncryptionEngine                                    ThreadEncryptProcedu

        private void ThreadEncryptProcedure(object poThreadParameter)
        {
            string lsEncryptedText;
            // Retrieve the thread number received in object poThreadParameter
            int liThreadNumber = (int)poThreadParameter;
            // ThreadNumber + 1          poThreadParameter  1
            int liStringNumber;

            // Create a new string list for the prlsSMSToEncrypt corresponding to the thread
            prlsEncryptedSMS[liThreadNumber] = new List<string>((prlsSMSToEncrypt.Count / priProcessorCount));

            priLastEncryptedString[liThreadNumber] = 0;

            liStringNumber = 0;
            int i;
            // steps the thread number
            string lsText;
            // Iterate through each string in the prlsSMSToEncrypt string list stepping by priProcessorCount
            // To distribute the work among each concurrent thread
            for (i = liThreadNumber; i < prlsSMSToEncrypt.Count; i += priProcessorCount)
            {
                lsText = prlsSMSToEncrypt[i];
                lsEncryptedText = Encrypt(lsText);
                // Append a string with the Encrypted text
                prlsEncryptedSMS[liThreadNumber].Add(lsEncryptedText);

                priLastEncryptedString[liThreadNumber]++;
                liStringNumber++;
            }
```

6. Stop the application and repeat the steps 1 to 5 to make sure you are not crazy because of parallelism, multithreading, and the FBI agents!

What just happened?

You are getting nervous about the debugging process! Do not worry. We will learn how to debug your encryption engine while the FBI agents kindly prepare a cup of fresh cappuccino for you.

The debugger executed each new `Thread` class instance call to the `Start` method, with this line:

```
prloThreadList[liThreadNumber].Start(liThreadNumber);
```

Then, it entered in the `ThreadEncryptProcedure` method (remember we used the same method for every created encryption thread) with different values for the `poThreadParameter` parameter. Therefore, you stayed in the same statement as many times as the threads were created (equivalent to the number of cores available in the computer) in the following line:

```
int liThreadNumber = (int)poThreadParameter;
```

 As we can see, debugging this way is very confusing, because the IDE switches from one thread to another, and you loose control over the statements that are going to be executed next. In a debugging process, you need to know in which part of the application you are.

As we tested our first attempt to debug a multithreaded application, we tried the same technique as with single-threaded applications. There are new subjects to learn and new techniques to use.

Debugging concurrent threads

When we need to inspect values, execute a procedure step-by-step, and find solutions to problems related to some specific code, the best way to achieve that with a multithreaded application is to work with it as a single-threaded application. But, how can we do that? It is very simple. We must run one thread at a time and **freeze** the other concurrent threads while we are debugging the thread in which we are interested and on which we are focusing.

When we debug single-threaded applications, we are aware of the method in which we are positioned and its context. In multithreaded applications, we must also be aware of the thread in which we are positioned. If we do not know in which thread we are executing statements, we will be completely confused in just a few seconds, as happened in our previous activity.

 We must tailor our multithreaded applications to simplify the debugging process. If we do not do this, the debugging process will be a nightmare. Indeed, we do not want that to happen!

Time for action – Finding the threads

You wonder where the threads are. How can you guess in which thread you are working while executing the application step-by-step? You are an excellent C# programmer, but multithreaded debugging is very confusing. You do not want the FBI agents to realize that you are in trouble. However, you must hurry up, because they have a great training in detecting nervous people in the course of their usual interrogations.

Now, we are going to use the IDE features to help us find the threads in a multithreaded application:

1. Using the same project that we used in the previous example, with the same breakpoint defined, press *F5* or select **Debug | Start Debugging** in the main menu.

2. Enter or copy and paste a long text (with more than 5,000 lines) in the `Textbox` labeled **Original SMS Messages** and click on the **Run in a thread** button. The line with the breakpoint defined is shown highlighted as the next statement that will be executed.

3. Select **Debug | Windows | Threads** in the main menu or press *Ctrl + Alt + H*. The **Threads** window will be shown, displaying all the threads created by the application process, as shown in the following image:

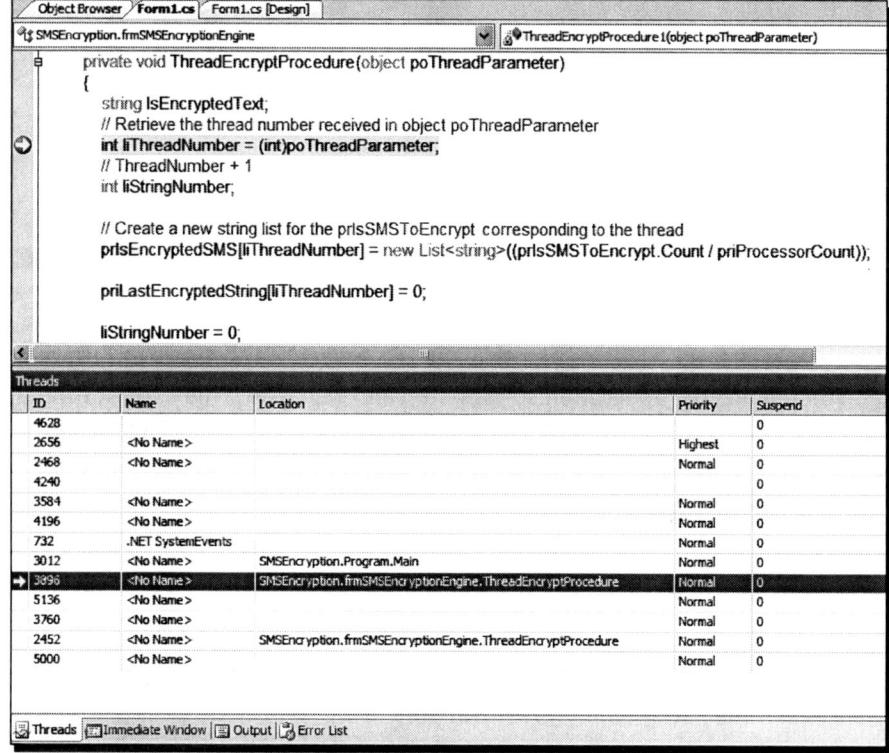

4. The yellow arrow in the left of the thread list points out the current thread—the thread for which the IDE is showing the current statement.

5. Press *F10* or select **Debug | Step Over** in the main menu. As you can see, the next statement is the same again, but the current thread pointed out in the thread list changes, as shown in the following image:

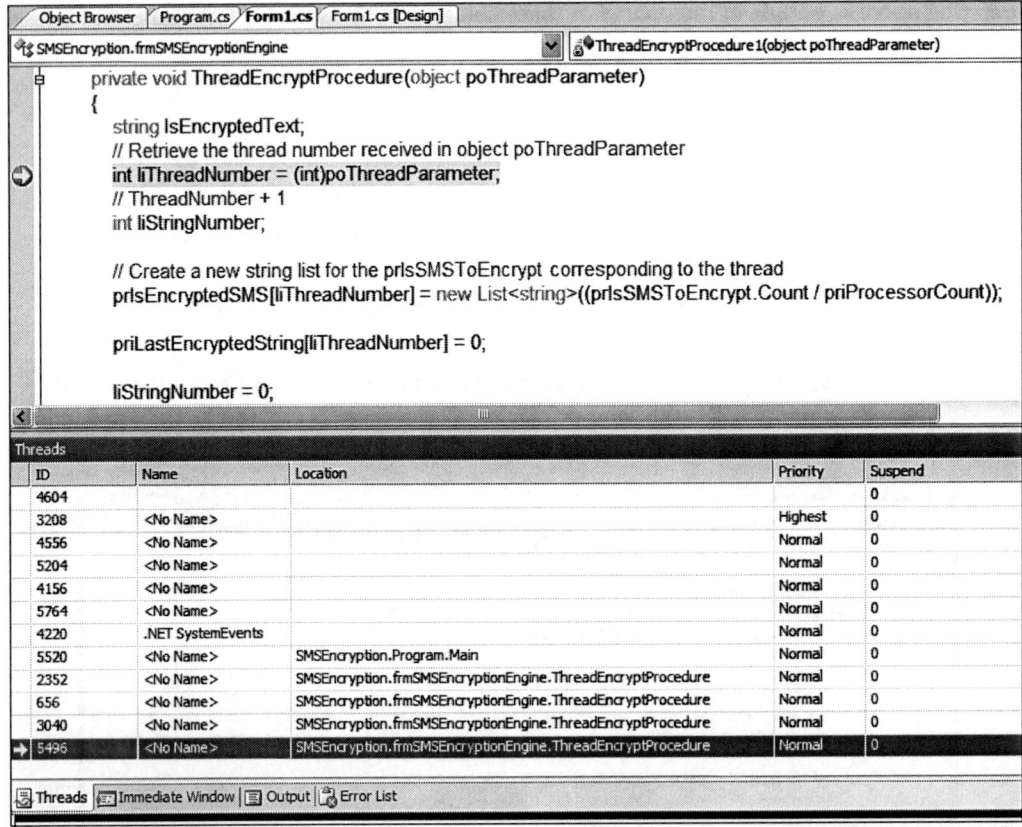

6. Go on running the application step-by-step and watch how the current thread changes. Observe the **Threads** window throughout your debugging process.

What just happened?

You found the threads in the debugging process. Now, you believe you will be able to make the necessary changes to the application if you learn a few debugging techniques quickly.

The **Threads** window displays the list of threads created by the application process. Many of them are created automatically by the C# runtime. The others are created by the Thread class instances and the BackgroundWorker component we have in the application.

Using the **Threads** window, we can easily determine in which thread we are executing when debugging a multithreaded application. It is indeed very helpful.

> Remember that each thread has its own **stack**.

Understanding the information shown in the Threads window

The **Threads** window displays the following information for each thread:

- **ID**: A unique numeric thread identifier.
- **Name**: The thread's name (the Name property). If the thread's Name property was not assigned, it has a null value, and the window will show **<No name>** in this column, as shown in the following image:

ID	Name	Location	Priority	Suspend
4604				0
3208	<No Name>		Highest	0
4556	<No Name>		Normal	0
5204				0
4156	<No Name>		Normal	0
5764	<No Name>		Normal	0
4220	.NET SystemEvents		Normal	0
5520	<No Name>	SMSEncryption.Program.Main	Normal	0
➡ 2352	<No Name>	SMSEncryption.frmSMSEncryptionEngine.ThreadEncryptProcedure	Normal	0
656	<No Name>	SMSEncryption.frmSMSEncryptionEngine.ThreadEncryptProcedure	Normal	0
3040	<No Name>	SMSEncryption.frmSMSEncryptionEngine.ThreadEncryptProcedure	Normal	0
5496	<No Name>	SMSEncryption.frmSMSEncryptionEngine.ThreadEncryptProcedure	Normal	0

- **Location**: The method the thread is running. In the previous image, the thread with its **Location** presented as **SMSEncryption.Program.Main** is the main thread and the threads with their **Location** set as **SMSEncryption.frmSMSEncryptionEngine. ThreadEncryptProcedure** are the ones created as instances of the Thread class by our dynamic thread-manufacturing algorithm.

- **Priority**: The priority assigned to the thread. The possible values are similar to the ones learned and experienced for the processes.

> No matter what the priority settings are, the results always depend on the scheduler decisions based on the number of running threads and their resources usage.

◆ **Suspend**. A `bool` value indicating whether the thread is running or paused. A **0** means the thread is running and a **1** means that it is suspended. When a thread is suspended, a pause icon is shown on the left, as shown in the following image:

	ID	Name	Location	Priority	Suspend
	4604				0
	3208	\<No Name\>		Highest	0
	4556	\<No Name\>		Normal	0
	5204				0
	4156	\<No Name\>		Normal	0
	5764	\<No Name\>		Normal	0
	4220	.NET SystemEvents		Normal	0
❚❚	5520	\<No Name\>	SMSEncryption.Program.Main	Normal	1
❚❙	2352	\<No Name\>	SMSEncryption.frmSMSEncryptionEngine.ThreadEncryptProcedure	Normal	1
❚❚	656	\<No Name\>	SMSEncryption.frmSMSEncryptionEngine.ThreadEncryptProcedure	Normal	1
	3040	\<No Name\>	SMSEncryption.frmSMSEncryptionEngine.ThreadEncryptProcedure	Normal	0
	5496	\<No Name\>	SMSEncryption.frmSMSEncryptionEngine.ThreadEncryptProcedure	Normal	0

Threads

The problem with our applications is that we did not use names for the threads, and they are using the same method (`ThreadEncryptProcedure`). We have to find a remedy for this.

Time for action – Assigning names to threads

You must identify each thread in the **Threads** window. This way, you will be able to easily find the problems in the encryption engine without getting confused.

Now, we are going to make some changes in the `Thread` class instances creating code, and to the BackgroundWorker in order to simplify the thread identification process during debugging:

1. Stay in the project, `SMSEncryption`.

2. Open the `Click` event in the button **butRutRunInThread**, and add the following code at the beginning:

```
// Give the main thread a name
Thread.CurrentThread.Name = "Main thread";
```

3. Add the following line of code before starting each thread with the line `prloThreadList[liThreadNumber].Start(liThreadNumber);` in the `for (liThreadNumber = 0; liThreadNumber < priProcessorCount; liThreadNumber++)` loop, in the `Click` event handler in the button **butRunInThread**:

```
// Give the thread a name
prloThreadList[liThreadNumber].Name = "Encryption #"
  + liThreadNumber.ToString();
```

4. Open the `DoWork` event in the BackgroundWorker **bakShowEncryptedStrings** and add the following code at the beginning:

```
// Give the BackgroundWorker thread a name
Thread.CurrentThread.Name = "bakShowEncryptedStrings";
```

5. Keep the breakpoint we defined in the previous example.

6. Define a new breakpoint in the line `priLastEncryptedStringShown = 0;` in the BackgroundWorker **bakShowEncryptedStrings** `DoWork` event.

7. Press *F5* or select **Debug | Start Debugging** in the main menu. Make sure the **Threads** window is visible.

8. Enter or copy and paste a long text (with more than 30,000 lines) in the `Textbox` labeled **Original SMS Messages** and click on the **Run in a thread** button. The line with the breakpoint defined in the `ThreadEncryptProcedure` procedure is shown highlighted as the next statement that will be executed. But, the threads are easily identified by their names in the **Threads** window, as shown in the following image:

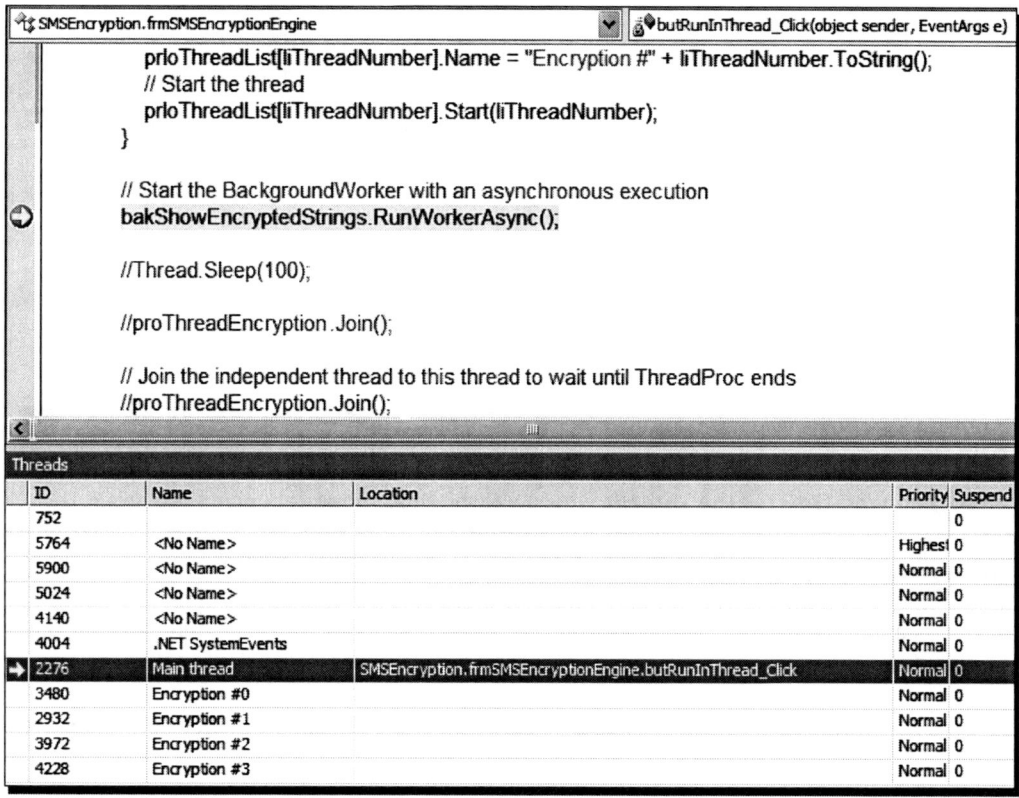

9. Press *F5* or select **Debug | Start Debugging** in the main menu many times until you reach the breakpoint defined in the BackgroundWorker code. You will see a new thread with the **bakShowEncryptedStrings** name defined, as shown in the following image:

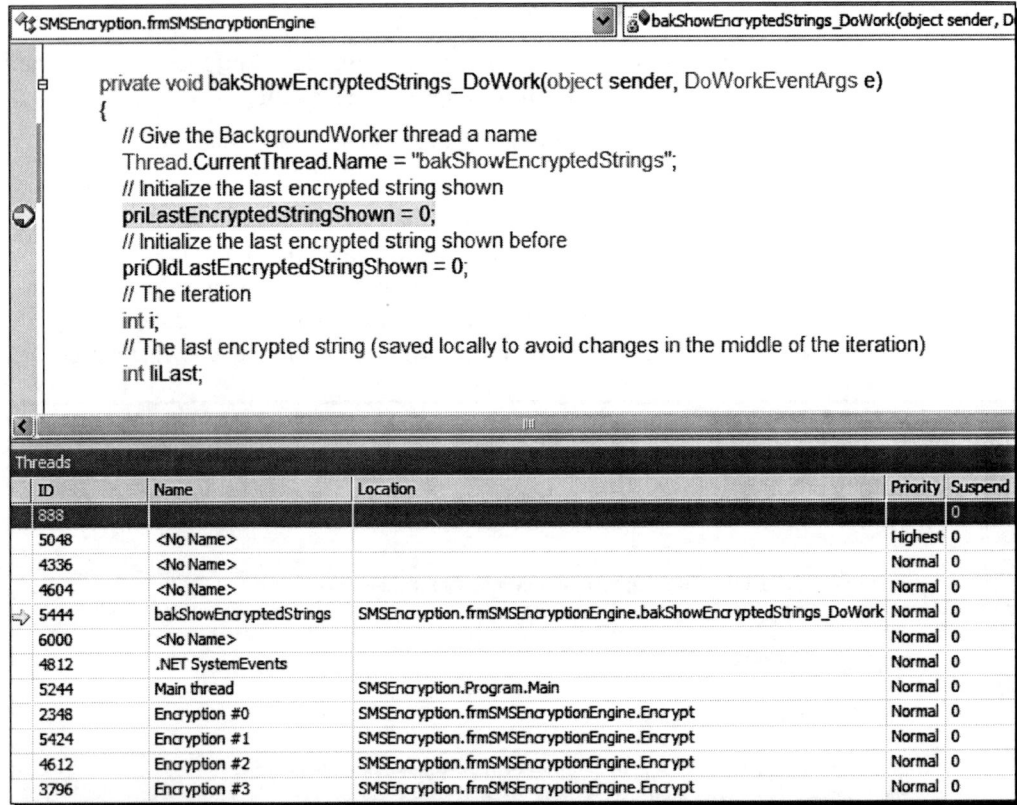

10. Go on running the application step-by-step and watch how the current thread changes. Observe the **Threads** window throughout your debugging process.

What just happened?

Now, you can easily identify each thread in the **Threads** window. The only thing you need is to isolate one thread, to understand what is going on in the encryption process.

Before starting with the threads, we assigned them a name. We did that for the main thread, the BackgroundWorker thread and the encryption threads. Thus, the **Threads** windows showed their names, and we can take control of the concurrent threads.

The following line assigns a string value to the **Name** property of the **Thread** class instance, taking into account the thread number (remember that we are creating them dynamically according to the number of available cores):

```
prloThreadList[liThreadNumber].Name = "Encryption #"
    + liThreadNumber.ToString();
```

If we have four cores available, the resulting names will be the following:

- Thread #0: "Encryption #0".
- Thread #1: "Encryption #1".
- Thread #2: "Encryption #2".
- Thread #3: "Encryption #3".

 It is a good practice to give each thread a name. It is very important to simplify the debugging process and to share code with other developers.

Identifying the current thread at runtime

A Thread class instance provides access to the Name property. As mentioned earlier, it allows us to set the name, and it is shown in the **Threads** windows. Nevertheless, the BackgroundWorker does not provide a direct method or property to set the name of the thread it creates.

For that reason, we use the CurrentThread property of the Thread (System. Threading.Thread) class. It offers access to a Thread instance of the currently running thread, that is, the thread running the current method. As it is an instance of the Thread class, it has a Name property.

The following line accesses the current thread of the BackgroundWorker and assigns the name for that thread, through Thread.CurrentThread:

```
Thread.CurrentThread.Name = "bakShowEncryptedStrings";
```

The current thread is the one created by the BackgroundWorker as we are in the `DoWork` event handler code. This is shown in the following image:

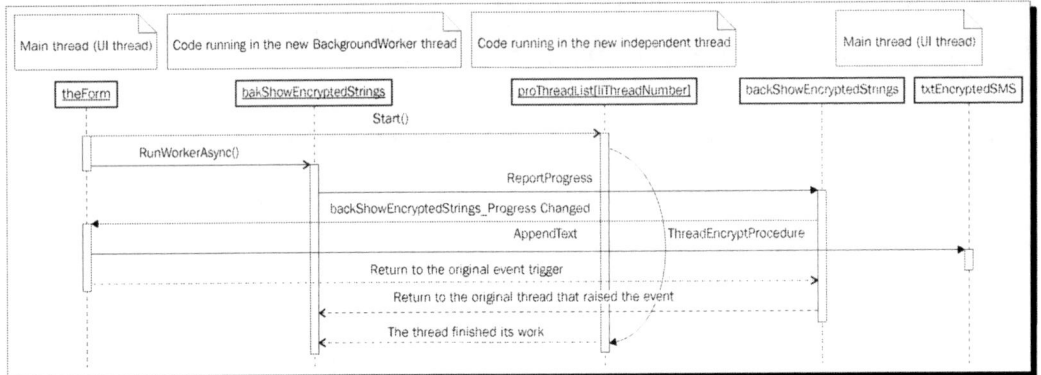

 Be careful with the BackgroundWorker because the `ProgressChanged` event handler code runs in the main thread and not in the thread created by the BackgroundWorker.

The following line accesses the current thread (the main thread) and assigns the name for that thread, again using `Thread.CurrentThread`:

```
Thread.CurrentThread.Name = "Main thread";
```

Of course, we can also use `Thread.CurrentThread` in the `ThreadEncryptProcedure` to assign the names for each created thread as the first instruction, instead of doing it before calling the `Start` method, as shown in the following line:

```
Thread.CurrentThread.Name = "Encryption #" + ((int)poThreadParameter).
ToString();
```

`Thread.CurrentThread` can also be used to access the current thread properties and methods. For example, we can access the `IsBackground` property with the following expression:

```
Thread.CurrentThread.IsBackground
```

Then, we can evaluate it for any purpose.

We can also evaluate the `Name` property of the current thread in order to execute conditional code, according to the thread. Identifying threads offers new opportunities in multithreaded applications because we are able to know in which thread the code is being executed at runtime. Moreover, it allows us to understand what is going on while we are debugging. It is too difficult to debug complex multithreaded code successfully without using names to identify each thread.

Debugging multithreaded applications as single-threaded applications

So far, we have identified threads created using both the BackgroundWorker component and the `Thread` class. We also identified the main application thread and we learned about the information shown by the **Threads** window. However, we must debug the encryption process to solve its problem without taking into account the other concurrent threads. How can we successfully debug the encryption engine focusing on one thread and leaving the others untouched?

We can use the **Threads** window to control the execution of the concurrent thread at runtime without having to make changes to the code. As we learned in the previous chapters, this will affect the performance results, but it will allow us to focus on a specific part of the code as if we were working in a single-threaded application.

This technique is suitable for solving problems related to a specific part of the code that runs in a thread. However, when there are problems generated by concurrency we must use other debugging tricks that we will learn later in this chapter.

The **Threads** window does a great job in offering good runtime information about the running threads while offering a simple way to watch, pause, and resume multiple threads.

Time for action – Leaving a thread running alone

You must run the encryption procedure called by `ThreadEncryptProcedure`. But you want to focus on just one thread, in order to solve the problem that the FBI agents detected. Changing the code is not an option, because it will take more time than expected, and you might introduce new bugs to the encryption engine. Thus, let's freeze the threads we are not interested in!

Now, we are going to leave one encryption thread running alone to focus on its code without the other threads disturbing our debugging procedure:

1. Stay in the project, `SMSEncryption`.

2. Clear all the breakpoints. Press *Ctrl + Shift + F9* or select **Debug | Delete All Breakpoints** in the main menu. Make sure the **Threads** window is visible.

3. Define a breakpoint in the line `int liThreadNumber = (int) poThreadParameter;` in the `ThreadEncryptProcedure` procedure code.

4. Enter or copy and paste a long text, using the same lines (with more than 30,000 lines) in the `Textbox` labeled **Original SMS Messages**, as shown in the following image:

5. Click on the **Run in a thread** button. The line with the breakpoint defined in the `ThreadEncryptProcedure` procedure is shown highlighted as the next statement that will be executed. The current thread will be shown with a yellow arrow on the left in the **Threads** window.

6. Right-click on each of the other encryption threads and select **Freeze** in the context menu that appears, in order to suspend them. If the current thread is **Encryption #1** and there are four cores available, you will freeze the following threads—**Encryption #0**, **Encryption #2**, and **Encryption #3**.

7. Right-click on the **Main thread** and select **Freeze** in the context menu that appears, in order to suspend it (we do not want the BackgroundWorker to start and interfere with our work). The only working thread that matters will be **Encryption #1**, as shown in the following image:

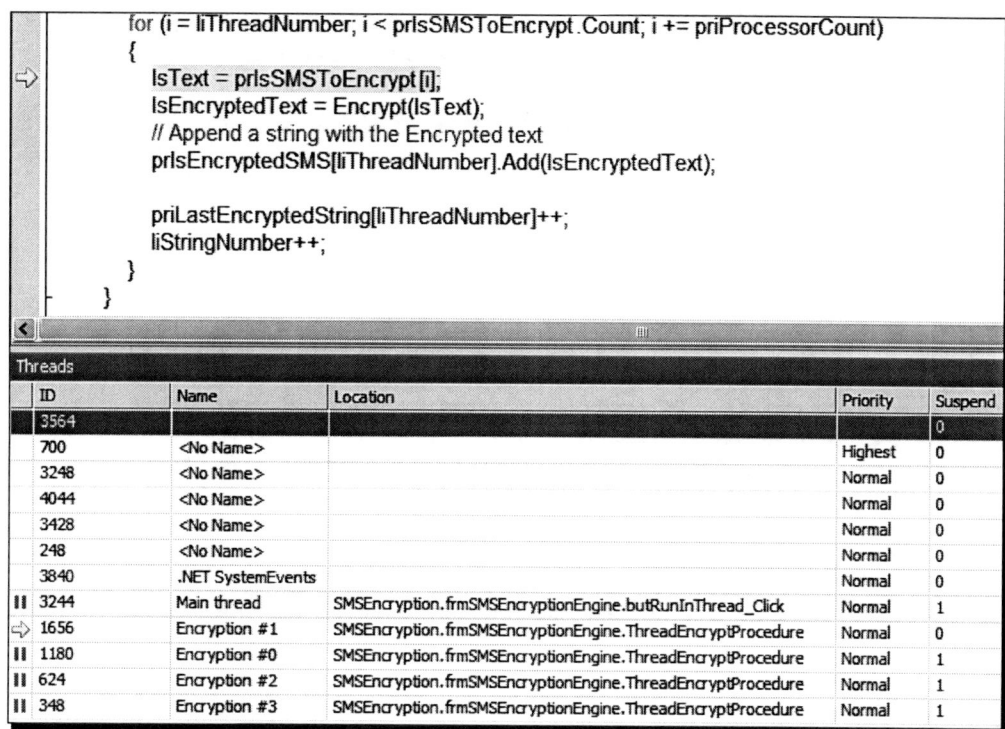

```
        for (i = liThreadNumber; i < prlsSMSToEncrypt.Count; i += priProcessorCount)
        {
            lsText = prlsSMSToEncrypt[i];
            lsEncryptedText = Encrypt(lsText);
            // Append a string with the Encrypted text
            prlsEncryptedSMS[liThreadNumber].Add(lsEncryptedText);

            priLastEncryptedString[liThreadNumber]++;
            liStringNumber++;
        }
    }
```

Threads

ID	Name	Location	Priority	Suspend
3564				0
700	<No Name>		Highest	0
3248	<No Name>		Normal	0
4044	<No Name>		Normal	0
3428	<No Name>		Normal	0
248	<No Name>		Normal	0
3840	.NET SystemEvents		Normal	0
3244	Main thread	SMSEncryption.frmSMSEncryptionEngine.butRunInThread_Click	Normal	1
1656	Encryption #1	SMSEncryption.frmSMSEncryptionEngine.ThreadEncryptProcedure	Normal	0
1180	Encryption #0	SMSEncryption.frmSMSEncryptionEngine.ThreadEncryptProcedure	Normal	1
624	Encryption #2	SMSEncryption.frmSMSEncryptionEngine.ThreadEncryptProcedure	Normal	1
348	Encryption #3	SMSEncryption.frmSMSEncryptionEngine.ThreadEncryptProcedure	Normal	1

8. Run the code step-by-step inspecting values as you do with single-threaded applications.

What just happened?

It is easy to debug a multithreaded application focusing on one thread instead of trying to do it with all the threads running at the same time.

We could transform a complex multithreaded application into a single-threaded application without making changes to the code. We did it at runtime using the multithreading debugging features offered by the C# IDE.

We suspended the execution of the concurrent threads that would disturb our step-by-step execution. Thus, we could focus on the code being executed by just one encryption thread.

Freezing and thawing threads

As we learned in the previous example, freezing a thread suspends its execution. However, in the debugging process, we would need to resume the thread execution.

It can be done at any point of time by right-clicking on a suspended thread and selecting **Thaw** in the context menu that appears, as shown in the following image:

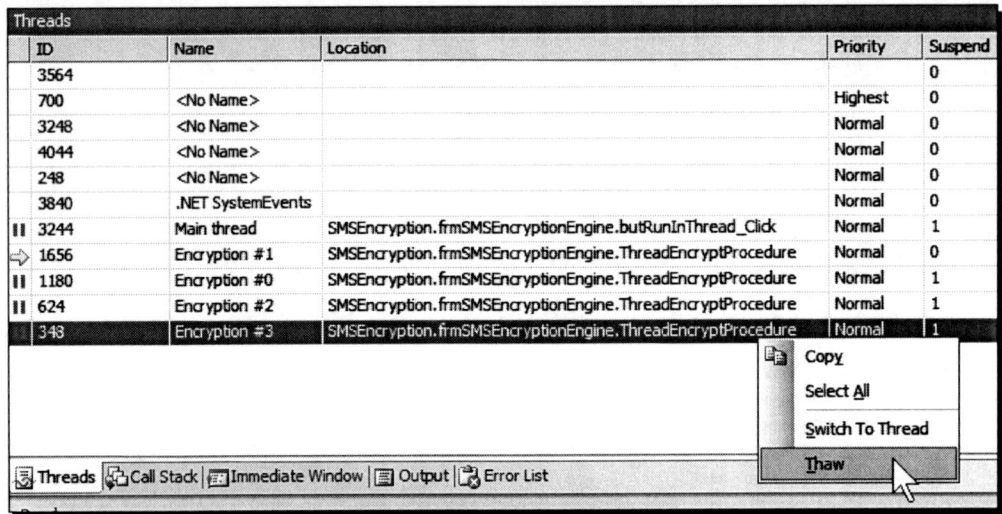

 By **Freezing** and **thawing** threads (suspending and resuming), we can have an exhaustive control over the threads running during the debugging process. It helps a lot when we have to solve bugs related to concurrency as we can easily analyze many contexts without making changes to the code—which could generate new bugs.

Nevertheless, when developing multithreaded applications, we must always test the execution with many concurrent threads running to make sure it does not have concurrency bugs.

The debugging techniques allow us to isolate the code for evaluation purposes, but the final tests must use the full multithreading potential.

Viewing the call stack for each running thread

Each thread has its own independent stack. Using the **Call Stack** window, we can move through the methods that were called, as we are used to doing so in single-threaded applications.

The main difference in doing this with multithreaded applications is that when the active thread changes, the **Call Stack** window will also show different content.

Debugging a multithreaded application using the techniques we are learning is an excellent way to understand how the different threads run and will improve our parallel programming skills.

To show the call stack for the active thread, press *Ctrl + Alt + C* or go to **Debug | Windows | Call Stack** in the main menu. Make sure the **Threads** window is also visible to take into account the active thread when analyzing the call stack, as shown in the following image:

```
        IsEncryptedText = "";
        for (i = 0; i <= (psText.Length - 1); i++)
        {
            loRandomChar = (char)(loRandom.Next(65535));
            // Current char XOR random generated char
            IsEncryptedText += ((char)(psText[i] ^ loRandomChar)).ToString();
            // Random generated char XOR 65535 - i
            // It is saved because we need it later for the decryption process
⇨          IsEncryptedText += ((char)(loRandomChar ^ (65535 - i))).ToString();
            // Another random generated char but just to add garbage to confuss the hackers
            loRandomChar = (char)(loRandom.Next(65535));
            IsEncryptedText += loRandomChar.ToString();
        }

        IsEncryptedTextWithFinalXOR = "";
        // Now, every character XOR 125
        for (i = 0; i <= (IsEncryptedText.Length - 1); i++)
```

Threads

	ID	Name	Location	Priority	Suspend
	3564				0
	700	<No Name>		Highest	0
	3248				0
	4044	<No Name>		Normal	0
	248	<No Name>		Normal	0
	3840	.NET SystemEvents		Normal	0
II	3244	Main thread	SMSEncryption.frmSMSEncryptionEngine.butRunInThread_Click	Normal	1
⇨	1656	Encryption #1	SMSEncryption.frmSMSEncryptionEngine.Encrypt	Normal	0
II	1180	Encryption #0	SMSEncryption.frmSMSEncryptionEngine.ThreadEncryptProcedure	Normal	1
II	624	Encryption #2	SMSEncryption.frmSMSEncryptionEngine.ThreadEncryptProcedure	Normal	1
II	348	Encryption #3	SMSEncryption.frmSMSEncryptionEngine.ThreadEncryptProcedure	Normal	1

Call Stack

Name
➡ SMSEncryption.exe!SMSEncryption.frmSMSEncryptionEngine.Encrypt(string psText = "THIS IS A MESSAGE TO BE ENCRYPTED") Line 86
SMSEncryption.exe!SMSEncryption.frmSMSEncryptionEngine.ThreadEncryptProcedure(object poThreadParameter = 1) Line 140 + 0xa bytes
[External Code]

🔁Call Stack | 🖼️Immediate Window | 📄 Output | 📋 Error List

Have a go hero – Debugging and enhancing the encryption algorithm

Using the multithreaded debugging techniques we have learned so far, develop a new version of this application with the encryption problem solved. Take into account everything we have studied about freezing and thawing threads.

 Check the randomly generated garbage and the way it is applied to the generated encrypted string. Making some changes to it, you can have a robust encryption process that differentiates each output with the same input text.

Improve the new versions you developed in the previous chapter. Use new randomly generated garbage to enhance the encryption algorithms.

Oh no! You have to explain to the agents the changes you made to the encryption procedure, and how it works.

Showing partial results in multithreaded code

So far, we have learned new debugging features provided by Visual C# that help us a lot in troubleshooting bugs in multithreaded applications without dying in action–transforming it into a single-threaded application without making changes in its code. However, sometimes, we must show partial results of a procedure to help us understand what is happening while it is running. How can we safely show partial results in procedures being executed in many concurrent threads?

We cannot show the partial results in the UI controls. We can do that using many BackgroundWorker components, but it would require lots of changes to the code and add a great complexity to the application. We do want to take a simpler approach.

Fortunately, the IDE offers us the **Immediate Window**, and it can help us in our task.

Time for action – Explaining the encryption procedure

The FBI agents want you to explain to them the encryption procedure, showing them partial results. Using the debugging techniques learned so far, you isolate an encryption thread and begin executing it step-by-step, inspecting variables to show the values. Nevertheless, they do not understand it this way. They want you to copy and paste the partial results in a document and then explain to them using what just happened. Do not worry; using the **Immediate Window**, it is very easy!

Now, we are going to add code to the `Encrypt` procedure to show partial results in the **Immediate Window** as the text is being encoded:

1. Stay in the project, `SMSEncryption`.

2. Clear all the breakpoints. Press *Ctrl + Shift + F9* or select **Debug | Delete All | Breakpoints** in the main menu. Make sure the **Threads** and the **Immediate Window** are visible.

3. Select **Tools | Options** in the main menu. The **Options** dialog box will appear. Make sure the option **Redirect all Output Window text to the Immediate Window** is checked in the **Debugging | General** page. This way, you will see the messages in the **Immediate Window**.

4. Add the following line of code at the beginning of the `Encrypt` procedure:

   ```
   // Show the original text in the Immediate Window
   System.Diagnostics.Debug.Print("Original text:" + psText);
   ```

5. Add the following line of code after the line `loRandomChar = (char)(loRandom.Next(65535));` in the `Encrypt` procedure:

   ```
   // Show the random char code (in numbers) generated in the
      Immediate Window
   System.Diagnostics.Debug.Print("Random char generated:" +  ((int)
                            loRandomChar).ToString());
   ```

6. Add the following line of code after the line `lsEncryptedText += loRandomChar.ToString();` in the `Encrypt` procedure:

   ```
   // Show how the encrypted text is being generated in the
      Immediate Window
   System.Diagnostics.Debug.Print("Partial encryption result char
              number: " + i.ToString() + ": " + lsEncryptedText);
   ```

7. Add the following line of code before the line `return lsEncryptedTextWithFinalXOR;` in the `Encrypt` procedure:

   ```
   // Show how the encrypted text is being generated in the
      Immediate Window
   System.Diagnostics.Debug.Print("Final encryption result with XOR:
                            " + lsEncryptedTextWithFinalXOR);
   ```

8. Enter or copy and paste a long text, using the same lines (with more than 30,000 lines) in the `Textbox` labeled **Original SMS Messages** and click on the **Run in a thread** button. You will see that partial results show in the **Immediate window** as shown in the following image:

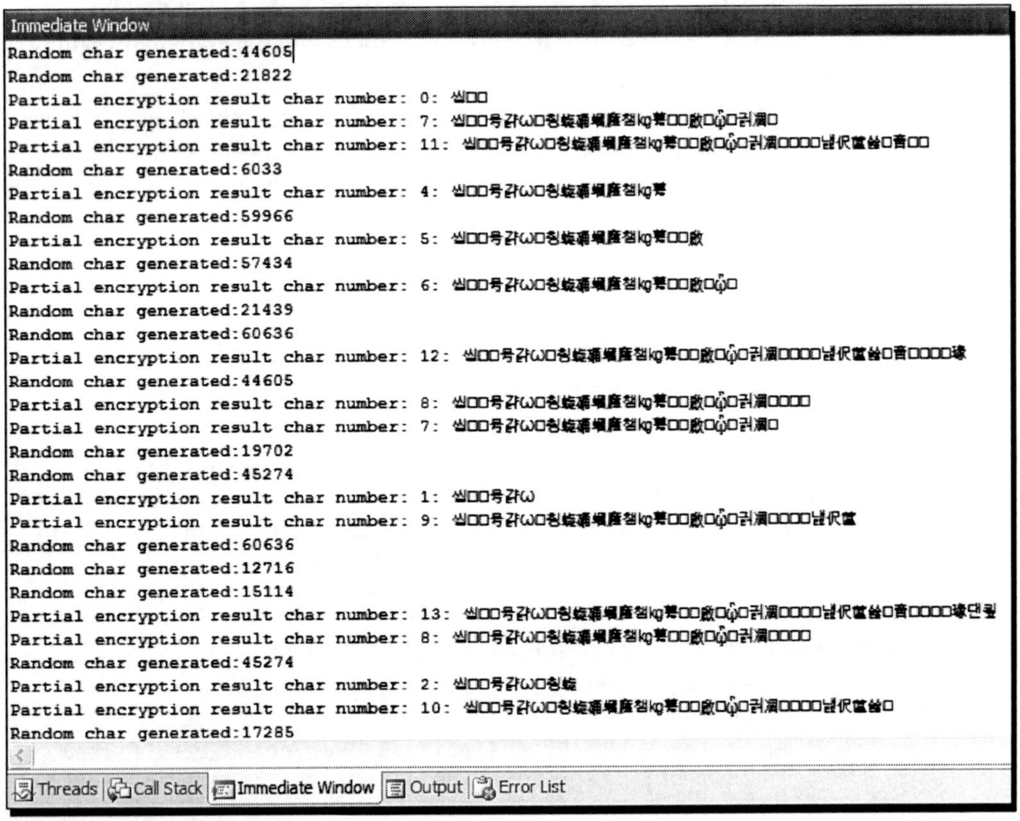

What just happened?

The results shown in the **Immediate Window** are a great mess. How can you explain that to the FBI agents? The answer would be to isolate an encryption thread and show the results for just that one thread using the debugging techniques learned. Then, you can copy the contents of the **Immediate Window** to a word processor!

The outputs shown in the **Immediate Window** are the results of the code executed in many concurrent threads. Therefore, it is very difficult to understand the real encryption execution sequence.

One possible solution is isolating one thread and running just that one. We have already learned how to do so.

The other is to show the information only when it is running on a certain thread. We can check it in the procedure executed by the thread using `Thread.CurrentThread` and comparing the name.

> As we can see, `Thread.CurrentThread` is very useful in defining conditional execution of certain code according to some information provided by the thread context in which the methods are being run. Besides, it is very useful while debugging.

Showing thread-safe output

The `System.Diagnostics.Debug.Print` method allows us to show information at runtime from many threads in a thread-safe way. Using it, the application can provide us with very important feedback to understand what happens when multiple concurrent threads are running at the same time.

Running a multithreaded application step-by-step, even without isolation, does not represent the real concurrent execution that happens at runtime without breakpoints. Therefore, it is very important to have some feedback to test certain conditions using the `System.Diagnostics.Debug.Print` method.

> However, we must remember that the application's performance will degrade when using the `System.Diagnostics.Debug.Print` method. Thus, the performance must be measured without calls to this method or any interfering debugging techniques.

Using this method, combined with all the debugging techniques known for single-threaded applications, such as inspecting values, setting breakpoints, and tracepoints, we will not have any trouble in solving bugs in multithreaded code.

Time for action – Isolating results

Using the debugging techniques learned to isolate a single thread, you can show the results of one encryption thread in the **Immediate Window**. This way, you will be able to explain to the FBI agents what just happened in the encryption procedure. Furthermore, finally, they will be happy with you!

Now, we are going to isolate the thread as we did in a previous example, but using our recently added code to the `Encrypt` procedure to show partial results in the **Immediate Window** as the text is being encoded:

1. Stay in the project, `SMSEncryption`.

2. Define a breakpoint at the line `int liThreadNumber = (int)` `poThreadParameter;` in the `ThreadEncryptProcedure` procedure code.

3. Enter or copy and paste a short text, using the same lines (with as many lines as cores available, for example, four in a computer with a quad-core microprocessor) in the `Textbox` labeled **Original SMS Messages**.

4. Click on the **Run in a thread** button. The line with the breakpoint defined in the `ThreadEncryptProcedure` procedure is shown highlighted as the next statement that will be executed. The current thread is shown with a yellow arrow on the left in the **Threads** window.

5. Freeze the threads you do not need as we learned to do in the previous examples and run the application to obtain the progress of the encryption procedure shown in the **Immediate Window**, as shown in the following image:

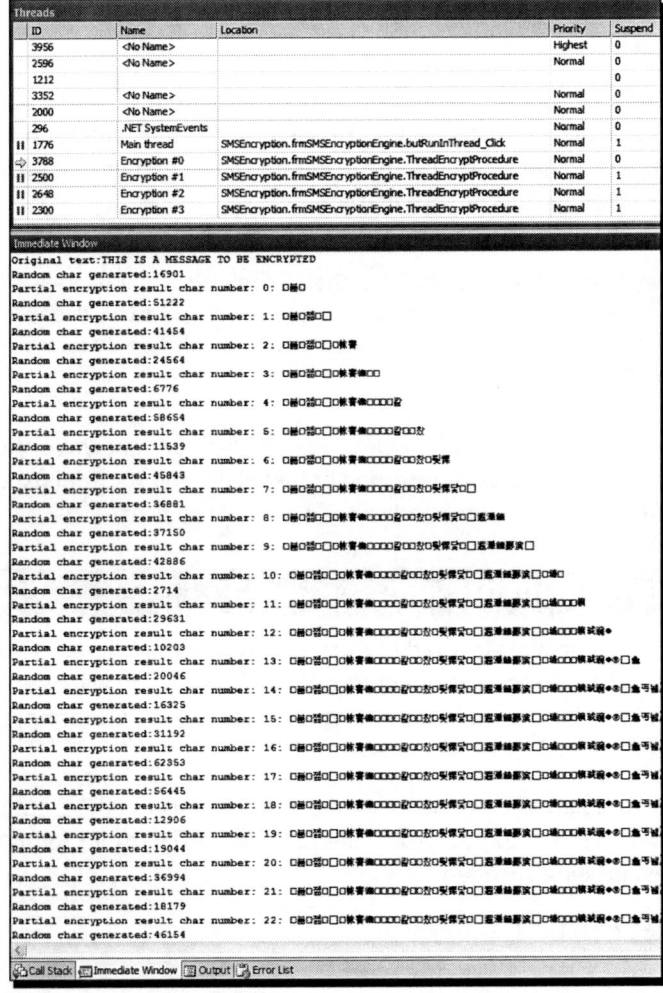

What just happened?

You explain the encryption procedure to the FBI agents, step-by-step with the example you obtained in the **Immediate Window**. They are amazed with the simplicity of your examples and your parallel processing skills! They think you are ready to cooperate with a very interesting project in NASA. But, before that, there is a new mission for you.

As we isolated one encryption thread, the text shown in the **Immediate Window** is the result of the linear execution of just one thread.

 Isolation is a great resource for debugging multithreaded applications. Using it, we can easily find and solve bugs.

Understanding thread information in tracepoints

When debugging multithreaded applications, the information shown by the **tracepoints** is usually useful. They can be used in a manner similar to their usage when debugging single-threaded applications. But they show us information about the running thread.

In order to solve bugs, sometimes we need to know whether a method was executed or not. In a multithreaded application, this can be more confusing, especially when we are writing our first parallelized structures.

To create a tracepoint, you must right-click the line of code and select **Breakpoints | Insert Tracepoint** in the context menu that appears. The **When Breakpoint Is Hit** dialog box will be shown, asking for the parameters for the behavior of the tracepoint, as shown in the following image:

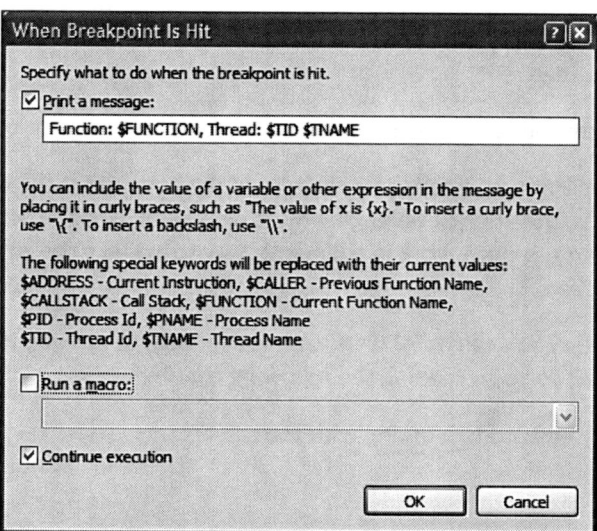

When debugging multithreaded applications, the **$TID** and **$TNAME** keywords are very important because they will give us information in the **Immediate Window** with the thread ID and its name, as shown in the following line:

Function: SMSEncryption.frmSMSEncryptionEngine.ThreadEncryptProcedure(object), Thread: 0x7FC Encryption #0

 When you need to know the methods the concurrent threads are running, using tracepoints is a very good choice, because you do not need to change the code to show results in the **Immediate Window**.

Have a go hero – Concurrent decryption

As mentioned earlier, there is still some work left to be done. The FBI wants to test the time needed to break the encryption. Remember, they have a computer with 16 quad-core microprocessors (64 cores). They do not want you to break the code, but they ask you to create a new application that decrypts each encrypted code. That is, you must decrypt the code simultaneously as the other threads are encrypting the original code. You have to use a queue scheme. The encryption threads add encrypted code to that queue, while the decryption threads remove code from it.

Using everything we have learned in the previous chapter and the debugging techniques studied in this one, develop a new version of the last application you developed in the previous chapter (the one that showed the incoming and outgoing SMS messages with their information in a grid). Use half of the processing power to encrypt and the other half to decrypt concurrently. The text to be decrypted must be entered or copied by the user. Therefore, the user interface must show the progress but must be responsive to the user.

While many threads are encrypting text, the user can copy the results and paste them in the decryption input TextBox.

The encryption and decryption processes must be launched by different buttons.

Enhance the new application detecting the activity of the concurrent threads. If there is no decryption process, the encryption engine must work with as many threads as cores available, and vice versa. It must work in a dynamic way to achieve the best possible performance at any time.

Do not be disappointed! You can do it! If you are not yet able to achieve the last application improvement, you will do so by reading the following chapters.

Now, NASA is looking forward to working with you!

Pop quiz

1. Which of the following lines of code assigns a name to a BackgroundWorker created thread positioned in the `DoWork` event handler?

   a. `backgroundWorker1.ThreadName = "Background thread";`

   b. `Thread.CurrentThread.Name = "Background thread";`

   c. `backgroundWorker1.Name = "Background thread";`

2. Which of the following lines of code assigns a name to an instance of the `Thread` class named `loThread` (positioned in the main thread)?

   a. `loThread.Name = "Encryption thread";`

   b. `loThread.ThreadName = "Encryption thread";`

   c. `Thread.CurrentThread.Name = "Background thread";`

3. In order to focus the debugging process in some methods called by a thread in a multithreaded application, a good practice is:

   a. To run the application step-by-step without any additional considerations

   b. To freeze the main thread and the other threads and leave only one thread running

   c. To make many changes to the code in order to launch only one thread

4. Each running thread:

   a. Has its own stack

   b. Shares the stack with the main thread

   c. Shares the stack with the group of threads created using the same class (`Thread`) or component (BackgroundWorker)

5. Partial results can be shown safely for debugging purposes:

   a. Changing the `Text` property of labels or other controls in the UI from any thread

   b. Calling `Thread.CurrentThread.ShowDebugInfo` from any thread

   c. Calling `System.Diagnostics.Debug.Print` from any thread

Right answers:

1. b.
2. a.
3. b.
4. a.
5. c.

Summary

We learned a lot in this chapter about debugging applications with many concurrent threads and coordinating the entire debugging process. Specifically, we covered:

- Preparing the multithreaded code to simplify the debugging and troubleshooting processes using names for the threads to identify them in the IDE
- Watching and inspecting the execution of multiple concurrent threads created with an instance of the `Thread` class or as a result of calling a BackgroundWorker component `RunWorkerAsync` method
- Freezing many threads to allow us to debug one thread at a time, without the problems related to concurrency while executing the application step-by-step
- Inserting breakpoints and tracepoints to simplify troubleshooting complex multithreaded applications
- Isolating the inspection of values when multiple threads are working on the variables that hold them
- Generating partial results information without creating problems for the multithreaded code

We also discussed the differences between single-threaded debugging and multithreading debugging and many tricks that will help us a lot in simplifying the debugging process. We learned this for threads created using BackgroundWorker and employing the `Thread` class.

Now that we've learned about the debugging techniques for finding and solving problems in methods running in concurrent threads in a C# application, we're ready to study many advanced ways to control the threads' execution and work out many issues related to concurrency, conflicts, and bottlenecks—which is the topic of the next chapter.

6
Understanding Thread Control with Patterns

In order to develop parallel algorithms successfully, without meeting the most difficult problems related to concurrency, we can apply some interesting code patterns that will help us in avoiding mistakes in future multithreaded applications. In this chapter, we will study new ways to keep control over the concurrent threads, and we will go on improving our parallel programming capabilities working with more challenging problems to solve. Reading it and following the exercises we shall:

- Find out how to apply innovative algorithms to generate portions from a huge piece
- Learn to create highly independent blocks of code to run in multiple threads avoiding many classic concurrency problems
- Discover how to use flags in multiple threads
- Find out how to apply new techniques to have exhaustive control over asynchronous and synchronous execution
- Learn techniques to use multithreading in non thread-safe components
- Improve the decoupling of the UI when we need to change the contents of controls with huge blocks of information
- Learn to rebuild results from independent portions

Starting, joining, pausing, and restarting threads

So far, we have worked with the BackgroundWorker component and the `Thread` class to create multithreaded applications. Parallel programming allowed us to achieve incredible performance enhancements and better UI feedback. We also learned new debugging techniques for troubleshooting bugs in multithreaded applications. However, there are other ways to control and queue multiple threads when we are working with huge information blocks, and we need to split their processing. How can we use threading and the `Thread` class to divide image processing algorithms into many concurrent blocks of code?

C# offers many techniques for working with images and bitmaps. However, many of them are not thread-safe. We cannot run many concurrent threads changing pixels in the same instance of the Bitmap (System.Drawing.Bitmap) class. Nevertheless, as we learned in the previous chapters, in order to apply parallel algorithms, we can avoid the problems instead of finding difficult solutions to them. We can split the original bitmap into a number of completely independent bitmaps. Each thread can work with its independent bitmap instance safely, and we can develop a new algorithm with great performance improvements over the single-threaded one. Besides, we can also add code to pause and then restart the threads. The performance results will depend upon the number of cores or processors available in the computer in which we run the application and many other factors. However, we will do some fine-tuning later in this chapter.

As happened in the previous chapters, each Thread class will create its own new independent thread. However, this time, the code dedicated to split the bitmap will be more complex as we are working with huge information blocks.

The Thread class, combined with smart algorithms that avoid the most difficult problems related to multithreaded programming, allows us to achieve incredible performance improvements, an impressive user experience, and great scalability with rational programming efforts.

Time for action – Defining methods for counting old stars

NASA has been working on a very important research project for many years. A group of scientists have been analyzing stellar family trees to detect the possibility of future black holes generated by the death of old stars which could cause great changes in the galaxies.

They know your parallel programming skills and they want you to use them to help them in developing a very complex application that has to detect the older stars from huge infrared portraits obtained by NASA's Spitzer Space Telescope. In the following image, you can see a wispy star-forming region, called **W5**:

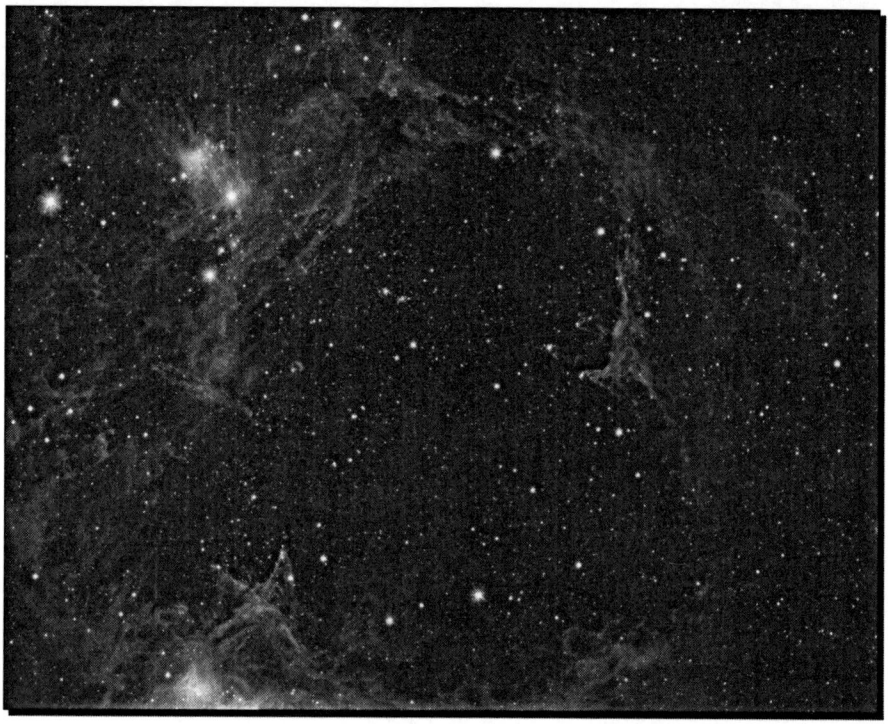

(Image Credit: NASA/JPL-Caltech/Harvard-Smithsonian CfA)

In this portrait, the oldest stars can be seen as blue dots, especially in the center of the two hollow cavities. The white knotty areas are where the youngest stars are forming.

This image contains some of the best evidence yet for the triggered star formation theory. Scientists analyzing the photo have been able to show that the ages of the stars become progressively and systematically younger with distance from the center of the cavities.

You have to work on a very fast and very efficient algorithm for detection of old stars, capable of changing the pixel colors of the old stars in the huge image to make them more visible to the scientists. They want you to use a fine-tuned, multithreading application that is capable of working with as many threads as the number of cores available in the computer where the stars detection algorithm is being executed.

First, we are going to build a new C# application, and we will put the program logic into methods for detecting old stars in any bitmap and preparing the bitmap input for many threads:

1. Create a new C# Project using the Windows Application template in Visual Studio or Visual C# Express. Use `OldStarsFinder` as the project's name.

2. Add the following lines of code at the beginning of the form class definition (as we are going to use the `System.Threading.Thread` class and `System.Drawing.Imaging` classes):

```
using System.Threading;
using System.Drawing.Imaging;
```

3. Add the following lines in the form class definition to declare three new private variables:

```
// The number of processors or cores available in the computer
   for this application
private int priProcessorCount = Environment.ProcessorCount;
// The bitmaps list
private List<Bitmap> prloBitmapList;
// The long list with the old stars count
private List<long> prliOldStarsCount;
```

4. Add the following function, `CropBitmap`. It will crop the bitmap received as a parameter and return the portion of the original defined by the `Rectangle` `proRectangle`:

```
private Bitmap CropBitmap(Bitmap proBitmap, Rectangle
                          proRectangle)
{
    // Create a new bitmap copying the portion of the original
       defined by proRectangle and keeping its PixelFormat
    Bitmap loCroppedBitmap = proBitmap.Clone(proRectangle,
                             proBitmap.PixelFormat);
    // Return the cropped bitmap
    return loCroppedBitmap;
}
```

5. Add the following function, `IsOldStar`. It will compare the pixel hue, saturation, and brightness to determine if their levels correspond to the typical color range offered by an old star in the infrared portraits:

```
public bool IsOldStar(Color poPixelColor)
{
    // Hue between 150 and 258
    // Saturation more than 0.10
    // Brightness more than 0.90
```

```
        return ((poPixelColor.GetHue() >= 150) &&
                (poPixelColor.GetHue() <= 258) &&
                (poPixelColor.GetSaturation() >= 0.10) &&
                (poPixelColor.GetBrightness() <= 0.90));
    }
```

6. Add the following procedure, `ThreadOldStarsFinder`. It will iterate through each pixel in the corresponding bitmap for the thread that launches it and count the old stars:

```
private void ThreadOldStarsFinder(object poThreadParameter)
{
    // Retrieve the thread number received in object
       poThreadParameter
    int liThreadNumber = (int)poThreadParameter;
    // The pixel matrix (bitmap) row number (Y)
    int liRow;
    // The pixel matrix (bitmap) col number (X)
    int liCol;
    // The pixel color
    Color loPixelColor;
    // Get my bitmap part from the bitmap list
    Bitmap loBitmap = prloBitmapList[liThreadNumber];

    // Reset my old stars counter
    prliOldStarsCount[liThreadNumber] = 0;
    // Iterate through each pixel matrix (bitmap) rows
    for (liRow = 0; liRow < loBitmap.Height; liRow++)
    {
        // Iterate through each pixel matrix (bitmap) cols
        for (liCol = 0; liCol < loBitmap.Width; liCol++)
        {
            // Get the pixel Color for liCol and liRow
            loPixelColor = loBitmap.GetPixel(liCol, liRow);
            if (IsOldStar(loPixelColor))
            {
                // The color range corresponds to an old star
                // Change its color to a pure blue
                loBitmap.SetPixel(liCol, liRow, Color.Blue);
                // Increase the old stars counter
                prliOldStarsCount[liThreadNumber]++;
            }
        }
    }
}
```

What just happened?

The code required to find and count potential old stars in any huge infrared bitmap portrait is now held in named functions and procedures, already prepared for dynamically created concurrent threads.

Why do we have to create a `CropBitmap` function? That is because we cannot access a single `Bitmap` instance pixel matrix from many different concurrent threads. If we do so, we will get an `InvalidOperationException`, as GDI+ is not prepared for multithreaded access.

Therefore, we must split the original `Bitmap` into as many independent portions as the number of concurrent threads that will be working on it. The `CropBitmap` function will allow us to obtain a specific portion of a `Bitmap` instance and generate a list of new `Bitmap` instances (`prloBitmapList`).

In this case, we cannot use other techniques learned in the previous chapters. For example, we cannot work with a pixel row per thread. We must create completely independent `Bitmap` instances. We are going to use a master-slave scenario.

Avoiding conflicts

As we have learned so far, there are many problems related to multithreaded applications and the parallel algorithms. Since there are many threads running concurrently, we must be very careful when changing the values of variables in different threads. The best solution to such concurrency problems is **avoiding them** or preventing them via **synchronization mechanisms**. However, synchronization mechanisms have to be used very carefully, because they can decrease performance and generate too many context switches. Besides, using them can introduce potential bugs that can be very difficult to debug.

How can we avoid the concurrency problems? It is very simple. As much as possible, we have to make each thread independent of the other concurrent threads working in the same global portion of resources.

We must count stars in a huge bitmap. Nevertheless, splitting the original bitmap using the very simple `CropBitmap` function avoids many conflicts related to concurrency that would have otherwise been very complex to troubleshoot. As each thread is going to work with its own bitmap, we are avoiding a potentially dangerous problem.

 Again, we must make a paradigm shift in the way we develop our applications. The changes are just a few, but they can spare us many problems related to concurrency. The solution patterns we are learning with our examples (in our recent missions) are very useful in any kind of applications with similar processes to be run in multithreaded code.

Another potential problem is counting the total number of old stars detected in the huge infrared bitmap portrait. If we used a shared member variable, we might have **locking problems**. If we have many threads concurrently changing the same variable value (at the same time), we will have to lock that variable each time its value is incremented. However, we want to avoid **locks**, as we must finish our application quickly and easily to astonish the NASA scientists. Locking a variable implies context switches and hence reduced performance. For this reason, we use the `prliOldStarsCount long` list. There is one counter for each thread, and we will obtain the total sum adding the n `prliOldStarsCount long` values to a new variable (where n is the number of start finder threads).

This way, we avoid locks as each thread has its own independent counter, and we achieve a better performance compared to a solution that would use the confusing and complex locks.

> Remember that modern microprocessors are optimized for parallelism, and their manufacturers are going to continue adding more capabilities in this area in the coming years. Therefore, avoiding concurrency conflicts and generating blocks of independent code will generate amazing performance improvements over single-threaded applications.

Splitting image processing

In order to process an image in many concurrent threads we must divide it into as many independent portions as the number of threads that will be running. As we have seen earlier, the `CropBitmap` function offers this utility.

Of course, this change in the image processing algorithm has its costs, and it is not free. In this case, we will be counting stars on a per pixel basis. However, when we must apply other more complex algorithms, we must consider many important additional changes in the basic code. We will continue with this topic later in this chapter.

Once each image part is processed, we must collect the results and recompose the original image with the changes made to its pixels.

> It is the same mechanism we used with string lists, but it has some changes because we are working with instances of the `Bitmap` class, which is slightly different and introduces new constraints for multithreading.

Understanding the pixels' color compositions

The infrared bitmap portrait does not have an exact blue (red = 0; green = 0; blue = 255) color for an old star. There is a complex technique used to determine a star's age according to color ranges. This is easy to understand for human beings, but difficult for computers.

However, it is simple to generate an algorithm obtaining the following three components of a `Color` (`System.Drawing.Color`) instance:

- **Hue**: Obtained by the `GetHue()` method
- **Saturation**: Obtained by the `GetSaturation()` method (from 0.01 to 1.00)
- **Brightness**: Obtained by the `GetBrightness()` method (from 0.01 to 1.00)

Using these color components, we can apply the following rules to determine whether a pixel in the infrared bitmap portrait corresponds to a potential old star or not:

- Hue is between 150 and 258
- Saturation is more than 10% (0.10)
- Brightness is more than 90% (0.90)

It is easier to work with Hue, Saturation, and Brightness values than with Red, Green, and Blue values in order to determine an old star.

The `IsOldStar` function receives a `Color` instance as a parameter and returns the results of applying the aforementioned rules to its Hue, Saturation, and Brightness in the following lines of code:

```
return ((poPixelColor.GetHue() >= 150)
    && (poPixelColor.GetHue() <= 258)
    && (poPixelColor.GetSaturation() >= 0.10)
    && (poPixelColor.GetBrightness() <= 0.90));
```

This function is called for each pixel in the infrared bitmap portrait, and it returns a `bool` value.

 One potential problem with the functions and procedures is that the `IsOldStar` function and the other methods can be called only from threads with independent bitmaps. If they are called from threads working in the same bitmap, they will fail and generate an `InvalidOperationException` exception. Therefore, we must be careful when designing the system architecture intended for parallelism.

Time for action – Running the stars counter in many concurrent threads

The NASA scientists showed you a single-threaded application recognizing the probable old stars and changing their pixels to pure blue. It took nearly an hour to complete the algorithm with a very huge infrared bitmap portrait. However, they have a server with 128 cores available. They think you can improve the performance using your multithreading skills. Of course you can! Let's work on a solution to improve this poor performance.

Now, we are going to create the UI and make some changes to create multiple threads dynamically to process each portion of a bitmap. In order to accomplish this, we must share data between the various threads, as we learned in the previous chapters:

1. Stay in the project, `OldStarsFinder`.

2. Open Windows Form `Form1` (**frmStarsFinder**) in the form designer, add the following controls, and align them as shown in the following image:

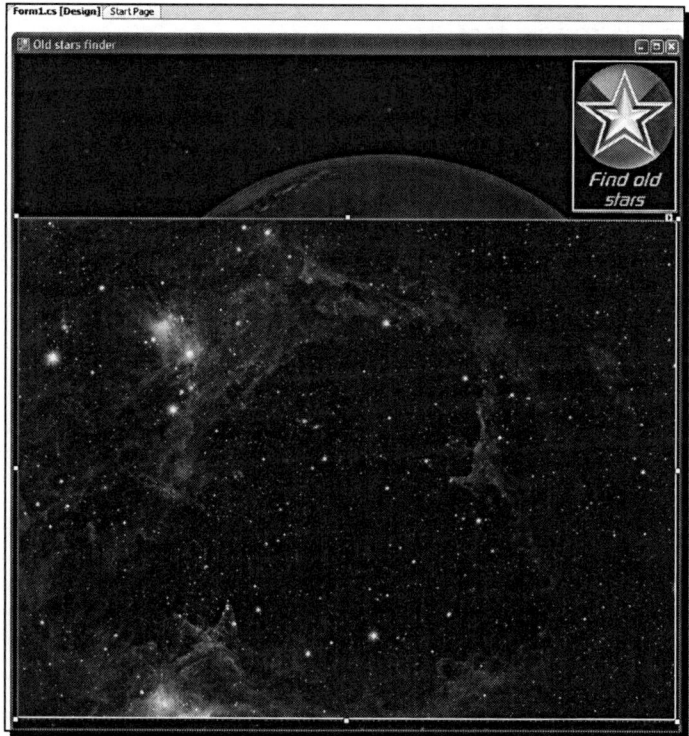

- ◆ One picturebox (`picStarsBitmap`) showing one of the infrared portraits obtained by NASA's Spitzer Space Telescope (you can find many of them on `www.nasa.gov` or `http://www.nasa.gov/multimedia/imagegallery/`), with its `SizeMode` property set to **StretchImage**.

◆ One button showing a star and its `Text` property set to **Find old star**
  (**butFindOldStars**). This button will start multiple old stars finder threads.

3. Add the following lines in the form's class definition to declare two new
private variables:

```
// The threads list
private List<Thread> prloThreadList;
// The original huge infrared bitmap portrait
Bitmap proOriginalBitmap;
```

4. Add the following procedure, `WaitForThreadsToDie`. It will make the main thread
sleep in order to wait until the many concurrent threads finish their work:

```
private void WaitForThreadsToDie()
{
    // A bool flag
    bool lbContinue = true;
    int liDeadThreads = 0;
    int liThreadNumber;
    while (lbContinue)
    {
        for (liThreadNumber = 0; liThreadNumber
            < priProcessorCount; liThreadNumber++)
        {
            if (prloThreadList[liThreadNumber].IsAlive)
            {
                // One of the threads is still alive, exit the
                    for loop and sleep 100 milliseconds
                break;
            }
            else
            {
                // Increase the dead threads count
                liDeadThreads++;
            }
        }
        if (liDeadThreads == priProcessorCount)
        {
            // All the threads are dead, exit the while loop
            break;
        }
        Thread.Sleep(100);
        liDeadThreads = 0;
    }
}
```

5. Add the following procedure, `ShowBitmapWithOldStars`. It will rebuild the bitmap adding each previously separated portion:

```
private void ShowBitmapWithOldStars()
{
    int liThreadNumber;
    // Each bitmap portion
    Bitmap loBitmap;
    // The starting row in each iteration
    int liStartRow = 0;

    // Calculate each bitmap's height
    int liEachBitmapHeight = ((int)(proOriginalBitmap.Height /
                         priProcessorCount)) + 1;

    // Create a new bitmap with the whole width and height
    loBitmap = new Bitmap(proOriginalBitmap.Width,
                         proOriginalBitmap.Height);
    Graphics g = Graphics.FromImage((Image)loBitmap);
    g.InterpolationMode = System.Drawing.Drawing2D.
                         InterpolationMode.HighQualityBicubic;

    for (liThreadNumber = 0; liThreadNumber < priProcessorCount;
        liThreadNumber++)
    {
        // Draw each portion in its corresponding absolute
           starting row
        g.DrawImage(prloBitmapList[liThreadNumber], 0,
                 liStartRow);
        // Increase the starting row
        liStartRow += liEachBitmapHeight;
    }
    // Show the bitmap in the PictureBox picStarsBitmap
    picStarsBitmap.Image = loBitmap;

    g.Dispose();
}
```

6. Open the `Click` event in the button **butFindOldStars**, and enter the following code:

```
proOriginalBitmap = new Bitmap(picStarsBitmap.Image);

// Thread number
int liThreadNumber;
// Create the thread list; the long list and the bitmap list
prloThreadList = new List<Thread>(priProcessorCount);
```

```
prliOldStarsCount = new List<long>(priProcessorCount);
prloBitmapList = new List<Bitmap>(priProcessorCount);

int liStartRow = 0;

int liEachBitmapHeight = ((int)(proOriginalBitmap.Height /
                        priProcessorCount)) + 1;

int liHeightToAdd = proOriginalBitmap.Height;
Bitmap loBitmap;

// Initialize the threads
for (liThreadNumber = 0; liThreadNumber < priProcessorCount;
    liThreadNumber++)
{
    // Just to occupy the number
    prliOldStarsCount.Add(0);

    if (liEachBitmapHeight > liHeightToAdd)
    {
        // The last bitmap height perhaps is less than the other
           bitmaps height
        liEachBitmapHeight = liHeightToAdd;
    }

    loBitmap = CropBitmap(proOriginalBitmap, new Rectangle(0,
            liStartRow, proOriginalBitmap.Width,
            liEachBitmapHeight));
    liHeightToAdd -= liEachBitmapHeight;
    liStartRow += liEachBitmapHeight;
    prloBitmapList.Add(loBitmap);

    // Add the new thread, with a parameterized start (to allow
       parameters)
    prloThreadList.Add(new Thread(new ParameterizedThreadStart
                    (ThreadOldStarsFinder)));
}

// Now, start the threads
for (liThreadNumber = 0; liThreadNumber < priProcessorCount;
    liThreadNumber++)
{
    prloThreadList[liThreadNumber].Start(liThreadNumber);
}
```

```
WaitForThreadsToDie();

ShowBitmapWithOldStars();
```

7. Build and run the application.

8. Click on the **Find old stars** button. After a few seconds (depending on the parallel processing capabilities of the computer) in the W5 wispy star-forming region, a huge infrared portrait will be shown with its probable old stars in pure blue, as shown in the following image:

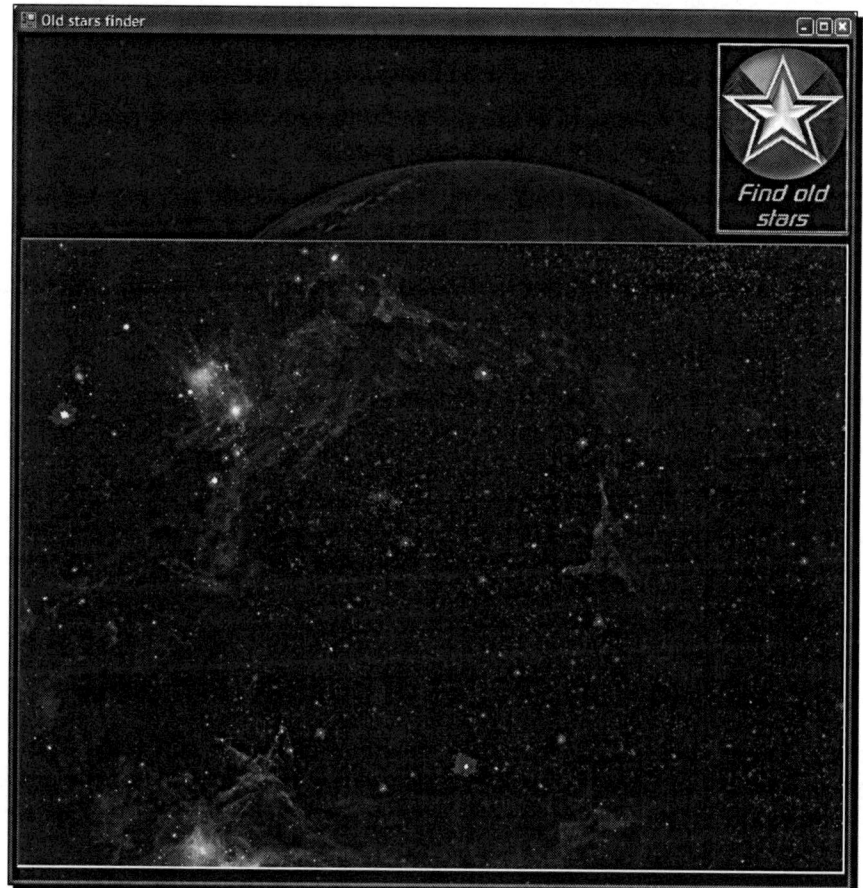

 Run the application using very large images. For example, an image with around 5000 x 3500 pixels would be adequate for this experiment.

What just happened?

The NASA scientists are amazed with the results. Your application ran faster than ever as it took full advantage of the parallel processing capabilities in the NASA servers. This is good news. However, as they are very excited with the results, they have a lot of additional work for you. Do not worry! They will not send you into space, not yet!

When the user clicks the **Find old stars** button, the process executes in the following manner:

1. The original image is divided into many independent bitmaps. Each portion will be assigned to a different thread.

2. Many threads are created and then started (executed asynchronously) with a parameter, so that they know which bitmap belongs to them.

3. The main thread waits until all the star finder threads finish their work, sleeping 100 milliseconds in each query of the threads' state.

4. Once all the threads finish their work, the main thread (the only one capable of touching the UI) rebuilds the divided bitmap and shows it in the picturebox control.

The focus used to generate a multithreaded version for an image processing application is very similar to the one applied to the string lists processing.

The application generated many dynamically generated input streams, processed them in multiple threads, and then collected the results offered by many output streams, decoupling the UI.

Besides, we used a classic linear programming technique, **flags**. However, we did this taking into account the requirements for working with loops and flags in concurrent and event-driven programming.

Creating independent blocks of concurrent code

Processing an image using multiple threads is something difficult in .NET with C# because GDI+ instances are not prepared for multithreaded access. Nevertheless, we could create self-sufficient blocks of safe concurrent code dividing the image into many independent images and adding a results collector.

This principle is the simplest way to transform a single-threaded algorithm into a multithreaded algorithm avoiding many complex problems related to concurrency.

Each thread works in its independent block, without disturbing or interfering with the other threads.

However, the code used for dividing the original bitmap dynamically into many smaller bitmaps is a bit complex. That is the price we have to pay for the performance enhancement and scalability of our application.

This line obtains a `Bitmap` instance from the `picStarsBitmap` picturebox (we begin decoupling the UI, as we cannot touch it from independent threads):

```
proOriginalBitmap = new Bitmap(picStarsBitmap.Image);
```

These lines create the thread list, the `long` numbers list and the bitmap list in order to let them grow dynamically at runtime depending upon the number of available cores in the computer where the application runs:

```
prloThreadList = new List<Thread>(priProcessorCount);
prliOldStarsCount = new List<long>(priProcessorCount);
prloBitmapList = new List<Bitmap>(priProcessorCount);
```

Now, we have a problem. We must prepare the application to run in computers having different cores and with diverse bitmaps. We must create as many bitmaps as the number of cores available, and that is a complex process. We use the rows to select a similar number of rows for each bitmap portion.

We define a variable `liStartRow` of type `int`, as the starting row from where we will begin cropping the original bitmap:

```
int liStartRow = 0;
```

Then, we must determine the approximate number of rows for each bitmap:

```
int liEachBitmapHeight = ((int)(proOriginalBitmap.Height /
                          priProcessorCount)) + 1;
```

However, depending on the number of cores and the original bitmap height, the result of this division might not be exact. That is another problem. Therefore, we use another `int` variable to calculate the height to be added to each iteration to solve that problem:

```
int liHeightToAdd = proOriginalBitmap.Height;
```

Then, the algorithm is simple; for each iteration of `liThreadNumber`:

```
if (liEachBitmapHeight > liHeightToAdd)
{
    liEachBitmapHeight = liHeightToAdd;
}
```

```
loBitmap = CropBitmap(proOriginalBitmap, new Rectangle(0, liStartRow,
                       proOriginalBitmap.Width, liEachBitmapHeight));
liHeightToAdd -= liEachBitmapHeight;
liStartRow += liEachBitmapHeight;
prloBitmapList.Add(loBitmap);
```

If the height calculated for each bitmap is greater than the height to be added (this could happen in the last bitmap portion to be cropped), we reduce this number from the height to be added, which is the result of this line in each iteration:

```
liHeightToAdd -= liEachBitmapHeight;
```

Besides, in each iteration, the starting row increases the height calculated for each bitmap.

> Each new portion of the original bitmap is completely independent of the previous one. Hence, it is completely safe for use in many independent concurrent threads.

The following image shows the results of applying this algorithm to the infrared portraits obtained by NASA's Spitzer Space Telescope with four threads:

Using our classic C# programming skills, we can generate smart algorithms for splitting the work into many independent blocks of safe concurrent code. Again, mastering the lists is indeed necessary in parallel programming.

Using flags to enhance control over concurrent threads

We used threads with parameters as we learned in the previous chapters, and we started them with an asynchronous execution with the following loop:

```
for (liThreadNumber = 0; liThreadNumber < priProcessorCount;
liThreadNumber++)
{
    prloThreadList[liThreadNumber].Start(liThreadNumber);
}
```

Nevertheless, we must wait until the concurrent stars finder threads finish their work in order to show the final modified bitmap in the UI. We do not want to use the BackgroundWorker component.

For this reason, we created the WaitForThreadsToDie procedure, which is called synchronously by the main application's thread. When this method returns, we can safely show the resulting bitmap in the UI because all the threads have finished their work. Of course, to achieve the same goal, we can also use the BackgroundWorker combined with the threads created as instances of the Thread class, as we learned in the previous chapters.

The code in the WaitForThreadsToDie procedure is complex because we have to check for each created thread and we know the number of threads at runtime, as they are dynamically aligned with the number of available cores. We use a bool flag to determine whether the while loop must go on running or not. However, in this case, we did not change the value of the flag, but there are other cases in which this code pattern could be useful for modifying the value of this variable used as a flag.

Once in the while (lbContinue) loop, we must check for each thread to finish its work. We use the well known IsAlive property:

```
for (liThreadNumber = 0; liThreadNumber < priProcessorCount;
    liThreadNumber++)
{
    if (prloThreadList[liThreadNumber].IsAlive)
    {
        break;
    }
    else
    {
        liDeadThreads++;
    }
}
```

If one thread is alive, we will exit the `for` loop. If all the threads are not alive, `liDeadThreads` will equal the total number of created threads. Hence, we will exit the outer loop:

```
if (liDeadThreads == priProcessorCount)
{
    break;
}
```

The `break;` line could be replaced by `lbContinue = false;` and we would achieve the same result.

If there is still a thread running, we call the `Sleep` method for the main thread and make it sleep for 100 milliseconds (0.1 seconds), and then reset the `liDeadThreads` variable:

```
Thread.Sleep(100);
liDeadThreads = 0;
```

The line with the call to the `Sleep` method is indispensable.

 One potential problem with the code above is that if we omit the call to the `Sleep` method, the `while` loop will simply consume the processing power of an entire core thereby making the application slow. We've explained this before, but it is very important to be considered when working with parallel and event-driven programming.

Using methods like these, and flags, we can have complete control over independent threads, without causing the classic problems related to concurrency, and the loss of control over the independent threads.

Rebuilding results to show in the UI

As mentioned earlier, when the call to the `WaitForThreadsToDie` method returns, we can safely show the resulting bitmap in the UI because all the threads have finished their work. Hence, we call the `ShowBitmapWithOldStars` procedure.

This method reproduces the work done when dividing the original bitmap into several independent portions, but in reverse order.

We repeat the height calculation process explained previously. Then, we must create a new bitmap with the whole width and height. This bitmap must hold the different portions aligned as they were extracted from the original bitmap:

```
loBitmap = new Bitmap(proOriginalBitmap.Width,
                      proOriginalBitmap.Height);
Graphics g = Graphics.FromImage((Image)loBitmap);
g.InterpolationMode = System.Drawing.Drawing2D.InterpolationMode.
                      HighQualityBicubic;
```

Therefore, we use the `Bitmap` constructor passing the original bitmap width and height as parameters to define its size. Then, we create a `Graphics` instance from the `Bitmap` typecast to an `Image` (the `Bitmap` class is a descendant of the `Image` class).

Once we have the `Graphics` instance, we must draw each bitmap image processed by each thread in its corresponding row (`liStartingRow`), which is calculated the same way we did it when separating the bitmap portions:

```
for (liThreadNumber = 0; liThreadNumber < priProcessorCount;
    liThreadNumber++)
{
    g.DrawImage(prloBitmapList[liThreadNumber], 0, liStartRow);
    liStartRow += liEachBitmapHeight;
}
```

Then, we are ready to show the rebuilt bitmap in the picturebox, `picStarsBitmap`:

```
picStarsBitmap.Image = loBitmap;
```

Besides, in each iteration, the starting row increases the height calculated for each bitmap.

 We are able to work with each bitmap processed by the independent threads because we are sure they have finished their work. We cannot do this when they are still changing pixels.

Decoupling the UI, we can generate impressive performance improvements changing basic linear programming algorithms.

The following image shows the results of applying this algorithm to the infrared portraits obtained by NASA's Spitzer Space Telescope processed by four threads:

The image shows the clear independency achieved by each thread.

Run the application changing the value of the `priProcessorCount` private variable from 1 to the number of available cores in your computer, and then compare the results.

> One of the most important drawbacks of this kind of multithreaded algorithms is that they require more memory to run than their single-threaded versions. Therefore, we must monitor their memory usage. The other is that some algorithms require cooperation between the concurrent threads. We will talk about this later.

Testing results with Performance Monitor and Process Explorer

Windows Performance Monitor can be helpful in monitoring the activities of the available cores while running these algorithms. When we are interested in achieving the best possible performance, we can test the results, monitoring each core's processing power usage.

The results of running the star finder process with four threads in a quad-core computer are shown in the following graph, with the four cores processing power usage generated by Windows Performance Monitor:

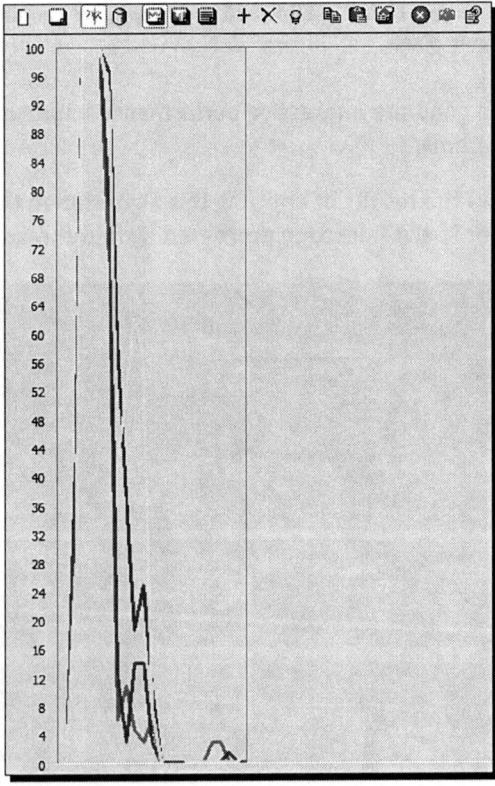

As we can see, the four cores work at full processing power concurrently in the first few seconds. That happens when the main application's thread and the four concurrent threads are running.

You still want to impress the NASA scientists with your knowledge on parallel programming. Hence, you show them the results of the application running in a quad-core notebook with a different number of concurrent threads, using the Process Explorer utility.

The following image shows the results with just one thread running the algorithm:

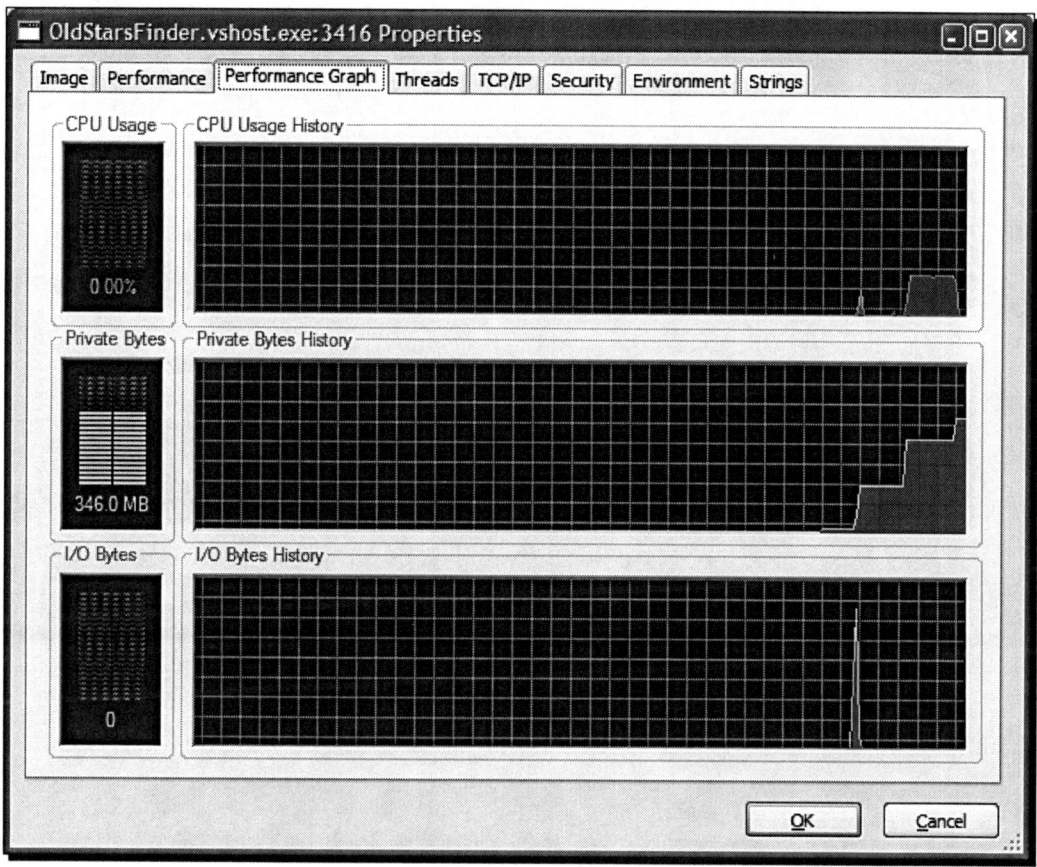

Now, look at the following image showing the results with only two threads running the algorithm:

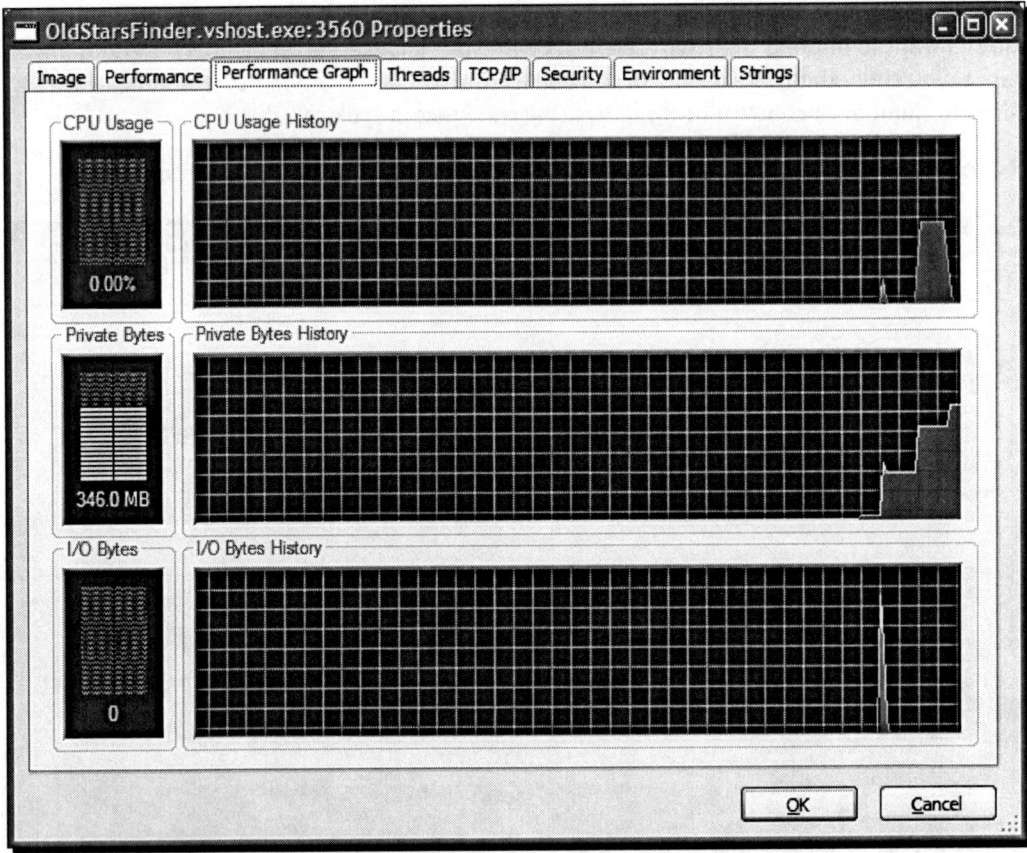

And now, the following image shows the results with four concurrent threads running the algorithm:

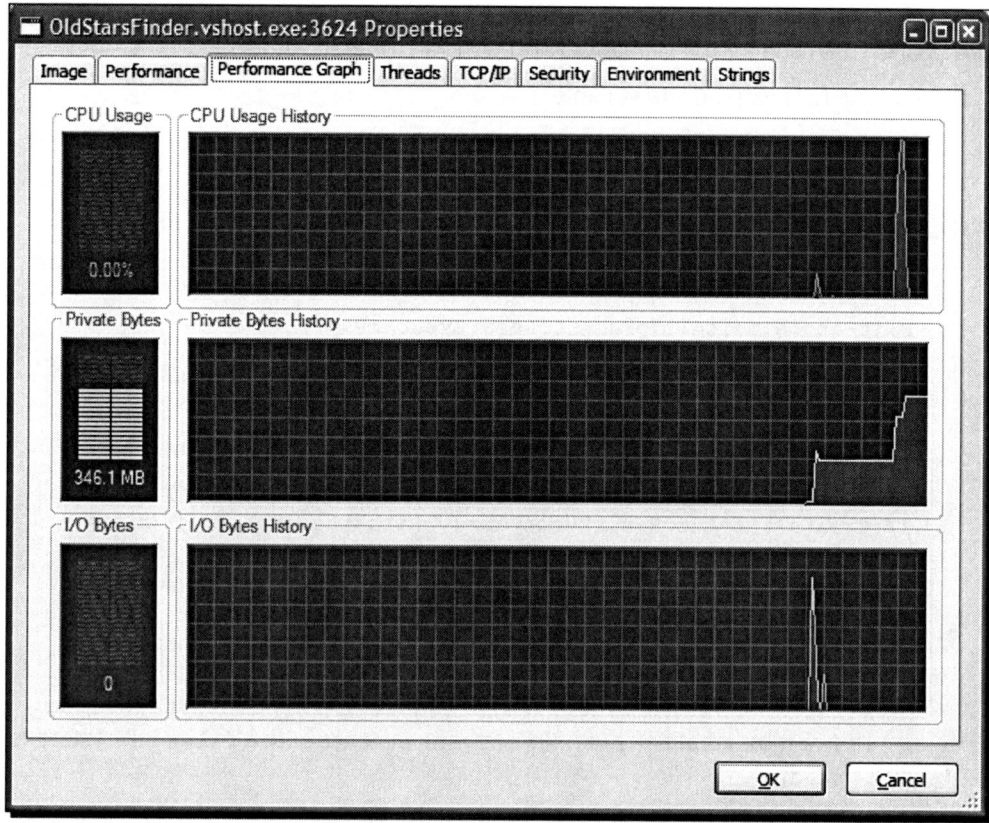

As we created completely independent processing blocks of code for each thread, we avoided bottlenecks and hence achieved a very high performance algorithm.

Congratulations! You have impressed the NASA scientists with your fantastic work!

Time for action –Waiting for the threads' signals

There are more elegant ways to wait for the various concurrent threads to finish their work. The WaitForThreadsToDie procedure is easy to understand, but is not as elegant as expected.

Now, we are going to make some changes to the code in order to use **event wait handles** instead of using a loop to check for the threads that are alive:

1. Stay in the project, OldStarsFinder.
2. Open the code for Program.cs.

3. Replace the line `[STAThread]` with the following line (before the `Main` method declaration):

```
[MTAThread]
```

4. Open the code for the Windows Form, `Form1` (**frmStarsFinder**).

5. Add the following private variable:

```
// The AutoResetEvent instances array
private AutoResetEvent[] praoAutoResetEventArray;
```

6. Replace the code in the `WaitForThreadsToDie` method with the following line:

```
// Just wait for the threads to signal that every work item has
    finished
WaitHandle.WaitAll(praoAutoResetEventArray);
```

7. Add the following line of code in the local variables declaration of the `ShowBitmapWithOldStars` method, before the line `int liStartRow = 0;` (we must create the array according to the number of available cores):

```
// Create the AutoResetEvent array with the number of cores
    available
praoAutoResetEventArray = new AutoResetEvent[priProcessorCount];
```

8. Add the following line of code in the thread creation loop in the `ShowBitmapWithOldStars` method, before the line `prloThreadList.Add (new Thread(new ParameterizedThreadStart(ThreadOldStarsFinde r)));` (we must create an `AutoResetEvent` instance with a `false` initial state for each thread):

```
// Create a new AutoResetEvent instance for that thread with its
    initial state set to false
praoAutoResetEventArray[liThreadNumber] = new
    AutoResetEvent(false);
```

9. Add the following line of code at the end of the `ThreadOldStarsFinder` method (we must signal that the work item has finished):

```
// The thread finished its work. Signal that the work item has
    finished.
praoAutoResetEventArray[liThreadNumber].Set();
```

10. Build and run the application.

11. Click on the **Find old stars** button. After a few seconds (depending on the parallel processing capabilities of the computer) the W5 wispy star-forming region will be shown in the huge infrared portrait with the probable old stars shown in pure blue. You will not notice any changes in the application.

What just happened?

When the user clicks the **Find old stars** button:

1. The original image is divided in many independent bitmaps. Each portion will be assigned to a different thread.

2. Many threads and their auto-reset event handlers are created to allow communications between the threads.

3. The threads are started (executed asynchronously) with a parameter, so that they know which bitmap belongs to them.

4. Once each thread finishes its work, it signals that the work is done, setting the auto-reset event.

5. The main thread waits until all the star finder threads finish their work, waiting for all the necessary signals from the multiple auto-reset events.

6. Once all the threads finish their work, the main thread (the only one capable of touching the UI) rebuilds the divided bitmap and shows it in the picturebox control.

The code used to wait for all the threads to finish their work is easier and more elegant.

Using the AutoResetEvent class to handle signals between threads

An `AutoResetEvent` instance allows us to notify a waiting thread that an event has occurred. It is a subclass of the `WaitHandle` and `EventWaitHandle` classes.

 Event wait handles encapsulate operating-system-specific objects that wait for exclusive access to shared resources. Using them, it is easier to wait for the threads' signals to continue working when their jobs are done.

First, we have to create as many event wait handles as the number of threads. We do it in the following line, in the `FindOldStarsAndShowResult` method:

```
praoAutoResetEventArray = new AutoResetEvent[priProcessorCount];
```

We use an array because the `WaitAll` method receives an array of wait handles as a parameter.

Before creating each new instance of the `Thread` class, we create a new `AutoResetEvent` instance for each thread, with its initial state (a `bool` state) set to `false`:

```
praoAutoResetEventArray[liThreadNumber] = new AutoResetEvent(false);
```

Thus, each independent thread can access its own `AutoResetEvent` instance. Once the thread finishes its work, it signals that the job is done calling the `Set` method, as shown in the following line, at the end of the `ThreadOldStarsFinder` procedure:

```
praoAutoResetEventArray[liThreadNumber].Set();
```

The event wait handle initial state was `false`; now it is `true`.

Using the WaitHandle class to check for signals

On the other side, the main UI thread has to wait until all the concurrent star finder threads finish their work in order to show the final modified bitmap in the UI. Thus, it must wait for all the event handles to have their state set to `true`, instead of the initial `false`.

That happens when all the threads have finished their work and have called the `Set` method for their corresponding `AutoResetEvent` instance.

We can check that using a single line of code in the `WaitForThreadsToDie` method:

```
WaitHandle.WaitAll(praoAutoResetEventArray);
```

The `WaitAll` method will monitor all the event handles, waiting for their signals to change (the threads' completion). It receives an array of event handles as a parameter.

> We must change the application's threading model to a multithreaded apartment in order to be able to use the `WaitHandle.WaitAll` method. If we do not do so, the method call will fail and generate an exception. Therefore, we have to replace the line `[STAThread]`, before the main method declaration, with `[MTAThread]`.

Have a go hero – Pausing and restarting threads with flags

As mentioned earlier, there is still some work to be done. The NASA scientists were so amazed with your application that they had almost forgotten they needed to know the number of probable old stars. The application is not showing the result of the counting process on the screen!

Each thread has its own counter. You must show the total number.

However, they have images bigger than the one you used for the first execution and they would like to see some kind of progress information shown. As they are very impatient and very smart, they need as much information as possible for the process.

The application is not as responsive as you would like it to be. We discussed that in the previous chapters. Therefore, you will have to develop a new version of this application.

First, use a BackgroundWorker component to show the overall progress and the number of partially counted stars. You will have to translate the code in the `WaitForThreadsToDie` procedure to the new BackgroundWorker.

Be careful and follow this rule:

> To avoid locking problems, a variable (irrespective of whether it is a flag or not) whose value is changed in one thread can be read in another thread. But do take care not to change the values in both the threads. For example, you can test a flag in a thread and change it only in another thread to control the behavior of an independent thread. Nevertheless, avoid making changes in both the threads simultaneously, as there are still many things to be learned.

Use a variable as a flag to enable the possibility of pausing and restarting the star finder threads. Add buttons to take full control of this in the UI. Take into account everything we have learned about combining the BackgroundWorker component and the threads created by instances of the `Thread` class. You can do it!

The application still lacks some animations.

Enhance the application, saving the following information about each old star found by each thread by using instances of a new class:

- Relative X position: The current X position in the partial bitmap.
- Relative Y position: The current Y position in the partial bitmap.
- Absolute X position: The calculated X absolute position in the whole bitmap.
- Absolute Y position: The calculated Y absolute position in the whole bitmap.

Adding a new BackgroundWorker component or using the existing one, show the pixels in blue as they are counted using the calculated absolute coordinates. This way, you will not need to regenerate the bitmap and can provide an impressive real-time UI feedback.

Do not worry, it is just the number of concurrent threads you will need for your following applications. However, you still have a lot of work coming your way from the NASA scientists!

Pop quiz

1. When waiting for threads to finish their work:

   a. We can use a classic while loop

   b. We can use the `WaitHandle.WaitAll` method passing an `AutoResetEvent` instances array (one instance for each thread)

   c. We can use the `WaitHandle.WaitForAllThreadsToDie` method without parameters

2. When processing bitmaps, the best results are achieved when:

   a. Each thread has full access to the whole bitmap

   b. Each thread has full access to the whole bitmap for reading, and partial access for writing

   c. Each thread has an independent portion of the original bitmap

3. The picturebox control:

   a. Can be modified directly by threads created by the `Thread` class

   b. Can be modified directly by threads created by the `Thread` class with its `CanModifyControls` property set to `true`

   c. Can be modified only by the code in the main thread

4. When using flags in threads:

   a. It is convenient to modify it in only one thread and read it in the others without changing it

   b. They cannot be modified by any thread

   c. They can be modified freely by any thread, but they must be declared using the `<threadflag>` modifier

5. When we need to count a total number using many threads, it is convenient to:

   a. Use a shared member variable for all the threads

   b. Use a method that modifies a shared member variable for all the threads

   c. Use an independent variable for each thread, or an independent item in a list

Right answers:

1. b.

2. c.

3. c.

4. a.

5. c.

Summary

We learned a lot in this chapter about working with independent blocks of code when concurrency is not allowed, managing and coordinating those using new techniques different from the ones offered by the `Thread` class. Specifically, we covered:

- Developing applications applying innovative algorithms to generate portions from a huge piece, and using them to create very independent blocks of code to be run in multiple threads, thereby avoiding many classic concurrency problems

- Programming specific procedures for controlling the multiple threads's execution using flags, and avoiding locks

- Achieving an exhaustive control over asynchronous and synchronous execution, combining everything we had learned in the previous chapters

- Rebuilding results from independent portions and controlling when it is safe to do so

- Improving the UI decoupling when we need to change the contents of controls with considerable streams of data

- Applying patterns to use multithreading in non thread-safe components offered by the .NET framework

We also learned how to apply parallel algorithms to image processing, and the solutions to the most common problems when working with components not enabled for multithreading.

Now that we've learned about a more advanced way to work with concurrent threads, using completely independent blocks of code in a C# application using new code patterns, we're ready to study many new ways to easily and dynamically split jobs into pieces—which is the topic of the next chapter.

7
Dynamically Splitting Jobs into Pieces—Avoiding Problems

In order to dynamically split jobs into pieces without huge memory consumption, we can generalize the splitting procedures using object-oriented capabilities offered by the C# programming language and some .NET runtime tricks. In this chapter, we will improve our capabilities to split linear algorithms into parallelized ones, and we will create classes to simplify our work. Reading it and following the exercises we shall:

- ◆ Solve and avoid memory problems related to running concurrent threads many times
- ◆ Optimize multithreaded algorithms to improve their performance
- ◆ Discover how to generalize the complex job-splitting process
- ◆ Learn to uses classes in order to create simpler multithreaded code, while avoiding concurrency problems
- ◆ Discover how to use independent instance variables in multiple threads
- ◆ Learn to reclaim the unused memory in high-performance multithreaded code

Running split jobs many times

So far, we have developed applications applying innovative algorithms to generate separate portions from a huge piece and used them to create very independent blocks of code to be run in multiple threads. We achieved a great performance improvement and a better UI feedback while avoiding classic concurrency problems. However, we have been working with algorithms running just once. How can we have performance improvements achieved while running the split jobs many times, and in different situations?

C# **safe code** (managed code) uses a service that automatically reclaims unused memory. It is known as the system **garbage collector**. This way, programmers do not have to worry about freeing resources used by the different objects and data types—making the developer's life easier. However, when we split jobs into many concurrent threads, and we do that repeatedly, many times over, the garbage could create some trouble and degrade our applications' performance.

Working with single-threaded applications, we did not pay much attention to the system's garbage collector behavior. However, with multithreaded applications, it is convenient to use some techniques to prevent performance degradation and unnecessary usage of huge amounts of memory.

> By adding just a few lines of code, we can achieve impressive performance and memory usage improvements. As we did in the previous chapters, using some code patterns and techniques with C#, we can take our applications to the next level, as though by magic.

Time for action – Defining new methods for running many times

The NASA scientists want to run your old star finder application in batch mode, processing all the images found in a hard disk folder, using your powerful parallel algorithm. You need to make some changes to the original application to allow this to happen. However, you have never run intensive multithreaded algorithms many times. Will you have memory problems? You trust the C# garbage collector when you program applications.

First, we are going to create a new method for processing an individual bitmap. This way, we will be able to call it many times for each bitmap found in a folder:

1. Stay in the project, `OldStarsFinder`.

2. Add the following procedure, `FindOldStarsAndShowResult`. It will split the old star finding algorithm into many threads. Once all the threads finish their work, the procedure will rebuild the divided bitmap and show it in the picturebox control. It does not receive parameters, because it will use the `private Bitmap proOriginalBitmap`:

   ```
   private void FindOldStarsAndShowResult()
   {

   }
   ```

3. Copy the code in the `Click` event in the button **butFindOldStars** and paste it into the above-mentioned procedure.

4. Now, remove the following line of code in the `FindOldStarsAndShowResult` procedure:

```
proOriginalBitmap = new Bitmap(picStarsBitmap.Image);
```

What just happened?

The code required to find old stars and show the resulting bitmap in the picturebox control is now held in a procedure, already prepared for creating as many threads as the number of available cores. We must assign the corresponding `Bitmap` instance to the private variable `proOriginalBitmap` before calling this new method.

Time for action – Running a multithreaded algorithm many times

Now, we are going to make some changes to the application to run the old star finder algorithm (now held in the previously defined method) in batch mode, processing all the images found in a hard disk folder:

1. Stay in the project, `OldStarsFinder`.

2. Add the following lines of code at the beginning of the form class definition (as we are going to use the `System.IO.DirectoryInfo` and `System.IO.FileInfo` classes):

```
using System.IO;
```

3. Add a button control showing a star finder icon and with its `Text` property set to **Run batch old stars finder (butRunBatch)**. This button will call the `FindOldStarsAndShowResult` method and start it for each image file found in a folder.

4. Open the `Click` event in the button **butRunBatch**, and enter the following code (replace `"C:\\NASA"` with your images folder path):

```
DirectoryInfo loDirectory;
FileInfo[] loImageFiles;

// Replace "C:\\NASA" with your images folder path
loDirectory = new DirectoryInfo("C:\\NASA");
// Get the JPG files stored in the path
loImageFiles = loDirectory.GetFiles("*.JPG");

// Process each JPG image file found
foreach (FileInfo loNextImageFile in loImageFiles)
{
    // Store the Bitmap to be processed in the proOriginalBitmap
        private variable
    proOriginalBitmap = new Bitmap(Image.FromFile(
                        loNextImageFile.FullName));
```

```
FindOldStarsAndShowResult();

// Let the PictureBox control update the image
Application.DoEvents();
}
```

5. Reset the `picStarBitmap` picturebox `Image` property, because the images are now going to be read from the folder, and we are going to analyze some memory problems.

6. Copy the images to be analyzed into the specified folder (the default is `"C:\\NASA"`). You will need more than 10 images with the resolutions as explained in the previous chapter.

7. Build and run the application.

8. Click on the **Run batch old stars finder** button. The images will be shown with the probable old stars in pure blue, one after the other, with a lag of a few seconds (depending on the parallel processing capabilities of the computer), as shown in the following image:

(Image Credit: NASA, SSC, JPL, Caltech, Nathan Smith (Univ. of Colorado), et al.)

What just happened?

The NASA scientists are very happy with your batch old star finder, and they are going to run it in the main server with 10,000 huge resolution images. Keep your fingers crossed! If the garbage collector does not work fine with this highly multithreaded batch processes, the server will run out of memory very quickly. Start running as fast as you can!

We could easily transform a complex multithreaded algorithm capable of taking full advantage of parallel processing capabilities into a method. We can call this method every time we need it, without worrying about threads and available cores.

Using classes, methods, procedures, and functions with multithreading capabilities

As we have learned so far, it is very easy to combine our new multithreading and parallel processing capabilities with C# language possibilities to encapsulate and write better and simpler code.

Code re-use, classes, methods, procedures, and functions can work with multiple threads to offer easy and transparent behavior to other developers.

A multithreading expert can create the most complex parallelized algorithms and encapsulate them into classes and methods. Other classic C# programmers can call them as they are used to doing in classic linear programming.

 You can achieve incredible performance enhancements making small changes to big applications, beginning with the most processor-intensive classes and transforming them to multithreaded versions. Of course, this process can be easily accomplished in applications with good software architectures, taking into account everything you are learning. Spaghetti code should be completely rewritten before being converted into multithreaded code.

Time for action – Analyzing the memory usage

The NASA scientists noticed that the application had some performance problems as more images were processed. They noticed a very intensive activity in the disk subsystem, and they used the Windows Task Manager to view the memory usage. The application used too much memory! Why? You used managed code, and the garbage collector is supposed to avoid these memory problems. What's going on? Let's use Windows Task Manager and Process Explorer to understand what happens with the multithreaded code running many times. Hurry up! You do not want to disappoint the NASA scientists.

Now, we are going to monitor the application memory usage with Windows Task Manager and Process Explorer while it is running. This way, we will be able to understand the problems related to the garbage collector with multithreaded applications:

1. Stay in the project, `OldStarsFinder`.

2. Run the application.

3. Open the Windows Task Manager in the **Performance** tab.

4. Open the Process Explorer. Right-click on the **OldStarsFinder.vshost.exe** process and select **Properties**. Show the **Performance graph** tab.

5. Click on the **Run batch old stars finder** button. The images will be shown with the probable old stars in pure blue, one after the other, with a lag of a few seconds. The Windows Task manager will show an increasing memory usage, as shown in the following image:

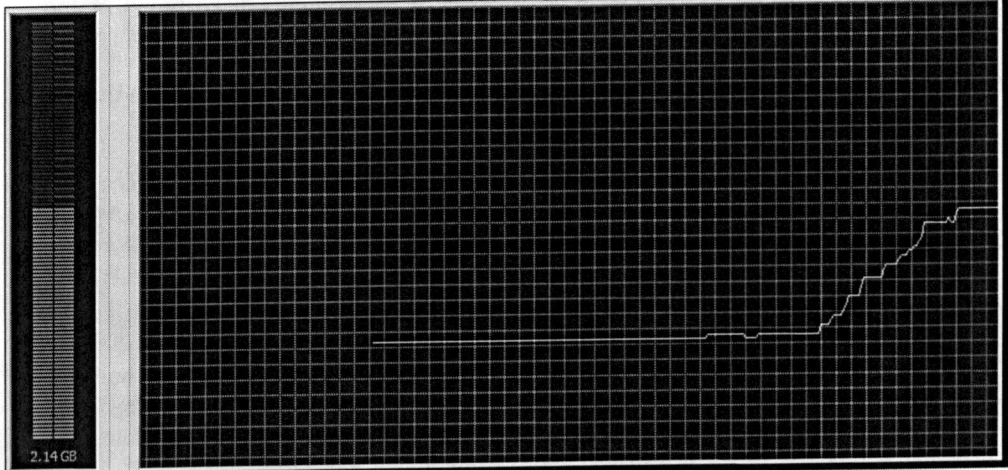

What just happened?

One of the main advantages C# has over older programming languages such as C++ and C is that it was born with a garbage collection system. Thus, the programmer does not have to focus on retrieving the memory used by created objects and data types. The runtime environment does that job. However, we have a memory problem with our application when we run the same algorithm many times.

Process Explorer shows the private bytes used by the application after running the algorithm on many images:

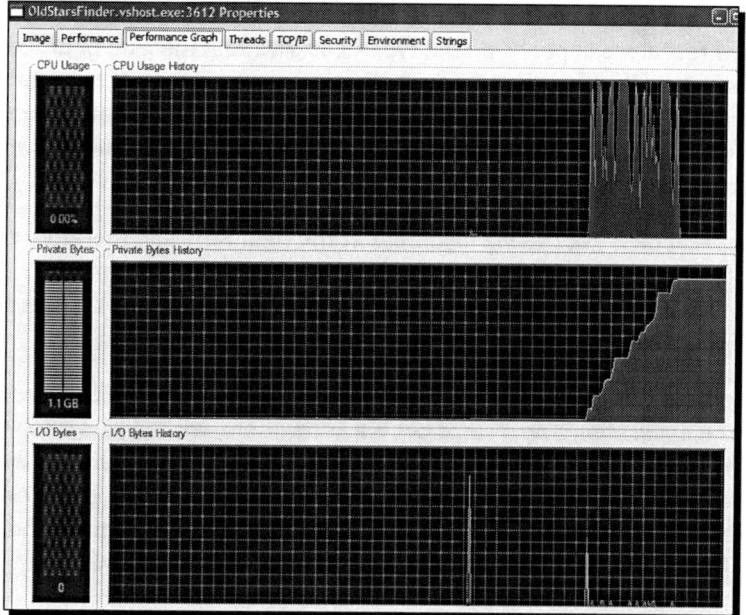

As we can see, the garbage collector is not guessing the right moment to reclaim the unused memory.

Does this mean that we must free every created resource as in old-fashioned C++ or C code? That is a nightmare for C# programmers!

Do not worry; it is not necessary to do that. Adding just a single line of code, in the right place, will solve the problem easily.

Understanding the garbage collector with multithreading

Using a garbage collection system has great advantages. The programmer forgets about freeing resources and focuses on creating efficient algorithms to solve problems. At runtime, a garbage collection system will free the unused memory when it considers it necessary.

However, it has two main disadvantages:

- The programmer loses control over the precise moment at which the resource is freed. Thus, the memory consumption and the available resources during certain circumstances become quite unpredictable.

- The garbage collection service is single-threaded! Yes, it runs in a single thread. Hence, when the garbage collection service is executed, our multithreaded application degrades its performance heavily.

It is very difficult to create a perfect garbage collection service, because the right time to free the unused resources depends on the type of application, the kind of process, the algorithms, and so on. Besides, the garbage collection service does not have fortune-telling abilities. It cannot guess precisely what the application is going to do next. Event-driven programming combined with multithreaded code is the most unpredictable world for a garbage collection service.

Our sample application is not freeing resources at the right time and therefore consumes a great quantity of memory, more than necessary to process the old star finder algorithm efficiently for each image. Besides, the application loses performance as it uses too much memory, and would have to be swapped to the hard disk soon.

How can we sort out this great mess? It is very simple. As the garbage collection service cannot guess the application's next steps but we know them, we can give it some advice and force it to do its work—collect the garbage at a certain time. This way, we can avoid huge memory consumption and poor performance. If the garbage collector service executes while the multiple threads are running, as it runs in a single thread, it will degrade the algorithm's performance. Hence, we must find the right time to force the collection.

It is just a single line of code in the right place. Leave the vacuum cleaner; it is not necessary for this kind of garbage!

Time for action – Collecting the garbage at the right time

The NASA scientists are waiting for you to solve the problem. They bring you a cappuccino, but then it reminds you of your exhausting work with the FBI agents. You prefer an orange juice!

Now, we are going to force the garbage collection service to free unused resources before running the algorithm on each image. This way, the memory consumption will not increase after each image is processed, and we will avoid the possibility of the garbage collection service being executed automatically in the middle of the intensive multithreaded code:

1. Stay in the project, `OldStarsFinder`.

2. Add the following line before the `for (liThreadNumber = 0; liThreadNumber < priProcessorCount; liThreadNumber++)` loop that calls the `Start` method for each created thread in the `FindOldStarsAndShowResult` procedure (this line forces a garbage collection):

```
// Call the garbage collector before starting each thread
GC.Collect(GC.MaxGeneration, GCCollectionMode.Forced);
```

3. Run the application.

4. Open the Windows Task Manager in the **Performance** tab.

5. Open the Process Explorer. Right-click on the **OldStarsFinder.vshost.exe** process and select **Properties**. Show the **Performance graph** tab.

6. Click on the **Run batch old stars finder** button. The Windows Task manager will show a very stable memory usage as shown in the following image:

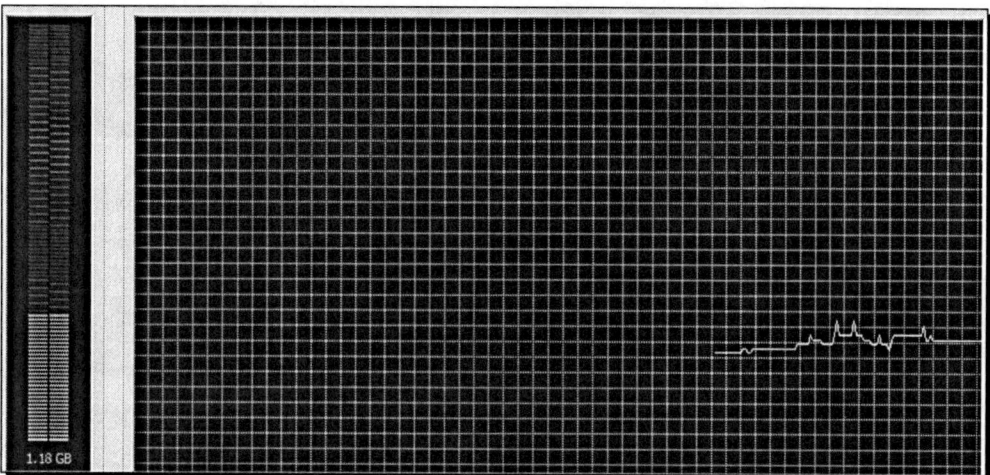

What just happened?

The NASA scientists have been running the application for twelve hours and the memory usage is completely stable. They are transferring huge images from other observatories all over the world because they want to process all of them with your high performance application. Just one line of code can make people so happy!

We did not have to free every used resource individually. Forcing the garbage collection service to do its work at the right time solved the memory problem and handled the degrading performance.

We can also see the difference in the private bytes used by the application after running the algorithm on many images with the Process Explorer, as shown in the following image:

Controlling the system garbage collector with the GC class

The key to controlling the system garbage collector is the `GC` (`System.GC`) class. This class offers many static methods to control its behavior.

We do not want to create a new optimized garbage collector based on the one offered by C# and .NET. We just want it to be more accurate when we are working with high performance multithreaded applications and want to avoid huge memory consumption.

The following line of code calls the `Collect` method:

```
GC.Collect(GC.MaxGeneration, GCCollectionMode.Forced);
```

This method has many implementations. We call it using two parameters:

◆ The maximum **generation** to be collected
◆ The collection mode

The garbage collection service takes into account how long the objects have been in memory in order to plan the memory reclaim process. Hence, the objects that can be reclaimed to free their memory belong to different **generations**. We can call the `Collect` method to collect a single generation or up to a specific generation number.

As we want to collect all the generations, we use the `GC.MaxGeneration` property that returns the maximum number of supported generations and ensures us a complete unused memory reclaim process, no matter which generation the objects belong to. We could use a fixed number, but we do want it to be compatible with future changes in the C# and .NET garbage collection service.

 No matter which way we force it to happen, the garbage collection service does not free objects that can be referenced. We are always talking about dead object references.

We want the garbage collection to happen before starting the new threads and not during their execution. Hence, we must tell the `Collect` method to force the collection to happen at that moment—with a synchronous execution. For that reason, we use the `GCCollectionMode.Forced` mode as the second parameter for the `GC.Collect` method call.

 It is a recommended practice to force a garbage collection to happen before starting an intensive multithreaded algorithm.

Avoiding garbage collection problems

In our experience, forcing a garbage collection at the right time could make big changes to our applications' performance. Nevertheless, forcing unnecessary garbage collections in multithreaded applications can also degrade performance. We must keep a reasonable balance.

Preparing applications to take full advantage of parallel processing capabilities requires taking control of some aspects that we usually leave in the hands of the compiler and the runtime environment. As modern applications are event-driven and multithreaded, we must help the runtime environment to take better decisions. Besides, as the programmers are the ones who know the best moment to force a garbage collection according to the multithreaded application architecture and their algorithms, there isn't just a single formula.

However, we must avoid garbage collection happening in the middle of multithreaded code, and we can easily detect automatic garbage collection problems and the memory usage dilemma using Process Explorer and even the Windows Task Manager while running our applications.

An inefficient single-threaded garbage collection can degrade our multithreaded performance improvements, because splitting jobs into pieces generates more work for the garbage collector service.

 Forcing the collection in the right place is the key to success. So do not trust the runtime environment's fortune-telling capabilities!

Avoiding inefficient processing usage problems

We could easily transform code placed in a button's `Click` event handler into a method that can perform intensive multithreaded processing many times. However, in this kind of batch processing, there is another issue to take into account.

Using the Process Explorer with four threads and a quad-core computer, we can see very clearly that there are times when one, two, or three cores are waiting for one thread to finish, as shown in the following image:

There is an inefficient processing usage problem caused by differences in the time it takes each thread to complete its part of the global job. The `WaitForThreadsToDie` procedure is guilty!

It does not matter whether `WaitForThreadsToDie` uses a loop or a call to the `WaitHandle.WaitAll` method. It generates the same problem in both the versions.

This method was useful when running the old star finder once, but when we call it time and again, it wastes available processing time. It will wait until all the threads finding the stars finish, to show the results. Therefore, the situation shown in the following diagram can happen:

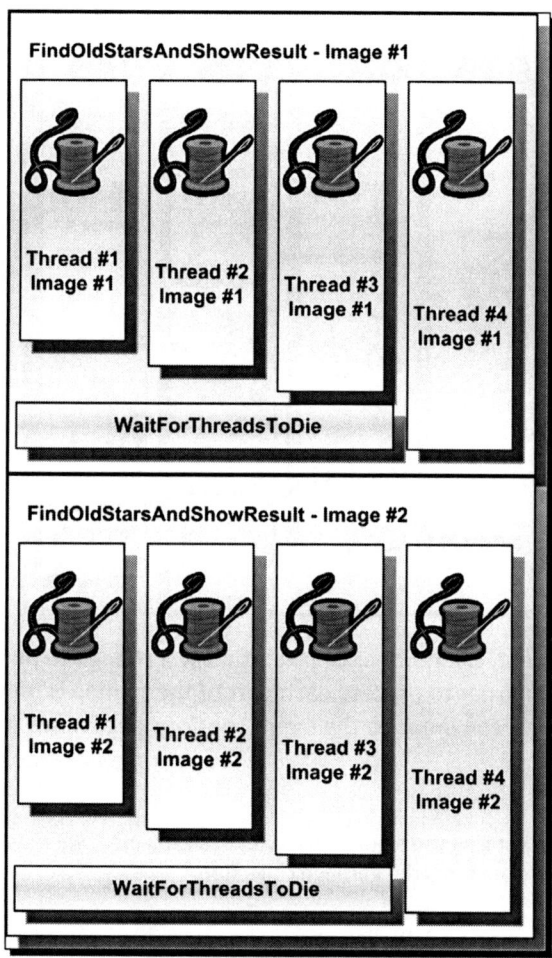

Some threads can finish before the others, and the cores in which they were running would be available for executing new threads. Nevertheless, as the `WaitForThreadsToDie` procedure is executed synchronously waiting for all the threads to finish, this processing power is wasted in the batch process.

We do not know which thread is going to finish first. It is impossible to know that, because the operating system is always running additional threads and processes. Therefore, we can achieve a better performance starting threads one after the other and beginning to process parts of the next image while waiting for the other threads to finish the current image.

We can see it more clearly in the following diagram, representing an ideal situation:

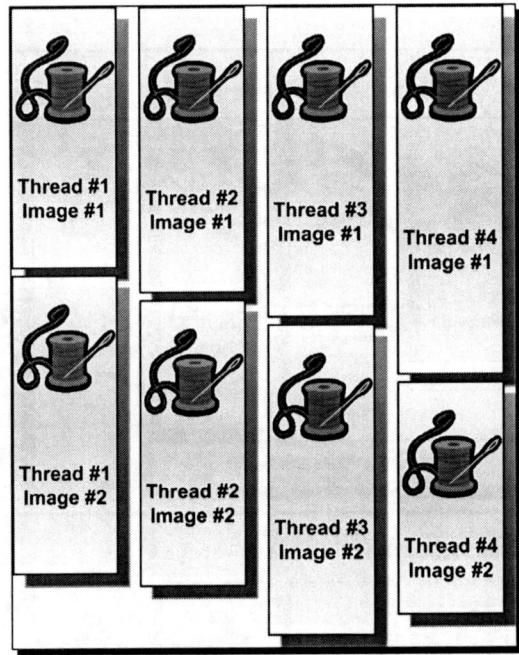

As the images are different, the number of pixels that will change to pure blue is diverse, and the time required in order to process each part of the bitmap is unknown. Queuing one thread after the other, we can improve the overall performance more than 20% in this kind of application.

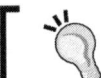 However, changing the algorithm to work as explained, we must modify the place where we force the garbage collection.

In this case, we could force a garbage collection based on the number of images processed because we do not have an exact point when there is a complete image. We cannot find an ideal situation, because the garbage collection service will run in a single thread, and will freeze the running threads for some milliseconds.

Parallel programming requires developers to be pragmatic and to test each critical process in order to determine which multithreaded algorithm achieves the best performance and memory consumption balance.

Have a go hero – Queuing threads and showing progress

The NASA scientists want to process as many images as possible in their servers. Thus, they request you to improve the performance a bit more. If you do this, they promise to let you play with your friends in a zero gravity cabin! That sounds cool! Imagine you and your friends bouncing uncontrollably about the cabin like human popcorn! Then you will find the required motivation to work with more multithreading!

Create a new version of this application that queues the threads for processing each part of the images one after the other, without wasting processing time.

Use a BackgroundWorker to show that each image is completely processed. You will have to translate the code in the `WaitForThreadsToDie` procedure to the new BackgroundWorker, and you have to make all the necessary changes to allow the application to begin processing a new image while other threads are finishing the previous one.

You will need some additional lists to save the previous image data. You can do it! We have been working with threads, lists, and the BackgroundWorker in many ways!

Be careful with the changes in the code and with the algorithm you use to determine the time to force the garbage collection.

Now, using the `GC.GetTotalMemory` function, create another version that forces the garbage collection when this method returns an amount of allocated memory space that you consider is too large for the application needs.

Show your results to the NASA scientists and enjoy the zero gravity cabin!

Retrieving the total memory thought to be allocated

The `GC.GetTotalMemory` function retrieves the number of bytes currently thought to be allocated by the managed runtime.

Calling this method, we can compare memory use with the amount of memory we consider our application should use, and force a garbage collection when necessary.

It receives a `bool` parameter. Passing it a `true` value will generate a garbage collection and then return a `long` with the number of bytes thought to be allocated (it is not the exact number, but a very precise approximation). As we studied another way to force a garbage collection, it is convenient to call it with a `false` value as a parameter in order to avoid two unnecessary garbage collections that would degrade performance.

Generalizing the algorithms for segmentation with classes

So far, we have been developing applications that split work into multiple independent jobs, improve performance, and offer a more responsive UI. We worked hard with lists, replaced linear algorithms with parallel ones, and collected many results to generate a single block while avoiding locking and memory usage problems. However, we used methods (procedures and functions) to create the jobs split into pieces. C# is an object-oriented programming language and offers many possibilities to generalize behaviors needed to simplify our code and to avoid repeating the same code on every new application. How can we use C# object-oriented capabilities to simplify the creation of segmented algorithms prepared for running each piece in an independent thread?

The answer is very simple; creating a new class with the most common needs for executing an algorithm in multiple threads. Thus, we can inherit from this base class to define new classes according to the needs of different kinds of algorithms. It sounds exciting because we can combine multithreading with object-oriented capabilities to reduce our development time.

 Besides, using a class to generalize the process of splitting a linear algorithm into many pieces will make it easier for the developers to focus on generating very independent parts that will work very well in a multithreading environment.

Time for action – Creating a parallel algorithm piece class

The NASA scientists are amazed with the miracles of parallel programming. Their servers are running your application, taking full advantage of the installed processing power. You enjoyed bouncing in the zero gravity cabin, but it is time to help them again.

Now, they want you to create new applications running different parallel algorithms to determine the young stars, the potential planets, and the comets based on many color analysis techniques that benefit from multithreading.

You are a legendary lover of object-oriented programming. Thus, you want to create classes to organize the process of splitting a linear algorithm into many pieces, and then fill the gaps in the skeleton to create each new application.

First, we are going to create a class to represent each piece of the parallel algorithm, and hold each `Thread` class instance. This way, we will be able to call a method for splitting any number of elements into pieces, and automatically distributing them without additional effort:

1. Stay in the project, `OldStarsFinder`.
2. Create a new class, `ParallelAlgorithmPiece`.

3. Add the following lines of code at the beginning of the class definition (as we are going to use many `System.Threading` classes):

```
using System.Threading;
```

4. Add the following private variables:

```
// The element to begin processing
private long priBegin = 0;
// The element to end processing (inclusive)
private long priEnd = 0;
// The thread number
private int priThreadNumber = 0;
// The thread
private Thread proThread;
// The AutoResetEvent instance for the thread
private AutoResetEvent proAutoResetEvent;
```

5. Add the following properties to access the private variables (we want to create a compact and reliable class):

```
public Thread poThread
{
    get
    {
        return proThread;
    }
    set
    {
        proThread = value;
    }
}

public long piBegin
{
    get
    {
        return priBegin;
    }
    set
    {
        priBegin = value;
    }
}

public long piEnd
{
    get
```

```
        {
            return priEnd;
        }
        set
        {
            priEnd = value;
        }
    }

    public long piThreadNumber
    {
        get
        {
            return priThreadNumber;
        }
    }

    public AutoResetEvent poAutoResetEvent
    {
        get
        {
            return proAutoResetEvent;
        }
        set
        {
            proAutoResetEvent = value;
        }
    }
}
```

What just happened?

The code to define the first and the last element to be processed by a thread is now held in the `ParallelAlgorithmPiece` class. The instances of this class will be a real independent part of an algorithm. Everything we need to access from each thread for the algorithm must be in the instance of this class.

For example, if we need a portion of a bitmap, we must add a new instance variable.

The properties are:

- `poThread`: The `Thread` class instance that will be in charge of this piece of the whole process
- `piBegin`: The first element to be processed by the thread
- `piEnd`: The last element to be processed by the thread

- ◆ `piThreadNumber`: The number of the thread for identification purposes
- ◆ `poAutoResetEvent`: The `AutoResetEvent` class instance that will allows us to notify a waiting thread that an event has occurred

Time for action – Using a generic method in order to create pieces

Creating the pieces and assigning the first and the last element numbers that correspond to each one is a complex task. We want it to be a generic algorithm to help us in focusing on the parallelization process, and not on the splitting problem.

Now, we are going to add some methods to the `ParallelAlgorithmPiece` class to simplify the splitting assignment:

1. Stay in the project, `OldStarsFinder`.

2. Add the following static function to return a list of `ParallelAlgorithmPiece` instances:

```
public static List<ParallelAlgorithmPiece> CreatePieces(long
 priTotalElements, int priTotalParts)
{
    // Always starts in element #0
    long liPieceSize;
    List<ParallelAlgorithmPiece> lloPieces;
    int i;
    long liTotalCovered = 0;

    liPieceSize = (long)(priTotalElements / priTotalParts);

    lloPieces = new List<ParallelAlgorithmPiece>(priTotalParts);
    for (i = 0; i < priTotalParts; i++)
    {
        lloPieces[i] = new ParallelAlgorithmPiece();
        lloPieces[i].priBegin = liTotalCovered;
        lloPieces[i].priEnd= liTotalCovered + (liPieceSize - 1);
        lloPieces[i].priThreadNumber = i;
        if (lloPieces[i].priEnd > (priTotalElements - 1))
        {
            lloPieces[i].priEnd = priTotalElements;
        }
        liTotalCovered += liPieceSize;
        if (liTotalCovered >= priTotalElements)
        {
            break;
        }
    }
    return lloPieces;
}
```

3. Add an empty `ThreadMethod` method (this is the method that will hold the thread code, having access to the instance variables):

```
public void ThreadMethod(object poThreadParameter)
{
    // This is the code that is going to be run by the thread
    // It has access to all the instance variable of this class
    // It receives the instance as a parameter
    // We must typecast poThreadParameter to
       ParallelAlgorithmPiece

    // When the work finishes, we must call
    // poAutoResetEvent.Set();
}
```

What just happened?

Now, we have a complete skeleton for the piece of algorithm defined in the `ParallelAlgorithmPiece` class.

Filling the gaps, we can split the most complex algorithms into independent pieces dynamically, according to the number of available cores or the number of cores designated to the application by the user.

The `ThreadMethod` method will hold the code for the thread. It receives the well-known `object poThreadParameter` parameter. However, it will be the corresponding instance of the `ParallelAlgorithmPiece` class assigned to that thread. Thus, casting the `object poThreadParameter` parameter to `ParallelAlgorithmPiece`, we will have a reference to the instance of `ParallelAlgorithmPiece` and hence, full access to the instance variables that are exclusive to the thread and completely independent of the others.

 Object-oriented programming provides excellent tools to avoid the most common threading problems. Each piece must be independent. Everything it needs to run must be an instance variable in the `ParallelAlgorithmPiece` class.

Once the work is finished, we must call the `poAutoResetEvent.Set` method to communicate that the thread has completed its job using an event handle.

Creating the pieces

The `CreatePieces` static function returns a list with as many `ParallelAlgorithmPiece` instances as specified in the `int priTotalParts` parameter.

For example, if we call this method with the following parameters, `priTotalElements = 10,000` and `priTotalParts = 4`, the result will be a list of `ParallelAlgorithmPiece` with the values shown in the following table:

List element #	priBegin	priEnd	priThreadNumber
0	0	2499	0
1	2500	4999	1
2	5000	7499	2
3	7500	9999	3

And, if we call this method with the following parameters, `priTotalElements = 9,000` and `priTotalParts = 3`, the result will be a list of `ParallelAlgorithmPiece` with the values shown in the following table:

List element #	priBegin	priEnd	priThreadNumber
0	0	2999	0
1	3000	5999	1
2	6000	8999	2

It does not matter whether the pieces are pixels, lines, elements of a list, or such. The class returns instances telling each thread where to begin and where to end.

The method uses a very simple algorithm for generalization of the segmentation. Using it, we can transform a great many linear algorithms into parallelized algorithms.

Time for action – Creating a parallel algorithm coordination class

We have the pieces, but we must now create the class to solve the puzzle. The class must offer us everything we need to know (up to this chapter) to create an efficiently parallelized algorithm:

1. Stay in the project, `OldStarsFinder`.

2. Create a new class, `ParallelAlgorithm`.

3. Add the following lines of code at the beginning of the class definition (as we are going to use many `System.Threading` classes):

   ```
   using System.Threading;
   ```

4. Add the following public variable (the list of pieces):

   ```
   public List<ParallelAlgorithmPiece> prloPieces;
   ```

5. Add the following private variable (the `AutoResetEvent` instances array):

```
// The AutoResetEvent instances array
private AutoResetEvent[] praoAutoResetEventArray;
```

6. Add the following public method to dynamically create the pieces and the corresponding threads according to the total number of elements and the parts into which they must be split:

```
public void CreateThreads(long priTotalElements,
                          int priTotalParts)
{
    // priTotalParts should be Environment.ProcessorCount in most
      cases
    prloPieces = ParallelAlgorithmPiece.CreatePieces(
              priTotalElements, priTotalParts);
    foreach (ParallelAlgorithmPiece loPiece in prloPieces)
    {
        // Create the new thread with parameters
        loPiece.poThread = new Thread(new
         ParameterizedThreadStart(loPiece.ThreadMethod));
        // Give the thread a name
        loPiece.poThread.Name = loPiece.piThreadNumber.
                                ToString();
        // Create a new AutoResetEvent instance for that thread
            with its initial state set to false
        loPiece.poAutoResetEvent = new AutoResetEvent(false);
        praoAutoResetEventArray[loPiece.piThreadNumber] =
         loPiece.poAutoResetEvent;
    }
}
```

7. Add the following public method to start creating the threads with an asynchronous execution and sending the corresponding `ParallelAlgorithmPiece` instance as a parameter:

```
public void StartThreadsAsync()
{
    foreach (ParallelAlgorithmPiece loPiece in prloPieces)
    {
        // Send the corresponding ParallelAlgorithmPiece instance
            as a parameter
        loPiece.poThread.Start(loPiece);
    }
}
```

What just happened?

Now, we have the code to call the piece creation function, assign a thread to each piece, and start it in the new `ParallelAlgorithm` class.

The `CreateThreads` method will receive the same parameters explained previously for the `ParallelAlgorithmPiece` class `CreatePieces` static function. In fact, it calls that function to create the number of requested pieces.

Completing the `ParallelAlgorithmPiece` class and using an instance of the `ParallelAlgorithm` class, we can split a complex algorithm and start executing its threads asynchronously. It is easier than coding from scratch for each new application. It represents an object-oriented approach, taking into account everything we have learned so far.

Starting the threads associated to the pieces

The following lines of code create a new instance of the `ParallelAlgorithm` class, create independent pieces and threads according to the number of available cores and the elements in a string list (`loStringList`), and start the threads' execution asynchronously:

```
ParallelAlgorithm loParallelAlgorithm;
loParallelAlgorithm = new ParallelAlgorithm();
loParallelAlgorithm.CreateThreads(loStringList.Count,
                                  Environment.ProcessorCount)
loParallelAlgorithm.StartThreadsAsync();
```

Of course, the string list parts should be accessible as instance variables of the `ParallelAlgorithmPiece` instances, and the `ThreadMethod` must be programmed to do something related to the algorithm.

 It is easier to focus on the algorithm using these classes, because we do not have to worry about the splitting process, the pieces, and the threads. We just have to think how to code each piece. The new classes do the rest!

Accessing instances and variables from threads' methods

A great advantage of these classes is to allow a thread to be encapsulated in an instance of the `ParallelAlgorithmPiece` class. It is easier to make the threads more independent, and we can make the necessary paradigm shift with less effort to reproduce the algorithm in a parallelized environment.

The `StartThreadsAsync` procedure calls the `Start` method for each thread and sends the corresponding `ParallelAlgorithmPiece` instance for that thread as a parameter:

```
public void StartThreadsAsync()
{
    foreach (ParallelAlgorithmPiece loPiece in prloPieces)
    {
        loPiece.poThread.Start(loPiece);
    }
}
```

Thus, as mentioned earlier, casting the thread method object parameter to `ParallelAlgorithmPiece`, we can access all the information we need for that thread and can save the results in instance variables, completely independent from the other threads.

We can use some tricks to access the information from the other threads, but we want to keep each piece as independent as possible to avoid complex concurrency problems. Our life in multithreaded land will be easier if we avoided unwanted problems.

Time for action – Adding useful classic coordination methods

Now that we have a `ParallelAlgorithm` class, we can add methods with the well-known techniques we've used so far, and can use them as needed in our applications. Remember that the class must offer us everything we know (up to this chapter) is needed for an efficiently parallelized algorithm:

1. Stay in the project, `OldStarsFinder`.

2. Add the following public static method to force a garbage collection:

```
public static void ForceGarbageCollection()
{
    GC.Collect(GC.MaxGeneration, GCCollectionMode.Forced);
}
```

3. Add the following public method to run the multiple created threads in a synchronous execution:

```
public void RunInParallelSync()
{
    StartThreadsAsync();
    WaitForMyThreadsToDie();
}
```

4. Add the following public method to wait for the threads to finish their execution and not return the control until that happens, using event handles:

```
WaitHandle.WaitAll(praoAutoResetEventArray);
```

5. Add an empty `CollectResults` method (this is the method that will hold the code to collect the results saved in the instance variables of the multiple `ParallelAlgorithmPiece` instances):

```
public void CollectResults()
{
    // Enter the results collection iteration through the results
        left in each ParallelAlgorithmPiece
}
```

What just happened?

Now we have a more complete `ParallelAlgorithm` class, with more methods to offer a skeleton for parallelizing different kinds of algorithms with lesser effort than involved in the previous examples.

Instead of remembering how to wait for the threads to die to go on with the results presentation method, we can now call the `WaitForMyThreadsToDie` method. Another way is to call the `RunInParallelSync` method instead of calling the `StartThreadsAsync` method.

The `WaitForMyThreadsToDie` method is very simple, because we are using event handles to synchronize information about the multiple threads. A non-elegant version of this method can allow us to understand how to wait for the threads to finish their work using more complex loops.

```
public void WaitForMyThreadsToDie()
{
    // A bool flag
    bool lbContinue = true;
    int liDeadThreads = 0;
    while (lbContinue)
    {
        foreach (ParallelAlgorithmPiece loPiece in prloPieces)
        {
            if (loPiece.poThread.IsAlive)
            {
                // One of the threads is still alive, exit the for
                    loop and sleep 100 milliseconds
                break;
            }
            else
```

```
            {
                // Increase the dead threads count
                liDeadThreads++;
            }
        }
        if (liDeadThreads == prloPieces.Count)
        {
            // All the threads are dead, exit the while loop
            break;
        }
        Thread.Sleep(100);
        liDeadThreads = 0;
    }
}
```

As we can see, using event handles simplifies the code when we must coordinate many dynamically created threads.

The `ParallelAlgorithm` class offers us the choice between synchronous and asynchronous execution of the multiple, dynamically generated threads.

Besides, we can combine this new class with the ease of use of the BackgroundWorker component to update the UI and show progress information.

When we need to force a garbage collection, we will not have to remember the parameters, as we will use the `ForceGarbageCollection` method added to the class.

Have a go hero – Splitting algorithms specializing classes

Now that you have the new classes, you must create new applications, and complete the `ParallelAlgorithmPiece` and the `ParallelAlgorithm` classes.

First, the NASA scientists want you to find planets very similar to Mars in the images corresponding to different galaxies. In these images, a planet like that will be represented by a pure red pixel. If you find a red pixel, you must not change the pixel color, but save the coordinates as you did in your mission in the previous chapter.

However, as you took some time to write the new classes you will have to use them in this new application. They want you to explain it to the NASA CIO (Chief Information Officer) who came from Massachusetts to see your work in person.

Do not modify the older code; create a new Windows form and make the necessary changes to the classes to find the planets and show the coordinates in a grid with absolute X and Y positions for each planet found. Use them combined with the BackgroundWorker component.

You can do it! We have been working with threads, lists, and the BackgroundWorker in many ways. Now, you have to use your object-oriented C# programming abilities.

Would you like to live in Massachusetts?

Pop quiz

1. In order to achieve the best performance when running multithreaded split jobs, it is convenient to:
    a. Force a garbage collection of all generations before starting the threads
    b. Force a garbage accumulation of all generations before starting the threads
    c. Force a garbage collection before calling the `Thread.Sleep` method

2. The `GC.GetTotalMemory` function:
    a. Retrieves the total number of bytes of memory used by the operating system
    b. Retrieves the number of bytes currently thought to be allocated by the managed runtime
    c. Retrieves the number of CPU cycles used by each memory access

3. The `ParallelAlgorithmPiece` class:
    a. Holds a thread as an instance variable
    b. Does not hold a thread as an instance variable
    c. Holds a thread created by a BackgroundWorker component

4. The `ParallelAlgorithm` class:
    a. Coordinates the BackgroundWorker components created by the `ParallelAlgorithmPiece` class instances
    b. Coordinates the `ParallelAlgorithmPiece` class instances and their threads
    c. Coordinates the operating system scheduler

5. Which of the following lines of code forces a garbage collection of all generations:
    a. `GarbageCollector.ForceAllGenerationsCollection();`
    b. `GC.PrepareForParallelCode(GC.MaxGeneration, GCCollectionMode.Forced);`
    c. `GC.Collect(GC.MaxGeneration, GCCollectionMode.Forced);`

Right answers:

1. a.
2. b.
3. a.
4. b.
5. c.

Summary

We learned a lot in this chapter about improving the memory usage in heavy multithreading applications, managing and coordinating the garbage collection service, and using an object-oriented approach for splitting jobs into well-managed pieces, easily and dynamically. Specifically, we covered:

♦ Calling specific methods to control the garbage collection and solving memory problems related to running concurrent threads many times

♦ Reclaiming unused memory at the right time to avoid running out of memory space in heavy duty algorithms

♦ Developing highly optimized multithreaded algorithms

♦ Creating new classes to easily generalize the complex job splitting process and to control everything related to parallelized algorithms with multiple threads

♦ Improving the independence of threads filling the gaps of classes with a generalized skeleton

We also learned how the garbage collection service works, and how to detect memory problems when working with multiple threads.

Now that we've learned about a more general way to work with parallel algorithms using classes in C#, we're ready to simplify the complexity of some advanced concurrent programming difficulties—which is the topic of the next chapter.

Simplifying Parallelism Complexity

In order to apply everything that we have learned so far, we must go on using the object-oriented capabilities offered by the C# programming language and design patterns to simplify parallelism complexity and avoid many concurrency pains. In this chapter, we will drastically simplify the creation of new parallelized code avoiding some advanced concurrent programming difficulties. Reading this chapter and following the exercises we shall:

- Learn to combine single-threaded code with multithreaded code
- Use of object-oriented design patterns to simplify the creation of parallelized code
- Solve various problems to specialize in segmentation algorithms and achieve thread affinity
- Encapsulate multithreaded algorithms to create high-performance and safer independent pieces
- Learn to avoid problems with design instead of solving them using very difficult-to-apply algorithms

Specializing the algorithms for segmentation with classes

So far, we have been developing applications that split work into multiple independent jobs and created classes to generalize the algorithms for segmentation. We simplified the creation of segmented and parallelized algorithms, generalizing behaviors to simplify our code and to avoid repeating the same code on every new application. However, we did not do that using **inheritance**, a very powerful object-oriented capability that simplifies code re-use. C# is an object-oriented programming language that supports inheritance and offers many possibilities to specialize behaviors to simplify our code and to avoid some **synchronization problems** related to parallel programming. How can we use C# object-oriented capabilities to define specific segmented algorithms prepared for running each piece in an independent thread using `ParallelAlgorithm` and `ParallelAlgorithmPiece` as the base classes?

The answer is very simple—by using inheritance and the **factory method** class creational pattern (also known as **virtual constructor**). Thus, we can advance into creating a complete framework to simplify the algorithm optimization process. Again, we can combine multithreading with object-oriented capabilities to reduce our development time and avoid synchronization problems.

 Besides, using classes to specialize the process of splitting a linear algorithm into many pieces will make it easier for the developers to focus on generating very independent parts that will work well in a multithreading environment, while avoiding **side-effects**.

Time for action – Preparing the parallel algorithm classes for the factory method

You made the necessary changes to the `ParallelAlgorithmPiece` and the `ParallelAlgorithm` classes to possibly find planets similar to Mars in the images corresponding to different galaxies.

NASA's CIO was impressed with your parallel programming capabilities. Nevertheless, he is an object-oriented guru, and he gave you the advice to apply the factory method pattern to specialize the parallel algorithm classes in each new algorithm. That could make the code simpler, more re-usable, and easier to maintain.

He asked you to do so. The NASA scientists would then bring you another huge image processing challenge for your parallel programming capabilities—a sunspot analyzer. If you resolve this problem using the factory method pattern or something like that, he will hire you! However, be careful, because you must avoid some synchronization problems!

First, we are going to create a new project with tailored versions of the `ParallelAlgorithmPiece` and `ParallelAlgorithm` classes. This way, later, we will be able to inherit from these classes and apply the factory method pattern to specialize in parallel algorithms:

1. Create a new C# Project using the Windows Forms Application template in Visual Studio or Visual C# Express. Use `SunspotsAnalyzer` as the project's name.

2. Open the code for `Program.cs`.

3. Replace the line `[STAThread]` with the following line (before the `Main` method declaration):

   `[MTAThread]`

4. Copy the file that contains the original code of the `ParallelAlgorithmPiece` and the `ParallelAlgorithm` classes (`ParallelAlgorithm.cs`) and include them in the project.

5. Add the `abstract` keyword before the declarations of the
`ParallelAlgorithmPiece` and the `ParallelAlgorithm` classes, as shown in
the following lines (we do not want to create instances directly from these
abstract classes):

```
abstract class ParallelAlgorithmPiece
abstract class ParallelAlgorithm
```

6. Change the `ThreadMethod` method declaration in the `ParallelAlgorithmPiece`
class (add the `abstract` keyword to force us to override it in subclasses):

```
public abstract void ThreadMethod(object poThreadParameter);
```

7. Add the following public abstract method to create each parallel algorithm piece in
the `ParallelAlgorithm` class (the key to the factory method pattern):

```
public abstract ParallelAlgorithmPiece
CreateParallelAlgorithmPiece(int priThreadNumber);
```

8. Add the following constructor with a parameter to the
`ParallelAlgorithmPiece` class:

```
public ParallelAlgorithmPiece(int priThreadNumberToAssign)
{
    priThreadNumber = priThreadNumberToAssign;
}
```

9. Copy the original code of the `ParallelAlgorithmPiece` class `CreatePieces`
method and paste it in the `ParallelAlgorithm` class (we move it to allow
creation of parallel algorithm pieces of different subclasses). Replace the
`lloPieces[i].priBegin` and `lloPieces[i].priEnd` private variables' access
with their corresponding public properties access `lloPieces[i].piBegin` and
`lloPieces[i].piEnd`.

10. Change the new `CreatePieces` method declaration in the `ParallelAlgorithm`
class (remove the static clause and add the `virtual` keyword to allow us to
override it in subclasses and to access instance variables):

```
public virtual List<ParallelAlgorithmPiece>
  CreatePieces(long priTotalElements, int priTotalParts)
```

11. Replace the line `lloPieces[i] = new ParallelAlgorithmPiece();` in the
`CreatePieces` method declaration in the `ParallelAlgorithm` class with the
following line of code (now the creation is encapsulated in a method, and also, a
great bug is corrected, which we will explain later):

```
lloPieces.Add(CreateParallelAlgorithmPiece(i));
```

12. Comment the following line of code in the `CreatePieces` method in the
`ParallelAlgorithm` class (now the new `ParallelAlgorithmPiece` constructor
assigns the value to `piThreadNumber`):

```
//lloPieces[i].piThreadNumber = i;
```

13. Replace the line `prloPieces = ParallelAlgorithmPiece.`
    `CreatePieces(priTotalElements, priTotalParts);` in the
    `CreateThreads` method declaration in the `ParallelAlgorithm` class with
    the following line of code (now the creation is done in the new `CreatePieces`
    method):

    ```
    prloPieces = CreatePieces(priTotalElements, priTotalParts);
    ```

14. Change the `StartThreadsAsync` method declaration in the `ParallelAlgorithm`
    class (add the `virtual` keyword to allow us to override it in subclasses):

    ```
    public virtual void StartThreadsAsync()
    ```

15. Change the `CollectResults` method declaration in the `ParallelAlgorithm`
    class (add the `abstract` keyword to force us to override it in subclasses):

    ```
    public abstract void CollectResults();
    ```

What just happened?

The code required to create subclasses to implement algorithms, following a variation of the
factory method class creational pattern, is now held in the `ParallelAlgorithmPiece` and
`ParallelAlgorithm` classes.

Thus, when we create new classes that will inherit from these two classes, we can easily
implement a parallel algorithm. We must just fill in the gaps and override some methods,
and we can then focus on the algorithm problems instead of working hard on the
splitting techniques.

We also solved some bugs related to the previous versions of these classes.

Using C# programming language's excellent object-oriented capabilities, we
can avoid many problems related to concurrency and simplify the development
process using high-performance parallel algorithms. Nevertheless, we must
master many object-oriented design patterns to help us in reducing the
complexity added by multithreading and concurrency.

Defining the class to instantiate

One of the main problems that arise when generalizing an algorithm is that the generalized
code needed to coordinate the parallel algorithm must create instances of the subclasses
that represent the pieces.

Using the concepts introduced by the factory method class creational pattern, we
solved this problem with great simplicity. We made the necessary changes to the
`ParallelAlgorithmPiece` and `ParallelAlgorithm` classes to implement a
variation of this design pattern.

First, we added a constructor to the `ParallelAlgorithmPiece` class with the thread or piece number as a parameter. The constructor assigns the received value to the `priThreadNumber` private variable, accessed by the `piThreadNumber` property:

```
public ParallelAlgorithmPiece(int priThreadNumberToAssign)
{
    priThreadNumber = priThreadNumberToAssign;
}
```

The subclasses will be able to override this constructor to add any additional initialization code.

We had to move the `CreatePieces` method from the `ParallelAlgorithmPiece` class to the `ParallelAlgorithm` class. We did this because each `ParallelAlgorithm` subclass will know which `ParallelAlgorithmPiece` subclass to create for each piece representation. Thus, we also made the method virtual, to allow it to be overridden in subclasses. Besides, now it is an instance method and not a static one.

There was an intentional bug left in the previous `CreatePieces` method. As you must master lists and collections management in C# in order to master parallel programming, you should be able to detect and solve this little problem. The method assigned the capacity, but did not add elements to the list. Hence, we must use the add method using the result of the new `CreateParallelAlgorithmPiece` method.

```
lloPieces.Add(CreateParallelAlgorithmPiece(i));
```

The creation is now encapsulated in this method, which is virtual, and allows subclasses to override it. The original implementation is shown in the following lines:

```
public virtual ParallelAlgorithmPiece CreateParallelAlgorithmPiece
(int priThreadNumber)
{
    return (new ParallelAlgorithmPiece(priThreadNumber));
}
```

It returns a new `ParallelAlgorithmPiece` instance, sending the thread or piece number as a parameter.

Overriding this method, we can return instances of any subclass of `ParallelAlgorithmPiece`. Thus, we let the `ParallelAlgorithm` subclasses decide which class to instantiate.

> This is the principle of the factory method design pattern. It lets a class defer instantiation to subclasses. Hence, each new implementation of a parallel algorithm will have its new `ParallelAlgorithm` and `ParallelAlgorithmPiece` subclasses.

We made additional changes needed to keep conceptual integrity with this new approach for the two classes that define the behavior of a parallel algorithm that splits work into pieces using multithreading capabilities.

Preparing the classes for inheritance

Apart from implementing a variation of the factory method design pattern, we had to prepare the classes for inheritance. We must override methods in order to create specialized classes. Therefore, we had to change some methods' declarations to make them **virtual**.

We must override the following methods in a `ParallelAlgorithmPiece` subclass:

♦ **The constructor**. This is used to call the base constructor and append any additional initialization code that is needed. Remember that constructors do not require the virtual keyword.

♦ **ThreadMethod**. This is the code that is going to be run by the thread.

We must override the following methods in a `ParallelAlgorithm` subclass:

♦ **The constructor**. This is used to call the base constructor and append any additional initialization code that is needed. Remember that constructors do not require the virtual keyword.

♦ **CreateParallelAlgorithmPiece**. This is used to return a new instance of a specific `ParallelAlgorithmPiece` subclass.

♦ **StartThreadsAsync**. This is used to append any additional code needed before or after starting the threads with an asynchronous execution.

♦ **CollectResults**. This is used to collect the results left in each `ParallelAlgorithmPiece` subclass instance.

Once the classes are prepared for a common parallel algorithm with job splitting capabilities, we must create the subclasses and fill in the gaps.

 In order to simplify parallel programming, it is very important to master inheritance and design patterns as well as many other object-oriented code re-use techniques. Simpler code is easier to maintain. C# is a very powerful language, and you can use that power to simplify multithreaded applications.

Time for action – Creating a specialized parallel algorithm piece subclass

Now, you have just created two subclasses and programmed the UI management code in order to create any split job, multithreaded algorithm. The NASA scientists have a keen interest in analyzing sunspots. However, the colors offered by the original, very high-resolution images make it difficult to generate the stream inputs necessary for the servers to make graphs about the sunspots' evolution.

They want you to help them in developing a simple application that has to invert the colors of many of these huge images, because there is no software that is able to work with this huge number of pixels. In the following image, you can see an image taken by Hinode's Solar Optical Telescope on November 20, 2006:

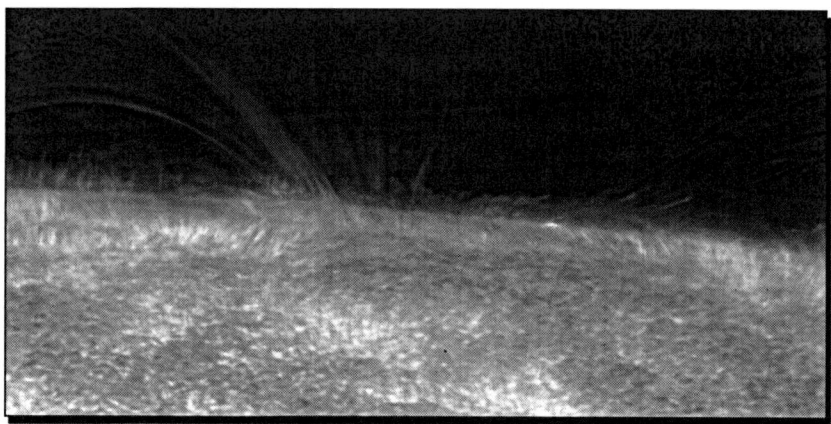

(Image credit: Hinode JAXA/NASA)

This image reveals the structure of the solar magnetic field rising vertically from a sunspot outward into the solar atmosphere. A sunspot is an area of strong magnetic field.

You have to work on a very fast and very efficient image color inverter, capable of changing the pixel colors to their opposite in the huge image, to make them capable of streaming to the statistics servers. NASA's CIO wants you to use a very fine-tuned multithreading application based on subclasses to demonstrate your object-oriented capabilities combined with parallel programming knowledge. Of course, the algorithm must be capable of working with as many threads as the number of cores available in the computer in which the sunspot analyzer algorithm is being executed.

First, we are going to create a subclass of the `ParallelAlgorithmPiece` class and fill in the gaps, overriding the necessary methods to define the code to be executed for each piece. Thus, we are going to represent each piece of the sunspot analyzer parallel algorithm:

1. Stay in the project, `SunspotsAnalyzer`.

2. Create a new class, `SunspotAnalyzerPiece` (a subclass of `ParallelAlgorithmPiece`) using the following declaration:

```
class SunspotAnalyzerPiece : ParallelAlgorithmPiece
```

3. Add the following lines of code at the beginning (as we are including the classes in a new application that does not know anything about drawing, we are going to use the `System.Drawing` classes):

```
using System.Drawing;
```

4. Add the following private variable:

```
// The resulting bitmap
private Bitmap proBitmap;
```

5. Add the following property to access the private variable (we want to create a compact and reliable class):

```
public Bitmap poBitmap
{
    set
    {
        proBitmap = value;
    }
    get
    {
        return proBitmap;
    }
}
```

6. Add a new constructor with a parameter that calls the base constructor:

```
public SunspotAnalyzerPiece(int priThreadNumberToAssign)
    : base(priThreadNumberToAssign)
{
    // Add any necessary additional instructions

}
```

7. Override the `ThreadMethod` method with the code that is going to be run by the thread:

```
public override void ThreadMethod(object poThreadParameter)
{
    // This is the code that is going to be run by the thread
    // It has access to all the instance variable of this class
    // It receives the instance as a parameter
    // We must typecast poThreadParameter to SunSpotAnalyzerPiece
        (inherited from ParallelAlgorithmPiece) to gain access to
```

```
        its members
SunspotAnalyzerPiece loPiece;
loPiece = (SunspotAnalyzerPiece)poThreadParameter;

// Retrieve the thread number received in object
   poThreadParameter, in piThreadNumber property
long liPieceNumber = loPiece.piThreadNumber;
// The pixel matrix (bitmap) row number (Y)
int liRow;
// The pixel matrix (bitmap) col number (X)
int liCol;
// The pixel color
Color loPixelColor;

// Iterate through each pixel matrix (bitmap) row
for (liRow = 0; liRow < proBitmap.Height; liRow++)
{
    // Iterate through each pixel matrix (bitmap) col
    for (liCol = 0; liCol < proBitmap.Width; liCol++)
    {
        // Get the pixel Color for liCol and liRow
        loPixelColor = proBitmap.GetPixel(liCol, liRow);
        // Change the pixel color (invert the color)
        proBitmap.SetPixel(liCol, liRow, Color.FromArgb((
            Int32.MaxValue - loPixelColor.ToArgb()))));
    }
}
}
```

What just happened?

The code to define the work done in the pieces of the algorithm is now held in the new `SunspotAnalyzerPiece` class (a subclass of `ParallelAlgorithmPiece`). The instances of this class are real independent parts of the sunspot analyzer algorithm. Everything we need to access from each thread for the algorithm resides in the instance of this class.

 Look at the code. It is very simple to understand, compared to the code in our previous examples. We needed a bitmap and the code to invert it. That was exactly what we added. We forgot about splitting the work into many pieces, because that is done by the `ParallelAlgorithmPiece` and `ParallelAlgorithm` superclasses.

Now we have completed the skeleton for the piece of an algorithm defined as a subclass of the `ParallelAlgorithmPiece` class.

Creating a complete piece of work

First, we added the variables and properties needed for the piece of work. We will be working with a portion of a bitmap. So, we defined the `proBitmap` private variable and its `poBitmap` property.

Then, we defined a constructor with the same parameter used in the base class:

```
public SunspotAnalyzerPiece(int priThreadNumberToAssign)
    : base(priThreadNumberToAssign)
```

This declaration calls the base constructor (`ParallelAlgorithmPiece` constructor) with the `priThreadNumberToAssign` received as a parameter, and allows us to add additional initialization code if any. We are therefore overriding the construction, but calling the base class constructor.

Then, we had to override the `ThreadMethod` method. This is the method that will run the code for each created thread (for each piece). We declared it with the same parameters as those in the base class:

```
public override void ThreadMethod(object poThreadParameter)
```

It receives the well-known `object poThreadParameter` parameter. However, it will be the corresponding instance of the `SunspotAnalyzerPiece` class assigned to that thread. Thus, casting the `object poThreadParameter` parameter to `SunspotAnalyzerPiece`, we will have a reference to the instance of `SunspotAnalyzerPiece` and hence, full access to the instance variables that are exclusive for the thread and completely independent of the others:

```
SunspotAnalyzerPiece loPiece;
loPiece = (SunspotAnalyzerPiece)poThreadParameter;
```

We define a `loPiece` local variable with the `SunspotAnalyzerPiece` type, in order to avoid having to cast to `SunspotAnalyzerPiece` many times. The code is easier to understand this way.

> If we create other subclasses of the `ParallelAlgorithmPiece`, we must change the casting according to the subclass name in order to gain access to all its member variables and properties.

Writing the code for a thread in an instance method

Developing multithreaded algorithms using static members is easy because most types of public static members are **thread-safe**. Nevertheless, writing real-life applications based on this rule is impossible.

You will find this text in Microsoft Visual Studio helpful in many cases:

> *All public static (Shared in Visual Basic) members of this type are thread-safe. No instance member is guaranteed to be thread-safe.*

We do need instance members for real-life applications. They create risks when we do not follow certain rules when programming multithreaded applications. However, it is the only way to create real-life applications and parallel algorithms that do something interesting—not just display numbers in the console output.

Hence, we write the code to be run in each thread in an instance method of the `SunspotAnalyzerPiece` class, which has access to those instance variables. It is a very independent block of code. Of course, it has some problems and trade-offs, but its main goal is to make it possible to split a huge task into many concurrent pieces.

Once the code retrieves its instance, it iterates through each pixel matrix (bitmap rows and columns) and inverts the colors in the following line of code:

```
proBitmap.SetPixel(liCol, liRow, Color.FromArgb((Int32.MaxValue -
                   loPixelColor.ToArgb()))));
```

We take the maximum value of the `Int32` data type to obtain the difference between this and the pixel color converted to an `Int32` Alpha, Red, Green, Blue value. It is simple, pure mathematics.

As we are working in our piece of the bitmap, we begin the row number in 0, and take into account its `Height` property:

```
for (liRow = 0; liRow < proBitmap.Height; liRow++)
```

 The possibility of accessing the instance corresponding to the thread makes it very easy to create highly independent blocks of code. Besides, it allows us to reduce the possibility of generating synchronization problems.

Time for action – Creating a specialized parallel algorithm coordination subclass

We have the pieces (instances of `SunspotAnalyzerPiece`), but now we must create the subclass to create and solve the sunspot analyzing algorithm.

We are going to create a subclass of the `ParallelAlgorithm` class and add the variables, properties, and methods needed for the sunspot analyzer algorithm. Thus, we are going to begin representing the sunspot analyzer parallel algorithm:

1. Stay in the project, `SunspotsAnalyzer`.

2. Create a new class, `SunspotAnalyzer` (a subclass of `ParallelAlgorithm`), using the following declaration:

```
class SunspotAnalyzer : ParallelAlgorithm
```

3. Add the following lines of code at the beginning, as we are going to use the `System.Drawing` classes):

```
using System.Drawing;
```

4. Add the following private variables (the original bitmap and the resulting one, the bitmaps list, and the total number of pieces or threads):

```
// The Bitmap
private Bitmap proOriginalBitmap;
// The resulting bitmap
private Bitmap proBitmap;
// The bitmaps list
private List<Bitmap> prloBitmapList;
// The total number of pieces
private int priTotalPieces;
```

5. Add the following properties to access the private variables (we want to create a compact and reliable class):

```
public Bitmap poBitmap
{
    get
    {
        return proBitmap;
    }
}
public int piTotalPieces
{
    get
    {
        return priTotalPieces;
    }
}
```

6. Add a constructor with a parameter (the bitmap to analyze or invert):

```
public SunspotAnalyzer(Bitmap proBitmap)
{
    proOriginalBitmap = proBitmap;
    // Create threads taking into account the number of lines in
        the bitmap and the number of available cores
```

```
      priTotalPieces = Environment.ProcessorCount;
      CreateThreads(proOriginalBitmap.Height, priTotalPieces);
      CreateBitmapParts();
}
```

7. Add the following function, `CropBitmap`. It will crop the bitmap received as a parameter and return the portion of the original defined by the `Rectangle` `proRectangle`:

```
private Bitmap CropBitmap(Bitmap proBitmap, Rectangle
                          proRectangle)
{
    // Create a new bitmap copying the portion of the original
       defined by proRectangle and keeping its PixelFormat
    Bitmap loCroppedBitmap = proBitmap.Clone(proRectangle,
                             proBitmap.PixelFormat);
    // Return the cropped bitmap
    return loCroppedBitmap;
}
```

8. Add the following procedure, `CreateBitmapParts`. It will assign the bitmap part corresponding to each piece:

```
private void CreateBitmapParts()
{
    // Create the bitmap list
    prloBitmapList = new List<Bitmap>(priTotalPieces);
    int liPieceNumber;

    Bitmap loBitmap;
    for (liPieceNumber = 0; liPieceNumber < priTotalPieces;
         liPieceNumber++)
    {
        loBitmap = CropBitmap(proOriginalBitmap, new Rectangle(0,
                   (int) prloPieces[liPieceNumber].piBegin,
                   proOriginalBitmap.Width, (int) (prloPieces
                   [liPieceNumber].piEnd -
                   prloPieces[liPieceNumber].piBegin + 1)));
        prloBitmapList.Add(loBitmap);

        // Assign the bitmap part corresponding to the piece
        ((SunspotAnalyzerPiece)prloPieces[liPieceNumber]).poBitmap
           = loBitmap;
    }
}
```

What just happened?

We added the necessary variables, properties, and methods strictly related to a bitmap algorithm. We could have created a `BitmapParallelAlgorithm` class instead of directly working on the `SunspotAnalyzer` class.

The code to work with specific Bitmap pieces is now held in the new `SunspotAnalyzer` class (a subclass of `ParallelAlgorithm`). The instance of this class will constitute a very simple-to-use algorithm. We must override everything we need to complete the methods, as the algorithm coordination resides in the instance of this class.

[ Look at the new code. It is very simple to add the necessary things we need to the new subclass, because we can focus on the algorithm problems and forget about the multithreading complexity. The complex coordination work is done by the `ParallelAlgorithm` superclass.]

Now we have completed the skeleton for the piece of an algorithm defined as a subclass of the `ParallelAlgorithmPiece` class.

Creating simple constructors

We created a very simple constructor that receives a `Bitmap` as a parameter:

```
public SunspotAnalyzer(Bitmap proBitmap)
```

It saves the original bitmap in the `proOriginalBitmap` private variable and creates the threads taking into account the number of lines in that bitmap and the number of available cores. However, this is accomplished by calling the `CreateThreads` method, defined in the `ParallelAlgorithm` superclass, using these simple lines:

```
priTotalPieces = Environment.ProcessorCount;
CreateThreads(proOriginalBitmap.Height, priTotalPieces);
```

It also saves the total number of pieces in the `priTotalPieces` private variable because we will need them later.

Then, it calls the specific `CreateBitmapParts` method. Again, we could have created a `BitmapParallelAlgorithm` class, but we must simplify the example.

The constructor leaves everything prepared to start running the threads without any additional method calls.

We already know the `CreateBitmapParts` method and the `CropBitmap` function. They work the same way they did in the previous examples. However, in this case, the `CreateBitmapParts` method takes into account the `piBegin` and `piEnd` properties for each piece defined, as shown in the following lines of code in the loop:

```
loBitmap = CropBitmap(proOriginalBitmap, new Rectangle(0,
    (int) prloPieces[liPieceNumber].piBegin, proOriginalBitmap.Width,
    (int) (prloPieces[liPieceNumber].piEnd
        - prloPieces[liPieceNumber].piBegin + 1)));
        prloBitmapList.Add(loBitmap);
    ((SunspotAnalyzerPiece)prloPieces[liPieceNumber]).poBitmap =
        loBitmap;
```

In the last line, it casts `prloPieces[liPieceNumber]` to `SunspotAnalyzerPiece` because it must access its `poBitmap` property, which is exclusive of the subclass. It assigns the bitmap part corresponding to that piece.

 These classes also help us to make a paradigm shift and begin thinking about the algorithms as pieces and a coordination work.

Time for action—Overriding methods in the coordination subclass

We have created the algorithm coordination subclass, and added the variables, properties, and methods needed for the sunspot analyzer algorithm.

Now, we are going to fill in the gaps overriding the necessary methods to define the code for creating and coordinating the pieces. Thus, we are going to represent the complete sunspot analyzer parallel algorithm:

1. Stay in the project, `SunspotsAnalyzer`.

2. Move to the `SunspotAnalyzer : ParallelAlgorithm` class code area.

3. Override the `StartThreadsAsync` method to force a garbage collection before starting the threads with an asynchronous execution:

```
public override void StartThreadsAsync()
{
    // Call the garbage collector before starting each thread
    ForceGarbageCollection();
    // Run the base code
    base.StartThreadsAsync();
}
```

4. Override the `CreateParallelAlgorithmPiece` method with the code that is going to create the specific piece instance:

```
public override ParallelAlgorithmPiece
    CreateParallelAlgorithmPiece(int priThreadNumber)
{
    return (new SunspotAnalyzerPiece(priThreadNumber));
}
```

5. Override the `CollectResults` method with the code that is going to join the pieces (in this case, the bitmaps):

```
public override void CollectResults()
{
    // Enter the results collection iteration through the results
    //    left in each ParallelAlgorithmPiece
    int liPieceNumber;
    // Each bitmap portion
    Bitmap loBitmap;

    // Create a new bitmap with the whole width and height
    loBitmap = new Bitmap(proOriginalBitmap.Width,
                            proOriginalBitmap.Height);
    Graphics g = Graphics.FromImage((Image)loBitmap);
    g.InterpolationMode = System.Drawing.Drawing2D.
                            InterpolationMode.HighQualityBicubic;

    for (liPieceNumber = 0; liPieceNumber < priTotalPieces;
        liPieceNumber++)
    {
        // Draw each portion in its corresponding absolute
        //    starting row
        g.DrawImage(prloBitmapList[liPieceNumber], 0,
                        prloPieces[liPieceNumber].piBegin);
    }
    // Assign the generated bitmap to proBitmap
    proBitmap = loBitmap;

    g.Dispose();
}
```

What just happened?

The code required to implement the sunspot analyzer algorithm is now held in the `SunspotAnalyzerPiece` and `SunspotAnalyzer` classes.

Thus, creating an instance of the `SunspotAnalyzer` class, we can easily invert any bitmap using as many threads as the number of available cores. We have filled in the gaps and have overridden some methods focusing on the algorithm problems instead of working hard on splitting techniques.

> Using C# object-oriented capabilities and some design patterns, we can design complete frameworks prepared for taking full advantage of parallel processing capabilities, avoiding the most common concurrency problems without too much code overhead.

Look at the code in the two subclasses. It is very easy to understand, and is also very well encapsulated.

We added a call to the `ForceGarbageCollection` method in the overridden `StartThreadsAsync` procedure. As we learned in the previous cases, forcing the garbage collector before starting the threads is a good practice. Then, we called the base code, because the behavior is then the same as in the superclass. The following line of code does that:

```
base.StartThreadsAsync();
```

Programming the piece creation method

We had to override the `CreateParallelAlgorithmPiece` method. This method will create the appropriate instance of a `ParallelAlgorithmPiece` subclass:

```
public override ParallelAlgorithmPiece
        CreateParallelAlgorithmPiece(int priThreadNumber)
{
    return (new SunspotAnalyzerPiece(priThreadNumber));
}
```

It returns a new `SunspotAnalyzerPiece` instance, sending the thread or piece number as a parameter.

Overriding this method, we can return instances of the `SunspotAnalyzerPiece` class (a subclass of `ParallelAlgorithmPiece`).

Programming the results collection method

We also had to override the `CollectResults` method. This method will collect the results left in each `SunspotAnalyzerPiece` subclass instance.

We already know the mechanism, since it is the same that we used in the previous examples. However, in this case, the `CollectResults` method takes into account the `piBegin` property for each piece defined, as shown in the following lines of code in the loop:

```
for (liPieceNumber = 0; liPieceNumber < priTotalPieces;
     liPieceNumber++)
{
    g.DrawImage(prloBitmapList[liPieceNumber], 0,
                prloPieces[liPieceNumber].piBegin);
}
```

Then, it assigns the generated bitmap to `proBitmap`, which can be accessed from the outside world by the `poBitmap` property:

```
proBitmap = loBitmap;
```

Time for action – Defining a new method to create an algorithm instance

Do not forget the NASA scientists and NASA's CIO. They are excited about your new application, and you do not want to disappoint them. You would rather work for the NASA and not the FBI or the hackers!

As they want to run the algorithm for a lot of images, first, we are going to create a new method for processing an individual bitmap. This way, we will be able to call it many times for each bitmap found in a folder:

1. Stay in the project, `SunspotsAnalyzer`.

2. Add the following procedure in the form's file, `AnalyzeSunspotsAndShowResult`. It will create a `SunspotAnalyzer` instance, run the algorithm, and show the resulting bitmap in a picturebox control. It receives a `Bitmap` as a parameter:

```
private void AnalyzeSunspotsAndShowResult(Bitmap proBitmap)
{
    SunspotAnalyzer loSunSpotAnalyzer;

    loSunSpotAnalyzer = new SunspotAnalyzer(proBitmap);
    loSunSpotAnalyzer.RunInParallelSync();
    loSunSpotAnalyzer.CollectResults();
    picSunspots.Image = loSunSpotAnalyzer.poBitmap;
}
```

What just happened?

The code required to analyze sunspots (inverting the bitmap colors) and show the resulting bitmap in the picturebox control is now held in a procedure already prepared for creating as many threads as the number of available cores with just a few lines of code. A `Bitmap` is received as a parameter for this method.

Forgetting about threads

Look at the code! There is nothing about threads, just a few lines creating an instance and calling two methods. The magic of object-orientation allows us to simplify several threading issues and reduce the parallelism complexity. The developer who writes this code could be a classic C# user interface or events programmer. He or she does not have to worry about multiple threads, cores, processors, and so on. Everything is encapsulated in the parallel algorithm-specific subclass.

First, it creates a `SunspotAnalyzer` instance, passing the entire bitmap received as a parameter to the constructor.

```
loSunSpotAnalyzer = new SunspotAnalyzer(proBitmap);
```

This call creates the pieces and gets everything prepared for an asynchronous execution. However, the method wants to return when everything is finished. Therefore, it calls the `RunInParallelSync` method:

```
loSunSpotAnalyzer.RunInParallelSync();
```

The threads are executed asynchronously. However, the `RunInParallelSync` method does not return until all the threads are finished with their work.

Then, it collects the results, leaving the processed bitmap accessible in the `poBitmap` property. Hence, it assigns it to the `picSunspots` picturebox:

```
loSunSpotAnalyzer.CollectResults();
picSunspots.Image = loSunSpotAnalyzer.poBitmap;
```

Using these classes as an initial pattern, we can create parallelized code encapsulated in classes in lesser time than initially expected and avoid lots of problems.

Time for action – Running the Sunspot Analyzer in many concurrent independent pieces

Now, we are going to create the UI and write some code to use the `SunspotAnalyzer` class and its encapsulated power:

1. Stay in the project, `SunspotsAnalyzer`.

2. Open the Windows Form `Form1` (**frmSunspotsAnalyzer**) in the form designer, add the following controls, and align them as shown in the image:

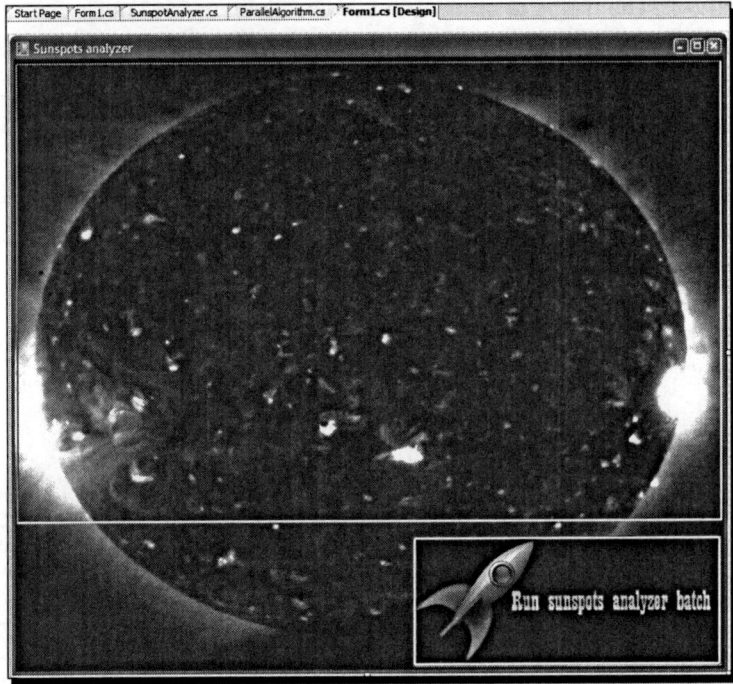

(Image credit: Hinode JAXA/NASA)

- ◆ One picturebox (`picSunspots`) with its `SizeMode` property set to **StretchImage**.
- ◆ One button showing a space shuttle and its `Text` property set to **Run sunspots analyzer batch (butRunBatch)**. This button will start an instance of the parallel algorithm subclass, calling the `AnalyzeSunspotsAndShowResult` method for each image file found in a folder.

3. Add the following lines of code at the beginning (as we are going to use the `System.IO.DirectoryInfo` and `System.IO. FileInfo` classes):

```
using System.IO;
```

4. Open the `Click` event in the button **butRunBatch**, and enter the following code (replace `C:\\NASASUNSPOT` with your images folder path):

```
DirectoryInfo loDirectory;
FileInfo[] loImageFiles;
Bitmap loBitmap;
```

```
// Replace "C:\\NASASUNSPOT" with your images folder path
loDirectory = new DirectoryInfo("C:\\NASASUNSPOT");
// Get the JPG files stored in the path
loImageFiles = loDirectory.GetFiles("*.JPG");

// Process each JPG image file found
foreach (FileInfo loNextImageFile in loImageFiles)
{
    // Store the Bitmap to be processed in the proOriginalBitmap
        private variable
    loBitmap = new Bitmap(Image.FromFile(loNextImageFile.
                    FullName));

    AnalyzeSunspotsAndShowResult(loBitmap);

    // Let the PictureBox control update the image
    Application.DoEvents();
}
```

5. Copy the images to be analyzed in the specified folder (the default is
   `C:\\NASASUNSPOT`). You will need more than 10 images with high resolutions
   to see the progress.

6. Build and run the application.

7. Click on the **Run sunspots analyzer batch** button. The images will be shown with their
   colors inverted, one after the other, with a delay (depending on the parallel processing
   capabilities of the computer) of a few seconds, as shown in the following image:

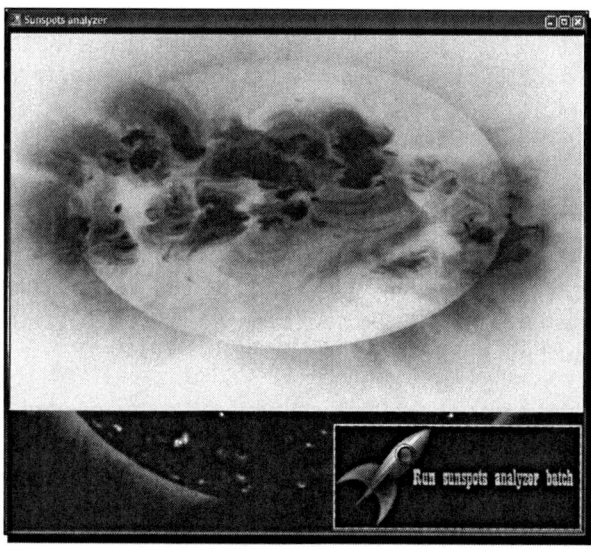

(Image credit: Hinode JAXA/NASA)

What just happened?

The NASA scientists and its CIO are very happy with your batch sunspot analyzer, and they are going to run it in the main server with 3,000 huge resolution images. You do not need to keep your fingers crossed, as the classes forced the garbage collector to run when needed. You are hired! However, you will need a more intensive training in avoiding some multithreading problems.

We could easily transform a new complex multithreaded algorithm capable of taking full advantage of parallel processing capabilities into subclasses of the generalized `ParallelAlgorithmPiece` and `ParallelAlgorithm` abstract superclasses. We can create instances of the subclass that represent the algorithm every time we need them, without worrying about threads and available cores thanks to object-oriented capabilities in the C# programming language.

Optimizing and encapsulating parallel algorithms

Look at the code in the final application! Using an object-oriented generalization process, we dramatically simplified the parallel algorithm creation process.

Now, we could create a parallelized bitmap processing algorithm by creating subclasses and making minor changes to the code.

Generalizing a parallel algorithm allows us to focus on the algorithm itself, and later we can easily optimize the algorithm making some changes to the methods.

 Achieving a good encapsulation is one of the most important tasks to reduce the difficulties associated with multithreaded applications. Working with well-defined pieces that are as independent as possible is the key to success in the parallel programming world.

Achieving thread affinity

Using and improving the classes and the encapsulation capabilities offered by the C# programming language, and accompanied by a good design, we can achieve the concept known as **thread** or **resource affinity**. We have been working on that without talking about it—sometimes you must run before you can walk!

Thread affinity promotes a task-oriented programming. We worked hard on splitting a job into highly independent tasks. Each task works in an independent thread with its instance variables and its local variables. It does not change the states of variables visible to other threads.

We worked on asking states or collecting states, but not changing them, except in the case of some very simple flags to interrupt the processing.

In real-life applications, it is nearly impossible to hide all the state changes by one thread from the other threads. It is possible, but it requires developing a very complex and also a processing-time-consuming framework. The performance improvements we achieve with multithreading could be lost with the instructions required to implement a very efficient affinity.

There are many techniques required to achieve thread affinity. Their usage depends on the kind of application we are developing. If we are working on a new multithreaded kernel, on a complex middleware, or on a low-level service, we will have to be very careful about the states, the affinity, and the problematic synchronization directives and objects.

The best and the simplest way to achieve a successful thread affinity is coding a good design to avoid concurrency problems, taking into account the paradigm shift we have learned so far.

To ensure thread affinity, we must not allow any foreign thread to make changes in the variables in which our threads are working, except some simple flags to control its behavior.

Avoiding locks and many synchronization nightmares

So far, we have been working with parallelized algorithms and we've used C# object-oriented capabilities to simplify the code and make it easier to understand. We have specialized classes using inheritance and many encapsulation techniques to simplify the parallel algorithm creation process. Hence, we avoided repeating the same code on every new application.

However, we have been avoiding some common nightmares related to multithreaded programming– **locks** and **synchronization** problems. How can we use C# and .NET capabilities to synchronize access to variables shared by several different threads?

The answer is very simple, avoiding locks and dodging synchronization problems. The best way to simplify these common concurrency problems is to avoid them as much as possible, because they are always big nightmares for the developers.

Using many encapsulation techniques and some programming rules like the ones we have been working on, we can avoid locks and dodge synchronization problems.

The best way to understand synchronization problems in multithreaded applications is to compare them with the concurrency problems found in databases used by many users at the same time.

If you need to work on the same table's records (rows), you have to be very careful with the updates. There are many approaches, corresponding to many different situations. Sometimes, you must lock the register until you are finished with writing the changes. Why? Because many users may be reading and writing concurrently to those records by using a different computer connected to the same database. The same happens with multiple threads in modern multiprocessing capable computers; many threads can change values at the same time. This is indeed very dangerous. We must be very careful when working with databases used by many users.

There are many synchronization classes, methods, and structures offered by C# and .NET. They allow us to block one or many threads until a certain condition is reached in another thread. They provide locking mechanisms to avoid changing the value of a variable in many threads simultaneously. However, our approach is to avoid using them as much as possible. This way, we can keep our code simpler, and can avoid many difficult-to-solve bugs related to the synchronization mechanism.

Have a go hero – Avoiding side-effects

NASA's CIO is very happy with your work so far. However, he thinks you are very individualistic; and now that he has hired you, he wants to test your capabilities to work in a group of developers. OK, you are a multithreading guru, but they have been working in NASA for many years! So, be quiet!

He wants you to teach the other developers how to use your classes. However, he warns you that they are very curious about object-oriented structures. As many of them had worked in Quality Assurance, they try to find as many bugs as possible using the classes in unexpected ways.

Therefore, you must avoid **side effects**. The classes must be prepared for unexpected concurrency, and they must avoid unauthorized changes in their states. You must create a new version of the classes and the application to achieve a pure thread affinity.

Each piece must work in an independent thread, but no other thread is allowed to be able to change its properties. You can do that exposing only properties and verifying whether the current thread is the original thread that created the instance. You must previously save the original thread that created the instance, and then you can compare it with `System.Threading.Thread.CurrentThread`.

The developers will add buttons to change unexpected values in other threads, while your multithreaded algorithm is running. For example, they will want to change the `SunspotAnalyzer` instance, `priTotalPieces`. Don't let this happen!

Then, create new subclasses of the `ParallelAlgorithmPiece` and the `ParallelAlgorithm` classes to develop a new algorithm to parallelize statistics about the emails that the NASA info inbox receives.

Use a good object-oriented design and have thread affinity in mind while doing it. Show the number of paragraphs, the number of sentences, and the number of words as they are found in very huge texts. Do not create global counters; instead collect them as and when needed from the pieces to show partial results and a progress bar.

You can do it; we have been working with the classes and with good object-oriented designs.

Do you like your new partners, or do you prefer your old hacker friends?

Pop quiz

1. Thread affinity promotes:

    a. An optimal garbage collection usage

    b. A task-oriented programming

    c. The use of global variables

2. Abstract methods:

    a. Must be overridden in subclasses

    b. Cannot be overridden in subclasses

    c. Can be overridden in superclasses

3. The `CollectResults` method in a `ParallelAlgorithm` subclass:

    a. Must be rewritten

    b. Must be erased

    c. Must be overridden

4. The `ParallelAlgorithm` class:

    a. Is responsible for the creation of the appropriate `ParallelAlgorithmPiece` subclass instance

    b. Is responsible for the creation of the appropriate `ParallelAlgorithm` subclass instances list

    c. Is responsible for the creation of the appropriate `ParallelAlgorithmPiece` superclass instance

5. In order to create the appropriate instance of a subclass of the `ParallelAlgorithmPiece` class, we used a variation of:

    a. The factory method class creational pattern

    b. The class creational pattern in the factory

    c. The pattern factory mechanism class creational

Right answers:

1. b.
2. a.
3. c.
4. a.
5. a.

Summary

We have learned a lot in this chapter about using object-oriented capabilities offered by the C# programming language, using design patterns for simplifying the parallelism complexity, and avoiding synchronization pains. Specifically, we covered:

- Using the factory method class creational pattern to create classes prepared for inheritance, and hence simplifying the creation of parallelized code
- Designing efficient and pragmatic object-oriented multithreaded code
- Creating instances and calling some methods in single-threaded code to create encapsulated and well-managed multithreaded code
- Encapsulating multithreaded algorithms in classes to simplify the development process and to allow a division of the development team in single-threaded and multithreaded code
- Creating safer, independent pieces of work filling the gaps in inherited classes
- Specializing segmentation algorithms, while avoiding synchronization pains and achieving thread affinity

We also learned the principles of thread affinity, and how to avoid the undesirable side-effects related to concurrent programming.

Now that we've learned simpler ways to create parallelized code in C# avoiding the complexity of some advanced concurrent programming difficulties, we're ready to work with parallelized input/output and data access—which is the topic of the next chapter.

9

Working with Parallelized Input/ Output and Data Access

In order to work with real-life applications, we must communicate with the I/O subsystem. We have to read from files, write to files, access tables in databases, and much more. In this chapter, we will combine everything we've learned so far with the possibilities offered by multiple threads to improve algorithms that require parallelized input/output operations, still avoiding some concurrent programming nightmares. Reading it and following the exercises we shall:

- ◆ Learn to easily manage a queue of jobs to be dispatched using a producer/consumer pattern
- ◆ Use object-oriented capabilities to transform single-threaded algorithms into multithreaded scalable jobs
- ◆ Improve the applications' scalability
- ◆ Learn to parallelize time-consuming, input/output operations
- ◆ Find solutions to avoid concurrency input/output bottlenecks
- ◆ Use multithreading to improve input/output performance

Queuing threads with I/O operations

So far, we have been working hard in parallelizing single algorithms in order to improve their performance. We created very simple classes to take full advantage of C# object-oriented capabilities of the C# programming language, and created a simple way to split work into multiple, independent jobs. However, some applications, like some engines, need to dispatch requests on demand. In those cases, which are very common in server applications or services, it is more convenient to process many requests in parallel, instead of splitting a single one into multiple pieces. How can we dispatch many requests using simple and efficient independent threads while reading and writing files?

The answer is simple—using a **pool of threads** provided by the .NET framework, which can be used to post work items and wait on behalf of other threads, among other uses. Thus, we can take full advantage of a framework class that simplifies queuing working threads. Now that we know a lot about parallel programming, it will be easier to understand how and when to use a pool of threads. Of course, we can also combine multithreading with object-oriented capabilities to reduce our development time and to avoid synchronization problems, as we learned in the previous chapters.

 It is very important to combine everything we learn in order to achieve the best performance, using the most appropriate pattern to suit the application's needs.

Time for action – Creating a class to run an algorithm in an independent thread

The NASA scientists are preparing a new edition of the Mars exploration Rover mission. The Mars exploration Rover mission is a part of NASA's Mars exploration program, a long-term effort aimed at a robotic exploration of the red planet. Nevertheless, this time, they are going to send thirty rovers—the robot geologists. They are going to be controlled by very simple commands encapsulated in text files.

The NASA's CIO knows your impressive work with encryption algorithms with the FBI agents. So, he asked you to develop a new encryption engine capable of saving encrypted copies of the original text files as they are being copied in a folder on a server. Remember he is an object-oriented guru. Therefore, you will begin coding a class!

First, we are going to create a new project with a class capable of reading a text file and writing an encrypted one. We will use the encryption algorithm developed in the previous chapters. This way, later, we will be able to work with a pool of threads using instances of this simple class, and the code will be very easy to understand while we avoid synchronization problems:

1. Create a new C# Project using the Windows Forms Application template in Visual Studio or Visual C# Express. Use `MarsEncrypter` as the project's name.

2. Create a new class, `Encrypter`.

3. Add the following line of code at the beginning (as we are going to use the `System.IO.StreamReader` and `System.IO.StreamWriter` classes):

   ```
   using System.IO;
   ```

4. Add the following private variables:

```
// The complete input file name (including the path)
private string prsInputFileName;
// The complete output (encrypted) file name (including the path)
private string prsOutputFileName;
// The list of strings to be encrypted
private List<string> pasTextToEncrypt;
```

5. Add the following properties to access the private variables (we want to create a compact and reliable class):

```
public string psInputFileName
{
    set
    {
        prsInputFileName = value;
    }
    get
    {
        return prsInputFileName;
    }
}
public string psOutputFileName
{
    set
    {
        prsOutputFileName = value;
    }
    get
    {
        return prsOutputFileName;
    }
}
```

What just happened?

The code to define the input and output file names and the list of strings to encrypt is now held in the `Encrypter` class. The instances of this class will represent a complete algorithm, and each instance is going to run in a new independent thread as files are copied in a folder. Everything we need to access for the algorithm must be in the instance of this class.

For example, if we need a temporary file name, we must add a new instance variable.

The properties are:

◆ `psInputFileName`: The complete input file name, including its path

◆ `psOutputFileName`: The complete output file name, including its path

Time for action – Putting the logic into methods to simplify multithreading

Object-oriented code is one of the most valuable friends of multithreaded applications. We want the `Encrypter` class to be simple, self-contained, and efficient. Achieving this will help us in focusing on parallelizing the requests, and help in solving the threading problem.

Now, we are going to add some methods to the `Encrypter` class to complete the algorithm:

1. Stay in the project, `MarsEncrypter`.

2. Open the code for the `Encrypter` class.

3. Add the following private method to load the text to encrypt into a string list from the specified input text file:

```
private void LoadTextToEncrypt()
{
    pasTextToEncrypt = new List<string>();

    try
    {
        // Create an instance of StreamReader to read from the
            input file
        // the using statement closes the StreamReader
        using (StreamReader loInputStream = new
                StreamReader(prsInputFileName))
        {
            String lsLine;
            // Read and add lines to lasTextToEncrypt from the
                file until its end is reached
            while ((lsLine = loInputStream.ReadLine()) != null)
            {
                pasTextToEncrypt.Add(lsLine);
            }
        }
    }
    catch (Exception e)
    {
        // Something went wrong
        System.Diagnostics.Debug.Print("The file could not be
                                        read:");
        System.Diagnostics.Debug.Print(e.Message);
    }
}
```

4. Add the following private method to encrypt each string in the list:

```
private void EncryptText()
{
    for (int i = 0; i < pasTextToEncrypt.Count; i++)
    {
```

```
        pasTextToEncrypt[i] = Encrypt(pasTextToEncrypt[i]);
    }
}
```

5. Add the following private method to save the encrypted strings in the specified output file:

```
private void SaveEncryptedText()
{
    try
    {
        // Create an instance of StreamWriter to write to the
            output file
        // the using statement closes the StreamWriter
        using (StreamWriter loOutputStream = new StreamWriter(
                prsOutputFileName, false, Encoding.Unicode))
        {
            foreach (string lsLine in pasTextToEncrypt)
            {
                loOutputStream.Write(lsLine);
            }
        }
    }
    catch (Exception e)
    {
        // Something went wrong
        System.Diagnostics.Debug.Print("The file could not be
                                        written:");
        System.Diagnostics.Debug.Print(e.Message);
    }
}
```

6. Copy and paste the `Encrypt` method from the `SMSEncryption` project (the one you developed to help the FBI agents) to this class. Change its visibility to `private`.

7. Remove or comment the lines used to show debugging information. They begin with `System.Diagnostics.Debug.Print`.

8. Add the following public method to do the entire work once the input and output files have been specified:

```
public void EncryptFile()
{
    LoadTextToEncrypt();
    EncryptText();
    SaveEncryptedText();
}
```

What just happened?

The code required to load a text file and save its encrypted version is now held in the `Encrypter` class.

Thus, creating an instance of this class and filling the properties with the corresponding input and output files, we can easily implement an independent algorithm that can be run in a self-sufficient thread, when each new file appears in a specific folder.

In order to run the encryption on a file, we must create an instance, fill the `psInputFileName` and `psOutputFileName` properties, and then call the `EncryptFile` method.

 Self-sufficient threads are very easy to achieve using instances of classes to encapsulate everything the algorithm needs to run in a thread. Engines running in servers that dispatch many concurrent requests can be prepared for great scalability using these principles.

Avoiding Input/Output bottlenecks

I/O bottlenecks are traditional in any programming model. Nevertheless, an inefficient concurrent I/O can keep all the running threads waiting for the I/O responses. We want to improve performance and scalability. Therefore, we have to avoid I/O bottlenecks as far as possible.

In this case, we are not worried about memory consumption. We have enough memory because the files are not very large (less than 100 megabytes). We want to run concurrent encryptions of different files. Thus, we must read and write data from the storage or from the network (according to the location of the files).

The following lines of code in the `EncryptFile` public method handle the complete algorithm, read the text to encrypt from the input file, process it, and save the results to a new output file:

```
LoadTextToEncrypt();
EncryptText();
SaveEncryptedText();
```

We read everything we need, and we store it in a private list of strings. This is done in the `LoadTextToEncrypt` method. We do this because we want to improve the reading process. Doing it line by line, without adding an encryption process in the middle will make it possible to specialize each moment and take full advantage of the modern hardware capabilities.

Concurrent threads reading and writing to files in a disordered way can create I/O bottlenecks, as storage subsystems have a better response time when focusing on one task or on buffered operations. We want to take full advantage of buffers, so we read everything and then we write everything.

Using concurrent streams

In order to work in different files concurrently from diverse threads, we can use many instances of certain `System.IO` classes, such as `System.IO.StreamReader` and `System.IO.StreamWriter`. Nevertheless, we have to remember that a file is not like a database, and the concurrent access for writing purposes is limited. We cannot write a file in parallel, but we can write a file collecting results as we did in our image processing samples.

The `StreamReader` provides a very simple way to read from an input stream. The following lines create and use a `StreamReader` instance to read text lines from the input file until it reaches the end (the line is equal to `null`):

```
using (StreamReader loInputStream = new StreamReader(
        prsInputFileName))
{
    String lsLine;
    while ((lsLine = loInputStream.ReadLine()) != null)
    {
        pasTextToEncrypt.Add(lsLine);
    }
}
```

The `using` statement closes the `StreamReader`. For this reason, we do not have to worry about closing statements.

As mentioned earlier, the lines are added to `pasTextToEncrypt`—a list of strings.

On the other hand, the `StreamWriter` provides a very simple way to write to an output stream. The following lines create and use a `StreamWriter` instance to write the encrypted lines to the output file:

```
using (StreamWriter loOutputStream = new StreamWriter(
        prsOutputFileName, false, Encoding.Unicode))
{
    foreach (string lsLine in pasTextToEncrypt)
    {
        loOutputStream.Write(lsLine);
    }
}
```

As with the `StreamReader`, the `using` statement closes the `StreamWriter`. The lines are taken from the `pasTextToEncrypt` list of strings, which at the time this method is called holds the list of encrypted strings.

The encryption algorithm relies on the complete Unicode character set. Thus, we need to create the `StreamWriter` specifying a Unicode encoding:

```
StreamWriter loOutputStream = new StreamWriter(prsOutputFileName,
                                  false, Encoding.Unicode)
```

We have to be very careful when developing applications with concurrent I/O operations. We have to avoid different threads trying to write in the same file. If we want an exclusive access, we have to use some flags or some other mechanisms to ensure that we are going to work on that file alone.

Controlling exceptions in threads

Exceptions mean problems and complexities. Handling exceptions is a difficult task in single-threaded applications. It makes code boring and difficult to understand. However, we need exceptions to take control of errors and unexpected situations at runtime.

When working with I/O operations, there are several possibilities of facing unexpected situations. Thus, we have to handle exceptions. Nevertheless, what happens with exceptions in multiple concurrent threads? Where are the exceptions that are raised caught, when they belong to a thread different from the main one?

To answer these questions, we would rather catch the exceptions in the methods that perform the I/O operations. Catching the exceptions in the code that runs in independent threads with asynchronous execution is a good practice to avoid unknown results.

The threads running the code for the instances of the `Encrypter` class will do that with an asynchronous execution. Thus, we do not know when the exceptions can be raised in the main thread's time.

Unhandled exceptions in multithreaded code can be a more serious nightmare than the synchronization problems. Hence, it is convenient to be conscious of such a situation and avoid unexpected situations by catching the exceptions and controlling them.

When working with classes whose instances represent a unit of work in a thread, it is simpler to handle exceptions, as we have control over the methods that we are calling.

In the `LoadTextToEncrypt` and `SaveEncryptedText` methods, we enclose the I/O operations in a `try...catch` block. If an exception occurs, we catch it and print debugging information in the **Immediate Window**, as shown in the following lines from the `LoadTextToEncrypt` method:

```
catch (Exception e)
{
    System.Diagnostics.Debug.Print("The file could not be read:");
    System.Diagnostics.Debug.Print(e.Message);
}
```

Raising unhandled exceptions in the threads independent of the main one is not recommended, as we can easily lose control over them. We must handle them before they leave the thread!

Time for action – Creating the methods for queuing requests

Now, we are going to write some code in methods to use the `Encrypter` class and to queue requests using a pool of threads provided by the `ThreadPool` class:

1. Stay in the project, `MarsEncrypter`.

2. Open the code for the Windows Form `Form1` (**frmMarsEncrypter**).

3. Add the following line of code at the beginning (as we are going to use the `System.Threading.ThreadPool` class):

   ```
   using System.Threading;
   ```

4. Open the `Form Load` event, and enter the following code—it is convenient to configure some `ThreadPool` class parameters to achieve optimal results:

   ```
   // Set the maximum number of requests to the thread pool that can
   //     be active concurrently equal to the number of available cores
   // All requests above that number remain queued until thread pool
   //     threads become available
   ThreadPool.SetMaxThreads(Environment.ProcessorCount,
                            Environment.ProcessorCount * 2);
   ```

5. Add the following private method—it will be run every time a new file appears:

   ```
   private void ThreadProc(Object stateInfo)
   {
       // An instance of Encrypter is passed in stateInfo
       Encrypter loEncrypter = (Encrypter) stateInfo;

       loEncrypter.EncryptFile();
   }
   ```

6. Add the following private method—it will be run every time a new file appears and will queue a `ThreadProc` method with an `Encrypter` instance as a parameter:

```
private void QueueFileEncryption(string psFileName)
{
    Encrypter loEncrypter;
    loEncrypter = new Encrypter();
    // Assign the input file name (received as a parameter)
    loEncrypter.psInputFileName = psFileName;
    // Generate the output file name replacing INPUT with OUTPUT
       in the path
    loEncrypter.psOutputFileName = psFileName.Replace("INPUT",
                                   "OUTPUT");
    // Queue the work passing an Encrypter instance as a
       parameter
    ThreadPool.QueueUserWorkItem(new WaitCallback(ThreadProc),
                                 loEncrypter);
}
```

What just happened?

NASA's CIO comes near you to see the code. He wants you to explain to him how to work with pools of threads using the `ThreadPool` class. However, he has a meeting and will return in half an hour. Hurry up and finish the application while you learn what the pools of threads are, and how they simplify your work with parallel programming!

The code required to queue a file encryption thread, preparing and using an instance of `Encrypter` class to run the encryption algorithm, and generate the output file is now held in methods in the form class.

Look at the code! We are not using the previously learned object-oriented generalization process. However, the code is very easy to understand. Nevertheless, is it multithreaded code? Yes, it is!

This time, we worked in an application optimized to work as a server and not as a client. For that reason, there are many differences in the parallelization approach. The application is not intended to run a batch process; it will be used to encrypt multiple concurrent files on demand. Hence, it is optimized for concurrency and for serving many clients.

Using a pool of threads with the ThreadPool class

The `ThreadPool` class provides and allows us to manage a pool of threads. We can use them to post work items, process asynchronous I/O operations, and process timers, among other tasks.

We already know the way the threads work. The `ThreadPool` class offers many interesting features, which can help us in certain kinds of applications.

In the Form Load event handler, the following line of code configured some parameters for the pool of threads:

```
ThreadPool.SetMaxThreads(Environment.ProcessorCount,
                    Environment.ProcessorCount * 2);
```

The `SetMaxThreads` method tells the `ThreadPool` class two things:

- The maximum number of worker threads that can run concurrently. We assigned the number of available cores (`Environment.ProcessorCount`) to this value. This way, the pool of threads will match the number of concurrent threads to the available cores.

- The maximum number of asynchronous I/O threads that can run concurrently. We assigned two times the number of available cores (`Environment.ProcessorCount * 2`) to this value. Asynchronous I/O operations do not tend to use huge processing time. Hence, it is a good practice to allow more threads than the number of available cores for these kinds of threads, generated automatically when we use asynchronous I/O operations.

 In this application, we are using I/O operations with a synchronous execution. However, the thread that calls them is run with an asynchronous execution.

The `QueueFileEncryption` method receives a file name with a path as a parameter. It creates a new instance of the `Encrypter` class, assigns the `psInputFileName` property with the parameter received, and then replaces the `"INPUT"` string in the path with the `"OUTPUT"` string to assign the `psOutputFileName` property:

```
Encrypter loEncrypter;
loEncrypter = new Encrypter();
loEncrypter.psInputFileName = psFileName;
loEncrypter.psOutputFileName = psFileName.Replace("INPUT", "OUTPUT");
```

If we use the following base path for the input files to be encrypted `"C:\MARSCOMMANDS\ INPUT"` and one file to be processed is `"C:\MARSCOMMANDS\INPUT\COMMANDS1.TXT"`, the encrypted output will be saved in the file `"C:\MARSCOMMANDS\OUTPUT\COMMANDS1.TXT"`.

We can create a thread in the pool, and hence queue a work item in a new independent thread, using the `QueueUserWorkItem`, as shown in the following line of code:

```
ThreadPool.QueueUserWorkItem(new WaitCallback(ThreadProc),
                    loEncrypter);
```

The threads generated by the ThreadPool class are **background threads**. We can check the bool value in the Thread.CurrentThread.IsBackground property. If you close an application, and there are background threads running, they will be finished. If you need **foreground threads**, they do not have to be created using the ThreadPool class. Foreground threads will keep the application alive until they finish their work.

Managing the thread queue in the pool

The QueueUserWorkItem creates a new background thread in the pool using a new WaitCallback referencing to a method as the first parameter. In our example, it is the ThreadProc method.

The second parameter is an object that will be sent as a parameter to the ThreadProc method that will run the new thread's code. We already know similar ways to send parameters to threads. Hence, we use our experience to send an instance of the Encrypter class with everything needed to complete the job (loEncrypter).

The code in the ThreadProc method is very easy. It unfolds the Encrypter instance in the stateInfo parameter (type: Object) and then calls the EncryptFile method, as shown in the following lines:

```
private void ThreadProc(Object stateInfo)
{
    Encrypter loEncrypter = (Encrypter) stateInfo;

    loEncrypter.EncryptFile();
}
```

The code running in the thread is very simple and completely self-contained. Combining object-oriented capabilities with multithreading is the best way to solve many concurrency problems.

However, there isn't a Start method call. When does the thread start its execution? The pool management system will decide that based on the parameters we defined previously.

The call to the QueueUserWorkItem method returns immediately. It is an asynchronous execution, but does not mean that the thread will begin executing the code immediately.

We defined the maximum number of worker threads that can run concurrently. We assigned the number of available cores to that value.

If there are no working threads in the pool, the thread starts executing the code immediately. Each running thread managed by the pool will reduce the number of available threads in the pool to start code execution.

If there are available threads in the pool (the maximum number of worker threads that can run concurrently - running threads managed by the pool > 0), the thread starts executing the code immediately.

If there are no available threads in the pool (the maximum number of worker threads that can run concurrently - running threads managed by the pool = 0), the thread will be arranged in a queue. Then, it will have to wait for the previous threads in the queue to be executed when the running threads managed by the pool begin finishing and leave space for new queued threads to begin running.

For example, if we have four available cores, the maximum number of worker threads that can run concurrently will be set to 4.

We will call the `QueueUserWorkItem` many times and explain what happens:

- First call to `QueueUserWorkItem`. The thread begins running. Available threads: 3 (4 − 1). Running threads: 1.

- Second call to `QueueUserWorkItem`. The thread begins running. Available threads: 2 (4 − 2). Running threads: 2.

- Third call to `QueueUserWorkItem`. The thread begins running. Available threads: 1 (4 − 3). Running threads: 3.

- Fourth call to `QueueUserWorkItem`. The thread begins running. Available threads: 0 (4 − 4). Running threads: 4.

- Fifth call to `QueueUserWorkItem`. The thread is queued (position #1 in queue). Available threads: 0 (4 − 4). Queued threads: 1. Running threads: 4.

- Sixth call to `QueueUserWorkItem`. The thread is queued (position #2 in queue). Available threads: 0 (4 − 4). Queued threads: 2. Running threads: 4.

- The first thread ends its execution. Available threads: 1 (4 − 3). Running threads: 3.

- The thread with the position #1 in the queue (fifth call to `QueueUserWorkItem`) begins running. Available threads: 0 (4 − 4). Queued threads: 1. Running threads: 4.

The `ThreadPool` offers a very simple way to work with a pool of threads and manage the queues. Using the right values for its parameters, we can achieve excellent results in certain kinds of applications.

Time for action – Running concurrent encryptions on demand using a pool of threads

Now, we are going to create the UI and write some code to use the `Encrypter` class and its encapsulated simplicity:

1. Stay in the project, `MarsEncrypter`.

2. Open the Windows Form `Form1` (**frmMarsEncrypter**) in the form designer, add the following controls and components, and align them as shown in the following image:

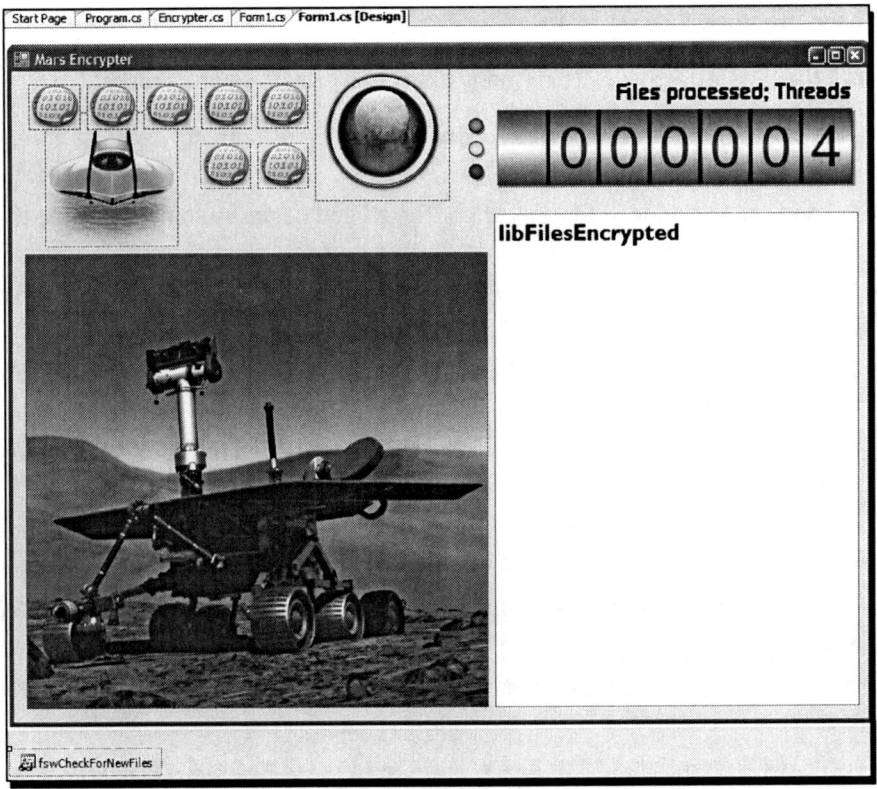

(Rover image credit: Courtesy NASA/JPL-Caltech)

- One listbox (**libFilesEncrypted**).
- One picturebox (**picRover**) with its `SizeMode` property set to **StretchImage**.
- One `FileSystemWatcher` component (**fswCheckForNewFiles**) with its `NotifyFilter` property set to **LastAccess**, its `EnableRaisingEvents` property set to **True,** and its `Path` property set to the input path for the original text files. In our sample, we will use `"C:\MARSCOMMANDS\INPUT"`.

3. Add the following lines of code at the beginning (as we are going to use the `System.IO.FileSystemEventArgs` **class**):

```
using System.IO;
```

4. Open the `CheckForNewFiles_Changed` **event handler in** `FileSystemWatcher` **fswCheckForNewFiles** and enter the following code:

```
// The file was last accessed, it is a new file ready to be
   encrypted
// Send it to the queue
   QueueFileEncryption(e.FullPath);
// Add its name to the ListBox
   libFilesEncrypted.Items.Add(e.Name);
```

5. Create the specified input folder (the default is `"C:\MARSCOMMANDS\INPUT"`).

6. Create the output folder (the default is `"C:\MARSCOMMANDS\INPUT"`).

7. Build and run the application.

8. Copy a dozen text files to be encrypted (around 10 megabytes in size to generate a processing impact) into the input folder while the application is running.

9. Open the Windows Explorer in the output folder. You will see the encrypted files appearing, and their names in the listbox, as shown in the following image:

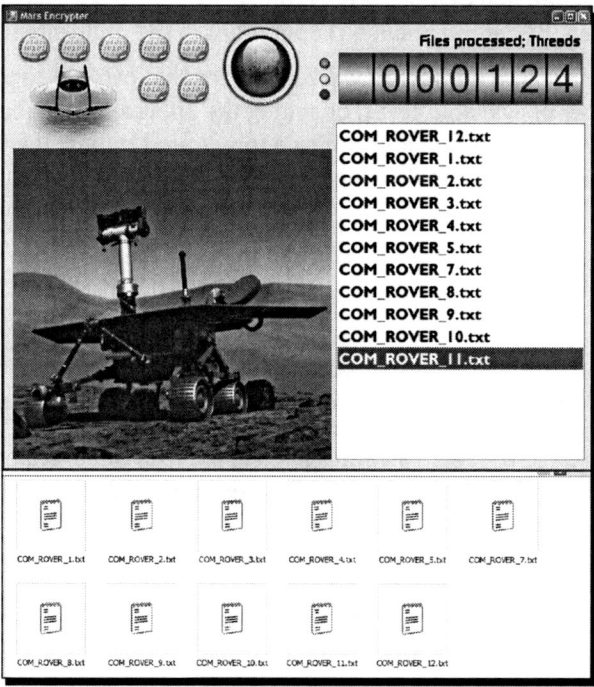

(Rover image credit: Courtesy NASA/JPL-Caltech)

What just happened?

NASA's CIO and the scientists are very happy, again! Now they have a server dispatching encrypted files as the original ones are copied in the folder. You discovered that multithreading makes people happy!

We could easily transform a single-threaded class into a very scalable engine capable of running as many concurrent threads as the number of available cores. Using the `ThreadPool` class capabilities, we simplified the complexity of managing a pool of threads and a queue of waiting threads.

 Once we understand the possibilities offered by concurrent programming, there is no way to go back to single-threaded programming. Welcome to the magic of the multithreaded world, where everything is possible!

Converting single-threaded tasks to a multithreaded pool

As we have seen, it is very easy to convert a single-threaded task into a job capable of running in a very flexible and scalable multithreaded pool. In order to do that, we must follow these simple steps:

1. Create a class capable of holding everything needed by the task. It must be self-contained. Be careful about I/O operations in the multithreaded world.

2. Assign the maximum number of worker threads that can run concurrently according to the number of available cores, or suiting the application's needs. For example, you can leave a thread free for running a foreground thread. It will depend on the kind of application you are developing.

3. Create a method that will run the code of the independent threads. Use the object received as a parameter as an instance of the class mentioned in step number 1. Unfold (typecast) it and run the main method. Let the instance do everything that is needed.

4. Create a method that creates an instance of that class, provides it the necessary property values, and sends it as a parameter to the `QueueUserWorkItem` method.

This is everything we need to create an application capable of being scaled up according to the number of available cores, using a pool of threads, as shown in the following diagram:

Of course, we must also take into account everything we've learned so far about parallel programming, concurrency, and multithreading. However, there is no need to mention that in the chapter!

Encapsulating scalability

Look at the code in the final application! It is very easy to understand. It does not have the complexity of multithreaded code. Using C# object-oriented capabilities, we offered a very simple solution to the scalability problem in applications that need to serve multiple users.

Now, we could create a multi-user encryption processing engine, encapsulating the code in a simple class, sending its instance with everything needed to a thread in a pool, and working almost the same way as qualified single-threaded code.

Encapsulating an algorithm in a class and combining that with the capabilities offered by the `ThreadPool` class, we could focus on the algorithm itself while achieving an unprecedented scalability level. Later, we can easily optimize the algorithm making some changes to the methods in the class.

Achieving a good encapsulation also helps in working with pools of threads. However, we can also combine the multithreaded algorithms with the pools of threads. With multithreaded applications, there are practically no limits for the scalability of an algorithm.

Thread affinity in a pool of threads

Programming the code for the threads that will run in a pool of threads like the one offered by the `ThreadPool` class using an independent class, we will achieve task-oriented programming.

We have been promoting task-oriented programming so far. However, it is a good practice to mention it in different situations.

The pool of threads is a very interesting way of achieving scalability without great effort. Combining it with thread affinity, we will avoid many concurrency problems.

Using the `ThreadPool` class and following the above-mentioned steps to achieve great scalability, we will be able to work with parallelized I/O algorithms that dispatch results to many concurrent requests without great effort, as shown in the following diagram:

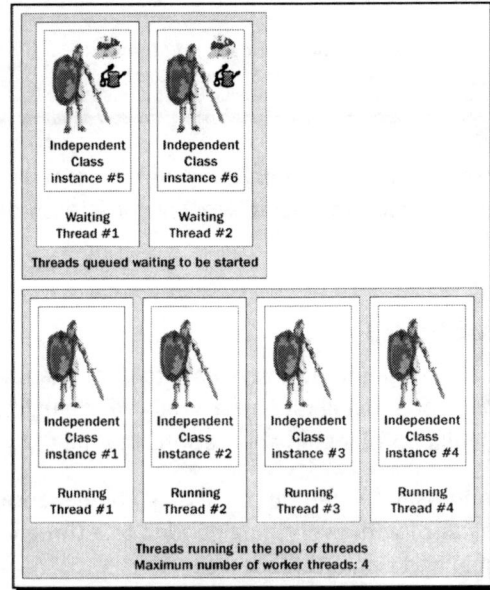

Besides, we will go on working on the paradigm shift needed for a successful life in the parallel programming world.

 Remember that threads running in pools must follow the same rules that we have already learned from the threads created with the Thread class and with the BackgroundWorker component. Consider them before starting your design and of course, before coding.

Have a go hero – Managing the pool of threads

Everybody is impressed with your application. However, a jealous developer in the group closed the application while it was running. The threads stopped running and the encrypted files were lost. Now, the scientists have to check which files are encrypted and which are not. That is a lot of work. And they had more than 15,000 files to process!

That is a horrible bug! You know the ThreadPool class creates background threads and they terminate when the application is closed. C# and .NET do not offer a property to change this behavior. Hence, you must use your multithreading knowledge in order to solve this problem.

Make the necessary changes to the application to avoid closing the application while some threads are still running or waiting in the queue.

Besides, the application does not provide nice UI feedback. Add the following feedback combining a BackgroundWorker with the threads running in the pool of threads:

- The number of files being processed
- The number of files processed
- The number of threads running
- The number of threads waiting in the queue

Again, use a good object-oriented design and have thread affinity in mind while doing it. Do not create global counters; instead collect them as needed from the threads created using the ThreadPool class.

The way to do it is complex, but you have all the information you need to do this job. Review the previous chapters!

Good luck, a parallelized database access is waiting for you!

Parallelizing database access

So far, we have been splitting work into multiple, independent jobs, and then we used a pool of threads to parallelize I/O operations without great effort. However, a database server is already very well prepared for parallelized access, as it is designed for serving a number of concurrent users. How can we optimize our client applications to take advantage of both multithreading and parallelized database access?

The answer is simple; it depends on the kind of application we need:

- If we need to optimize something that runs like a time-consuming batch process, we will use specialized subclasses of our well-known `ParallelAlgorithmPiece` and `ParallelAlgorithm` classes to develop a new algorithm for parallelizing database access and collecting results.

- If we need to dispatch many concurrent independent jobs, we will use a pool of threads provided by the `ThreadPool` class, combined with an independent class, to run the code for each thread.

As database servers are optimized for concurrency and usually have more processing power than client machines for parallelizing algorithms, we can achieve unprecedented scalability and performance enhancements. However, the network will become a great bottleneck, and we must work hard to avoid it.

Have a go hero – Creating a parallelized data access algorithm

The encryption dispatcher works great, but the NASA's CIO asks you to improve its performance. He tells you about a great database server, with 128 cores. You believe it is convenient to create a new application with a very optimized, parallelized, data access algorithm to encrypt lines that are stored as rows in a database table in that huge server.

Create a database table with the following fields, making the necessary changes to match your database server specifications:

- ID (an auto incremented value)
- Input (memo / text)
- Output (memo / text)
- Processed (`bool`)

Populate the table with thousands of rows with lines of text in the input field.

Then, create new subclasses of the `ParallelAlgorithmPiece` and the `ParallelAlgorithm` classes to develop a new algorithm to encrypt rows of the database table and save the results in the output field while setting the processed `bool` value to `true` or its numeric representation in the database server.

In order to divide the work into pieces, use the ID field. Get the max ID and split the work. Let each thread go to the database, query for the data to be processed (from the first ID to the last), and then process each row updating the encrypted text in the corresponding output field.

Provide the UI with feedback about the progress using a BackgroundWorker component.

Databases are very well prepared for parallelized access. Therefore, you will achieve excellent performance results compared to a single-threaded approach.

You can do it! You know about database access, and you can work with object-oriented designs.

Are you bored of encrypting? Do not worry, there are many new interesting tasks waiting for your multithreading capabilities.

Pop quiz

1. The `ThreadPool` class creates:
    a. Foreground threads
    b. Ground threads
    c. Background threads

2. Using a pool of threads you can:
    a. Manage multiple concurrent threads and a queue of waiting threads
    b. Transform multithreaded applications into single-threaded queues
    c. Manage multiple cores according to the number of threads

3. To achieve the best performance in most cases, it is convenient:
    a. To read, process, and then write in each thread, taking full advantage of buffered mechanisms
    b. To read and write from many concurrent threads no matter the order
    c. To read, process, and then write in each pool, taking full advantage of the threading mechanisms

4. When an application is closed, the background threads:
    a. Are terminated two seconds later
    b. Go on running until they finish their work
    c. Are terminated immediately

5. If there are no available threads in the pool (the maximum number of worker threads that can run concurrently - running threads managed by the pool = 0), the created thread will be:

    a. Terminated and collected by the garbage collector

    b. Arranged in a queue

    c. Sent to the trash can

Right answers:

1. c.

2. a.

3. a.

4. c.

5. b.

Summary

We learned a lot in this chapter about using pools and parallelized input/output operations in many ways. Again, we used object-oriented capabilities offered by the C# programming language for achieving great scalability in converting single-threaded algorithms to multithreaded scalable jobs, while avoiding the pains of multithreading. Specifically, we covered:

- Using the `ThreadPool` class and its pool of threads to easily manage a queue of jobs to be dispatched using a producer/consumer pattern

- Encapsulating single-threaded algorithms in classes to simplify their use in multithreaded scalable jobs using a pool of threads

- Improving the input/output performance using multithreaded streaming and taking full advantage of buffers while avoiding common bottlenecks

- Achieving a great deal of scalability without great effort using a pool of threads to dispatch jobs

- Using very simple algorithms to parallelize the access to database tables in multiple threads

We also learned the differences between background and foreground threads, the thread affinity issues, and how to manage a complex pool of threads.

Now that we've learned simple ways to create parallelized Input/Output access with files and databases avoiding bottlenecks, we're ready to work with a parallelized user interface—which is the topic of the next chapter.

10

Parallelizing and Concurrently Updating the User Interface

In order to see the advantages of parallel algorithms and concurrency, we must create a continuous and precise user interface feedback. We have to provide information to the user about the things that are happening and the progress being made. In this chapter, we will combine everything we have learned so far with the possibilities offered by many specific structures to improve the user interface feedback, avoiding some concurrent programming nightmares. Reading it and following the exercises we shall:

- ◆ Learn to make safe changes to the user interface from concurrent programming
- ◆ Use the programming language capabilities to provide safe user interface updates without degrading performance
- ◆ Improve the user interface feedback for parallelized algorithms
- ◆ Use techniques to generate global information without the use of difficult collection procedures
- ◆ Learn to manage a queue of user interface update jobs to be dispatched
- ◆ Combine our concurrent programming knowledge with our user interface update abilities

Updating the UI from independent threads

So far, we have been working with parallelized algorithms splitting jobs into pieces, job dispatchers using pools of threads, and C# programming language object-oriented capabilities applied to concurrency. The BackgroundWorker component was always there to help us in providing feedback to the user interface. However, using loops in the BackgroundWorker to synchronize the changes in the threads to update the user interface is annoying. Some applications need to update the user interface at specific times known by the independent threads, which are unable to make direct changes to the UI controls. How can we make changes to the user interface from any independent thread without causing problems and without using BackgroundWorker loops? Is it possible to do that?

Yes, and it is very simple to do that for any independent thread. It doesn't matter if it was created as a new `Thread` instance or as a worker thread in the `ThreadPool` class.

> There are many ways to update the user interface making certain calls from independent threads—different than the UI thread. Nevertheless, we have to be pragmatic and we must learn a simple way to synchronize our user interface updates easily. Regardless of whether it is a white cat or a black cat, as long as it can catch mice, it is a good cat!

The simplest way to update the user interface from independent threads without using the BackgroundWorker component is programming a method in the UI class and invoking a **delegate** to call it. The syntax to do it is a bit complicated, but we can do that because we are in Chapter 10!

Time for action – Creating a safe method to update the user interface

The quality assurance team discovered a bug in the encryption dispatcher. As they were working with huge files, they realized that the file names were appearing in the listbox before the encryption job began. That sounds confusing. They want you to change the application and add the file names in the listbox as soon as the work gets completed.

That sounds easy for a BackgroundWorker component, but this time, you cannot use it because you would have to introduce a loop in the BackgroundWorker thread. Instead, you can invoke a delegate from the worker thread to update the user interface safely.

Now, we are going to add a new method and a delegate to the form in order to allow the UI to be updated from other threads invoking that delegate:

1. Stay in the project `MarsEncrypter`, created in the previous chapter.

2. Open the code for the Windows Form `Form1` (**frmMarsEncrypter**).

3. Add the following declaration in the instance variables zone:
   ```
   private delegate void AddToListBoxCaller(string psText);
   ```

4. Add the following public method to add a string to the listbox, invoking a delegate when the calling thread is different than the UI thread:
   ```
   public void AddToListBox(string psText)
   {
       // InvokeRequired compares the thread ID of the
       // calling thread to the thread ID of the creating thread.
       // If they are different, it will return true.
       if (libFilesEncrypted.InvokeRequired)
       {
           // The calling thread is different than the UI thread
           // Create the delegate
   ```

```
                AddToListBoxCaller ldAddToListBox = new
                            AddToListBoxCaller(AddToListBox);
            // Invoke the delegate
            // The current thread will block until the delegate has
               been executed
            this.Invoke(ldAddToListBox, new object[] { psText });
        }
        else
        {
            // The calling thread is the same as the UI thread
            // Add the string received as a parameter to the ListBox
               control
            libFilesEncrypted.Items.Add(psText);
        }
    }
```

5. Comment the following line of code in the **FileSystemWatcher fswCheckForNewFiles** changed event handler (the listbox does not have to show the file when the encryption begins):

```
//libFilesEncrypted.Items.Add(e.Name);
```

What just happened?

The code required to update the user interface safely from any thread is now held in a new public method defined in the main form class.

Thus, calling the `AddToListBox` public method with the string to add as a parameter from any thread, we can easily update the `libFilesEncrypted` listbox with each encrypted file when the corresponding thread finishes its work.

We commented the line with the purpose of adding the file when the encryption thread began running, because the listbox has to show the files when the encryption is finished, and the output folder holds the new encrypted text file.

 Delegates are not easy to understand. It is true. However, they add powerful **cross-thread call** capabilities with synchronous or asynchronous executions. In this case, we will be using a synchronous execution.

Creating delegates to make cross-thread calls

We already know that we cannot make changes to the user interface from a thread different from the one that created the controls.

Therefore, in order to make this possible and to synchronize some situations with some user interface feedback, we can use a delegate.

A **delegate** is a **data structure** that refers to a method—a static method or an instance method. It is very useful to allow making cross-thread calls with synchronous or asynchronous executions. Thus, the use of a delegate allows us to call methods in the UI thread from other threads. This way, we can have a precise control over the UI feedback provided by multiple independent threads.

First, we added the delegate declaration, in the instance variables zone:

```
private delegate void AddToListBoxCaller(string psText);
```

This line uses the `private delegate` keywords (visibility + `delegate` keyword) followed by a method declaration: `void AddToListBoxCaller(string psText)`.

We called it `AddToListBoxCaller` because it will hold a reference to the public `AddToListBox` method. We added the `Caller` suffix to specify that it is a delegate and hence a method caller.

The following line declared the public method:

```
public void AddToListBox(string psText)
```

Moreover, the following line declared the delegate for that method:

```
private delegate void AddToListBoxCaller(string psText);
```

 Creating a delegate to update the user interface is easy. You have to add a public method that makes the changes in the UI, with the necessary parameters and then declare a delegate to reference that method using the same method declaration combined with the desired visibility and the delegate keyword as mentioned earlier.

Figuring out the right thread to make the call to the UI

Let's focus on the public `AddToListBox` method. As mentioned earlier, it receives a string as a parameter. That string (`psText`) has to be added to the `libFilesEncrypted` ListBox control.

One of the simplest lines of code to perform that task would be as follows, if no cross-thread call capabilities were considered:

```
libFilesEncrypted.Items.Add(psText);
```

Nevertheless, we need the possibility to call this public method from any independent thread created by the `ThreadPool` class. It sounds complicated and indeed, there is a bit of additional complexity in the code.

It is a method with public visibility. For that reason, any thread that has a reference to the form class instance can call it. Therefore, the first thing that we must do is to check whether the calling thread (the current one) is the same as the thread that created the control or the UI elements to be updated. We can find that out by checking the `bool` value of the `InvokeRequired` property of the `libFilesEncrypted` **listbox** control.

 The `InvokeRequired` property is available for all the controls. It gets a value indicating whether the caller must call an invoke method when making method calls to the control because the caller is on a thread different from the one the control was created on (the UI thread).

The following lines take into account the value of the `InvokeRequired` property:

```
if (libFilesEncrypted.InvokeRequired)
{
    AddToListBoxCaller ldAddToListBox = new AddToListBoxCaller(
                                        AddToListBox);
    this.Invoke(ldAddToListBox, new object[] { psText });
}
else
{
    libFilesEncrypted.Items.Add(psText);
}
```

If the `InvokeRequired` property value for the `libFilesEncrypted` listbox control is false, there will be no problem in making a direct call to the controls methods and properties. In that case, the code in the `else` section will be executed, and it is the same, simple line of code mentioned earlier:

```
libFilesEncrypted.Items.Add(psText);
```

 We can use the `InvokeRequired` property or the other techniques explained in the previous chapters to achieve thread and resource affinity. It is the same concept, but this time, using a property available to all controls.

Avoiding UI update problems with a delegate

If the `InvokeRequired` property value for the `libFilesEncrypted` listbox control is true, it means we are calling the method from a different thread. Therefore, we must invoke the delegate to send a message on the queue for the UI thread to process.

In this case, we want to invoke a synchronous execution. This means that the calling thread (current thread) will block until the delegate has been executed. Moreover, we want to send data to the delegate, file name of the file whose encryption has been completed.

First, we create a new instance of the `AddToListBoxCaller` delegate, sending the main method name as a parameter (`AddToListBox`), as shown in the following line:

```
AddToListBoxCaller ldAddToListBox = new
                        AddToListBoxCaller(AddToListBox);
```

Then, we can call the `Invoke` method. It executes the specified delegate on the thread that owns the control's underlying window handle, with a synchronous execution. We need to execute the `ldAddToListBox` delegate, but we must send a parameter to it (a string with the encrypted file's name). The list of arguments for the delegate is specified as an array of objects, in the second parameter to the `Invoke` method, as shown in the following line of code:

```
this.Invoke(ldAddToListBox, new object[] { psText });
```

Calling the `Invoke` method puts a message on the queue for the UI thread to process. The UI thread will not process many delegates concurrently; therefore there will be no concurrency in the UI. As it is a queue, one message will be processed after the other. The current thread will be blocked until the delegate has been executed, as the `Invoke` method follows a synchronous execution. It would be very useful to control the specific time at which we want to update the UI without requiring loops in a BackgroundWorker component.

The `Invoke` method will switch to the UI thread and call the `AddToListBox` method sending the argument specified as a parameter for the method. However, this time the `InvokeRequired` property of the `libFilesEncrypted` listbox control will hold a false value, because we are in the UI thread. Thus, the code in the `else` part is going to be executed in order to add the string received as a parameter to the listbox control:

```
libFilesEncrypted.Items.Add(psText);
```

Retrieving results from a synchronous delegate invoke

The `Invoke` method returns an `Object` that contains the return value from the delegate being invoked, or a null reference if the delegate has no return value.

In this case, we are using the `Invoke` method to execute a delegate that does not return a value. Nevertheless, sometimes, it is very useful to use it in order to call functions that do return a value.

For example, if we need the `AddToListBox` method to return an instance of the `EncrypterView` class (a new class not included in the sample code), the following line will declare the public method in the form class:

```
public EncrypterView AddToListBox(string psText)
```

Moreover, the following line will declare the delegate for that method:

```
private delegate EncrypterView AddToListBoxCaller(string psText);
```

Furthermore, the following line will typecast the results of the `Invoke` method to obtain the resulting `EncrypterView` instance:

```
EncrypterView loEncrypterView = (EncrypterView) this.
            Invoke(ldAddToListBox, new object[] { psText });
```

 Running the samples step-by-step is very useful in understanding how delegates work.

Time for action – Invoking a user interface update from a thread

Now, we are going to make the necessary changes to the `Encrypter` class to allow it to invoke a user interface update when it completes the encryption algorithm:

1. Stay in the project, `MarsEncrypter`.

2. Open the code for the `Encrypter` class.

3. Add the following line of code at the beginning:

```
using System.Windows.Forms;
```

4. Add the following private variable:

```
private frmMarsEncrypter proForm;
```

5. Add the following properties to access the private variable (we want to create a compact and reliable class):

```
public frmMarsEncrypter poForm
{
    set
    {
        proForm = value;
    }
    get
    {
        return proForm;
    }
}
```

 In this case, to simplify the examples, we will use a delegate to make a direct call to a method in the form, holding a reference to it in the `Encrypter` class. We must take into account that decoupling the UI by design is more convenient than this approach. However, sometimes, we must run before we can walk. We have to understand how to make cross-thread calls via delegates using the simplest code. Nevertheless, we can also do that using an **MVC (Model-View-Controller)** design. This would be more appropriate and a good practice in bigger applications. In order to implement a successful MVC design using delegates, we can also trust the **observer** object behavioral design pattern, also known as **dependents** and **publish-subscribe**. It allows us to achieve a simple UI decouple while keeping a model to request modifications and notify changes.

6. Add the following line of code at the end of the `EncryptFile` method:

```
// Call the form's method to update the UI using a safe delegate
proForm.AddToListBox(prsInputFileName);
```

7. Open the code for the Windows Form `Form1` (**frmMarsEncrypter**).

8. Add the following line of code in the `QueueFileEncryption` method, before the line `ThreadPool.QueueUserWorkItem(new WaitCallback(ThreadProc), loEncrypter);`:

```
// Fill the property with the reference to this form
loEncrypter.poForm = this;
```

9. Build and run the application.

10. Copy a dozen text files to be encrypted (around 10 megabytes in size to generate a processing impact) into the input folder while the application is running.

11. Open the Windows Explorer in the output folder. You will see the encrypted files appearing, and their names in the listbox, when the encryption has finished (and not when it begins), as shown in the following image:

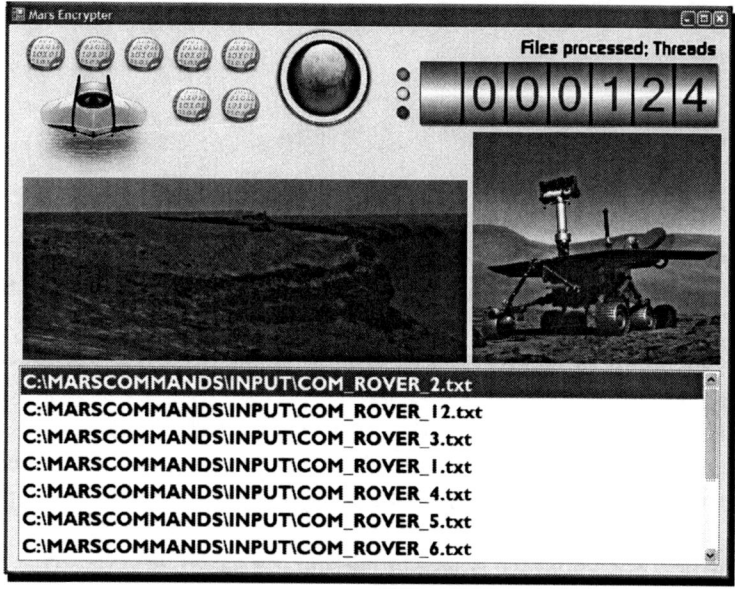

(Rover image credits: Courtesy NASA/JPL-Caltech and NASA/JPL/Cornell)

What just happened?

You solved the problem discovered by the quality assurance team in the encryption dispatcher. Now, they can see the file names appearing in the listbox exactly when the work is completed. It is easy to provide precise user interface feedback using delegates. The team is very happy because they believe you are able to solve many complex multithreading problems!

Following simple steps, we could easily create a delegate to update the UI from any independent thread created by the `ThreadPool` class. Using delegates, we simplified the complexity of updating the UI at specific times without having to use the BackgroundWorker component.

> Once we understand the possibilities offered by delegates to update the UI, we can have complete control over UI feedback with concurrent programming.

Providing feedback when the work is finished

First, we added a property to the `Encrypter` class to hold a reference to the instance of the `frmMarsEncrypter` class that represents the user interface and updates the form.

Then, we changed the `EncryptFile` method. Now the method has the following lines of code:

```
LoadTextToEncrypt();
EncryptText();
SaveEncryptedText();
proForm.AddToListBox(prsInputFileName);
```

The last line simply calls the public `AddToListBox` method found in the instance of the `frmMarsEncrypter` class held by the `proForm` private variable associated to the `poForm` public property. Yes, we can make a direct call to this method without delegates. It is possible because it is a safe method that invokes a delegate when necessary, as previously explained.

 Remember that the current thread will be blocked until the code in the `AddToListBox` method and the code in the delegate called by it has been executed. We did it with a synchronous execution.

Hence, after the new encrypted file is saved to disk in the `SaveEncryptedText` method, the `libFilesEncrypted` listbox adds the input file name to the list of processed files.

We could provide a precise feedback to the UI when the work of a thread is finished using a delegate.

Time for action – Identifying threads and giving them names

Now, we are going to make some changes to the code in order to identify the threads. We are going to give them names:

1. Stay in the project, `MarsEncrypter`.
2. Open the code for the Windows Form `Form1` (**frmMarsEncrypter**).
3. Open the `Form Load` event and add the following code; we want to identify the UI thread:
   ```
   // Give a name to identify the thread that creates the UI
   Thread.CurrentThread.Name = "UI Thread";
   ```

4. Add the following line of code in the `ThreadProc` method, before the line, `loEncrypter.EncryptFile();`. We want to identify each thread created by the ThreadPool:

```
// Give the thread a name
Thread.CurrentThread.Name = "ThreadPool: " + loEncrypter.
                            psInputFileName;
```

What just happened?

Now, each thread has a name that identifies it. We are able to identify the thread that created the UI from the worker threads produced by the `ThreadPool` class.

Time for action – Understanding how to invoke delegates step-by-step

Now, we are going to execute the code in the `AddToListBox` method step-by-step, to have a better understanding of how delegates work in order to update the UI from worker threads:

1. Stay in the project, `MarsEncrypter`.
2. Open the code for the Windows Form `Form1` (**frmMarsEncrypter**).
3. Define a new breakpoint in the line `if (libFilesEncrypted.InvokeRequired)` in the `AddToListBox` method.
4. Press *F5* or select **Debug | Start Debugging** in the main menu. Make sure the **Threads** window is visible.
5. Copy just one text file to be encrypted (around 10 megabytes in size to generate a processing impact) into the input folder while the application runs.

6. After a few seconds, when the working thread finishes the encryption process, the line with the breakpoint defined in the `AddToListBox` method is shown highlighted as the next statement that will be executed. The current thread is the worker thread created by the `ThreadPool` class, as shown in the following image:

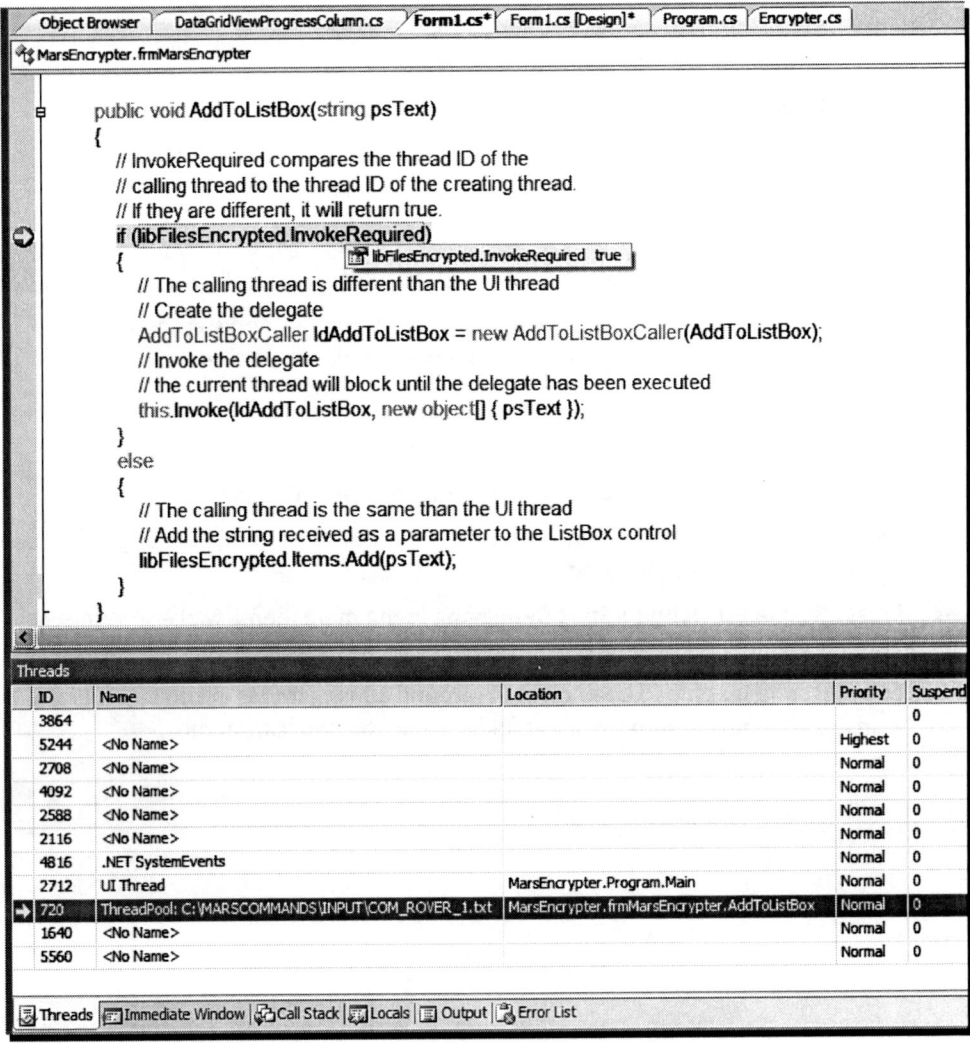

7. Inspect the value of the `InvokeRequired` property. This time, it is **true** because the current thread is the worker thread created by the `ThreadPool` class.

8. Go on running the application step-by-step and watch how the call to the `Invoke` method sends us again to the line with the defined breakpoint. However, now the current thread is the thread that created the UI, as shown in the following image:

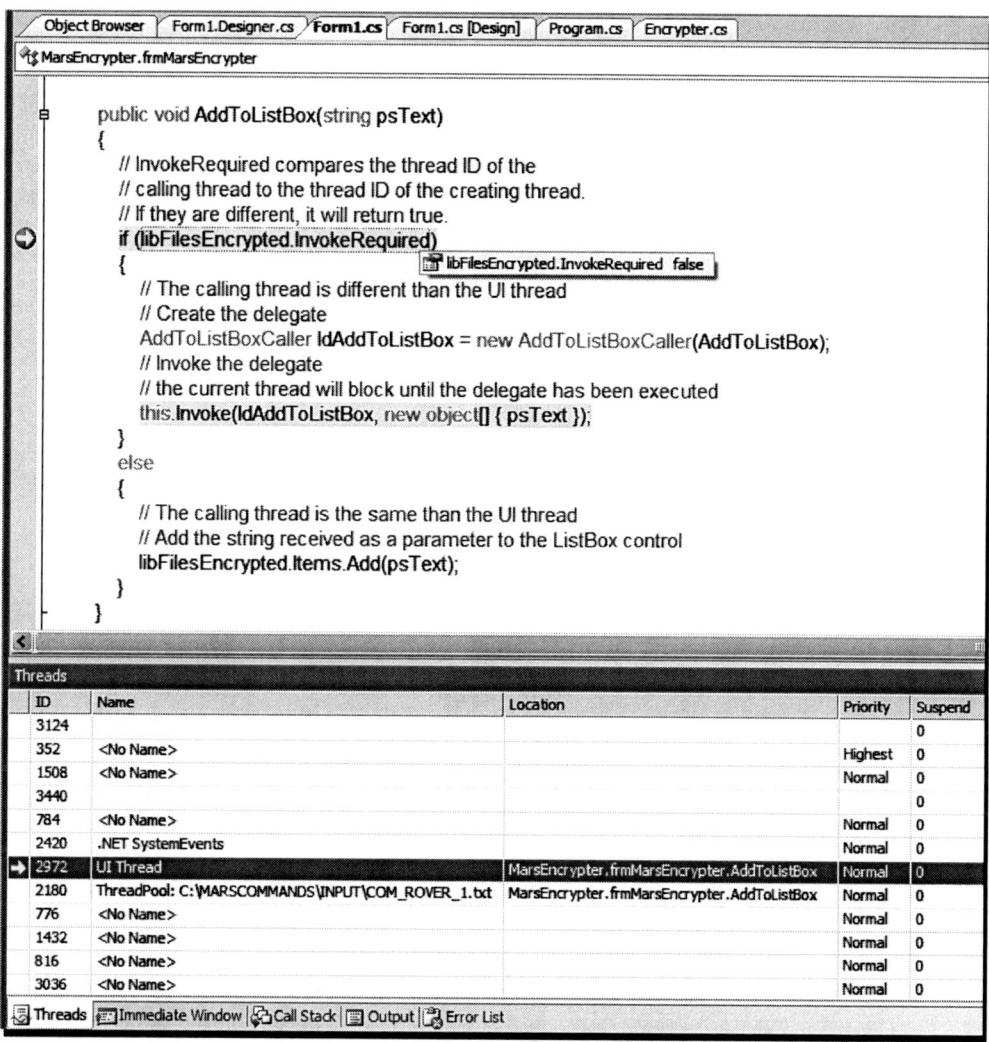

9. Now, inspect the value of the `InvokeRequired` property. This time, it is **false**, because the current thread is the one that created the UI.

10. Go on running the application step-by-step and watch how the current thread is again the worker thread created by the `ThreadPool` class, when it returns from the method called in the UI thread by the `Invoke` method, as shown in the following image:

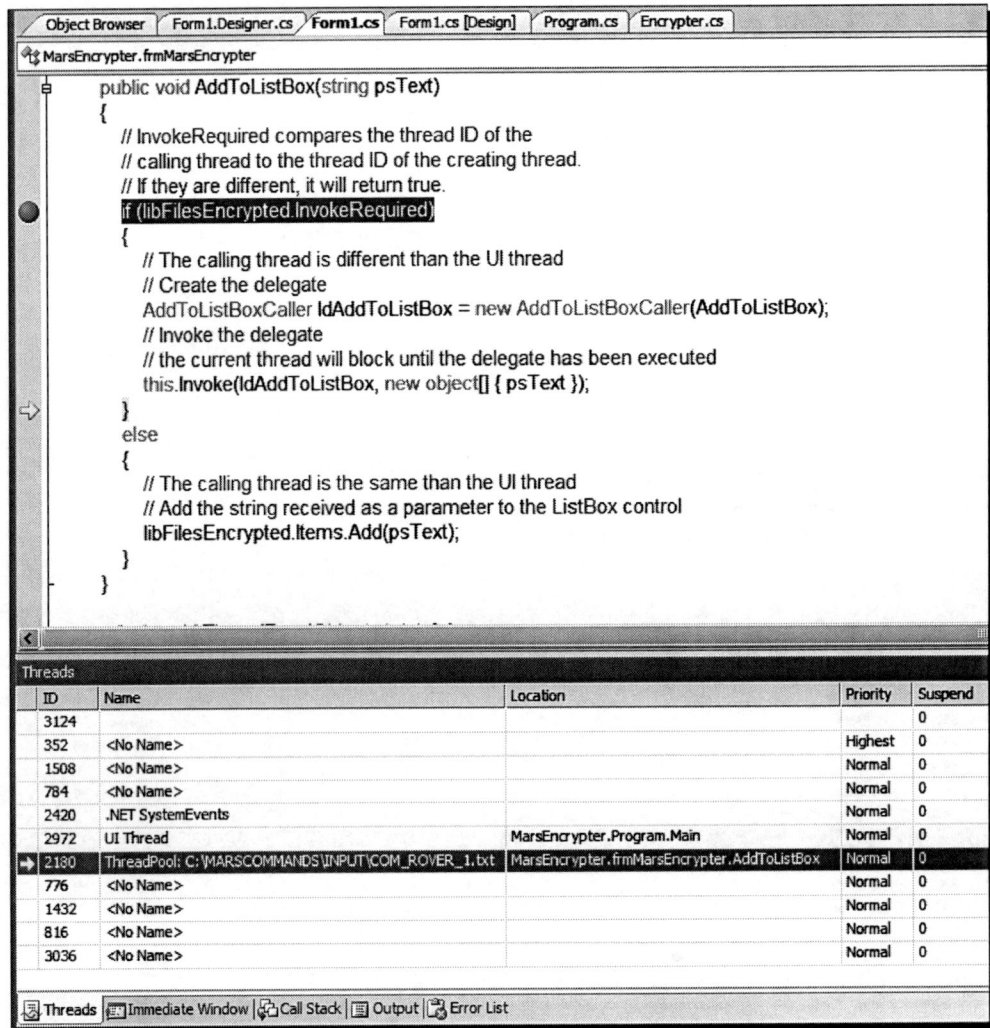

What just happened?

It is easy to understand how delegates help us to update the UI and make cross-thread calls, debugging the application and running it step-by-step, with the **Threads** window visible.

Following the steps explained here, we could create delegates and methods to update the UI from any thread.

Delegates add some complexity to the code, but they are very powerful and they allow us to create more responsive user interfaces with extreme precision.

Decoding the delegates and concurrency puzzle

In the following sequence diagram, we can see the interaction between instances and the different threads involved when using a delegate to make cross-thread calls:

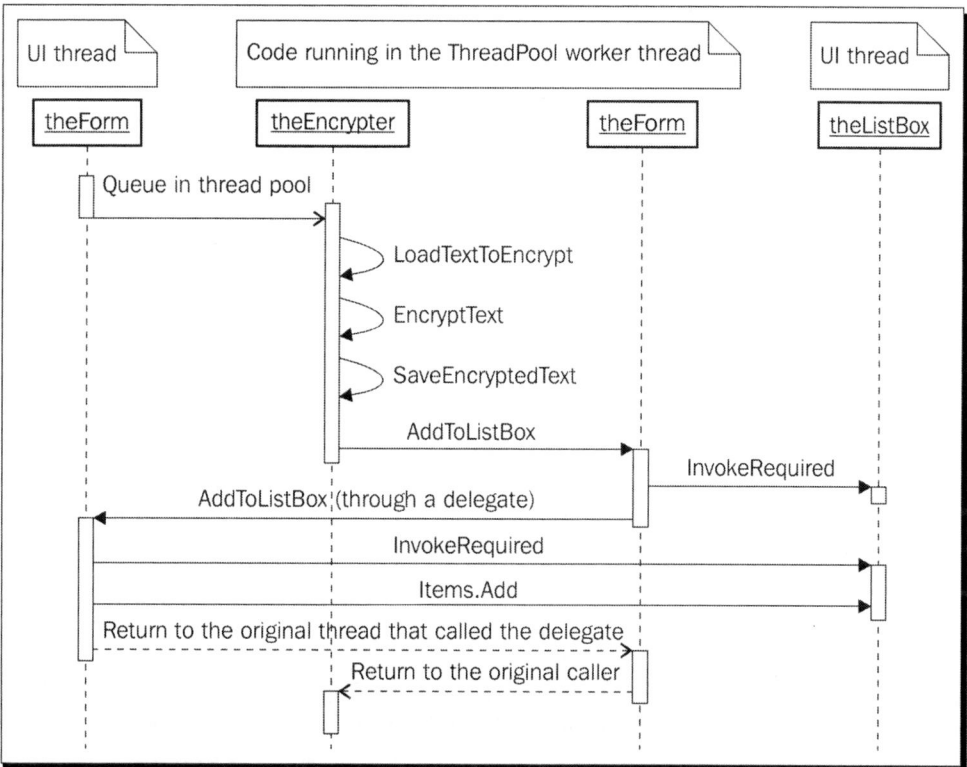

There is some code in the form running in the UI thread and some code running in the ThreadPool worker thread. Traditional sequence diagrams prepared for single-threaded applications are not useful in understanding concurrency problems. Therefore, we added notes to specify the thread in which the instance is running, and hence we will be able to have a better understanding of these cross-thread calls using delegates.

The diagram represents the following sequence:

1. The form, running in the UI thread, queues an `Encrypter` instance to run in the pool of threads, with an asynchronous execution. Therefore, the UI thread can go on dispatching messages and can run code concurrently with the code that is run by the `Encrypter` instance.

2. The `Encrypter` instance calls some internal methods to encrypt the file and save the results in a new output file. Then, it calls the `AddToListBox` method in the form, while running in the worker thread created by the `ThreadPool` class. It is the same form, but in a thread different from the UI one.

3. Therefore, the method checks the value of the `InvokeRequired` property of the listbox. As the thread is different from the UI thread, it holds a `true` value.

4. Thus, the `AddToListBox` method that is still running in the worker thread created by the `ThreadPool` class invokes a delegate to run the `AddToListBox` method (the same method), but this time, using the UI thread to do so.

5. Now, the method checks the value of the `InvokeRequired` property of the listbox. As the thread is the same as the UI thread, it holds a `false` value.

6. Next, it calls the `Items.Add` method of the listbox to make the necessary changes in the control to provide the feedback to the UI.

7. As there is no additional code in the `AddToListBox` method in the form, it returns to the original thread, and the original method that called the delegate through the `Invoke` method, which is the `AddToListBox` method running in the worker thread created by the `ThreadPool` class. Thus, it completes the cross-thread call, returning to the original thread.

8. As there is no additional code in the `AddToListBox` method in the form running in the worker thread created by the `ThreadPool` class, it returns to the original caller in the `Encrypter` instance.

Time for action – Creating safe counters using delegates and avoiding concurrency problems

The quality assurance team discovered another bug in the renewed encryption dispatcher. It displays a very nice counter image, but is not updated as the files are being encrypted. They want you to change the application to add an encrypted files counter and to increase it exactly when each work item is completed.

Again, that sounds easy for a BackgroundWorker component, but this time, you cannot use it because you would have to introduce a loop in the BackgroundWorker thread to collect the results. Instead, you can take advantage of the delegate invocation from the worker thread to update the user interface safely and increase the counter.

Now, we are going to add a counter and a method to update it, taking advantage of the delegate invocation previously made in this project:

 We are going to use a label control to display the counter. However, we will show a **Dundas gauge GaugeContainer (Dundas.Gauge.Wincontrol.GaugeContainer)** because it offers a nice representation to impress NASA's staff. You can download fully functional demos of **Dundas Data Visualization products** from `http://www.dundas.com/`.

1. Stay in the project, `MarsEncrypter`.

2. Add a label control (**lblCounter**) to the form in order to display the counter (files processed and the maximum number of concurrent threads that are going to be used), as shown in the following image:

3. Open the code for the Windows Form `Form1` (**frmMarsEncrypter**).

4. Add the following private variable (the counter):

```
// The total number of files encrypted
private int priTotalFilesEncrypted = 0;
```

5. Add the following method to increase and update the counter (as it is going to be run by the delegate, we are sure it will not have concurrency problems, and is therefore safe):

```
private void IncreaseAndShowCounter()
{
    // Increase the number of total files encrypted
    priTotalFilesEncrypted++;
    // Update the counter
    lblCounter.Text = string.Format("{0};{1}",
    priTotalFilesEncrypted, Environment.ProcessorCount);
}
```

6. Add the following line of code in the `AddToListBox` method, after the line `libFilesEncrypted.Items.Add(psText);`:

```
// Increase and show the counter (safely because we are in the UI
    thread when we make this call)
IncreaseAndShowCounter();
```

7. Build and run the application.

8. Copy a dozen text files to be encrypted (around 10 megabytes in size to generate a processing impact) in the input folder while the application is running.

9. Open the Windows Explorer in the output folder. You will see the encrypted files appearing, their names in the listbox when the encryption has finished (and not when it begins), and the counter being increased as shown in the following image:

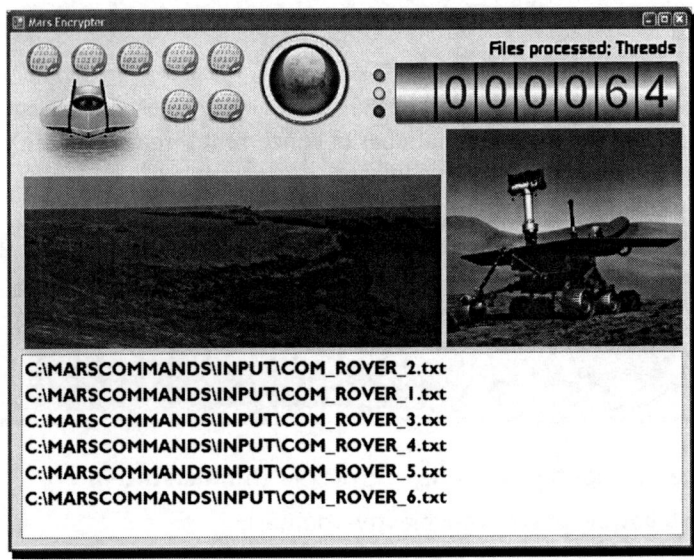

(Rover image credits: Courtesy NASA/JPL-Caltech and NASA/JPL/Cornell)

What just happened?

Again, you solved the problem discovered by the quality assurance team in the encryption dispatcher. Now, they can see a very nice counter increasing its number when the encryption of each file completes. We took advantage of the delegate to provide precise user interface feedback. However, as NASA's CIO is amazed with the UI feedback with a highly multithreaded application, he is going to ask you to create an even more responsive UI. More work coming your way!

Taking advantage of the single-threaded UI to create safe counters

As mentioned earlier, the UI thread queues the incoming messages and processes the method calls one after the other, with a single-threaded synchronous approach. Therefore, it offers an excellent execution mechanism for creating safe counters, avoiding locks and loops to collect information from many threads.

 The UI thread will never have concurrency problems because it does not allow concurrency. It offers warranties for safe code to be executed without synchronization pains and avoids locks.

First, we added a private instance variable for the form, `priTotalFilesEncrypted`, to hold the total number of encrypted files. As the UI thread will never have concurrency and is single-threaded, we can work safely with this private variable in this thread:

```
private int priTotalFilesEncrypted = 0;
```

We initialized the variable in the declaration.

The worker threads created by the `ThreadPool` class do not see this variable because it has a private visibility. Thus, they are not able to change its value.

Then, we created a method (`IncreaseAndShowCounter`) to increase that variable and show the counter in the UI. This method will always run in the UI thread. An `InvalidOperationException` would be raised if we called it from another thread, although that is not possible because the `priTotalFilesEncrypted` variable has a private visibility.

We increase the total number of files encrypted without the need to implement locks or synchronization mechanisms because we are sure it is going to run in the UI thread and without concurrency. Thus, the counter will always reflect the real number of files processed. Then, we update the UI, changing the label text:

```
priTotalFilesEncrypted++;
lblCounter.Text = string.Format("{0};{1}", priTotalFilesEncrypted,
                    Environment.ProcessorCount);
```

The call to the `IncreaseAndShowCounter` method takes place in the `AddToListBox` method, which is called by a delegate when the `InvokeRequired` property holds a `true` value.

For each call to the delegate, there is a new message on the queue for the UI thread to process.

If many concurrent worker threads created by the `ThreadPool` class finish the encryption process at the same time, there will be many messages on the queue for the UI thread to process. However, as they will be processed one after the other, the counter is safe from concurrency, and the information shown in the UI is consistent.

Combining the advantage of the single-threaded UI with the power of delegates, we can solve many concurrency problems without the synchronization pains and avoid the conception of difficult-to-solve bugs. Creativity is a great competitive advantage for solving concurrency problems.

Have a go hero – Implementing a Model-View-Controller design

Do you remember that NASA's CIO is an object-oriented guru? He is amazed with your precise user interface feedback. Nevertheless, he loves great object-oriented designs, as he was a **Smalltalk** programmer. So, he is a big fan of the Model-View-Controller (MVC) design.

Develop a new version of this application using a Model-View-Controller design, using everything you've learned about delegates, to provide precise UI updates, while simultaneously establishing a subscribe/notify protocol between the model and the view.

The way to do this is a bit complex, but you have all the information you need to do the job. Review the previous chapters if you need more data!

Good luck, a more complex UI feedback combined with concurrency is waiting for you!

Reporting progress to the UI from independent threads

So far, we have been using delegates with a synchronous execution to update the user interface from independent threads, without the need to implement loops using the BackgroundWorker component. How can we make many changes to the user interface from any independent thread without causing problems and avoiding great performance degradation?

We can do that in a very simple way using delegates with an asynchronous execution to update the UI many times in a thread without blocking it.

The thread is not going to be blocked until the delegate completes the execution. However, the messages queued in the UI thread will be dispatched one after the other, with a synchronous execution. The only thing that changes is that the thread gains control almost instantly after the delegate's asynchronous invocation.

The syntax to do it is almost the same as the one learned previously. Thus, we will be able to focus on a new case without having to explain the code in deep detail.

Time for action – Creating the classes to show a progress bar column in a DataGridView

NASA's CIO wants you to make some changes to the encryption dispatcher to improve the UI feedback. He would like to see all the files being encrypted shown in a DataGridView control with the following columns:

- The input file name
- A progress bar showing the percentage completed

That sounds complex, because you have to create a custom DataGridViewImageCell to show a rectangle filling up, while the file is being encrypted. However, it would be an excellent experience to practice for improving other applications that need this kind of UI feedback. So, let's do that!

First, we are going to create new classes to create the custom DataGridViewImageCell, capable of displaying a progress bar in a DataGridView cell:

1. Stay in the project, MarsEncrypter.

2. Create a new class, DataGridViewProgressCell.

3. Add the following lines of code at the beginning:

```
using System.ComponentModel;
using System.Data;
using System.Drawing;
using System.Windows.Forms;
```

4. Change the class declaration to the following (it must inherit from DataGridViewImageColumn):

```
public class DataGridViewProgressCell : DataGridViewImageCell
```

5. Add the following static variable:

```
static Image proEmptyImage;
```

6. Add the following constructor:

```
public DataGridViewProgressCell()
{
    ValueType = typeof(int);
}
```

7. Add the following static method:

```
static DataGridViewProgressCell()
{
    // The custom cell must be consistent with a
    DataGridViewImageCell
```

```
proEmptyImage = new Bitmap(1, 1, System.Drawing.Imaging.
                           PixelFormat.Format32bppArgb);
}
```

8. Add the following overridden method to return a formatted value:

```
protected override object GetFormattedValue(object value,
  int rowIndex, ref DataGridViewCellStyle cellStyle,
  TypeConverter valueTypeConverter, TypeConverter
  formattedValueTypeConverter, DataGridViewDataErrorContexts
  context)
{
    // This method is required to make the ProgressCell
       consistent with the default ImageCell.
    return proEmptyImage;
}
```

9. Add the following overridden method to perform the custom cell paint, showing a progress bar (a rectangle filling up and a percentage text):

```
protected override void Paint(System.Drawing.Graphics g,
  System.Drawing.Rectangle clipBounds, System.Drawing.Rectangle
  cellBounds, int rowIndex, DataGridViewElementStates cellState,
  object value, object formattedValue, string errorText,
  DataGridViewCellStyle cellStyle, DataGridViewAdvancedBorderStyle
  advancedBorderStyle, DataGridViewPaintParts paintParts)
{
    int liProgressPercentage;

    if (value == null)
    {
        liProgressPercentage = 0;
    }
    else
    {
        liProgressPercentage = (int)value;
    }
    float lfPercentage = ((float) liProgressPercentage / 100.0f);
    Brush loForeColorBrush = new SolidBrush(cellStyle.ForeColor);
    // Draws the grid for the cell
    base.Paint(g, clipBounds, cellBounds, rowIndex, cellState,
               value, formattedValue, errorText, cellStyle,
               advancedBorderStyle, (paintParts &
               ~DataGridViewPaintParts.ContentForeground));
    if (lfPercentage > 0.0)
    {
        // Draw the progress bar
        g.FillRectangle(new SolidBrush(Color.FromArgb(163, 189,
                        242)), cellBounds.X + 2,
                        cellBounds.Y + 2, Convert.
                        ToInt32((lfPercentage * cellBounds.Width
```

```
                                       - 4)), cellBounds.Height - 4);
                // Draw a string showing the percentage value
                g.DrawString(liProgressPercentage.ToString() + "%",
                        cellStyle.Font, loForeColorBrush,
                        cellBounds.X + 6, cellBounds.Y + 2);
        }
        else
        {
            if (this.DataGridView.CurrentRow == null)
            {
                // Draw a string showing the percentage value
                g.DrawString(liProgressPercentage.ToString() + "%",
                        cellStyle.Font, loForeColorBrush,
                        cellBounds.X + 6, cellBounds.Y + 2);
            }
            else
            {
                if (this.DataGridView.CurrentRow.Index == rowIndex)
                {
                    // Draw a string showing the percentage value
                    //    using the selection fore color
                    g.DrawString(liProgressPercentage.ToString() +
                    "%", cellStyle.Font, new SolidBrush(cellStyle.
                    SelectionForeColor), cellBounds.X + 6,
                    cellBounds.Y + 2);
                }
                else
                {
                    // Draw a string showing the percentage value
                    g.DrawString(liProgressPercentage.ToString() +
                            "%", cellStyle.Font,
                            loForeColorBrush, cellBounds.X + 6,
                            cellBounds.Y + 2);
                }
            }
        }
    }
```

10. Create a new class, `DataGridViewProgressColumn`:

```
public class DataGridViewProgressColumn : DataGridViewImageColumn
```

11. Add the following line of code at the beginning:

```
using System.Windows.Forms;
```

12. Add the following constructor:

```
public DataGridViewProgressColumn()
{
    CellTemplate = new DataGridViewProgressCell();
}
```

What just happened?

The code required to create a custom `DataGridViewImageCell` to show a rectangle filling up while the file is being encrypted is now held in the `DataGridViewProgressCell` and the `DataGridViewProgressColumn` classes. We are now going to create a class to hold the information to allow the application to show the progress in this new custom cell.

Time for action – Creating a class to hold the information to show in the DataGridView

Now, we are going to create a new class that implements the `INotifyPropertyChanged` interface because we want it bound to a `DataGridView`. It is going to offer the necessary properties to show the information in the `DataGridView` columns:

1. Stay in the project, `MarsEncrypter`.
2. Open the code for the `Encrypter` class.
3. Change the existing `Encrypter` class visibility to public:

   ```
   public class Encrypter
   ```

4. Create a new class, `FileToEncryptProgress`, implementing the `INotifyPropertyChanged` interface, using the following declaration:

   ```
   public class FileToEncryptProgress : INotifyPropertyChanged
   ```

5. Add the following line of code at the beginning:

   ```
   using System.ComponentModel;
   ```

6. Add the following private variables:

   ```
   private string prsInputFileName = String.Empty;
   private int priProgress = 0;
   ```

7. Add the following properties to access the private variable (we want to create a compact and reliable class, and we need the properties to bind them to the `DataGridView` columns):

   ```
   public string psInputFileName
   {
       set
       {
           if (value != prsInputFileName)
           {
               // The value changed
               prsInputFileName = value;
               NotifyPropertyChanged("psInputFileName");
           }
       }
       get
   ```

```
        {
            return prsInputFileName;
        }
    }

    public int piProgress
    {
        set
        {
            if (value != priProgress)
            {
                // The value changed
                priProgress = value;
                NotifyPropertyChanged("piProgress");
            }
        }

        get
        {
            return priProgress;
        }
    }
```

8. Add the following public event:

```
public event PropertyChangedEventHandler PropertyChanged;
```

9. Add the following private method:

```
private void NotifyPropertyChanged(String info)
{
    if (PropertyChanged != null)
    {
        PropertyChanged(this, new PropertyChangedEventArgs(
                        info));
    }
}
```

10. Create the following constructor with parameters:

```
public FileToEncryptProgress(string parsInputFileName,
                             int pariProgress)
{
    prsInputFileName = parsInputFileName;
    priProgress = pariProgress;
}
```

What just happened?

The code required creation of a new class that implements the `INotifyPropertyChanged` interface with the following properties held in the `FileToEncryptProgress` class:

- ◆ `psInputFileName`: The complete input file name, including its path
- ◆ `piProgress`: The progress percentage of the encryption process (0 to 100)

Every time an encryption job is queued by the `ThreadPool` class, a new instance of the `FileToEncryptProgress` class must be shown as a new row in a `DataGridView`.

Time for action – Invoking multiple asynchronous user interface updates from many threads

Now, we must add a `DataGridView` and create a new delegate to update the user interface from many threads using an asynchronous execution to avoid performance degradation:

1. Stay in the project, `MarsEncrypter`.

2. Open Windows Form `Form1` (**frmMarsEncrypter**) in the form designer and add a `DataGridView` control, **dgvFilesToEncryptProgress**.

3. Open the code for the Windows Form `Form1` (**frmMarsEncrypter**).

4. Add the following declaration in the instance variables zone:

   ```
   // The list to hold the FileToEncryptProgress instances for each
      new file to encrypt
   List<FileToEncryptProgress> paoFilesToEncryptProgress = new
     List<FileToEncryptProgress>();
   ```

5. Add the following declaration in the instance variables zone (a new delegate to update the UI showing the progress in a `DataGridView`):

   ```
   private delegate void UpdateProgressCaller();
   ```

6. Add the following public method to invalidate the `DataGridView` column that shows the progress, invoking an asynchronous delegate when the calling thread is different from the UI thread:

   ```
   public void UpdateProgress()
   {
       // InvokeRequired compares the thread ID of the calling
          thread to the thread ID of the creating thread.
       // If they are different, it will return true.
       if (dgvFilesToEncryptProgress.InvokeRequired)
       {
           // The calling thread is different than the UI thread
           // Create the delegate
   ```

```
        UpdateProgressCaller ldUpdateProgress = new
         UpdateProgressCaller(UpdateProgress);
        // Invoke the delegate asynchronously
        // the current thread will not block until the delegate
           has been executed
        this.BeginInvoke(ldUpdateProgress);
    }
    else
    {
        // The calling thread is the same as the UI thread
        // Invalidate the progress column of the grid control (to
           avoid repainting all the grid)
        dgvFilesToEncryptProgress.InvalidateColumn(1);
    }
}
```

7. Add the following procedure to bind or rebind the `DataGridView` with the list of files to be encrypted with their progress values:

```
private void ShowFilesToEncryptProgressGrid()
{
    // Do not generate the DataGridView columns automatically
    dgvFilesToEncryptProgress.AutoGenerateColumns = false;
    // Bind the DataGridView to the list of encrypted files
    dgvFilesToEncryptProgress.DataSource =
     paoFilesToEncryptProgress;
    dgvFilesToEncryptProgress.Columns.Clear();
    // Add the Input file name column
    dgvFilesToEncryptProgress.Columns.Add(new
     DataGridViewTextBoxColumn());
    dgvFilesToEncryptProgress.Columns[0].DataPropertyName =
     "psInputFileName";
    dgvFilesToEncryptProgress.Columns[0].HeaderText = "File name
     to encrypt";
    // Add the Progress column
    dgvFilesToEncryptProgress.Columns.Add(new
     DataGridViewProgressColumn());
    dgvFilesToEncryptProgress.Columns[1].DataPropertyName =
     "piProgress";
    dgvFilesToEncryptProgress.Columns[1].HeaderText = "Encryption
     progress";
}
```

8. Add the following lines of code before the `loEncrypter.poForm = this;` statement in the `QueueFileEncryption` method (we need to create a new instance of the `FileToEncryptProgress` class, add it to the list, and bind or rebind the `DataGridView`):

```
FileToEncryptProgress loFileToEncryptProgress;
loFileToEncryptProgress = new FileToEncryptProgress(psFileName,
                                                     0);
paoFilesToEncryptProgress.Add(loFileToEncryptProgress);
// Update the data grid binding it again to the data source
ShowFilesToEncryptProgressGrid();
loEncrypter.poFileToEncryptProgress = loFileToEncryptProgress;
```

> The `Encrypter` class does not have the `poFileToEncryptProgress` property. The code is going to be completed in the forthcoming sections.

What just happened?

The code required to update the `DataGridView` safely from any thread is now held in a new public method defined in the main form class.

Thus, calling the `UpdateProgress` public method without parameters from any thread, we can easily update the `dgvFilesToEncryptProgress` grid column that shows a progress bar when the corresponding thread reports an increase in the progress percentage.

> Now that we understand how delegates work, we have no problems in updating the UI. We can do it whenever we want to do it. However, this time, we are making **cross-thread calls** with an asynchronous execution.

Creating a delegate without parameters

We already know that we cannot make changes to the user interface from a thread different from the one that created the controls. In this case, we have a list bounded to the `DataGridView` control. However, in order to update the data displayed in the corresponding column as a progress bar, we must call the `Invalidate` method for that control.

Therefore, in order to make it possible and to synchronize the progress with this user interface feedback, we can use a new delegate. Nevertheless, this time, the delegate is going to be called 100 times for each file that is being encrypted. As we will have a number of concurrent threads with encryption jobs, we do not want to degrade performance. Hence, we use an asynchronous execution for the delegate.

First, we added the delegate declaration, in the instance variables zone:

```
private delegate void UpdateProgressCaller();
```

As previously explained, this line uses the `private delegate` keywords (visibility + `delegate` keyword) followed by a method declaration—`void UpdateProgressCaller()`.

We called it `UpdateProgressCaller` because it will hold a reference to the public `UpdateProgress` method. We added the `Caller` suffix to specify that it is a delegate and hence a method caller.

The following line declared the public method:

```
public void UpdateProgress()
```

Invoking a delegate asynchronously to avoid performance degradation

Now, let's focus on the public `UpdateProgress` method. It has a structure very similar to the `AddToListBox` method, explained previously.

It uses the well-known `InvokeRequired` property. The following lines take into account the value of the `InvokeRequired` property:

```
if (dgvFilesToEncryptProgress.InvokeRequired)
{
    // The calling thread is different than the UI thread
    // Create the delegate
    UpdateProgressCaller ldUpdateProgress =
     new UpdateProgressCaller(UpdateProgress);
    // Invoke the delegate
    // the current thread will block until the delegate has been
        executed
    this.BeginInvoke(ldUpdateProgress);
}
else
{
    // The calling thread is the same as the UI thread
    // Invalidate the progress column of the grid control (to avoid
        repainting all the grid)
    dgvFilesToEncryptProgress.InvalidateColumn(1);
}
```

If the `InvokeRequired` property value for the `dgvFilesToEncryptProgress`
`DataGridView` control is `false`, there will be no problem in making a direct call to the
control methods and their properties. In that case, the following line of code in the `else`
section will be executed:

```
dgvFilesToEncryptProgress.InvalidateColumn(1);
```

If the `InvokeRequired` property value for the `dgvFilesToEncryptProgress`
`DataGridView` control is `true`, it means that we are calling the method from a different
thread. Therefore we must invoke the delegate to send a message on the queue for the UI
thread to process.

In this case, we want to invoke an asynchronous execution. This means that the calling
thread (current thread) will not block until the delegate has been executed. Thus, it will send
the message to the UI thread to be processed, and it will return without waiting for that
message to finish its execution. This way, the worker thread can go on encrypting the file.

First, we create a new instance of the `UpdateProgressCaller` delegate, sending the main
method name as a parameter (`UpdateProgress`), as shown in the following line of code:

```
UpdateProgressCaller ldUpdateProgress = new
        UpdateProgressCaller(UpdateProgress);
```

Then, we can call the `BeginInvoke` method. It executes the specified delegate on the
thread that owns the control's underlying window handle, with an asynchronous execution.
We need to execute the `ldUpdateProgress` delegate without parameters:

```
this.BeginInvoke(ldUpdateProgress);
```

Calling the `BeginInvoke` method puts a message on the queue for the
UI thread to process and returns control to the calling thread immediately.
Nevertheless, again, the UI thread will not process many delegates concurrently.
Therefore there will be no concurrency in the UI. As it is a queue, messages
will be processed sequentially. Using the `BeginInvoke` method, the current
thread will not be blocked until the delegate has been executed because this
method follows an asynchronous execution. It is very useful in controlling the
specific time at which we want to update the UI, when we need to make many
calls and do not want to block the worker threads.

The `BeginInvoke` method will return control to the worker thread, and then it will switch
over to the UI thread when it becomes available, and call the `UpdateProgress` method.
However, this time the `InvokeRequired` property of the `dgvFilesToEncryptProgress`
listbox control will hold a `false` value, because we are in the UI thread, while the worker
threads continues to process instructions. Thus, the code in the `else` part is going to
be executed in order to invalidate and repaint the `DataGridView` column, showing the
progress bars:

```
dgvFilesToEncryptProgress.InvalidateColumn(1);
```

Time for action – Updating progress percentages from worker threads

Now, we are going to make the necessary changes to the `Encrypter` class to allow it to invoke many user interface updates, while the progress percentages increase during the encryption algorithm:

1. Stay in the project, `MarsEncrypter`.

2. Open the code for the `Encrypter` class.

3. Add the following private variable:

```
private FileToEncryptProgress proFileToEncryptProgress;
```

4. Add the following properties to access the private variable (we want to create a compact and reliable class):

```
public FileToEncryptProgress poFileToEncryptProgress
{
    set
    {
        proFileToEncryptProgress = value;
    }
    get
    {
        return proFileToEncryptProgress;
    }
}
```

5. Replace the `EncryptText` method with the following:

```
private void EncryptText()
{
    int liProgress;
    int liOldProgress = 0;

    for (int i = 0; i < pasTextToEncrypt.Count; i++)
    {
        pasTextToEncrypt[i] = Encrypt(pasTextToEncrypt[i]);
        liProgress = (i * 100 / pasTextToEncrypt.Count);
        if (liProgress > liOldProgress)
        {
            liOldProgress = liProgress;
            proFileToEncryptProgress.piProgress = liProgress;
            // Update the UI
            // Call the form's method to update the UI using a
               safe delegate
            proForm.UpdateProgress();
        }
    }
}
```

```
        // All the strings were encrypted
        // Thus, 100% must be shown
        proFileToEncryptProgress.piProgress = 100;
        proForm.UpdateProgress();
    }
```

6. Build and run the application.

7. Copy a dozen text files to be encrypted (around 10 megabytes in size to generate a processing impact) into the input folder while the application is running.

8. Open Windows Explorer in the output folder. You will see a grid reporting the progress of each file being encrypted, as shown in the following image:

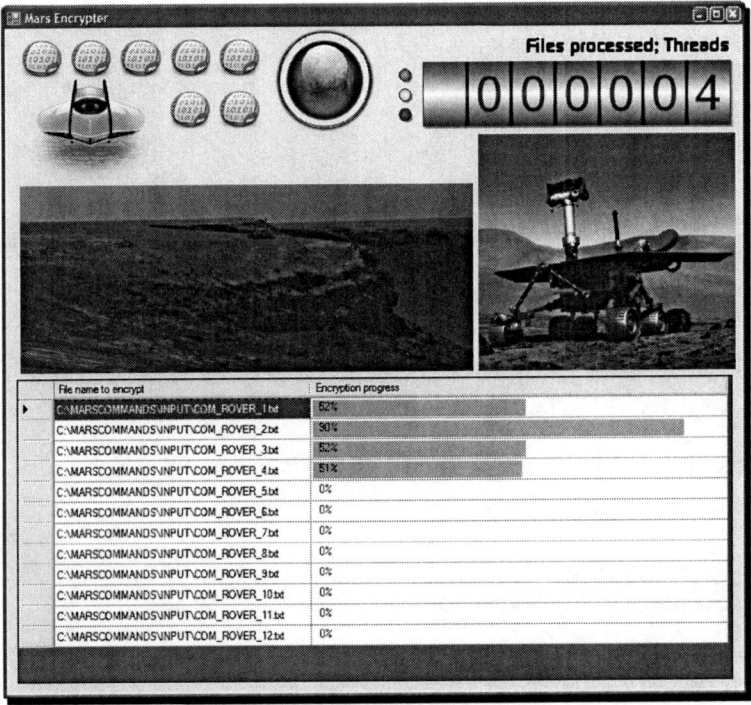

(Rover image credits: Courtesy NASA/JPL-Caltech and NASA/JPL/Cornell)

What just happened?

The user interface is very responsive and it is indeed amazing to see how the multiple progress bars are filled up concurrently. The jealous developers now believe that you are a multithreading god and they respect you!

Following simple steps, we could easily create a new delegate to update the UI multiple times from any independent thread created by the `ThreadPool` class. Using delegates with an asynchronous execution, we simplified the complexity of updating the UI at several times without having to use the BackgroundWorker component. The progress bars in the grid are the best examples of how a pool of threads works, because they make it very easy to understand what is going on with the jobs being processed.

> Delegates offer a very complete control over the UI feedback with concurrent programming. Showing the concurrency while keeping the UI alive is one of the most difficult tasks to be achieved. And we have done it!

Providing feedback while the work is being done

In our previous case, we added a property to the `Encrypter` class to hold a reference to the instance of the `frmMarsEncrypter` class that represents the user interface to update the form. So, we won't do it again.

First, we added a new property to this class to hold a reference to the instance of the `FileToEncryptProgress` class that represents the information to be shown in the `DataGridView` row (the list that contains the instance is bound to it).

Then, we changed the `EncryptText` method. Now the method calculates and increases the progress percentage in the `piProgress` property of the `FileToEncryptProgress` instance it is associated with. However, this happens only when the value increases in units (+1) to avoid updating the UI millions of times.

This happens in the following lines of code:

```
proFileToEncryptProgress.piProgress = liProgress;
proForm.UpdateProgress();
```

The last line simply calls the public `UpdateProgress` method found in the instance of the `frmMarsEncrypter` class held by the `proForm` private variable associated with the `poForm` public property. Yes, we can make a direct call to this method without delegates. It is possible because it is a safe method that invokes a delegate when necessary, as explained previously.

> Remember that the current thread will not be blocked until the code in the `UpdateProgress` method and the code in the delegate called by it have been executed. We did it with an asynchronous execution.

Hence, when the progress percentage increases by a unit or more, the main worker thread's grid column that shows the progress bars is invalidated to force its update, showing the value held in the `piProgress` property for each row.

We could provide multiple precise feedback to the UI, while the work is being executed in many threads, using a delegate with an asynchronous execution.

Have a go hero – Creating a parallelized user interface

The encryption dispatcher is a masterpiece, but NASA's CIO asks you to improve the star finder application with new user interface feedback.

He wants you to make a new version of that application with the following behavior:

♦ Running as a dispatcher for many input images.

♦ Showing the progress in a `DataGridView` for each image being processed (using safe counters as you learned in this chapter).

♦ Showing the stars as they are found in thumbnails, and allowing the user to click on a thumbnail and display a new window. The new window must not be modal, and it must show the progress if that image is being processed.

♦ Try to do that using an MVC and creating strong, highly cohesive classes and methods. Do not forget object-oriented best practices.

As you can see, he wants an impressive UI combined with great performance.

You can do it; using delegates everything is possible!

Pop quiz

1. Using delegates is useful to:

    a. Make cross-thread calls with synchronous or asynchronous executions

    b. Make **IPC (Inter-Process Communication)** with synchronous or asynchronous executions

    c. Make **RPC (Remote Procedure Calls)** with synchronous or asynchronous executions

2. A control's `InvokeRequired` property will return `true` when:

    a. The calling thread is the UI thread

    b. The calling thread is different from the UI thread

    c. The UI thread is busy

3. For invoking the `ldShowUpdate` delegate instance with a synchronous execution, sending `piProcessedPiece` and `psText` as parameters, the following line of code has the right syntax:

   a. `this.Invoke(ldShowUpdate, psText, piProcessedPiece);`

   b. `this.Invoke(ldShowUpdate, new object[]`
      `{ psText, piProcessedPiece });`

   c. `this.Invoke(ldShowUpdate, { psText, piProcessedPiece });`

4. Calling the `Invoke` method:

   a. Puts a message on the queue for the current thread to process

   b. Puts a message on the stack for the current thread to process

   c. Puts a message on the queue for the UI thread to process

5. Moreover, using delegates is useful for:

   a. Creating safe concurrency, as the code is executed in the concurrency message queue

   b. Creating safe garbage collectors, as the code is executed in the garbage collector queue, without the possibility of concurrency

   c. Creating safe counters related to threads, as the code is executed in the safe UI message queue, without the possibility of concurrency

Right answers:

1. a.
2. b.
3. b.
4. c.
5. c.

Summary

We learned a lot in this chapter about providing a more responsive user interface, using synchronous and asynchronous delegates. We were able to combine the parallelized operations with a precise user interface feedback while avoiding some multithreading pains. Specifically, we covered:

- Using delegates to make cross-thread calls and update the user interface from independent threads safely
- Achieving a great responsive user interface without great efforts, using synchronous and asynchronous delegates to dispatch changes to the UI thread
- Using techniques to update the user interface many times without degrading performance
- Creating counters and other global information without collecting results, taking advantage of the single-threaded model for the UI thread
- Updating progress bar columns in many rows of a grid from multiple worker threads
- Combining our concurrent programming knowledge with our user interface update abilities

We also learned how to add a progress bar to a `DataGridView` control, use new techniques to create safe counters, and how to combine a pool of threads with a responsive user interface.

Now that we've learned many ways to update the user interface with great precision, we're ready to work with .NET parallel extensions—which is the topic of the next chapter.

11

Coding with .NET Parallel Extensions

In order to take full advantage of the parallel processing capabilities offered by modern hardware, there are new libraries being developed for C# and other Visual Studio programming languages. They can help us in developing parallel algorithms and concurrent programs with more flexibility and less code. In this chapter, we will take a close look at the new features that will be a part of the new versions of C# and Visual Studio to improve our applications and to prepare our code to be compatible with them. Reading it and following the exercises we shall:

- ♦ Learn to install and use parallel extensions being developed by Microsoft
- ♦ Use third-party libraries in our parallel algorithms
- ♦ Combine different execution techniques with automatically parallelized structures
- ♦ Simplify the code needed to run tasks in parallel
- ♦ Work with producer-consumer schemes running in parallel
- ♦ Learn different techniques to parallelize statistics, improving the overall performance
- ♦ Combine our concurrent programming knowledge with future improvements in the C# programming language and runtime

Parallelizing loops using .NET extensions

So far, we have relied on concurrency structures offered by both Visual C# 2.0 and 3.0 (2005 and 2008) and on the object-oriented capabilities of the C# programming language, applied to offer clean solutions to some concurrency problems. However, Microsoft is working hard on a new parallel library to be part of Visual Studio 2010. It is available as a **CTP (Community Technology Preview)** for use in Visual Studio 2008 (C# 3.0). Besides, this library is also available in Visual Studio 2010 CTP (C# 4.0). How can we use these new **Parallel Extensions** to improve the performance of our applications? Is it safe to use them?

As they are CTPs, it means that they are a beta releases (pre-releases), continuously changing from version to version, and can have some new features added and some others removed. Therefore, it is not convenient to use them in the final releases of our applications. Nevertheless, it would be useful to take a look at the new structures we will find in future Visual C# versions. Of course, we have to be pragmatic, and there is **no silver bullet** in the new parallel extensions. We must take into account everything we have learned so far.

The simplest way to work with parallelism is not always the most efficient one. As we will be working on a CTP during this chapter, some features are going to change in the final release. We must know everything we have learned so far to achieve an efficient parallelization. Sometimes, the parallel extensions will be useful, while in other cases, they will not be as efficient as expected, and we can use manual threading.

Knowing both worlds gives us the opportunity to choose which one is better for each case!

Time for action – Downloading and installing the .NET Parallel Extensions

Let's return to stars with NASA! A nebula is an interstellar cloud of dust, gas, hydrogen, and plasma. It is the first stage of a star's life cycle. As you would expect, NASA has millions of images of nebulae taken from thousands of telescopes around the world. This huge image library is difficult to process as they are receiving thousands of new images per day.

Using your multithreading capabilities, NASA's CIO wants you to parallelize as much as possible and take full advantage of available servers, to optimize the execution of a nebula finder algorithm. They will provide you with a graphics library to help you in that process, but you must test the capabilities offered by the Parallel Extensions (June 2008) CTP or the Visual Studio 2010 CTP offered by Microsoft. Why? Because helping Microsoft to test them will make it possible for NASA to obtain 500 free Visual Studio 2010 licenses when they become available. That sounds amazing and you will be a hero! Now, you are very well-known for your multithreading capabilities. For this reason, your opinions about the Parallel Extensions are going to be taken into account as a parallel guru's feedback. Come on, let's test the Parallel Extensions!

To complete the following exercises, we need Visual C# 2008 (.NET Framework 3.5) with Service Pack 1 or greater installed. The Parallel Extensions do not run with Visual C# 2005. English language versions of both Windows and Visual Studio/Visual C#/Visual Basic are recommended because the Parallel Extensions CTP has not been tested extensively on other platforms. We will be working with a beta version of a library; therefore, we can face unexpected results.

First, we are going to download and install the most recent Parallel Extensions CTP release, create a new project and add references to this library in order to use them. We can also use Visual Studio 2010 CTP (it includes the parallel extensions). This way, later, we will be able to use the new features offered by the Parallel Extensions in our parallelized nebula finder algorithms:

1. Download the following files from the latest Parallel Extensions CTP available at `http://msdn.microsoft.com/en-us/concurrency/bb896007.aspx`:

   ◆ `ParallelExtensions_Jun08CTP.msi`—the installer

   ◆ `ParallelExtensions_Jun08CTP_Help.zip`—the help file in `.CHM` format

2. We are going to work with the June 2008 CTP, which can be downloaded from `http://www.microsoft.com/downloads/details.aspx?FamilyId=348F73FD-593D-4B3C-B055-694C50D2B0F3&displaylang=en`.

3. Uninstall any previously installed CTP of the Parallel Extensions using the **Add/Remove programs** feature in any Windows version **Control Panel**.

4. Run the `ParallelExtensions_Jun08CTP.msi` installer and follow the steps to complete the installation wizard.

5. The following are the default installation folders :

   ◆ `C:\Program Files\Microsoft Parallel Extensions Jun08 CTP\` On 32-bit operating systems

   ◆ `C:\Program Files (x86)\Microsoft Parallel Extensions Jun08 CTP\` On 64-bit operating systems

6. Once the installation has finished, create a new C# Project using the Windows Forms Application template in Visual Studio 2008 or Visual C# Express 2008 (or later). Use `BlobCounter` as the project's name.

7. Now, we must add a reference to the installed library to access the Parallel Extensions. Select **Project | Add Reference...** from the main menu. The **Add Reference** dialog box will appear.

8. Stay in the **.NET** tab and select the **System.Threading** element, as shown in the following image:

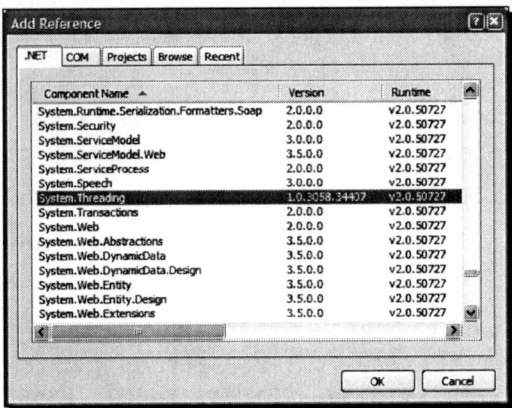

9. Click **OK**. The Parallel Extensions will be available for use in our new project.

10. Open the **Solution Explorer**.

11. Unfold the **References** container.

12. Right-click on **System.Threading** and select **Properties** in the context menu that appears. Check the description; it must be **Parallel Extensions to the .NET Framework**, and the path must be the one in which the new libraries were installed, as shown in the following image:

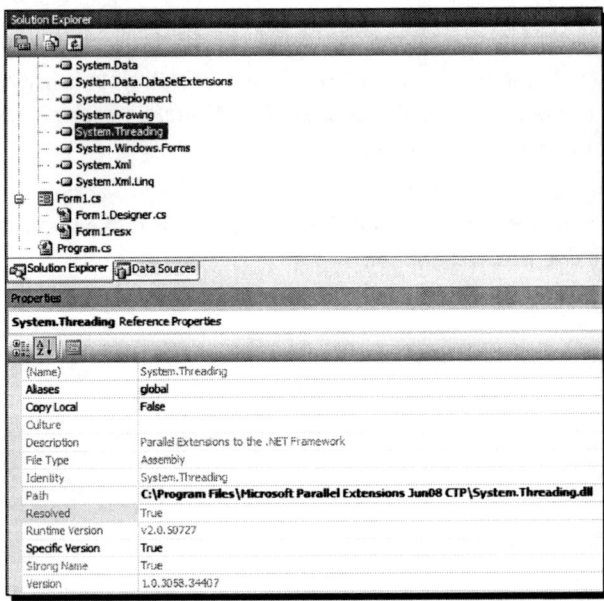

What just happened?

The Parallel Extensions CTP library was installed and added as a reference for our new project that will use them. The previously mentioned steps are necessary for every project in which we intend to work with the Parallel Extensions. Again, we can also use Visual Studio 2010 CTP.

 Remember that using a CTP means risks! It is a pre-release—so, it can have lots of changes before a final release, and it has bugs. If you have to develop an application that needs to take full advantage of parallel processing capabilities offered by modern hardware, it is recommended to use the techniques learned in the previous chapters. Microsoft presents the CTP with the following sentences: "This CTP is for testing purposes only. Features and functionality may change before the final release, and Microsoft may choose not to provide a final release". So, be careful.

No silver bullet

It is very important to take into account that everything we've learned so far is also useful when using the Parallel Extensions library. It provides several new ways to express parallelism in the code and new coordination data structures to avoid the synchronization nightmare. Nevertheless, in order to achieve the most efficient results, we still have to work on a paradigm shift and consider a good design to avoid side effects and concurrency issues.

One of the great problems we will find in the Parallel Extensions library is that when using some of the parallelized loop structures, we lose some control over each running thread.

Time for action – Downloading and installing the imaging library

In order to count and separate the potential nebulae in an image we can use a **blob counter**. It is a very useful feature and can be applied in many different applications, as it can count objects on a binary image and extract them.

As it is a complex algorithm, we are going to use an excellent open source imaging library, AForge.NET, developed and maintained by Andrew Kirillov (http://code.google.com/u/andrew.kirillov/). AForge.NET is a C# framework designed for developers and researchers in the fields of computer vision and artificial intelligence, image processing, neural networks, genetic algorithms, and machine learning among others.

We are going to use AForge.NET 1.7.0, which is thread-safe. Nevertheless, it offers single-threaded functions; therefore, it does not take full advantage of parallelization. We will have to run many instances in parallel to improve the performance of our nebula finder.

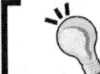

> AForge.NET is very useful, and it is open source. Besides, it is a very active project.

Now, we are going to download and install AForge.NET 1.7.0 and add references to this library in order to use this framework. This way, later, we will be able to combine the Parallel Extensions with the functions provided by AForge.NET to create our nebula finder:

1. Download the `AForge-1.7.0.exe` file from the AForge.NET framework repository in Google Code (`http://code.google.com/p/aforge/downloads/list`).

2. We are going to work with AForge.NET 1.7.0, which can be downloaded from `http://aforge.googlecode.com/files/AForge-1.7.0.exe`.

3. Run the `AForge-1.7.0.exe` installer and follow the steps to complete the installation wizard.

4. The default installation folder is: `C:\Program Files\AForge.NET`.

5. Once the installation has completed, stay in the project `BlobCounter`.

6. Now, we must add a reference to the installed libraries to access the AForge. NET framework. Select **Project | Add Reference...** from the main menu. The **Add Reference** dialog box will appear.

7. Click on the **Browse** tab, go to the AForge.NET installation folder (`C:\Program Files\AForge.NET`) and then to the `Release` subfolder. Select the `AForge.dll` file and click **OK**.

8. Then, repeat steps 6 and 7 for the following files:
   - `AForge.Imaging.dll`
   - `AForge.Math.dll`

9. Open the **Solution Explorer**.

10. Unfold the **References** container and check that the three references are added to the project, as shown in the following image:

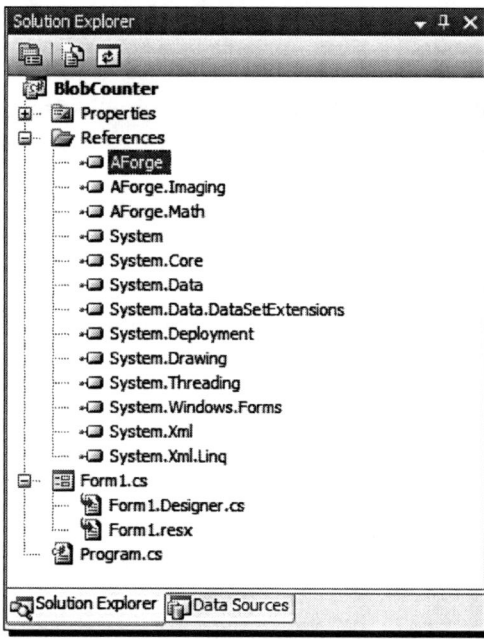

What just happened?

The AForge.NET 1.7.0 framework was installed and added as a reference for our nebula finder project that will use it.

Now, we have everything we need to begin coding our parallelized nebula finder using .NET Parallel Extensions and the AForge.NET 1.7.0 framework.

Time for action – Creating an independent class to run in parallel without side effects

The best way to achieve a parallelized execution without problems is to create a class that contains all the code to be run concurrently in order to avoid undesired and problematic side effects. Yes, we will be using .NET Parallel Extensions, but that does not mean we have to forget about side effects and concurrency problems.

Now, you just have to create a class with independent code to be run in parallel using the .NET Parallel Extensions. Many instances of this class will be running in parallel according to the number of available cores.

You have to work in a very fast and very efficient blob counter that will be able to run concurrently and avoid side effects.

First, we are going to create the class that runs the blob counter for a binary image file (a `.GIF` image with two colors—black and white, converted to grayscale):

1. Stay in the project, `BlobCounter`.

2. Create a new class, `NebulaFinder`.

3. Add the following lines of code at the beginning because we are going to use AForge.NET classes and the `System.Drawing` classes):

   ```
   using System.Drawing;
   using AForge;
   using AForge.Imaging;
   using AForge.Imaging.Filters;
   using AForge.Math;
   ```

4. Add the following private variables:

   ```
   // The image file name
   private string prsFileName;
   // The resulting bitmap
   private Bitmap proBitmap;
   // The resulting list of blobs
   private List<Blob> praoBlobs;
   // The resulting list of potential nebula blobs
   private List<Blob> praoNebulaBlobs;
   ```

5. Add the following properties to access the private variables (we want to create a compact and reliable class):

   ```
   public string psFileName
   {
       get
       {
           return prsFileName;
       }
   }
   public Bitmap poBitmap
   {
       get
       {
           return proBitmap;
       }
   }
   public List<Blob> paoBlobs
   ```

```
{
    get
    {
        return praoBlobs;
    }
}
public List<Blob> paoNebulaBlobs
{
    get
    {
        return praoNebulaBlobs;
    }
}
```

6. Add the following public static method to force a garbage collection (we still have to worry about the garbage collector):

```
public static void ForceGarbageCollection()
{
    GC.Collect(GC.MaxGeneration, GCCollectionMode.Forced);
}
```

7. Add the following public method to count the blobs and the potential nebulae detected in the image file received as a parameter:

```
public void CountBlobs(string parsFileName)
{
    Bitmap loBitmap;

    prsFileName = parsFileName;
    // Load the binary bitmap from the file
    loBitmap = (Bitmap)System.Drawing.Bitmap.
            FromFile(parsFileName);
    // Format the image according to AForge.NET needs to apply
       the filter
    AForge.Imaging.Image.FormatImage(ref loBitmap);
    // Create an instance of the blob counter algorithm
    AForge.Imaging.BlobCounter loBlobCounter = new AForge.
            Imaging.BlobCounter();
    // Process the binary image (find the blobs)
    loBlobCounter.ProcessImage(loBitmap);
    // Retrieve the array of found blobs and convert it to a List
       of Blob instances
    praoBlobs = loBlobCounter.GetObjects(loBitmap).
            ToList<Blob>();
```

```
// Create a new image with a 24 bpp pixel format
// We use System.Drawing.Image because there is also an
    AForge.Imaging.Image
System.Drawing.Image loNewBitmap = new Bitmap(loBitmap.Width,
 loBitmap.Height, System.Drawing.Imaging.PixelFormat.
 Format24bppRgb);
// Create the graphics from the new image
Graphics g = Graphics.FromImage((System.Drawing.
            Image)loNewBitmap);
// Draw the image
g.DrawImage(loBitmap, 0, 0);
// Create the a new potential nebula list
praoNebulaBlobs = new List<Blob>();
using (Pen loPen = new Pen(Color.CornflowerBlue, 2))
{
    // Process the blobs found in the image
    foreach (Blob loBlob in praoBlobs)
    {
        if ((loBlob.Rectangle.Size.Width * loBlob.Rectangle.
            Size.Height) > 150)
        {
            // If the area is greater than 150 pixels, it is
                a potential nebula
            praoNebulaBlobs.Add(loBlob);
            // Draw a rectangle using the pen in the
                resulting image
            g.DrawRectangle(loPen, loBlob.Rectangle);
        }
    }
}
// Assign the generated bitmap to proBitmap
proBitmap = (Bitmap)loNewBitmap;
g.Dispose();
}
```

What just happened?

The code to find the blobs and determine the potential nebulae from a binary image is now held in the `NebulaFinder` class. The instances of this class will represent a complete algorithm, and each instance is going to run in a new independent thread, parallelizing the nebula finder for as many images as the number of cores available. Everything we need to access for the algorithm must be in the instance of this class. Besides, the output produced is stored in each instance property.

For example, if we need an output file name, we must add a new instance variable. As explained in the previous chapters, using C# object-oriented capabilities allows us to avoid side effects.

These are the properties:

- `psFileName`: The complete input image file name, including its path
- `psBitmap`: The resulting bitmap image with the rectangles showing the potential nebulae detected drawn on it
- `paoBlobs`: The resulting complete list of blobs found in the image, irrespective of their area
- `paoNebulaBlobs`: The resulting list of potential nebula blobs found in the image, the ones whose area is greater than 150 pixels

Thus, creating an instance of this class and calling the `CountBlobs` method while sending the image file name as a parameter, we can easily implement an independent algorithm that can be run in a self-sufficient thread, thus avoiding side effects.

Self-sufficient parallelizable code without side effects is very easy to achieve using instances of classes to encapsulate everything the algorithm needs to run concurrently. We must provide safe code to be successful using the .NET Parallel Extensions. We do not have to forget everything we have learned so far.

Counting and showing blobs while avoiding side effects

The `CountBlobs` method is going to be run concurrently as many times as the number of available cores that use the .NET Parallel Extensions. It uses AForge.NET capabilities to find blobs and return their positions and rectangles to generate a new image showing the potential nebulae using a cornflower blue pen.

The method requires the name of a binary (indexed black and white converted to grayscale) image file. It loads the binary image from the file and then formats it according to the requirements of AForge.NET to apply the blob counter filter:

```
loBitmap = (Bitmap)System.Drawing.Bitmap.FromFile(parsFileName);
AForge.Imaging.Image.FormatImage(ref loBitmap);
```

Then, it creates an instance of the blob counter algorithm and processes the binary image:

```
AForge.Imaging.BlobCounter loBlobCounter = new AForge.Imaging.
                                  BlobCounter();
loBlobCounter.ProcessImage(loBitmap);
```

Once the filter has run, it retrieves an array of the blobs found and converts it into a list of instances of the `Blob` class:

```
praoBlobs = loBlobCounter.GetObjects(loBitmap).ToList<Blob>();
```

Then, it creates a new image with a 24 bpp pixel format using the original bitmap width and height and draws that bitmap in the new image:

```
System.Drawing.Image loNewBitmap = new Bitmap(loBitmap.Width,
                loBitmap.Height, System.Drawing.Imaging.
                PixelFormat.Format24bppRgb);
Graphics g = Graphics.FromImage((System.Drawing.Image)loNewBitmap);
g.DrawImage(loBitmap, 0, 0);
```

This is done because it is not possible to work with indexed images. Once the new image is created, we must find the potential nebulae. They are the blobs that have an area greater than 150 pixels.

Therefore, it creates a new list of instances of the `Blob` class and adds each blob whose rectangular area is greater than 150 pixels:

```
praoNebulaBlobs = new List<Blob>();
using (Pen loPen = new Pen(Color.CornflowerBlue, 2))
{
    // Process the blobs found in the image
    foreach (Blob loBlob in praoBlobs)
    {
        if ((loBlob.Rectangle.Size.Width * loBlob.Rectangle.Size.
            Height) > 150)
        {
            // If the area is greater than 150 pixels, it is a
                potential nebula
            praoNebulaBlobs.Add(loBlob);
            // Draw a rectangle using the pen in the resulting image
            g.DrawRectangle(loPen, loBlob.Rectangle);
        }
    }
}
```

Each potential nebula found is drawn as a rectangle in the new image. Then, the generated bitmap is stored to be accessed by the `poBitmap` property.

```
proBitmap = (Bitmap)loNewBitmap;
g.Dispose();
```

Hence, the results are available in the corresponding instance of the `NebulaFinder` class. Thus, we avoid side effects and allow many instances to run in parallel without unexpected problems.

> The code to be run in parallelized loops using .NET Parallel Extensions must avoid side effects.

Time for action – Running concurrent nebula finders using a parallelized loop

Now, we are going to create the UI and write some code to use the `NebulaFinder` class and its encapsulated simplicity combined with the .NET Parallel Extensions:

1. Stay in the project, `BlobCounter`.

2. Open the Windows Form `Form1` (**frmNebulaFinder**) in the form designer, add the following controls and components, and align them as shown in the following image:

- One picturebox (**picResultingBitmap**) with its `SizeMode` property set to **StretchImage**

- One button (**butShowResults**) with its `Text` property set to **Show results**

- One button (**butRunBatch**) with its `Text` property set to **Run batch**
- One BackgroundWorker component (**bakDisplayImages**)

3. Add the following lines of code at the beginning (as we are going to use the .NET Parallel Extensions and `System.IO` classes):

```
using System.Threading;
using System.Threading.Collections;
using System.IO;
```

4. Add the following private variable (it will hold a concurrency safe queue of the `NebulaFinder` instances):

```
private ConcurrentQueue<NebulaFinder> praoNebulaFinders;
```

5. Open the `Click` event in the button **butRunBatch**, and enter the following code (replace `"C:\\NASABLOB"` with your images folder path):

```
DirectoryInfo loDirectory;
FileInfo[] loImageFiles;

// Replace "C:\\NASABLOB" with your images folder path
loDirectory = new DirectoryInfo("C:\\NASABLOB");
// Get the JPG files stored in the path
loImageFiles = loDirectory.GetFiles("*.GIF");

// Call the garbage collector before starting each thread
NebulaFinder.ForceGarbageCollection();
// Create a concurrent queue
praoNebulaFinders = new ConcurrentQueue<NebulaFinder>();

try
{
    Parallel.ForEach<FileInfo>(loImageFiles, delegate(FileInfo
                                loNextImageFile)
    {
        // Create a new instance of the nebula finder
        NebulaFinder loNebulaFinder = new NebulaFinder();
        // Count the blobs for the image file
        loNebulaFinder.CountBlobs(loNextImageFile.FullName);
        // Add the nebula finder instance to the safe concurrent
            queue
        praoNebulaFinders.Enqueue(loNebulaFinder);
    });
}
catch (System.Threading.AggregateException loAggregateException)
{
```

```
foreach (Exception loInnerException in
         loAggregateException.InnerExceptions)
{
    // Something went wrong
    System.Diagnostics.Debug.Print(loInnerException.
                                   ToString());
}
}
// Call the garbage collector to remove unused memory
NebulaFinder.ForceGarbageCollection();
```

6. Create the specified input folder (the default is `C:\NASABLOB`).

7. Copy a dozen binary image files (`.GIF` black & white image files converted to grayscale) in the input folder to be analyzed by our nebula finder.

8. Build and run the application.

9. Click the **Run batch** button. The algorithm is going to run parallelized depending on the number of available cores. However, as we did not program any UI feedback, you will see no results. We have already created a solution for this problem!

What just happened?

Combining .NET Parallel Extensions with an independent class capable of running code without side effects, you could create a concurrent processor for the nebula finder algorithm for the binary image files found in the specified folder.

Each image file is going to be processed in an independent thread. However, the threading is managed by the .NET Parallel Extensions.

Suppose the following image file is processed by the nebula finder in one of the concurrent threads:

Then, the results will have, as in the following image, the potential nebulae shown using rectangles:

Programming the code for the loop that will run in parallel like the one offered by the `Parallel.ForEach` loop using an independent class, we will achieve task-oriented programming.

We have been promoting task-oriented programming so far. However, it is good practice to mention it in different situations, when using the .NET Parallel Extensions.

 Threads and tasks created automatically by .NET Parallel Extensions follow most of the rules we have already learned for threads created with the `ThreadPool` class, the `Thread` class, and the BackgroundWorker component. Consider them before starting your design, and of course, before coding.

Using a parallelized ForEach loop

We want to execute the `CountBlobs` method for each image file in the specified input folder. It is very simple; we use a `DirectoryInfo` instance passing the folder name as a parameter and then calling the `GetFiles` method with the `*.GIF` file filter. This happens in the following lines of code:

```
loDirectory = new DirectoryInfo("C:\\NASABLOB");
loImageFiles = loDirectory.GetFiles("*.GIF");
```

Then, we can use a classic `foreach` loop. Nevertheless, we do not want to execute each `CountBlobs` method sequentially. We want to do that concurrently, in parallel, using the new instructions provided by .NET Parallel Extensions. We can take advantage of `Parallel.ForEach` (`System.Threading.Parallel.ForEach`), as shown in the following lines of code:

```
Parallel.ForEach<FileInfo>(loImageFiles, delegate(FileInfo
loNextImageFile)
{
    NebulaFinder loNebulaFinder = new NebulaFinder();
    loNebulaFinder.CountBlobs(loNextImageFile.FullName);
    praoNebulaFinders.Enqueue(loNebulaFinder);
});
```

However, as we can see, it has a syntax different from that of the classic `foreach` loop. `Parallel.ForEach` can work in many ways. The one used here specifies the type name `<FileInfo>` and receives the `IEnumerable` source and a **delegate** with the `FileInfo` instance as a parameter, as shown in the following line of code:

```
Parallel.ForEach<FileInfo>(loImageFiles, delegate(FileInfo
                          loNextImageFile)
```

The code that defines the delegate will run in parallel as many times as the number of available cores, or run taking into account the different task creation options (`System.Threading.TaskCreationOptions`). The .NET Parallel Extensions will create the necessary threads to complete the work in parallel.

> Using a parallelized `ForEach` loop is similar to starting many threads in parallel running the code in the delegate using the `ThreadPool` class. However, using the .NET Parallel Extensions, we lose some control over the way the threads work, because it is done automatically and not manually.

Coding with delegates in parallelized loops

The code in the delegate method is very easy; it creates a new `NebulaFinder` instance and then calls the `CountBlobs` method, sending the full name of the image file to be processed as a parameter. This full name is obtained from the `FileInfo` instance generated by the parallelized `ForEach` loop (`loNextImageFile`), as shown in the following lines:

```
NebulaFinder loNebulaFinder = new NebulaFinder();
loNebulaFinder.CountBlobs(loNextImageFile.FullName);
```

The code running in the delegate for each parallelized execution is very simple and completely self-contained. Combining object-oriented capabilities with .NET Parallel Extensions is the best way to solve many concurrency problems.

However, there is neither a `Start` method call, nor a thread management directive. When does each thread created by the .NET Parallel Extensions start its execution? It will create a block with a synchronous execution. The control will return to the calling thread when the parallelized `ForEach` loop has completed the entire work. The pool management system managed by .NET Parallel Extensions will coordinate each thread.

> The .NET Parallel Extensions parallelized loop structures work with a synchronous execution. However, they parallelize work using independent threads as needed. In order to achieve the best performance results, only the outer loop must be parallelized using `Parallel.ForEach` or other concurrent loops using .NET Parallel Extensions. If we review the code in the `NebulaFinder` class, it works with classic loops. A single-threaded algorithm is prepared to be executed in parallel when needed.

Hence, we created an application capable of scaling according to the number of available cores, using an automatically parallelized loop provided by .NET Parallel Extensions. The number of threads created and the tasks scheduled for each thread will be determined automatically by the .NET Parallel Extensions. As we are working with a CTP, this may change in future Visual C# 2010.

However, as the loop has a synchronous execution, and the code is running in the main thread (the UI thread), it will be blocked until the loop ends. The .NET Parallel Extensions are not magical, and sometimes, it is more convenient to develop our own dispatchers to have more control over the threads and their desired execution.

Again, of course, we must also take into account everything learned so far about parallel programming, concurrency, and multithreading.

Working with a concurrent queue

The last line of code programmed in the delegate that runs for each file found in the folder in parallel is the following:

```
praoNebulaFinders.Enqueue(loNebulaFinder);
```

It adds the created and processed instances of the `NebulaFinder` class, with the results stored in its instance variables. Nevertheless, we are not using a standard list or collection. Why? Because it would not be thread-safe to do that, as the code is going to run in parallel.

One technique would be storing each instance in a specific position of a list. However, the .NET Parallel Extensions offer some new safe collections prepared for use in concurrent code in the `System.Threading.Collections` namespace. One of them is the `ConcurrentQueue`, declared as a private instance variable in the form class with the following line:

```
private ConcurrentQueue<NebulaFinder> praoNebulaFinders;
```

The queue would be created in the following line before entering the parallel loop:

```
praoNebulaFinders = new ConcurrentQueue<NebulaFinder>();
```

The `ConcurrentQueue` represents a thread-safe **First-In-First-Out(FIFO)** collection of objects. Thus, it is safe to call the `Enqueue` method to add an object in the code that will be run in the delegate in the parallel loop.

 The code running in the parallel loop does not need a special order because there is no warranty on when each file will be processed. That is an important fact to take into account when using parallel loops. The same thing happened when using the pool of threads managed by the `ThreadPool` class.

We cannot use a list with this line:

```
praoNebulaFinders.Add(loNebulaFinder);
```

Because `List<NebulaFinder>` is a mutable data structure that is shared by all the threads used to execute tasks generated by the call to `Parallel.ForEach`. Calling the `Add` method on a supposed results list would result in an undesired race condition under certain specific circumstances.

Nevertheless, using the `ConcurrentQueue` implies some coordination costs. It must lock the queue when one thread is adding an element. Besides, it must lock the queue when one thread is removing (de-queuing) an element. The locks reduce the overall performance because they generate many context switches. However, using the `ConcurrentQueue` simplifies the code.

The .NET Parallel Extensions provide two more classes for managing collections of data in a thread-safe manner (both implementing the common `IConcurrentCollection` interface):

- `BlockingCollection`: Provides blocking and binding capabilities for thread-safe collections
- `ConcurrentStack`: Represents a variable size **Last-In-First-Out (LIFO)** collection of instances of the same arbitrary type

Controlling exceptions in parallelized loops

Everything that we have learned about controlling exceptions in code that was going to be run in independent threads applies to parallelized loops with .NET Parallel Extensions.

We must handle these exceptions before they leave the thread! This must also be considered in the classes that will run code in the parallelized loops.

However, there are still some unexpected exceptions that can be raised by the code. In order to handle them when working with parallelized loops using .NET Parallel Extensions, we can catch the new `System.Threading.AggregateException` introduced in the library.

An `AggregateException` represents multiple errors that occur during the execution of many independent threads—the ones created during the execution of the parallelized loop. Thus, catching and iterating through each exception contained in the `InnerExceptions` read-only collection, we can know the problems generated during the execution of the automatically generated multiple concurrent threads.

The following code does that and shows all the exceptions contained in the `InnerExceptions` read-only collection in the Immediate Window:

```
try
{
    Parallel.ForEach<FileInfo>(loImageFiles, delegate(FileInfo
                              loNextImageFile)
    {
        NebulaFinder loNebulaFinder = new NebulaFinder();
        loNebulaFinder.CountBlobs(loNextImageFile.FullName);
        praoNebulaFinders.Enqueue(loNebulaFinder);
    });
}
catch (System.Threading.AggregateException loAggregateException)
{
    foreach (Exception loInnerException in loAggregateException.
            InnerExceptions)
    {
        System.Diagnostics.Debug.Print(loInnerException.ToString());
    }
}
```

Using a `foreach` loop, we can iterate through the collection and make sure that we have the exceptions under control when working with parallelized loops.

Time for action – Showing the results in the UI

The application is boring, because it does not show any results in the UI. You have to change this for the good, because the NASA scientists have great expectations from your work.

Now, we are going to show the results in the UI, using a BackgroundWorker combined with a delegate to work in the UI thread:

1. Stay in the project, `BlobCounter`.

2. Open Windows Form `Form1` (**frmNebulaFinder**) in the form designer.

3. Set the BackgroundWorker **bakDisplayImages WorkerSupportsCancellation** property to **True**.

4. Open the code for the Windows Form `Form1` (**frmNebulaFinder**).

5. Add the following declaration in the instance variables zone:

```
private delegate void ShowImageCaller(Bitmap poBitmap);
```

6. Add the following public method to display an image in the picture box—invoking a delegate with an asynchronous execution when the calling thread is different than the UI thread:

```
public void ShowImage(Bitmap poBitmap)
{
    // InvokeRequired compares the thread ID of the
    // calling thread to the thread ID of the creating thread.
    // If they are different, it will return true.
    if (picResultingBitmap.InvokeRequired)
    {
        // The calling thread is different than the UI thread
        // Create the delegate
        ShowImageCaller ldShowImage = new ShowImageCaller(
                                    ShowImage);
        // Invoke the delegate with an asynchronous execution
        // the current thread will not block until the delegate
           has been executed
        this.BeginInvoke(ldShowImage, new object[] { poBitmap });
    }
    else
    {
        // The calling thread is the same as the UI thread
        // Add the string received as a parameter to the ListBox
           control
        picResultingBitmap.Image = poBitmap;
    }
}
```

7. Open the `DoWork` event in the BackgroundWorker **bakDisplayImages** and enter the following code:

```
// Assign a name to the BackgroundWorker thread to identify it in
   the Threads Window
Thread.CurrentThread.Name = ((BackgroundWorker)sender).
                                ToString();
NebulaFinder loNebulaFinder;
```

```
while (!((BackgroundWorker)sender).CancellationPending)
{
    while (praoNebulaFinders.TryDequeue(out loNebulaFinder))
    {
        // A NebulaFinder instance could be dequeued from the
           praoNebulaFinders thread-safe queue
        ShowImage(loNebulaFinder.poBitmap);
        Thread.Sleep(1000);
    }
    Thread.Sleep(1000);
}
```

8. Open the `Click` event in the button **butShowResults** and enter the following code to start the BackgroundWorker:

```
// Start the BackgroundWorker thread
bakDisplayImages.RunWorkerAsync();
```

9. Build and run the application.

10. Click the **Run batch** button. The algorithm is going to run in parallel, depending on the number of available cores. However, as the loop is executed with a synchronous execution, we will have to wait till it finishes, for us to touch a control.

11. Click the **Show results** button. You will see the images appearing one after the other, with the potential nebulae with a rectangle drawn around them, as shown in the following image:

What just happened?

Wow, your nebula finder application shows very impressive results. The NASA scientists are very happy with the algorithm execution. However, they were expecting a more responsive UI. Your multithreading capabilities now generate more expectations for your applications. They would like to see the images as they are being processed. They do not like to press a button after the processing has ended. That happens because your applications usually offer a more responsive UI and now, you cannot go back to a synchronous execution world!

> Once you provide more performance and a more responsive UI, users will expect those results in all your applications. Be careful; multithreading is too addictive for the users!

Combining delegates with a BackgroundWorker

In this application, we used the BackgroundWorker component in a non-traditional way. We combined its capabilities to create an independent thread with an asynchronous execution, using a delegate to update the UI. Yes, we could have achieved the same goal calling the `ReportProgress` method. Nevertheless, it is interesting to combine everything we have learned so far. Now, we are multithreading experts, and we can defy most of the challenges related to concurrency!

The `ShowImage` method uses the well-known `InvokeRequired` property and the `BeginInvoke` method to call a delegate with an asynchronous execution in the UI thread.

The code in the BackgroundWorker `DoWork` event handler calls the form's `ShowImage` method, passing the `Bitmap` stored in the retrieved `NebulaFinder` instance as a parameter:

```
ShowImage(loNebulaFinder.poBitmap);
```

Retrieving elements from a concurrent queue in a producer-consumer scheme

The code programmed in the BackgroundWorker `DoWork` event handler represents a classic **producer-consumer** problem solved using a concurrent queue.

The threads running the parallelized loop add elements to the concurrent queue, with the following line:

```
praoNebulaFinders.Enqueue(loNebulaFinder);
```

The queue grows as each image finishes its processing.

On the other side, the BackgroundWorker retrieves the elements added to that queue (which can go on growing) and takes each element out of the queue with the following line:

```
while (praoNebulaFinders.TryDequeue(out loNebulaFinder))
```

In this case, the BackgroundWorker does not begin its execution while the parallel loop is adding elements to the queue, because it works with a synchronous execution, hence blocking the UI thread. Nevertheless, sometimes, it is possible to work in a producer-consumer scheme.

The **producer** is the parallel loop, composed of many concurrent threads that add elements to the queue calling the thread-safe `Enqueue` method.

The **consumer** is the Background thread that removes elements from the queue calling the thread-safe `TryDequeue` method, as shown in the following image:

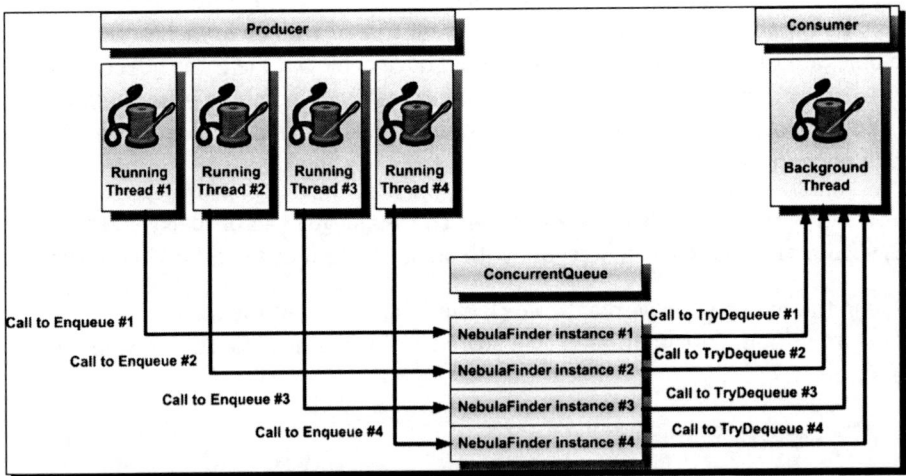

This method returns a `bool` value indicating whether or not an object was successfully removed from the queue. So, we used it in the `while` loop. If it returns `true`, the removed instance of the `NebulaFinder` class will be stored in `loNebulaFinder`, and the following lines will be executed each time it happens:

```
ShowImage(loNebulaFinder.poBitmap);
Thread.Sleep(1000);
```

The ConcurrentQueue is very useful for working with multiple threads using a **producer-consumer** scheme, without having to take into account the synchronization problems, because they are solved by .NET Parallel Extensions in the background. We do not need to worry about locks as they are made inside the calls to the methods provided by the ConcurrentQueue class.

Time for action – Providing feedback to the UI using a producer-consumer scheme

Now, we are going to make some changes to the application to provide a more responsive UI running the parallelized loop with an asynchronous execution to unblock the UI thread:

1. Stay in the project, BlobCounter.

2. Open the code for the Windows Form Form1 (**frmNebulaFinder**).

3. Open the Click event in the button **butRunBatch** and add the following line of code:

```
// Start the BackgroundWorker (the consumer)
bakDisplayImages.RunWorkerAsync();
```

After the line praoNebulaFinders = new ConcurrentQueue<NebulaFinder>(); (we want the BackgroundWorker to run concurrently with the parallelized loop).

4. Enclose the try...catch block including the Parallel.ForEach block of code with the following (we want to run the parallel loop with an asynchronous execution):

```
System.Threading.Tasks.Task.Create(delegate(object poObject)
{
    // try...catch block
});
```

5. Build and run the application.

6. Click the **Run batch** button. The algorithm is going to run in parallel according to the number of available cores, and you will see the images appearing one after the other, displaying the potential nebulae with a rectangle drawn around them, while you can keep control over the UI (moving the window, changing its size, and so on), as shown in the following image:

What just happened?

When the user clicks on the **Run batch** button, the nebula finder application shows a more responsive UI. Now the application is more appropriate, taking into account your parallel programming experience. Microsoft will be happy with these results, and there is a great possibility to win the Visual Studio 2010 licenses!

> Combining a parallel loop with a synchronous execution and an asynchronous launcher, and using the `ConcurrentQueue`, we could create a producer-consumer scheme without having to worry about synchronization problems because they are solved by .NET Parallel Extensions in the background. Combining our parallel programming knowledge is the key to the success of multithreaded applications.

Creating an asynchronous task combined with a synchronous parallel loop

The main problem we had was that the parallel loop was executed concurrently but synchronously in the UI thread. Thus, the UI was blocked until the loop finished its execution. Therefore, we could not use delegates or a BackgroundWorker component to provide the UI with some feedback. Why? Because the UI thread was blocked! The messages being sent to the UI thread would not be processed until the loop finished.

We do not like this kind of applications anymore. We want a great performance improvement through parallelism, while providing great UI feedback. How can we avoid the parallel loop blocking the UI thread? The answer is simple– by running it asynchronously in another thread.

We already know how to do that using the `ThreadPool` class. However, we can use the new `Task` class (`System.Threading.Tasks.Task`) provided by the .NET Parallel Extensions to represent an asynchronous operation. Instances of this class can only be created using its factory methods.

Enclosing the `try...catch` block including the `Parallel.ForEach` block of code with the `Task` creation, and specifying a delegate with an `object` parameter, we schedule the parallel loop to run asynchronously:

```
System.Threading.Tasks.Task.Create(delegate(object poObject) {
```

With that simple line, we can schedule a task to run asynchronously. Thus, the UI thread is not blocked, and this allows us to provide feedback to the UI.

In this case, we used a producer-consumer scheme combined with a BackgroundWorker, which acts as a consumer. It is started asynchronously with the following line of code:

```
bakDisplayImages.RunWorkerAsync();
```

 This task uses the default `TaskCreationOptions` and runs in the default `TaskManager`. We can change them to fine-tune the task scheduling and the worker threads' behavior.

Changing the threads' names while debugging

Working with Visual Studio 2008 or later, we can change a thread's name by right-clicking on it in the Threads Window, and selecting **Rename** while debugging an application. It will allow us to simplify the debugging process, especially while using the .NET Parallel Extensions.

Besides, it shows each thread's category, as shown in the following image:

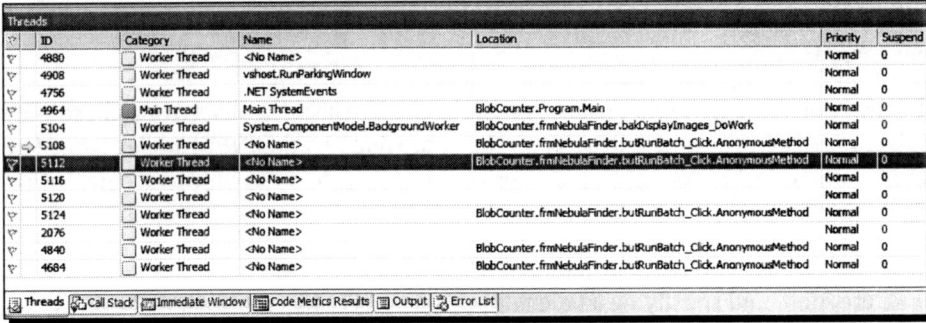

	ID	Category	Name	Location	Priority	Suspend
▽	4880	Worker Thread	<No Name>		Normal	0
▽	4908	Worker Thread	vshost.RunParkingWindow		Normal	0
▽	4756	Worker Thread	.NET SystemEvents		Normal	0
▽	4964	Main Thread	Main Thread	BlobCounter.Program.Main	Normal	0
▽	5104	Worker Thread	System.ComponentModel.BackgroundWorker	BlobCounter.frmNebulaFinder.bakDisplayImages_DoWork	Normal	0
▽ ⇨	5108	Worker Thread	<No Name>	BlobCounter.frmNebulaFinder.butRunBatch_Click.AnonymousMethod	Normal	0
▽	5112	Worker Thread	<No Name>	BlobCounter.frmNebulaFinder.butRunBatch_Click.AnonymousMethod	Normal	0
▽	5116	Worker Thread	<No Name>		Normal	0
▽	5120	Worker Thread	<No Name>		Normal	0
▽	5124	Worker Thread	<No Name>	BlobCounter.frmNebulaFinder.butRunBatch_Click.AnonymousMethod	Normal	0
▽	2076	Worker Thread	<No Name>		Normal	0
▽	4840	Worker Thread	<No Name>	BlobCounter.frmNebulaFinder.butRunBatch_Click.AnonymousMethod	Normal	0
▽	4684	Worker Thread	<No Name>	BlobCounter.frmNebulaFinder.butRunBatch_Click.AnonymousMethod	Normal	0

Sometimes, the .NET Parallel Extensions create more threads than expected to parallelize a work. For example, in a quad-core microprocessor, they create eight threads for this parallel loop. There is a great difference between having an exhaustive control over our application's threads and letting the .NET Parallel Extensions decide how to do the work.

> In some cases, using .NET Parallel Extensions is useful and simpler than manual threading. In other cases, manual threading is easier and more functional. As always, there isn't a simple answer to which method is preferable. Nevertheless, we must not use a CTP for a final release. We will have to wait to use the final release of .NET Parallel Extensions in Visual Studio 2010. CTP is for test purposes only!

Time for action – Invoking a UI update from a task

You want to impress the NASA scientists with the speed of your nebula finder. Now that the parallel loop does not block the UI thread, you can use everything you know about delegates to provide precise UI feedback. Hence, you can amaze the scientists with the speed of your nebula finder queuing the UI thread with messages to show the images as they are being processed, instead of using a BackgroundWorker with sleeps.

Now, we are going to make the necessary changes to the application to allow it to invoke a user interface update from the asynchronous task when it completes processing each image in the parallel loop:

1. Stay in the project, `BlobCounter`.

2. Open the code for the Windows Form `Form1` (**frmNebulaFinder**).

3. Open the `Click` event in the button **butShowResults** and comment the following line of code (we do not want the BackgroundWorker to run concurrently with the parallelized loop):

```
// Start the BackgroundWorker (the consumer)
// bakDisplayImages.RunWorkerAsync();
```

4. Open the `Click` event in the button **butRunBatch**. Add the following line of code

```
// Call the form's method to update the UI using a safe delegate
ShowImage(loNebulaFinder.poBitmap);
```

After the line, `praoNebulaFinders.Enqueue(loNebulaFinder);`.

5. Build and run the application.

6. Click the **Run batch** button. The algorithm is going to run in parallel, depending upon the number of available cores. You will see the images appearing one after the other precisely when they finish their processing ,faster than in the previous version of the application, highlighting the potential nebulae with a rectangle drawn around them. Meanwhile, you can continue to control the UI (moving the window, changing its size, and so on), as shown in the following image:

What just happened?

When the user clicks on the **Run batch** button, the nebula finder application shows a very fast and responsive UI, representing the speed achieved by the algorithms. Now the application is precise in providing UI feedback. Do you like Visual Studio 2010?

> Once we avoid blocking the UI with the parallel loops provided by .NET Parallel Extensions, we can use everything that we have learned so far to provide a precise UI feedback.

Providing feedback when each job is finished

Why didn't we invoke the form's method to update the UI using a safe delegate in the first version? It was just as easy as writing a line of code. We could not do that in the first version because the parallel loop was blocking the UI thread! This was the big problem we had to solve first.

Now that we have encapsulated the parallel loop in an asynchronous task, separating it from the UI thread, we can call the form's method to update the UI precisely when each nebula finder job is finished with this line:

```
ShowImage(loNebulaFinder.poBitmap);
```

The messages are queued in the UI thread to be dispatched one after the other, as previously explained.

We could provide a precise feedback to the UI when the job done by one of the many tasks created by the loop is finished using a delegate.

Using lambda expressions to simplify the code

We can also use **lambda expressions** introduced in C# 3.0 to shorten the code.

> A lambda expression is an anonymous function that can contain expressions and statements, and can be used to create delegates or expression tree types. They are useful in simplifying the code when we use delegates. All lambda expressions use the lambda operator => (read as **goes to**). Lambda expressions are described in depth in *WCF Multi-tier Services Development with LINQ* by Mike Liu, Packt Publishing.

We can change the code that defines the new task to run the loop asynchronously through the following code, using lambda expressions:

```
System.Threading.Tasks.Task.Create(poObject =>
{
    try
    {
        Parallel.ForEach<FileInfo>(loImageFiles, loNextImageFile =>
        {
```

It replaces the following lines:

```
System.Threading.Tasks.Task.Create(delegate(object poObject) {
    try
    {
        Parallel.ForEach<FileInfo>(loImageFiles, delegate(FileInfo
                            loNextImageFile)
        {
```

Parallelizing loops with ranges

Previously, we have been creating threads manually to split a work into many independent jobs using ranges. To do the same while taking advantage of the .NET Parallel Extensions, we can use the `Parallel.For` loop (`System.Threading.Parallel.For`), which is similar to the `for` statement, but since it is parallelized, it is named `Parallel.For`.

If we want to execute the `CountBlobs` method for each image file in the specified input folder using a `Parallel.For` loop, instead of a `Parallel.ForEach` one, we can make the following changes to the initial loop code (using lambda expressions):

```
System.Threading.Tasks.Task.Create(poObject =>
{
    try
    {
        Parallel.For(0, loImageFiles.Count(), i =>
        {
            NebulaFinder loNebulaFinder = new NebulaFinder();
            loNebulaFinder.CountBlobs(loImageFiles[i].FullName);
```

However, as can be seen, it has a syntax that is different from the classic `for` loop. `Parallel.For` can work in many ways. The one used specifies an `int` from (inclusive), an `int` to (exclusive), and a delegate with an `int` as a parameter, as shown in the following line (without lambda expressions):

```
Parallel.For(0, loImageFiles.Count(), delegate(int i)
```

The code that defines the delegate will run in parallel as many times as the number of available cores, or will run taking into account different task creation options (`System.Threading.TaskCreationOptions`). The .NET Parallel Extensions will create the necessary threads to complete the work in parallel.

Using a parallelized `for` loop is similar to starting many threads in parallel, running the code in the delegate using the `ThreadPool` class. However, using the .NET Parallel Extensions, we loose some control over the way the threads work, because it is done automatically and not manually, as explained previously for the `Parallel.ForEach` loop.

Parallelizing queries

So far, we have been working with parallel loops using the .NET Parallel Extensions combined with everything we had learned about updating the UI and making cross-thread calls. However, one of the most interesting jobs to improve performance and provide a more responsive UI is to run large queries and certain statistics. How can we use these new parallel extensions to improve the performance of queries and statistics in our applications? Is there any simple way to achieve that goal?

LINQ (Language-Integrated Query) was introduced in C# 3.0 and is very useful for processing queries for many different data sources. The simplest way to parallelize a query is to use **PLINQ (Parallel Language-Integrated Query)**, introduced in the .NET Parallel Extensions CTP and a future part of Visual Studio 2010.

The features of LINQ and its usage in real-life scenarios are described in-depth in *LINQ Quickly (A Practical Guite to Programming Language Integrated Query with C#)* by N. Satheesh Kumar, Packt Publishing.

Time for action – Parallelized counter

Now that you have completed the nebula finder application, a team of scientists think you have a data warehouse, and they want your help in creating some interesting statistics about these images. They begin asking you questions about the potential nebulae, using different widths, heights, formulas, and things like that! Collecting all the blobs into a single list and using LINQ, you can query the objects using methods. However, using PLINQ can provide a better performance, as it is able to parallelize the queries. So now, let us learn to use PLINQ!

Now, we are going to use PLINQ to count the number of potential nebulae using the same technique as earlier, but we are going to leave the code prepared for generating new statistics without great effort:

1. Stay in the project, `BlobCounter`.
2. Open the Windows Form `Form1` (**frmNebulaFinder**) in the form designer.
3. Add a new button control (**butCountNebulas**). Set its `Text` property to **Count potential nebulas**.
4. Open the code for the Windows Form `Form1` (**frmNebulaFinder**).

5. Add the following lines of code at the beginning because we are going to use the
   `AForge.Imaging.Blob` class:

   ```
   using AForge.Imaging;
   ```

6. Add the following public static function to determine whether a blob represents a
   potential nebula according to its dimensions:

   ```
   public static bool IsPotentialNebula(Blob poBlob)
   {
       return ((poBlob.Rectangle.Size.Width * poBlob.Rectangle.
               Size.Height) > 150);
   }
   ```

7. Add the following public static function to count the potential nebulae using PLINQ:

   ```
   public static int CountPotentialNebulasParallel(IEnumerable<Blob>
                                                   paoSource)
   {
       return paoSource.AsParallel().Where(s =>
               IsPotentialNebula(s)).Count();
   }
   ```

8. Open the `Click` event in the button **butCountNebulas** and enter the
   following code:

   ```
   List<Blob> laoNebulaFinderList = new List<Blob>();
   // First, collect the blobs in a single unified list
   foreach (NebulaFinder loNebulaFinder in praoNebulaFinders)
   {
       laoNebulaFinderList.AddRange(loNebulaFinder.paoBlobs);
   }
   // Count the potential nebulae
   int liCount = CountPotentialNebulasParallel(laoNebulaFinderList);
   // Show a message box with the potential nebula count
   System.Windows.Forms.MessageBox.Show(string.Format("The potential
           nebulas are {0}", liCount));
   ```

9. Build and run the application.

10. Click the **Run batch** button.

11. Once the batch finished, click the **Count potential nebulas** button. The application
    will show the potential nebula count in a message box.

What just happened?

In a few seconds, you've added to the application the capability to count the number of
potential nebulae using a function that can be easily modified according to the current
needs. It is very easy to parallelize a query combining PLINQ with a thread-safe code that
avoids side effects. This way, you can make people happy without having to write a lot
of code.

PLINQ is one of the most exciting features offered by the .NET Parallel Extensions. However, when data needs to be ordered, its performance is not as good compared to its performance with disordered data.

Parallelizing LINQ queries with PLINQ

As we are working with parallel loops, we have to collect the results in a single list first. We do it in the following lines of code:

```
List<Blob> laoNebulaFinderList = new List<Blob>();
foreach (NebulaFinder loNebulaFinder in praoNebulaFinders)
{
    laoNebulaFinderList.AddRange(loNebulaFinder.paoBlobs);
}
```

We've created a unified list of `Blob` instances, which contain the data for all the images analyzed so far.

The `IsPotentialNebula` function must be called for every instance, in order to determine whether the blob is a potential nebula or not. This function is very important because it is going to be parallelized by PLINQ. So it is important that the function does not produce any side effects, and we have to be very careful when designing and coding it.

```
public static bool IsPotentialNebula(Blob poBlob)
{
    return ((poBlob.Rectangle.Size.Width * poBlob.Rectangle.Size.
        Height) > 150);
}
```

In this case, the code is very simple. As we are multithreading gurus, there is no need to explain what can happen if the code was not considered for concurrent execution.

The `CountPotentialNebulasParallel` function received an `IEnumerable<Blob>`, in this case, the list with the collected results.

The key to parallelize a LINQ query is to add the call to the `AsParallel()` extension method, as shown in the following line of code:

```
return paoSource.AsParallel().Where(s =>
    IsPotentialNebula(s)).Count();
```

A classic, sequential LINQ version of the above code would be:

```
return paoSource.Where(s => IsPotentialNebula(s)).Count();
```

 Not all queries achieve better performance when using PLINQ, as compared to their LINQ version. There are many issues related to PLINQ performance, which are similar to those explained for any kind of parallelization. We must take into account everything we've learned so far to decide whether or not to use the `AsParallel()` extension method.

Specifying the degree of parallelism for PLINQ

We can also specify the degree of parallelism desired for the query execution, that is, the number of threads that the query must use to achieve a better performance. Why would we do that? Because some queries take too long to execute, and perhaps we want to leave one core free for running other threads while the query is being executed.

For example, if we want the aforementioned query to leave one core free for the other threads, we could use the following line of code:

```
return paoSource.AsParallel(Environment.ProcessorCount - 1)
        .Where(s => IsPotentialNebula(s)).Count();
```

It will use `Environment.ProcessorCount - 1` threads to parallelize the query.

Parallelizing statistics and multiple queries

Sometimes, you must execute synchronous code that is very independent from a precedent result. Therefore, it is code that can be parallelized.

A classic case is statistics. You must run many queries under the same data. Perhaps, parallelizing a single query does not improve performance, but running many queries using classic single-threaded LINQ in parallel can improve the overall performance.

It can be done using the `Parallel.Invoke` method, as shown in the following lines of code (using lambda expressions and methods that call sequential LINQ):

```
Parallel.Invoke(
    () => CountPotentialNebulasSequential(laoNebulaFinderList),
    () => CountPotentialGreatNebulasSequential(laoNebulaFinderList),
    () => CountPotentialOldStarsSequential(laoNebulaFinderList)
);
```

The current thread will be blocked until the three methods return from their execution in parallel.

If we want the parallelized code to run asynchronously, we can do that the same way we did using the `Task` class (`System.Threading.Tasks.Task`) provided by the .NET Parallel Extensions to represent an asynchronous operation. Remember that we can do this using the `ThreadPool` class as well.

The `Parallel.Invoke` method provides a very easy way to launch many tasks in parallel without the need to write too much code.

Have a go hero – Creating a parallelized user interface

The Visual Studio 2010 licenses are on the way! However, there's more work waiting for your concurrent programming capabilities!

NASA's CIO wants you to develop a new application using the features offered by .NET Parallel Extensions. It is a multiple producer-consumer problem (you can use the `ConcurrentQueue` combined with everything you've learned in this chapter):

- One producer must search all the image files in folders and sub-folders, beginning with a folder specified by the user.
- One consumer must take each new file found and generate a thumbnail.
- Another consumer must take each generated thumbnail and convert it to a sepia palette.
- Another consumer must update the UI as the thumbnails are converted to sepia.

Configure the producers and consumers in a way that takes full advantage of any hardware in which the application could run. Also, provide a very responsive user interface, offering the user the possibility to interrupt and continue the work as desired at any moment.

Hey! Is this related to NASA's research? No, it is not. NASA's CIO wants to arrange his family photographs using this application!

You can do it! Combining asynchronous and synchronous executions with .NET Parallel Extensions, everything is possible!

Pop quiz

1. The execution of concurrent threads created by the `Parallel.ForEach` and `Parallel.For` loops is:

   a. Asynchronous

   b. Synchronous

   c. Automatically switched from synchronous to asynchronous according to the block of code that is to be executed after the loop (decided at runtime by .NET Parallel Extensions AI algorithms)

2. The exceptions raised and not caught in the code running in the delegate in a parallelized loop with `Parallel.ForEach` or `Parallel.For` are caught as a:

    a. `System.Threading.AggregateException`

    b. `System.Threading.ExceptionCollection`

    c. `System.Threading.ConcurrentException`

3. The `ConcurrentQueue` is very useful for:

    a. Creating a collection with blocking and binding capabilities

    b. Working with multiple threads using a producer-consumer scheme, without having to take into account synchronization problems

    c. Working with multiple processes using a producer-consumer scheme, using IPC

4. `System.Threading.Tasks.Task` represents:

    a. An asynchronous operation

    b. A synchronous operation

    c. A user interface message to be queued in the UI thread

5. In order to update the UI in the code of a delegate called by a `Parallel.ForEach` or a `Parallel.For` loop, we must:

    a. Run the parallel loop in the UI thread and use a delegate to make a cross-thread call

    b. Run the parallel loop in an independent thread or task and make a direct call to the UI

    c. Run the parallel loop in an independent thread or task and use a delegate to make a cross-thread call

Right answers:

1. b.

2. a.

3. b.

4. a.

5. c.

Summary

We've learned a lot in this chapter about parallelizing the execution of code, taking advantage of the .NET Parallel Extensions. We were able to combine different execution techniques with automatically parallelized structures that will be available in Visual Studio 2010. Specifically, we covered:

- Downloading and installing .NET Parallel Extensions CTP
- Combining asynchronous executions with synchronous parallelized loops and other automatically parallelized structures
- Using delegates to make cross-thread calls, and safely update the user interface from independent tasks scheduled and coordinated by the .NET Parallel Extensions
- Achieving scalability combining calls to third-party libraries in our parallel algorithms
- Reducing the code needed to run tasks in parallel using the C# 3.0 lambda expressions
- Running queries in parallel using PLINQ and multiple LINQ invocations
- Creating producer-consumer schemes running in multiple threads without synchronization pains
- Taking advantage of future improvements in the C# programming language and runtime

We also learned how to transform a single-threaded imaging library into a parallelized algorithm, and how to combine the .NET Parallel Extensions with a responsive user interface.

Now that we've learned many ways to take advantage of the .NET Parallel Extensions, we're ready to join the pieces in a complete application—which is the topic of the next chapter.

12

Developing a Completely Parallelized Application

In order to combine everything we have learned so far, we must follow certain rules and structures. In this chapter, we will join all the pieces in a complete application, parallelizing the execution as much as possible to offer great scalability, an impressive performance, and an incredibly responsive user interface. Reading it and following the exercises we shall:

- ◆ Create parallelized effects in the UI
- ◆ Combine different kinds of parallelized tasks in a single application
- ◆ Provide a very responsive UI, while showing multiple windows
- ◆ Learn techniques to keep the UI more responsive
- ◆ Learn different techniques to combine parallelized tasks, and improve the overall performance and achieve great scalability
- ◆ Take full advantage of modern hardware in every part of a whole application
- ◆ Know tools to provide useful information about the code to run in many concurrent threads

Joining many different parallelized pieces into a complete application

So far, we have been working with parallelized algorithms and UI updates using different techniques and many classes and components offered by Visual C# 2.0, 3.0, and future 4.0 (2005, 2008, and 2010) versions. However, they were used in applications based on one window in the UI. How can we combine many different parallelized pieces into a complete application with an entirely multithreaded programming scheme?

We can work with many windows combining everything we have learned so far, offering the user a more responsive application at every moment, while he or she can work faster to complete jobs!

 Remember that Parallel Extensions CTP is a pre-release available only for Visual Studio 2008 (C# 3.0), or later. Thus, we are not going to base our last case on this preview. However, by making many changes, you can use the same base to create your version using Parallel Extensions and the lambda expressions.

Time for action – Creating an opacity effect in an independent thread

Your work on parallelized algorithms with NASA was great! They are very happy with your multithreaded applications. However, there is more work to be done!

Adjusting a digital photograph's brightness is fast when you work with small resolution images. Nevertheless, when you do that with huge resolution images (for example, photographs taken by 10 or 12 mega pixels digital cameras), it takes some time to get the brightness adjustment right.

You are going to travel to many countries to understand the NASA scientists' needs around the world. You will take lots of pictures with your new 24 mega pixels camera—a gift from NASA's CIO for your excellent work in the last few weeks. You have experience working with AForge.NET, the excellent open source imaging library. Thus, you can create an application to preview high quality thumbnails of one image with different brightness adjustments, using your multithreading knowledge.

You will run the application to select the best brightness adjustment for each image using the power available in the NASA servers and their exclusive **XHD (eXtreme High Definition)** displays!

First, we are going to create a new project with a class capable of running a transparency and opacity effect on a Windows form, using an independent thread to allow a responsive UI. This way, we will be able to use this class later, in the main application's form:

1. Create a new C# project using the Windows Forms Application template in Visual Studio or Visual C# Express. Use `ImageBrowser` as the project's name.

2. Open the code for `Program.cs`.

3. Replace the line `[STAThread]` with the following line (before the `Main` method declaration):

   `[MTAThread]`

4. Change the form's name to **frmMain**.

5. Create a new class, `OpacityEffect`.

6. Add the following lines of code at the beginning:

```
using System.Windows.Forms;
using System.Threading;
```

7. Add the following private variable (a reference to the form):

```
private frmMain proForm;
```

8. Create the following constructor with a parameter:

```
public OpacityEffect(frmMain paroForm)
{
    // Store a reference to the form
    proForm = paroForm;
}
```

9. Add the following private method to be run by an independent thread (receiving an instance of the `OpacityEffect` class as a parameter):

```
private void ThreadProc(object poThreadParameter)
{
    // An instance of OpacityEffect is passed in
       poThreadParameter
    OpacityEffect loOpacityEffect =
                    (OpacityEffect)poThreadParameter;
    // Call the RunEffect method for the instance
    loOpacityEffect.RunEffect();
}
```

10. Add the following private method to be called by the instance in the independent thread; it will invoke a form's delegate to update the UI:

```
private void RunEffect()
{
    for (double liOpacity = 0; liOpacity < 1; liOpacity += .05)
    {
        // Invoke the delegate to update the UI
        proForm.ChangeOpacity(liOpacity);
        // Sleep the thread for 100 milliseconds
        Thread.Sleep(100);
    }
    // To solve a horrible bug in +0.05 with double in some CPUs
    proForm.ChangeOpacity(1);
}
```

11. Add the following public method to be called by the form to run the effect in an independent thread with an asynchronous execution:

```
public void RunAsync()
```

```
{
      // Add a new independent thread, with a parameterized start
         (to allow parameters)
      Thread loThread = new Thread(new
            ParameterizedThreadStart(ThreadProc));
      // The thread is going to be a background thread
      loThread.IsBackground = true;
      // Start the thread with an asynchronous execution
      loThread.Start(this);
}
```

What just happened?

We created a class that will be able to change the form's opacity value from 0 to 100% in 5% increments, running the code in a new independent thread to allow the UI to go on working while the effect is being shown. The form to which the effects is to be applied is received as a parameter in the class's constructor.

Running code out of the UI thread

We want the code to run out of the UI thread. Why? Because we want a very responsive user interface when the application starts. We want the user to be capable of moving, maximizing, or minimizing the window while its opacity increases.

The RunAsync method creates a new independent thread using the well-known Thread class. The thread is going to be a background thread, because we do not want it to go on running if the user closes the window. This method will run the code in the thread with an asynchronous execution using the Start method with this instance as a parameter that immediately returns to the caller:

```
Thread loThread = new Thread(new
      ParameterizedThreadStart(ThreadProc));
loThread.IsBackground = true;
loThread.Start(this);
```

The thread procedure is easy to understand because we are working the same way we did in the previous cases. The RunEffect method invokes a delegate to update the UI every 100 milliseconds, with a new opacity sent as a parameter.

Running the code out of the UI threads would be very useful when we want to offer a responsive user interface. Moreover, we need to do this when we are going to have an application that is able to show many windows on the desktop.

Time for action – Creating a safe method to change the opacity

Now, we are going to add a new method and a delegate to the form in order to allow the UI to be updated from the other threads, which are running the transparency and opacity effect, that invoke the delegate:

1. Stay in the project, ImageBrowser.

2. Open the Windows Form Form1 (**frmMain**) in the form designer, add the following controls, and align them as shown in the image:

- ◆ One status strip (**staStatusStrip**) with its Dock property set to **Bottom**
- ◆ One tool strip progress bar (**tstThumbnailsProgress**) added to the **staStatusStrip** status strip
- ◆ One flow layout panel (**pnlFlowLayoutPanel**) with its AutoScroll property set to **true** and its Dock property set to **Fill**

3. Set the form's DoubleBuffered property value to **true** and its Opacity property value to **0%**. The form must be transparent when shown for the first time.

4. Open the code for the Windows Form Form1 (**frmMain**).

5. Add the following declaration in the instance variables zone:

```
private delegate void ChangeOpacityCaller(double pariOpacity);
```

6. Add the following public method to change the form's opacity, invoking a delegate when the calling thread is different from that of the UI thread:

```
public void ChangeOpacity(double pariOpacity)
{
    // InvokeRequired compares the thread ID of the
    // calling thread to the thread ID of the creating thread.
    // If they are different, it will return true.
    if (this.InvokeRequired)
    {
        // The calling thread is different than the UI thread
        // Create the delegate
        ChangeOpacityCaller ldChangeOpacity = new
                    ChangeOpacityCaller(ChangeOpacity);
        // Invoke the delegate
        // the current thread will block until the delegate has
            been executed
        this.Invoke(ldChangeOpacity, new object[] { pariOpacity
                    });
    }
    else
    {
        // The calling thread is the same as the UI thread
        // Change the form's opacity value
        this.Opacity = pariOpacity;
    }
}
```

7. Open the Load event in the form, and enter the following code:

```
OpacityEffect loOpacityEffect = new OpacityEffect(this);
loOpacityEffect.RunAsync();
```

8. Build and run the application. The form will appear slowly incrementing its opacity, as shown in the following image:

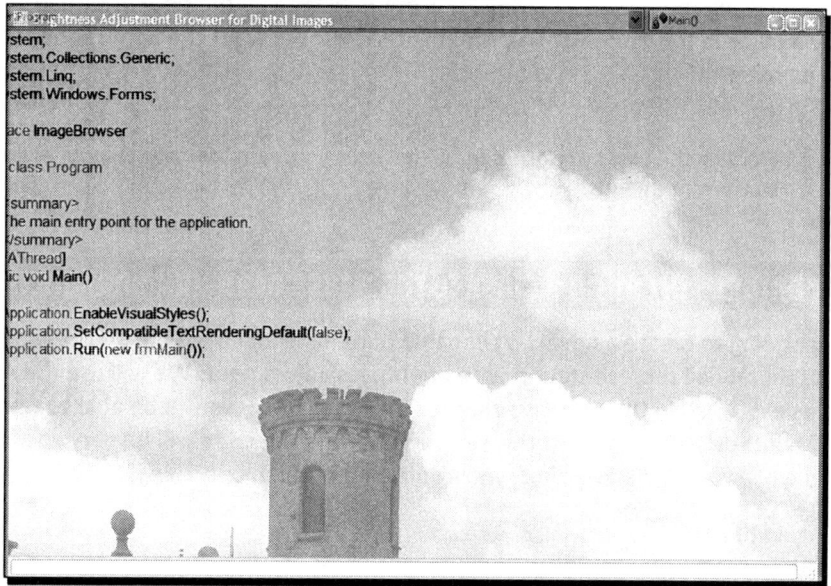

What just happened?

The code required to update the opacity safely from any thread is now held in a new public method defined in the main form class.

Thus, calling the `ChangeOpacity` public method with the opacity value as a parameter from any thread, we can easily update the form's transparency.

Blocking the UI—Forbidden with multithreading code

When the form is shown, it is completely transparent. Then, the effect will begin running in an independent thread, leaving the UI thread free to go on running the code. Some messages to update the form's opacity will be queued to the UI thread every 100 milliseconds.

The user can move the window, resize it, minimize it, or maximize it while the effect is running. Moreover, we will be able to run code to update the UI while the transparency effect is running, creating a very impressive user interface.

The following lines added to the form's load event do everything needed to run our effect in an independent thread; again, taking advantage of C# object-oriented capabilities:

```
OpacityEffect loOpacityEffect = new OpacityEffect(this);
loOpacityEffect.RunAsync();
```

Any code added after the last line will be executed immediately, because the effect is being run in an independent thread, with an asynchronous execution. Besides, it does it in a thread created using the `Thread` class. As it is not managed by the pool of threads, it does not occupy a place in the `ThreadPool` running threads. We want the application to offer maximum parallelism!

> Blocking the user interface is forbidden once you learn to program using multiple concurrent threads.

Time for action – Creating a class to run a task in an independent thread

Now, we are going to create a new class capable of reading an image file and generating a high quality thumbnail representation with brightness adjustment. We will use the AForge. NET libraries explained in the previous chapter. This way, later, we will be able to work with a pool of threads using instances of this simple class, and the code will be very easy to understand while we will be avoiding synchronization problems:

1. Stay in the project, `ImageBrowser`.

2. Create a new class, `ThumbnailBrightnessAdjuster`.

3. Add the references to the installed libraries so as to access the AForge.NET framework, as we did in the previous chapter.

4. Add the following lines of code at the beginning because we are going to use the AForge.NET classes and the `System.Drawing` classes:

```
using System.Drawing;
using AForge;
using AForge.Imaging;
using AForge.Imaging.Filters;
using AForge.Math;
```

5. Add the following private variables:

```
// The brightness delta
private double priBrightnessDelta;
// The thumbnail image size to generate
private Size proThumbnailSize;
// The original image file name
private string prsImageFileName;
// The thumbnail image generated
private System.Drawing.Image proThumbnailImage;
```

6. Add the following properties to access the private variables (we want to create a compact and reliable class):

```
public double piBrightnessDelta
{
    get
    {
        return priBrightnessDelta;
    }
}
public string psImageFileName
{
    get
    {
        return prsImageFileName;
    }
}
public System.Drawing.Image poThumbnailImage
{
    get
    {
        return proThumbnailImage;
    }
}
```

What just happened?

The code to define the image file name and the brightness adjustment to create a processed thumbnail is now held in the `ThumbnailBrightnessAdjuster` class. The instances of this class will represent a complete algorithm, and each instance is going to run in a new independent thread as thumbnails with different brightness deltas need to be generated. Everything we need to access for the algorithm must be in the instance of this class.

Time for action – Putting the logic into methods to simplify running tasks in a pool of threads

As mentioned earlier, object-oriented code is one of the most valuable friends of multithreaded applications. We want the `ThumbnailBrightnessAdjuster` class to be simple, self-contained, and efficient. Achieving this will help us focus on parallelizing the requests and not on threading problems.

Now, we are going to add some methods to the `ThumbnailBrightnessAdjuster` class to complete the adjusted high quality thumbnail generation algorithm:

1. Stay in the project, `ImageBrowser`.

2. Open the code for the `ThumbnailBrightnessAdjuster` class.

3. Add the following constructor:

```
public ThumbnailBrightnessAdjuster(string parsImageFileName,
        Size paroThumbnailSize, double pariBrightnessAdjustment)
{
    prsImageFileName = parsImageFileName;
    priBrightnessDelta = pariBrightnessAdjustment;
    proThumbnailSize = paroThumbnailSize;
}
```

4. Add the following private method to create a high quality thumbnail from the specified image file, the size of the thumbnail:

```
private Bitmap CreateThumbnail()
{
    // Read the original image
    System.Drawing.Image loImage = new Bitmap(prsImageFileName);

    // Create a new rectangle for displaying the original image
    Rectangle loDestinationRectangle = new Rectangle(new Point(0,
            0), proThumbnailSize);

    // Create a new bitmap with the thumbnail width and height
    Bitmap loBitmap = new Bitmap(proThumbnailSize.Width,
                                 proThumbnailSize.Height);
    Graphics g = Graphics.FromImage((System.Drawing.
                                    Image)loBitmap);
    g.InterpolationMode = System.Drawing.Drawing2D.
                            InterpolationMode.HighQualityBicubic;
    // Draw the image resized to the thumbnail width and height
    //   using a high quality bicubic interpolation
    g.DrawImage(loImage, loDestinationRectangle, 0, 0,
                loImage.Width, loImage.Height,
                GraphicsUnit.Pixel);

    g.Dispose();

    return loBitmap;
}
```

5. Add the following private method to adjust the brightness of the thumbnail image received as a parameter:

```
private void AdjustThumbnailBrightness(Bitmap loBitmap)
{
    // Format the image according to AForge.NET needs to apply
        the filter
    AForge.Imaging.Image.FormatImage(ref loBitmap);
    // Create an instance of the brightness correction filter
    AForge.Imaging.Filters.BrightnessCorrection
            loBrightnessCorrection = new AForge.Imaging.Filters.
            BrightnessCorrection(priBrightnessDelta);
    // Process the image (correct the brightness)
    proThumbnailImage = loBrightnessCorrection.Apply(loBitmap);
    Graphics g = Graphics.FromImage((System.
                Drawing.Image)proThumbnailImage);
    g.InterpolationMode = System.Drawing.Drawing2D.
                    InterpolationMode.HighQualityBicubic;
    // Create the string to draw
    string loString = string.Format("Brightness value: {0}",
                            priBrightnessDelta);
    // Create the font and the brush
    Font loFont = new Font("Arial", 12);
    SolidBrush loBrush = new SolidBrush(Color.CornflowerBlue);
    // Create the point for the upper-left corner of drawing
    PointF loPoint = new PointF(10.0F, (proThumbnailSize.
                        Height - 50.0F));
    // Draw string to the thumbnail
    g.DrawString(loString, loFont, loBrush, loPoint);
    // Draw a rectangle around the thumbnail
    g.DrawRectangle(new Pen(loBrush, 10), new Rectangle(0, 0,
                proThumbnailImage.Width, proThumbnailImage.
                Height));

    g.Dispose();
}
```

6. Add the following public method to do the entire work, once the necessary private variables are filled in by the constructor:

```
public void GenerateThumbnailImage()
{
    // Create the high quality thumbnail
    Bitmap loBitmap = CreateThumbnail();
    // Run the brightness adjustment
    AdjustThumbnailBrightness(loBitmap);
}
```

What just happened?

The code required to load an image and create a high quality thumbnail with a specific size and a brightness adjustment is now held in the `ThumbnailBrightnessAdjuster` class.

Thus, by creating an instance of this class and sending the corresponding parameters to the constructor, we can easily implement an independent algorithm that can be run in a self-sufficient thread when thumbnails with different brightness deltas need to be generated.

In order to create a thumbnail with a specific brightness adjustment, we must create an instance, sending the image file name, the desired thumbnail size, and the brightness delta as parameters to the constructor and then call the `GenerateThumbnailImage` method.

The generated thumbnail image will be available in the `poThumbnailImage` property.

> Using instances of classes to encapsulate everything the algorithm needs to run in a thread, we will be able to develop an application prepared for great scalability.

Time for action – Queuing requests, running threads, and updating the UI

Now, we are going to make the necessary changes to the main form to show the thumbnails with many brightness adjustments, while the opacity effect runs in another thread:

1. Stay in the project, `ImageBrowser`.

2. Open the code for the Windows Form `Form1` (**frmMain**).

3. Add the following lines of code at the beginning (as we are going to use the `System.Threading.ThreadPool` class):

   ```
   using System.Threading;
   ```

4. Add the following private variables:

   ```
   // The thumbnails size
   private Size poThumbnailSize = new  Size(200, 200);
   // The image file name
   private string psImageFileName;
   // The beginning brightness adjustment
   double piBeginningBrightness = -1;
   // The ending brightness adjustment
   double piEndingBrightness = 1;
   // The step
   double piBrightnessStep = 0.01F;
   // The total number of thumbnails with brightness adjustments
      that are going to be shown
   int piTotalThumbnails;
   // The thumbnails already shown in the form
   int piThumbnailsShown;
   ```

5. Add the following declaration in the instance variables zone:

```
private delegate void AddThumbnailCaller(System.Drawing.
        Image paroThumbnailImage, double pariBrightnessDelta);
```

6. Add the following public method to call a method for adding a picture box that displays the generated thumbnail in the form's layout panel, thereby invoking a delegate when the calling thread is different from the UI thread:

```
public void AddThumbnail(System.Drawing.Image paroThumbnailImage,
                        double pariBrightnessDelta)
{
    // InvokeRequired compares the thread ID of the
    // calling thread to the thread ID of the creating thread.
    // If they are different, it will return true.
    if (this.InvokeRequired)
    {
        // The calling thread is different than the UI thread
        // Create the delegate
        AddThumbnailCaller ldAddThumbnail = new
            AddThumbnailCaller(AddThumbnail);
        // Invoke the delegate
        // The current thread will block until the delegate has
            been executed
        this.Invoke(ldAddThumbnail, new object[] {
                    paroThumbnailImage, pariBrightnessDelta });
    }
    else
    {
        // The calling thread is the same as the UI thread
        // Add a new picture box showing the thumbnail in a
            layout panel
        AddThumbnailInLayoutPanel(paroThumbnailImage,
                            pariBrightnessDelta);
    }
}
```

7. Add the following private method to add a picture box displaying the generated thumbnail in the form's layout panel and save the brightness delta in the picture box's `Tag` property:

```
private void AddThumbnailInLayoutPanel(System.Drawing.Image
        paroThumbnailImage, double pariBrightnessDelta)
{
    PictureBox loPictureBox = new PictureBox();

    loPictureBox.Size = poThumbnailSize;
    loPictureBox.SizeMode = PictureBoxSizeMode.CenterImage;
```

```
pnlFlowLayoutPanel.Controls.Add(loPictureBox);
loPictureBox.Image = paroThumbnailImage;
// A safe counter to track the total number of thumbnails
    shown
piThumbnailsShown++;
// Update the toolstrip progress bar
tstThumbnailsProgress.Value = (int)((piThumbnailsShown * 100)
                                        / piTotalThumbnails);
// Store the brightness delta in the picture box Tag property
loPictureBox.Tag = pariBrightnessDelta;
}
```

8. Add the following private method. It will be run every time a new thumbnail with a specific brightness adjustment is added:

```
private void QueueBrightnessThumbnailThreadProc(Object stateInfo)
{
    // An instance of ThumbnailBrightnessAdjuster is passed in
        stateInfo
    ThumbnailBrightnessAdjuster loThumbnailBrightnessAdjuster =
      (ThumbnailBrightnessAdjuster)stateInfo;

    loThumbnailBrightnessAdjuster.GenerateThumbnailImage();
    AddThumbnail(loThumbnailBrightnessAdjuster.poThumbnailImage,
            loThumbnailBrightnessAdjuster.piBrightnessDelta);
}
```

9. Add the following private method. It will be run every time a new thumbnail with a specific brightness adjustment is added, and will queue a QueueBrightnessThumbnailThreadProc method with a ThumbnailBrightnessAdjuster instance as a parameter:

```
private void QueueBrightnessThumbnail(double
        pariBrightnessAdjustment)
{
    ThumbnailBrightnessAdjuster loThumbnailBrightnessAdjuster;
    loThumbnailBrightnessAdjuster = new
      ThumbnailBrightnessAdjuster(psImageFileName,
      poThumbnailSize, pariBrightnessAdjustment);

    // Queue the work passing a ThumbnailBrightnessAdjuster
        instance as a parameter
```

```
ThreadPool.QueueUserWorkItem(new WaitCallback(
            QueueBrightnessThumbnailThreadProc),
            loThumbnailBrightnessAdjuster);
}
```

10. Add the following code to the form `Load` event. It would be convenient to configure some `ThreadPool` class parameters to achieve optimal results (replace `"C:\MYPHOTOS\DSC01470.JPG"` with your high resolution image path and name to test the application):

```
// Set the maximum number of requests to the thread pool that can
    be active concurrently equal to the number of available cores
// All requests above that number remain queued until thread pool
    threads become available
ThreadPool.SetMaxThreads(Environment.ProcessorCount,
                        Environment.ProcessorCount * 2);


// Specify the image file name (replace it with your image file
    name)
psImageFileName = @"C:\MYPHOTOS\DSC01470.JPG";


// Initialize the safe counter
piThumbnailsShown = 0;
piTotalThumbnails = (int)((piEndingBrightness -
                        piBeginningBrightness) / piBrightnessStep);
double liBrightnessAdjustment = piBeginningBrightness;
while (liBrightnessAdjustment <= piEndingBrightness)
{
    QueueBrightnessThumbnail(liBrightnessAdjustment);
    liBrightnessAdjustment += piBrightnessStep;
    liBrightnessAdjustment = Math.Round(liBrightnessAdjustment,
                                        3);
}
```

11. Build and run the application. The form will appear slowly with increasing opacity, while showing the thumbnails with different brightness adjustments, and updating the progress bar at the bottom of the window, as shown in the following image:

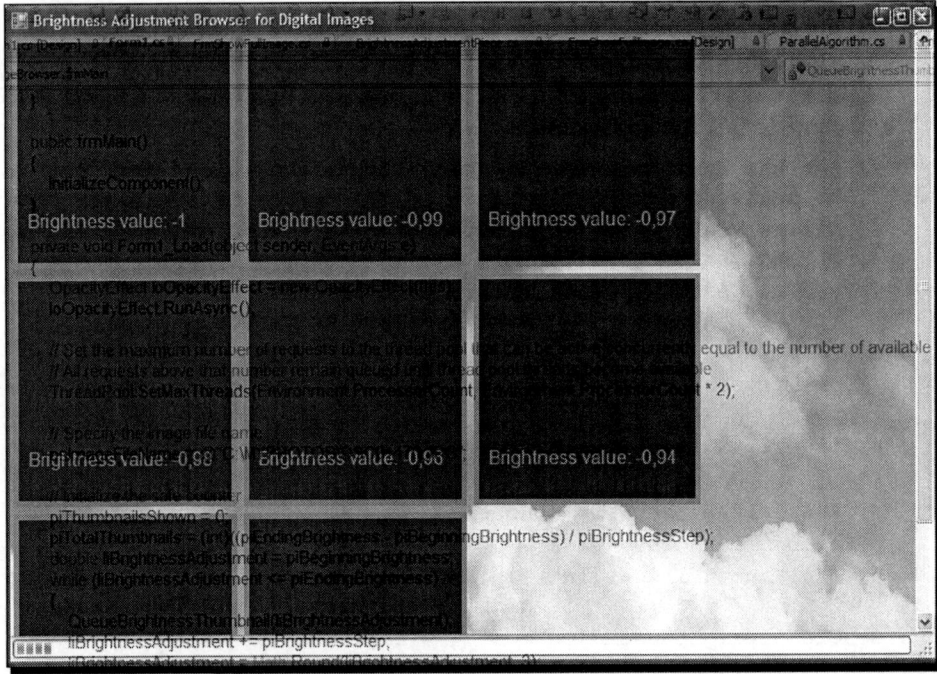

What just happened?

We could easily create a very responsive user interface. The window's opacity changes while the thumbnails with different brightness adjustments are being added to the layout panel. Simultaneously, the user can move the window, change its size, minimize it, or maximize it. The UI is alive and is using a safe counter in the UI thread. We can show an overall progress at the bottom of the window.

The code is easy to understand because we used everything that we have already learned in the previous chapters.

Once the opacity effect is completed, we can browse the thumbnails showing the image, with a text displaying the brightness adjustment value, as shown in the following image:

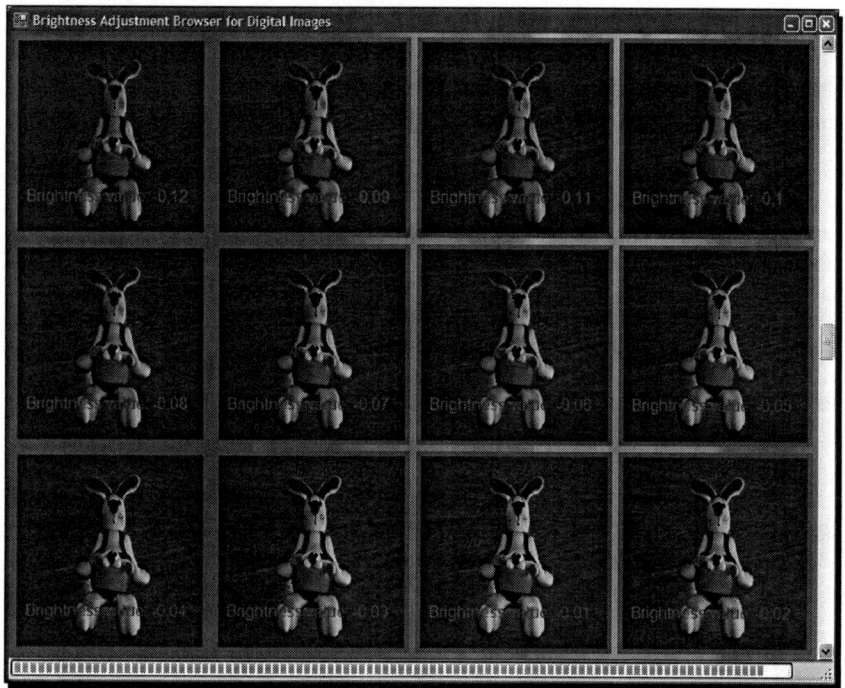

Combining threads with a pool of threads and the UI thread

We combined a background thread created with the `Thread` class and a pool of threads created with the `ThreadPool` class. Why? Because we want them to run concurrently. We want to display a transparency effect at the time when the thumbnails begin appearing.

The simplest way to organize the thumbnails to appear is to use a pool of threads, taking full advantage of the coordination and schedule facilities offered by the `ThreadPool` class. Nevertheless, we do not want the effect to be a part of the pool of threads because it must run in parallel with the latter.

And, taking advantage of the single-threaded approach of the UI thread, we have created a safe counter avoiding locks and concurrency problems to track the number of thumbnails shown, and to report an overall progress.

The form's `piThumbnailsShown` private variable holds that counter. However, in order to show an overall progress percentage, we need to know the total number of thumbnails to be shown. This is calculated in the following line:

```
piTotalThumbnails = (int)((piEndingBrightness -
                        piBeginningBrightness) /
                        piBrightnessStep);
```

We know the beginning brightness value, the ending value, and the step. It is easy to determine the total number of thumbnails that will be generated. Thus, we can show the progress using the toolstrip progress bar. It is done in the `AddThumbnailInLayoutPanel` method:

```
// A safe counter to track the total number of thumbnails shown
   piThumbnailsShown++;
// Update the toolstrip progress bar
   tstThumbnailsProgress.Value = (int)((piThumbnailsShown * 100) /
                                       piTotalThumbnails);
// Store the brightness delta in the picture box Tag property
   loPictureBox.Tag = pariBrightnessDelta;
```

The thumbnail size is determined by the `poThumbnailSize` private variable.

 Using everything that we have learned in the previous chapters, we can create applications with a very responsive UI and take full advantage of the parallel processing capabilities offered by the modern computers.

Time for action – Creating a specialized parallel algorithm piece subclass to run concurrently with the pool of threads

The application is very attractive, showing high quality thumbnails with a very responsive UI. However, you may want to see the whole image with the brightness adjustment. You can do that when you click on the thumbnail's picture box. Nevertheless, you may still want to have a responsive UI and the best possible performance. To achieve that, you can have the brightness adjustment run using a parallelized algorithm to allow it to use the available cores. It makes sense to do that with huge resolution images.

 This is very easy to do using our well-known `ParallelAlgorithmPiece` and `ParallelAlgorithm` classes.

First, we are going to create a subclass of the `ParallelAlgorithmPiece` class and fill in the gaps overriding the necessary methods to define the code to be executed for each piece. Thus, we are going to represent each piece of the brightness adjustment algorithm:

1. Stay in the project, `ImageBrowser`.

2. Copy the original code of the `ParallelAlgorithmPiece` and `ParallelAlgorithm` classes and paste it in a new class file, `ParallelAlgorithm. cs` (from the `SunspotsAnalyzer` project, in the previous chapters). Replace the namespace `SunspotsAnalyzer` with the namespace of this new project.

3. Create a new class, `BrightnessAdjustmentPiece` (as a subclass of `ParallelAlgorithmPiece`), using the following declaration:

```
class BrightnessAdjustmentPiece : ParallelAlgorithmPiece
```

4. Add the following lines of code at the beginning. We are going to use the `System.Drawing`, `System.Threading`, and AForge.Net classes:

```
using System.Drawing;
using System.Threading;
using AForge;
using AForge.Imaging;
using AForge.Imaging.Filters;
using AForge.Math;
```

5. Add the following private variable:

```
// The resulting bitmap
private Bitmap proBitmap;
// The brightness adjustment value
private double priBrightnessDelta;
```

6. Add the following property to access the private variables (we want to create a compact and reliable class):

```
public Bitmap poBitmap
{
    set
    {
        proBitmap = value;
    }
    get
    {
        return proBitmap;
    }
}
public double piBrightnessDelta
{
    set
    {
        priBrightnessDelta = value;
    }
    get
    {
        return priBrightnessDelta;
    }
}
```

7. Add a new constructor with a parameter that calls the base constructor:

```
public BrightnessAdjustmentPiece(int priThreadNumberToAssign)
    : base(priThreadNumberToAssign)
{
    // Add any necessary additional instructions
}
```

8. Override the `ThreadMethod` method with the code that is going to be run by the thread:

```
public override void ThreadMethod(object poThreadParameter)
{
    // This is the code that is going to be run by the thread
    // It has access to all the instance variable of this class
    // It receives the instance as a parameter
    // We must typecast poThreadParameter to
       BrightnessAdjustmentPiece (inherited from
       ParallelAlgorithmPiece) to gain access to its members

    BrightnessAdjustmentPiece loPiece;
    loPiece = (BrightnessAdjustmentPiece)poThreadParameter;

    // Retrieve the thread number received in object
       poThreadParameter, in piThreadNumber property
    long liPieceNumber = loPiece.piThreadNumber;

    // Format the image according to AForge.NET needs to apply
       the filter
    AForge.Imaging.Image.FormatImage(ref proBitmap);
    // Create an instance of the brightness correction filter
    AForge.Imaging.Filters.BrightnessCorrection
            loBrightnessCorrection = new AForge.Imaging.Filters.
            BrightnessCorrection(priBrightnessDelta);
    // Process the image (correct the brightness)
    loBrightnessCorrection.ApplyInPlace(proBitmap);

    // The thread finished its work. Signal that the work item
       has finished.
    poAutoResetEvent.Set();
}
```

What just happened?

The code to define the work done in the pieces of the algorithm is now held in the new `BrightnessAdjustmentPiece` class (a subclass of `ParallelAlgorithmPiece`). The instances of this class are really independent parts of the brightness adjustment algorithm. Everything we need to access from each thread for the algorithm resides in the instance of this class.

Now, we have completed the skeleton for the piece of an algorithm defined as a subclass of the `ParallelAlgorithmPiece` class.

Time for action – Creating a specialized parallel algorithm coordination subclass to run concurrently with the pool of threads

We have the pieces (instances of `ParallelAlgorithmPiece`), but now we must create the subclass to build and solve the brightness adjustment algorithm.

We are going to create a subclass of the `ParallelAlgorithm` class and add the variables, properties, and methods needed for the brightness adjustment algorithm:

1. Stay in the project, `ImageBrowser`.

2. Create a new class, `BrightnessAdjustment` (a subclass of `ParallelAlgorithm`), using the following declaration:

```
class BrightnessAdjustment : ParallelAlgorithm
```

3. Add the following lines of code at the beginning. We are going to use the `System.Drawing` classes:

```
using System.Drawing;
```

4. Add the following private variables (the original bitmap and the resulting one, the bitmaps list, the total number of pieces or threads, and the brightness delta):

```
// The Bitmap
private Bitmap proOriginalBitmap;
// The brightness adjustment value
private double priBrightnessDelta;
// The resulting bitmap
private Bitmap proBitmap;
// The bitmaps list
private List<Bitmap> prloBitmapList;
// The total number of pieces
private int priTotalPieces;
```

5. Add the following properties to access the private variables (we want to create a compact and reliable class):

```
public Bitmap poBitmap
{
    get
    {
        return proBitmap;
    }
}
```

```
public int piTotalPieces
{
    get
    {
        return priTotalPieces;
    }
}
```

6. Add a constructor with a parameter (the bitmap to adjust its brightness):

```
public BrightnessAdjustment(Bitmap paroBitmap,
                            double pariBrightnessDelta)
{
    proOriginalBitmap = paroBitmap;
    priBrightnessDelta = pariBrightnessDelta;
    // Create threads taking into account the number of lines in
        the bitmap
    // And the number of available cores
    priTotalPieces = Environment.ProcessorCount;
    CreateThreads(proOriginalBitmap.Height, priTotalPieces);
    CreateBitmapParts();
}
```

7. Add the following function, `CropBitmap`. It will crop the bitmap received as a parameter and return the portion of the original defined by the rectangle `proRectangle`:

```
private Bitmap CropBitmap(Bitmap proBitmap, Rectangle
                          proRectangle)
{
    // Create a new bitmap copying the portion of the original
        defined by proRectangle and keeping its PixelFormat
    Bitmap loCroppedBitmap = proBitmap.Clone(proRectangle,
                             proBitmap.PixelFormat);
    // Return the cropped bitmap
    return loCroppedBitmap;
}
```

8. Add the following procedure, `CreateBitmapParts`. It will assign the bitmap part corresponding to each piece:

```
private void CreateBitmapParts()
{
    // Create the bitmap list
    prloBitmapList = new List<Bitmap>(priTotalPieces);
    int liPieceNumber;

    Bitmap loBitmap;
```

```
for (liPieceNumber = 0; liPieceNumber < priTotalPieces;
    liPieceNumber++)
{
    loBitmap = CropBitmap(proOriginalBitmap,
        new Rectangle(0, (int)prloPieces[liPieceNumber].
                    piBegin, proOriginalBitmap.Width,
                    (int)(prloPieces[liPieceNumber].
                    piEnd - prloPieces[liPieceNumber].piBegin
                    + 1)));
    prloBitmapList.Add(loBitmap);

    // Assign the bitmap part corresponding to the piece
    ((BrightnessAdjustmentPiece)prloPieces[liPieceNumber])
    .poBitmap = loBitmap;
    // Assign the brightness adjustment value to the piece
    ((BrightnessAdjustmentPiece)prloPieces[liPieceNumber])
    .piBrightnessDelta = priBrightnessDelta;
}
}
```

What just happened?

We added the necessary variables, properties, and methods strictly related to a bitmap's brightness adjustment algorithm.

The code to work with specific bitmap pieces is now held in the new BrightnessAdjustment class (a subclass of ParallelAlgorithm). The instance of this class will constitute a very simple-to-use algorithm. Everything that we need to complete the methods (we must override a few methods for the algorithm coordination) resides in the instance of this class.

Now we have completed the skeleton for the piece of an algorithm defined as a subclass of the ParallelAlgorithmPiece class that will run in threads independent of the threads created in the pool of threads (by the ThreadPool class).

Time for action – Overriding methods in the brightness adjustment coordination subclass

We have created the algorithm coordination subclass, we have added the variables, properties, and methods needed for the brightness adjustment algorithm.

Now, we are going to fill in the gaps overriding the necessary methods to define the code for creating and coordinating the pieces. Thus, we are going to represent the complete brightness adjustment algorithm:

1. Stay in the project, `ImageBrowser`.

2. Move to the `BrightnessAdjustment : ParallelAlgorithm` class code area.

3. Override the `StartThreadsAsync` method to force a garbage collection before starting the threads with an asynchronous execution:

```
public override void StartThreadsAsync()
{
    // Call the garbage collector before starting each thread
    ForceGarbageCollection();
    // Run the base code
    base.StartThreadsAsync();
}
```

4. Override the `CreateParallelAlgorithmPiece` method with the code that is going to create the specific piece instance:

```
public override ParallelAlgorithmPiece
        CreateParallelAlgorithmPiece(int priThreadNumber)
{
    return (new BrightnessAdjustmentPiece(priThreadNumber));
}
```

5. Override the `CollectResults` method with the code that is going to join the pieces (in this case, the bitmaps):

```
public override void CollectResults()
{
    // Enter the results collection iteration through the results
        left in each ParallelAlgorithmPiece
    int liPieceNumber;
    // Each bitmap portion
    Bitmap loBitmap;
    // Create a new bitmap with the whole width and height
    loBitmap = new Bitmap(proOriginalBitmap.Width,
                        proOriginalBitmap.Height);
    Graphics g = Graphics.FromImage((System.Drawing.
                                Image)loBitmap);
    g.InterpolationMode = System.Drawing.Drawing2D.
                        InterpolationMode.HighQualityBicubic;

    for (liPieceNumber = 0; liPieceNumber < priTotalPieces;
        liPieceNumber++)
```

```
    {
        // Draw each portion in its corresponding absolute
            starting row
        g.DrawImage(prloBitmapList[liPieceNumber], 0,
                    prloPieces[liPieceNumber].piBegin);
    }
    // Assign the generated bitmap to proBitmap
    proBitmap = loBitmap;

    g.Dispose();
}
```

What just happened?

The code required to implement the parallelized brightness adjustment algorithm is now held in the BrightnessAdjustmentPiece and BrightnessAdjustment classes.

Thus, creating an instance of the BrightnessAdjustment class, we can easily adjust the brightness of any bitmap, using as many threads as the number of available cores. We filled in the gaps and overrode some methods focusing on the algorithm problems, instead of working hard on its splitting techniques.

The code in the two subclasses is very easy to understand, and it is very well encapsulated.

As the base classes use threads created by the Thread class, they can run in parallel with the threads created by the ThreadPool class.

Time for action – Starting new threads in a new window

Now, we have to create a new windows form to show the full image, having made its the brightness adjustments:

1. Stay in the project, ImageBrowser.
2. Add a new Windows form (**frmShowFullImage**).
3. Open Windows form **frmShowFullImage** in the form designer and add a picturebox control (picImage) to it.
4. Open the code for the Windows form **frmShowFullImage**.
5. Add the following lines of code at the beginning (as we are going to use the System.Threading.Thread class):

```
using System.Threading;
```

6. Add the following private variables:

```
// The brightness adjustment value
private double priBrightnessDelta;
// The image file name
private string prsImageFileName;
// The bitmap to show with the brightness adjustment
private Bitmap proBitmap;
```

7. Add the following properties to access the private variables (we want to create a compact and reliable class). They will be filled by the form's caller:

```
public double piBrightnessDelta
{
    get
    {
        return priBrightnessDelta;
    }
    set
    {
        priBrightnessDelta = value;
    }
}
public string psImageFileName
{
    get
    {
        return prsImageFileName;
    }
    set
    {
        prsImageFileName = value;
    }
}
```

8. Add the following declaration in the instance variables zone:

```
private delegate void ShowImageCaller(System.Drawing.Image
                                      paroImage);
```

9. Add the following public method to call a method to display the adjusted image in the picture box by invoking a delegate, when the calling thread is different from the UI thread:

```
public void ShowImage(System.Drawing.Image paroImage)
{
    // InvokeRequired compares the thread ID of the calling
        thread to the thread ID of the creating thread.
```

```
        // If they are different, it will return true.
        if (this.InvokeRequired)
        {
            // The calling thread is different than the UI thread
            // Create the delegate
            ShowImageCaller ldAddThumbnail = new ShowImageCaller(
                                            ShowImage);
            // Invoke the delegate
            // The current thread will block until the delegate has
               been executed
            this.Invoke(ldAddThumbnail, new object[] { paroImage });
        }
        else
        {
            // The calling thread is the same as the UI thread
            // Show the image in the picture box and assign its size
            picImage.Size = paroImage.Size;
            picImage.Image = paroImage;
        }
    }
```

10. Add the following private method to be run by an independent thread (receiving an instance of the frmShowFullImage class as a parameter):

```
private void ThreadProc()
{
    BrightnessAdjustment loBrightnessAdjustment;

    proBitmap = new Bitmap(psImageFileName);
    loBrightnessAdjustment = new BrightnessAdjustment(proBitmap,
                                priBrightnessDelta);
    loBrightnessAdjustment.RunInParallelSync();
    loBrightnessAdjustment.CollectResults();
    // Invoke the image assignation and resize
    ShowImage(loBrightnessAdjustment.poBitmap);
}
```

11. Add the following public method to be executed by the form's caller in order to start running the parallelized algorithm in an independent background thread:

```
public void RunAsync()
{
    // Add a new independent thread
    Thread loThread = new Thread(new ThreadStart(ThreadProc));
    // If the user closes the form, we want the threads to be
       cancelled
    // Therefore, it must be a background thread
    loThread.IsBackground = true;
```

```
        // Start the thread with an asynchronous execution
        loThread.Start();
    }
```

12. Open the `Load` event in the form and enter the following code:

```
// Set the form's title
this.Text = psImageFileName + string.Format("; Brightness value:
                                {0}", priBrightnessDelta);
// Run in an independent thread to avoid blocking the UI thread
RunAsync();
```

What just happened?

A new form will run the parallelized algorithm to adjust an image's brightness. However, it will not run the algorithm directly in the UI thread. It will create a background thread to call the algorithm there. This way, the form will not block the UI thread, and many forms could be launched by the main form, while the thumbnails continue to show on that window.

Creating threads inside other threads

We are using the same technique that we used with the opacity effect. We run threads inside a background thread to avoid blocking the UI thread. We need the UI thread to be free in order to process the messages that are continuously queued by the multiple threads that invoke delegates to update the UI.

The form needs two properties to be filled in by its caller:

♦ `psImageFileName`: The name of the image file to be processed

♦ `piBrightnessDelta`: The brightness adjustment value (it was saved in the thumbnail's picture box `Tag` property)

The `Load` event handler does not run code to block the UI thread. Instead, it calls the `RunAsync` method:

```
this.Text = psImageFileName + string.Format("; Brightness value:
                                {0}", priBrightnessDelta);
RunAsync();
```

The `RunAsync` method creates a new independent background thread using the `Thread` class (it will not be a part of the threads managed by the pool of threads). If the user closes the form, we want the threads to be cancelled. Therefore, it must be a background thread and it starts with an asynchronous execution—again, to avoid blocking the UI thread:

```
Thread loThread = new Thread(new ThreadStart(ThreadProc));
loThread.IsBackground = true;
loThread.Start(this);
```

The `ThreadProc` procedure runs in an independent thread. It creates a new bitmap from the file received in the property and creates an instance of the `BrightnessAdjustment` class to run the algorithm with the bitmap and the brightness adjustment value:

```
proBitmap = new Bitmap(psImageFileName);
loBrightnessAdjustment = new BrightnessAdjustment(proBitmap,
                        priBrightnessDelta);
loBrightnessAdjustment.RunInParallelSync();
loBrightnessAdjustment.CollectResults();
ShowImage(loBrightnessAdjustment.poBitmap);
```

Then, it waits for the threads to finish using the `RunInParallelSync` method. But since it is called from an independent thread, it does not block the UI thread. The results are collected, and the image is shown by invoking a delegate to update the UI thread.

The code is a bit more complicated, but it allows us to offer a very responsive user interface, while achieving an incredible performance enhancement.

Time for action – Showing new windows without blocking the user interface

Now, we have to add an event handler to display the form when the user clicks on the thumbnail's picture box, without blocking the user interface:

1. Stay in the project, `ImageBrowser`.

2. Open the code for the Windows Form `Form1` (**frmMain**).

3. Now, we will create a generic procedure for handling the picturebox control click event, receiving the same parameters as the corresponding event handler:

```
private void PictureBoxClickProcedure(object sender,
            System.EventArgs e)
{
    PictureBox loPictureBox = (PictureBox)(sender);
    frmShowFullImage loForm = new frmShowFullImage();
    loForm.psImageFileName = psImageFileName;
    loForm.piBrightnessDelta = (double)loPictureBox.Tag;
    loForm.Show(this);
}
```

4. Add the following line of code to the `AddThumbnailInLayoutPanel` method. We have to attach an event handler to each generated thumbnail's picture box:

```
// Attach an event handler making reference to the procedure that
   contains the code that will be triggered by the Click event
loPictureBox.Click += new System.
            EventHandler(PictureBoxClickProcedure);
```

5. Build and run the application. The form will appear slowly, with increasing opacity, and will show the thumbnails with different brightness adjustments and also update the progress bar at the bottom of the window.

6. Click on a thumbnail, and a window will be shown with the whole image and its brightness adjustment value, while the background window continues to show new thumbnails and report the progress, as shown in the following image:

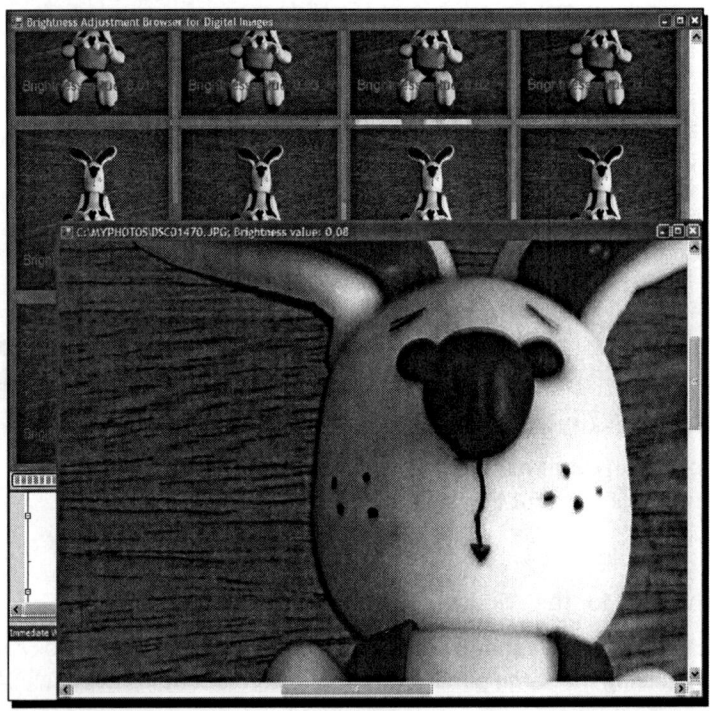

What just happened?

Combining everything that we learned in the previous chapters, we could easily create a very responsive user interface using multiple windows.

When the user clicks on the thumbnail's picture box, the generic event handler procedure code retrieves the sender picture box casting the `sender` parameter:

```
PictureBox loPictureBox = (PictureBox)(sender);
```

Then, it creates a new `frmShowFullImage` form instance, assigns the necessary properties and calls the `Show` method that will run the code in the `Load` event and execute the brightness adjustment parallelized algorithm without blocking the UI thread:

```
frmShowFullImage loForm = new frmShowFullImage();
loForm.psImageFileName = psImageFileName;
```

```
loForm.piBrightnessDelta = (double)loPictureBox.Tag;
loForm.Show(this);
```

 Leaving the UI thread unblocked allows us to offer a parallelized and a very responsive user interface.

Multiple windows and one UI thread for all of them

Although we are showing multiple windows, the UI thread is shared by all of them. Thus, we do not have to block the UI thread in order to allow all the windows to update their controls from the same message queue.

This is the main reason why we had to use an asynchronous background thread to run the code in each new window. Thus, we avoid blocking the UI thread, and by combining the `ThreadPool` threads with the ones created by the `Thread` class, we achieve a very responsive UI.

Clicking on many thumbnails, we can parallelize the work and take full advantage of the most impressive parallel hardware, as shown in the following image:

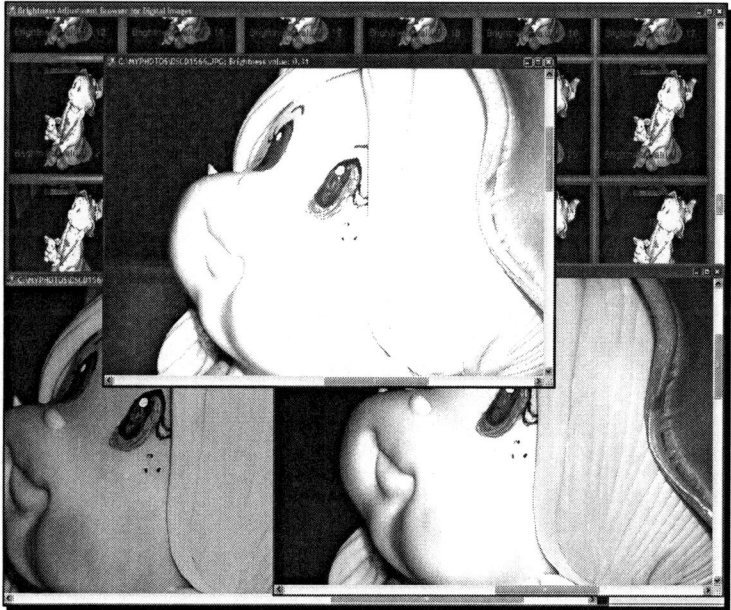

 If we had coded directly in the form's load event handler, the UI thread would have been blocked, and the application would not present a responsive UI. Using these techniques, we can deliver the most responsive applications ever seen.

Rationalizing multithreaded code

As mentioned earlier, when creating highly multithreaded code, we have to be careful to avoid some common mistakes. Luckily, many tools can help us in learning how to code better to avoid side effects and other problems related to multithreaded code.

One of them is **NDepend**, developed by SMACCHIA.COM S.A.R.L., which is an excellent tool that simplifies the management of a complex .NET code base. One of its most interesting features, relating to multithreaded code, is its ability to check for specific design rules and its capability to analyze very complex code structures.

 S.A.R.L. stands for "Société à Responsabilité Limitée" in French, as SMACCHIA. COM is a French company.

It supports the **Code Query Language (CQL)** that can help the developer find answers to questions about the code base, and it integrates with many Visual Studio versions. It offers advice on how to constrain your classes, so that these are immutable, and how to determine which code might potentially corrupt states. That is excellent advice for safe multithreaded code.

The following image shows an analysis result provided by this tool, inherent to multithreaded code:

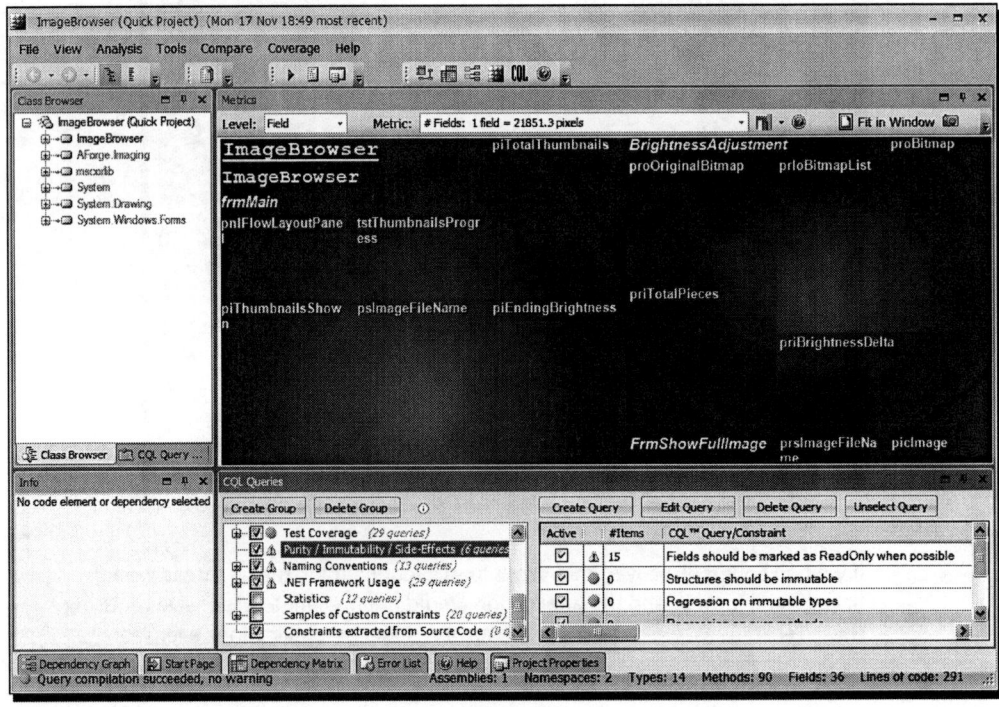

NDepend is commercial software. However, it does offer a trial edition. To download and evaluate it, visit the software's main web site: `http://www.ndepend.com`.

Nevertheless, we must not forget that we live in a pragmatic world. The guidelines offered by tools of this kind are always helpful, but not definitive.

Using some confident code metrics and guidelines will indeed be very helpful in developing safe multithreaded code.

Have a go hero – Improving the application and solving bugs

The application is great. However, it has some defects. You are a multithreading guru, and you want your travel photographs to be the most impressive ones. Therefore, you must make the necessary changes to the application to show your multithreading capabilities.

The thumbnails are shown without an order, as shown in the following image:

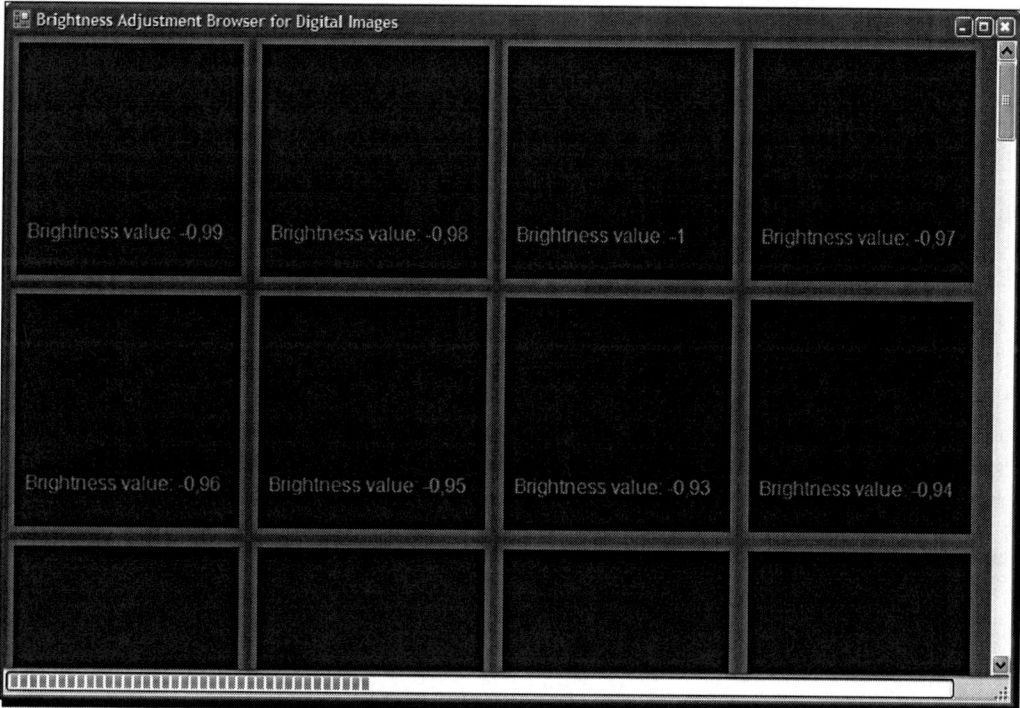

Make the necessary changes to show them in a specific order, and add some toolbar buttons to allow the user to modify the order on the fly.

When the application windows are closed, the following message may appear sometimes in the Immediate Window: **A first chance exception of type 'System.ObjectDisposedException' occurred in System.Windows.Forms.dll**. Add an exception handler and capabilities to stop the running threads to avoid this problem. You know how to do that.

When the whole image is processed in the window and the user clicks the thumbnail, no progress report is shown. Make the necessary changes to show a progress report for the brightness adjustment algorithm.

Do you have Visual Studio 2010 or the .NET Parallel Extensions CTP? Develop a new version of this application using the features that you learned in the previous chapter. Microsoft will be happy to know that you are testing the new features!

Have a go hero – Creating parallel, multithreaded applications using the C# programming language

In today's world, we have numerous situations such as the following:

◆ Millions of computer users own a multi-core CPU. They want applications that take full advantage of their processing power. They need parallelized algorithms.

◆ Millions of computer users do not want the UI to be blocked while some processing occurs. They want a more responsive UI. They need multithreaded applications.

◆ Thousands of servers are prepared for scaling while their applications are not. They need scalable applications depending upon the number of available processors.

◆ Thousands of companies require architects, developers, and testers with great knowledge on parallel algorithms and concurrent programming. They need multithreading experts.

◆ Billions of **aliens** around the universe are looking forward to hiring your services!

You worked with hackers, FBI agents, and then you developed the most complex parallelized algorithms for NASA! You can develop the best multithreaded applications that take full advantage of modern hardware while offering a very responsive UI indeed!

You can do it—combining everything you have learned so far. Everything is possible!

Pop quiz

1. Using multithreaded code, you can:

   a. Create a more responsive user interface

   b. Develop applications that offer a great performance in hardware with parallel processing capabilities

   c. Improve your software development skills

2. Using a pool of threads you can develop better:

   a. Client applications

   b. Server applications

   c. Batch jobs

3. Combining everything you learned in this book, you can:

   a. Dazzle your boss and co-workers

   b. Find a better job

   c. Take full advantage of your multiple-core computers

4. Now, you are able to develop multithreaded applications and parallel algorithms with:

   a. C# 2.0 (2005)

   b. C# 3.0 (2008)

   c. C# 4.0 (2010)

5. Using your multithreading abilities, you can parallelize:

   a. The UI updates

   b. Queries

   c. Statistics

Right answers:

1. a, b, and c!
2. a, b, and c!
3. a, b, and c!
4. a, b, and c!
5. a, b, and c!

Summary

We learned a lot in this chapter about joining all the pieces in a complete application, parallelizing the execution as much as possible to offer great scalability, an impressive performance, and an incredibly responsive user interface. We were able to combine different parallelized tasks with multiple-window UIs, always offering the best possible performance, and the most responsive UI. Specifically, we covered:

- Combining asynchronous and synchronous executions, independent threads and threads from pools to create parallelized effects in the UI

- Running different kinds of parallelized tasks in a single application, taking advantage of each threading technique's outstanding features

- Using delegates to provide a very responsive UI, while showing multiple windows

- Starting threads from asynchronous independent threads to avoid blocking the shared UI thread

- Taking advantage of the present and future hardware with parallel execution capabilities in every part of an application

- Understanding the available tools to rationalize more complex multithreaded code

We also learned how to create a whole application from scratch with completely multithreaded code offering a responsive user interface for every event.

Now that we've learned to develop a completely parallelized application, we're ready for real-life parallelized software development using C#!

Index

A

affinity 37
algorithms
  about 218
  class, defining to instantiate 234-236
  classes, preparing for inheritance 236
  classic coordination methods, adding 226, 227
  instance creating, new method defining 248
  instances, accessing from threads methods 225
  locks, avoiding 253
  methods, overriding in coordination
      subclass 245-247
  parallel algorithm classes, preparing for factory
      classes 232-234
  parallel algorithm coordination class,
      creating 223-225
  parallel algorithm piece class, creating 218, 219
  ParallelAlgorithmPiece subclass 236
  parallel algorithm piece subclass,
      creating 237-239
  parallel algorithms, encapsulating 252
  parallel algorithms, optimizing 252
  piece creation method, programming 247
  pieces, creating 222
  pieces creating, generic method used 221
  results collection method,
      programming 247, 248
  side-effects, avoiding 254, 255
  simple constructor, creating 241
  simple constructors, creating 244, 245
  specialized parallel algorithm coordination
      subclass, creating 241-244
  specializing 231

  SunspotAnalyzer class, running in many
      concurrent independent pieces 249-252
  thread affinity, achieving 252, 253
  threads, starting 225
  variables, accessing from threads methods 226
ALU 10
AMP 14-16
Arithmetic and Logic Unit. *See* **ALU**
ASMP. *See* **AMP**
asymmetrical multiprocessing. *See* **AMP**
asymmetrical multiprocessing, multiprocessor
      systems 14-16
asynchronous execution
  about 75
  step-by-step process 76-78

B

background threads 268
BackgroundWorker components
  about 65
  application, enhancing 102
  application, monitoring 75, 104
  CodeBreaker application 68-70
  code, breaking in single thread 67
  code, enhancing 109
  creating, in run-time 105-109
  multiple BackgroundWorker components,
      working with 94, 95
  quiz 109
  Rapid thread creation (RTC) 65
  UI elements, adding 75
  using, in thread class 132
  using, to break code 94-96

using, to cancel the job 85, 86
using, to detect job 87
vs timer component 104
BackgroundWorker components, creating
code, enhancing 109
in run-time 105
bandwidth between processors 21
bottlenecks, avoiding 21-23

C

C#
advantages over C and C++ 208, 209
BackgroundWorker components 65
components, advantages 65, 67
mono-processor systems 8
multi-processor systems 13
multithreaded code, rationalizing 384
parallelized application 353
performance waterfall 11
processes 35
threads 53
XOR (Exclusive OR) operation 118
callbacks 79
Code Query Language. *See* **CQL**
Community Technology Preview. *See* **CTP**
CTP 315
concurrent code
independent blocks, creating 186-188
concurrent threads
control enhancing, flags used 189, 190
debugging 150
debugging, difficulties 148-150
coordination cost, formula 17-21
CQL 384

D

database access
parallelized data access algorithm,
creating 276, 277
parallelizing 276
delegate 282

E

encryption algorithm
debugging 164

enhancing 164
Event wait handles 197
exceptions, controlling in parallelized loops
about 334
results, showing in UI 334-337
exceptions, controlling in threads 264

F

flags
concurrent threads control, enhancing 189, 190
Floating Point Unit. *See* **FPU**
FPU 10
Front Side Bus. *See* **FSB**
FSB 7

G

garbage collector
about 204
advantages 209
inefficient processing usage problems,
avoiding 214-216
problems, avoiding 213, 214
system garbage collector controlling,
GC class used 212
total memory allocation, retrieving 217
using 210, 211

I

IDE 37
independent thread
opacity effect, creating 354-356
inefficient processing usage problems,
avoiding 214-216
Input/Output. *See* **I/O**
Input; Processing; Output. *See* **IPO**
Integrated Development Environment. *See* **IDE**
Inter-Process Communication. *See* **IPC**
I/O
operations, threads queuing with 257, 258
I/O bottlenecks
avoiding 262, 263
IPC 51
IPO 8

J

job, cancelling
advantages 84
application, enhancing 92, 93
BackgroundWorker used 85, 86
BackgroundWorker, using to detect job 87- 89
e.Argument property 89, 93
e.Result property 89
e.Result property, results 93
parameters, working with 89, 90
results, working with 89-92

L

Language-Integrated Query. *See* **LINQ**
LINQ 346
load balancing, multi-processors systems
about 29
traditional procedures 30
loops parallelizing, .NET extensions used
AForge.NET 1.7.0, downloading 320
asynchronous task combined with
    synchronous parallel loop,
    creating 340, 341
blobs, counting 325
blobs, showing 326
code simplifying, lambda expressions
    used 344, 345
concurrent nebula finders,
    running 327-330
concurrent queue, working with 332, 333
delegates, coding with 331
delegates, combining with
    BackgroundWorker 337
elements, retrieving from from a concurrent
    queue in producer-consumer
    scheme 337-339
exceptions, controlling 333, 334
feedback, providing on finishing job 344
feedback providing to UI, producer-consumer
    scheme used 339, 340
imaging library, downloading 319
independent class, creating 321-325
.NET parallel extensions, downloading 316-318
.NET parallel extensions, installing 317, 318
parallelized ForEach loop, using 330
threads name, changing while debugging 341
UI update, invoking from task 342-344
with ranges 345

M

mono-processor systems
about 8
multiplexing 9
multi-users system 10
single core 8, 9
von-Neumanns bottleneck 10
multi-core 23
multi-users system 10
multiple threads
concurrent threads, debugging 150
concurrent threads debugging,
    difficulties 148, 149, 150
threads, finding 151-153
multiplexing 9
multiprocessing systems
linear code, problems 44
parallelism capabilities, testing 48-51
parallel performance tester 44, 45
processes, running in parallel 44, 45
process explorer, using 51
multi-processor systems
asymmetrical multiprocessing 14
bottlenecks, avoiding 21, 22
bottlenecks, detecting 23
load balancing 29, 30
multi-core 23
multiple execution cores 23, 24
operating systems 31
parallelism 31
performance improvements, estimating 16
scalability, measuring 27
scalability problems, detecting 29
symmetrical multiprocessing 13
tasks distributing, procedures 13
virtual machines 31
multithreaded application. *See also*
    multithreaded code
classes, using 207
concurrency problems, avoiding 178, 179

debugging, as single-threaded
    application 159, 160
functions, using 207
garbage collector 209
image processing, splitting 179
memory usage, analyzing 207, 208
methods, using 207
procedures, using 207
multithreaded code
    application, improving 385, 386
    bugs, solving 385, 386
    concurrent decryption 170
    encryption, procedure 164
    partial results, showing 164
    rationalizing 384
    results, isolating 167
    thread information, in tracepoints 169
    thread-safe output, displaying 167

N

NASA
    old stars, detecting 174-178
NDepend 385
number of processors 17-19

O

object-oriented programming language 231
over-clocking 23

P

ParallelAlgorithm classes
    preparing, for factory method 232- 236
ParallelAlgorithmPiece subclass
    constructor 236
    ThreadMethod 236
ParallelAlgorithm subclass
    CollectResults 236
    constructor 236
    CreateParallelAlgorithmPiece 236
    methods, overriding 236
    StartThreadsAsync 236
parallel extensions. *See* **loops parallelizing, .NET
    extensions used**

parallelism 31, 32
parallelism complexity. *See* **algorithms**
parallelized application
    code, running out of UI thread 356
    methods, overriding in the brightness adjust-
        ment coordination subclass 375, 377
    multiple windows 383
    new threads, starting in new window 377-380
    new windows, showing without blocking user
        interface 381-383
    opacity effect, creating in independent
        thread 354-356
    safe method, creating to change
        opacity 357-359
    specialized parallel algorithm coordination
        subclass, creating 373-375
    specialized parallel algorithm piece subclass,
        creating 370-373
    threads, combining with pool of
        threads 369-370
    threads, creating inside other threads 380, 381
    UI, blocking 359, 360
Parallel Language-Integrated Query. *See* **PLINQ**
performance waterfall
    about 11, 12
    Front Side Bus (FSB) 11
PLB 30
PLINQ 346-348
pool of threads
    concurrent encryptions, running on
        demand 270
    managing 275
    thread, affinity 274, 275
    thread queue, managing 268
    using, with ThreadPool class 266, 267
processes
    about 35
    and threads, diagrammatic representation 54
    cores, changing 39
    CPU-intensive loop, coding 37
    CPU time 36
    linear code, problems 44
    parallelism capabilities, testing 48
    parallel performer test 40
    priority, changing 42

process explorer, using 51
relating, to cores 41
running, in parallel 42
process explorer. *See* **also threads**
about 51,52
context switch, analyzing 57,58
multiple threads in clients 59-63
multiple threads in servers 59
multi threaded application, searching 57
threads, listing 55-57
processes, relating to cores
about 41
process priority, changing 41-43
progress, reporting
in UI , BackgroundWorker used 79-84
ways 84
Processing Load Balancing. *See* **PLB**
progress, reporting to UI from independent
threads. *See* **UI**

Q

queries, parallelizing
degree of parallelism, specifying for PLINQ 349
LINQ queries, parallelizing with PLINQ 348, 349
multiple queries, parallelizing 349
parallelized counter 346, 347
parallelized user interface, creating 350
statistics, parallelizing 349

R

Rapid thread creation. *See* **RTC**
RTC 65

S

scalability, encapsulating 273, 274
single core 8
Single Instruction, Single Data. *See* **SISD**
SISD 8
split jobs
multithreaded algorithm,
running 205-207
running 203, 204
running, new methods defining 204, 205

symmetrical multiprocessing. *See* **SMP**
SMP 13
symmetrical multiprocessing, multiprocessors
systems 13
synchronous execution 78
system garbage collector
controlling, GC used 212, 213

T

thread class. *See* **also threads**
data, retrieving from threads 125
encryption algorithm 114
Int32 structure 123
new thread, creating 124, 125
new thread, encrypting 119-122
string decrypting, methods 117, 118
string encrypting, methods 114-116
thread safety 123
threads, creating with 113, 114
UI, decoupling 122, 123
threads
about 53, 54
affinity, in pool of threads 274, 275
and processes, diagrammatic representation 54
AutoResetEvent class, using to handle
signals 197, 198
background threads 268
BackgroundWorker component used 132
call stack, viewing 162
combining with pool of threads 369, 370
concurrency problems, avoiding 178, 179
concurrent encryption algorithms 136
concurrent encryptions, running on
demand 270, 271
concurrent streams, using 263, 264
concurrent threads control enhancing,
flags used 189, 190
context switch analyzing, process explorer
used 57, 58
creating, with thread class 113, 114
data, retrieving from 125
data, sharing 125-130
data, sharing between threads 125, 126, 181
encryption algorithm, debugging 164
encryption algorithm, enhancing 164

exceptions, controlling 264, 265
executing, synchronously 133-135
finding, in multithreaded application 151-153
freezing 161
identifying, at runtime 157, 158
independent blocks, creating 186, 187
inefficient processing usage problems,
        avoiding 214-216
join method 135
listing, process explorer used 55, 56
multiple threads, in clients 59, 60
multiple threads, in servers 59
multithreaded applications, searching 57
names, assigning to 154-156
old stars, detecting 174-176
old stars, detecting process 186
parameters, passing 136-139
parameters, receiving 142, 143
pausing, flags used 198, 199
pixels color composition 180
pool of threads, managing 275
pool of threads, using 266, 268
queue, managing in pool 268, 269
queuing, I/O operations used 257, 258
restarting, flags used 198
result, showing in UI 190
results testing, windows performance
        monitor used 192, 193
scalability, encapsulating 273
signals, waiting for 195, 196
single-threaded tasks, converting to
        multithreaded pools 272
specific data, sharing between threads 130
start method 135
StreamReader 263
thawing 162
ThreadPool class 266
UI, updating 126
WaitHandle class, using to check for signals 198
window, information 153
threads, combining with pool of threads 369
threads, creating inside other threads 380
threads, parameters passing 136
threads, parameters receiving 142
threads window

current thread, identifying 157
information, understanding 153
names, assigning to threads 154-156
timer component
vs BackgroundWorker component 104

U

UI 37
blocking 359
class, creating to hold information to show in
        DataGridView 302, 303
classes, creating to show progress bar column in
        DataGridView 299, 300
concurrency problems, avoiding 294
delegate, creating without parameters 306
delegate, invoking asynchronously 307
delegates, creating to make
        cross-thread calls 281
delegates, decoding 293, 294
delegates, invoking step-by-step 289, 290
feedback, providing 287
Model-View-Controller design,
        implementing 298
multiple asynchronous user interface updates
        from many threads, invoking 304
parallelized user interface, creating 312
progress percentages, updating from worker
        threads 309, 310
progress, reporting from independent
        threads 298
results, retrieving from synchronous
        delegate invoke 284
right thread, figuring out 282, 283
safe counters creating, delegates used 294, 296
single-threaded UI, handling 296, 298
threads, identifying 288, 289
threads, naming 288, 289
unblocking, new windows
        showing 381-383
update from thread, invoking 285, 286
update problems avoiding, delegate used 283
updating, from independent threads 279, 280
updating, safe method creating 280
UI, blocking

about 359, 360
class, creating to run task in independent
thread 360, 361
logic, putting into methods 361-364
request, queuing 364-368
threads, running 364-368
UI, updating 364-368
UI thread
code, running out 356
safe method, creating to change
opacity 357-359
User Interface. *See* **UI**

V

virtual constructor 232
von-Neumanns bottleneck 10

W

windows performance monitor 192-195
windows task manager. *See also* processes
processes 35
starting, actions 40

X

XOR (Exclusive OR) operation 119, 118

Thank you for buying
C# 2008 and 2005 Threaded Programming: Beginner's Guide

About Packt Publishing

Packt, pronounced 'packed', published its first book "*Mastering phpMyAdmin for Effective MySQL Management*" in April 2004 and subsequently continued to specialize in publishing highly focused books on specific technologies and solutions.

Our books and publications share the experiences of your fellow IT professionals in adapting and customizing today's systems, applications, and frameworks. Our solution based books give you the knowledge and power to customize the software and technologies you're using to get the job done. Packt books are more specific and less general than the IT books you have seen in the past. Our unique business model allows us to bring you more focused information, giving you more of what you need to know, and less of what you don't.

Packt is a modern, yet unique publishing company, which focuses on producing quality, cutting-edge books for communities of developers, administrators, and newbies alike. For more information, please visit our website: www.packtpub.com.

Writing for Packt

We welcome all inquiries from people who are interested in authoring. Book proposals should be sent to author@packtpub.com. If your book idea is still at an early stage and you would like to discuss it first before writing a formal book proposal, contact us; one of our commissioning editors will get in touch with you.

We're not just looking for published authors; if you have strong technical skills but no writing experience, our experienced editors can help you develop a writing career, or simply get some additional reward for your expertise.

ASP.NET 3.5 Social Networking

ISBN: 978-1-847194-78-7   Paperback: 556 pages

An expert guide to building enterprise-ready social networking and community applications with ASP. NET 3.5

1. Create a full-featured, enterprise-grade social network using ASP.NET 3.5

2. Learn key new ASP.NET topics in a practical, hands-on way: LINQ, AJAX, C# 3.0, n-tier architectures, and MVC

3. Build friends lists, messaging systems, user profiles, blogs, message boards, groups, and more

ASP.NET 3.5 Application Architecture and Design

ISBN: 978-1-847195-50-0   Paperback: 239 pages

Build robust, scalable ASP.NET applications quickly and easily.

1. Master the architectural options in ASP.NET to enhance your applications

2. Develop and implement n-tier architecture to allow you to modify a component without disturbing the next one

3. Design scalable and maintainable web applications rapidly

Please check **www.PacktPub.com** for information on our titles

Lightning Source UK Ltd.
Milton Keynes UK
UKOW020727280513

211353UK00001B/9/P